READINGS
IN THE QUR'ĀN

READINGS
IN THE QUR'ĀN

Selected and translated by

KENNETH CRAGG

sussex
ACADEMIC
PRESS

BRIGHTON • PORTLAND

2 4 6 8 10 9 7 5 3 1

First published by Collins Religious Publishing, HarperCollins
Publishers, in 1988. Re-published 1999
in Great Britain by
SUSSEX ACADEMIC PRESS
Box 2950
Brighton BN2 5SP

and in the United States of America by
SUSSEX ACADEMIC PRESS
5804 N.E. Hassalo St.
Portland, Oregon 97213–3644

Cover photos: the Opening Surah and first page of Surah 2 from the Qur'ān, MS. Bodl.
Or. 95, fols 4v–5r, by permission of the Bodleian Library, Oxford.

The arabic verse above the part titles, chapter titles and each of the themes is the
opening verse of the Qur'ān. It is the invocation of the divine Name and mercy which
properly begins all Muslim acts.

British Library Cataloguing in Publication Data
A CIP catalogue record for this book is available from the British Library.

Library of Congress Cataloging-in-Publication Data
Koran. English. Selections.
Readings in the Qu'rān / selected and translated with an introductory essay
by Kenneth Cragg.
p. cm.
Originally published: San Francisco : Collins, 1988.
ISBN 1–902210–31–X (pbk. : alk. paper)
BP110 1999
297.1'22521—dc21 99–24296
CIP

Printed by Biddles Ltd, Guildford and King's Lynn

Contents

Preface

Any translation of the Holy Qur'ān has to anticipate a very wide diversity of readers. Among them will be newcomers to the sacred Scripture of Islam with only a minimal or modest familiarity with its historical context or its contents. Others, however, will be well versed in scholarship concerning Muhammad and the decisive role in the faith, law and culture of Muslims of the Book to which he was instrumental. There will be Muslim readers, as well as outsiders, legitimately alert to how their treasured text fares in English rendering and anxious to discover whether the translator has been adequately aware of the susceptibilities of the faithful. These readers will be more wary in the present case since the version offered here has the added liability of selection. Though an Index shows that no accent or emphasis of the Qur'ān has been omitted in the abridgement (by less than one third of the total length of the whole), Muslims will rightly look for an adequate explanation of why the translator sees selection as an aid to the Qur'ān's impact in the contemporary world. To facilitate intelligent comprehension of the Qur'ān wherever the English language goes is certainly a right intention at a time of increasing need for informed understanding between religions in their cultures and communities. Whether custodians, teachers, citizens, pilgrims, tourists or sceptics, we all need a lively reckoning with the faiths that others live by, and their Scriptures are the place to begin.

Such a range of readership, however, means that this publication needs to explain itself on several levels. Accordingly, the Introductory Essay has four parts.

The first section, 'The Qur'ān at First Meeting', offers an elementary review of the background of the Book, the career (or *Sīrah*) of the Prophet Muhammad, and the significance of the Scripture as Muslims receive, venerate and fulfil it. This section need not concern those who are already familiar with the Qur'ān. They can proceed straight to the other three sections. Similarly, those who want only a general introduction can omit the rest of the Introductory Essay and go straight to the text, perhaps returning later if they wish to satisfy any need for elucidation the text may have aroused. In that way the Qur'ān can come to them disencumbered of the minutiae of scholarship.

However, these are by no means 'minutiae' to the initiated. Selection, translation and contemporary study all require careful argument and justification. For they comprise a nest of 'problems' — if we are problem-minded — or from another point of view they make lively demands on what we might call the 'art' of readership. The second section, 'The Qur'ān and its themes' therefore, takes up in some detail my logic for selection. I have tried to make the selection consonant with the Qur'ān's own character as well as conducive to its appreciation by those outside Islam. The steady repetition of his message, in a context of scorn and incredulity, was the hallmark of Muhammad's vocation through his great preaching years in Mecca. Today's readers need not so much the repetition as the perspective of the whole as a living legacy; they need to appreciate but no longer be immersed in the vicissitudes of its incidence at the time.

Hence the second section of the Introduction studies the Qur'ān by its great themes, around which the selected texts have been grouped. There need be no hesitation about what these themes are. We must begin and end with God. Among the first instincts of such living theology is the theme of praise. Praise and worship celebrate the trust of the created order and acknowledge the calling and destiny of man as tenant-master of the good earth, on God's behalf. This 'trust' of the world, yielding both the sciences of control and the arts of wonder, is the theme of revealed law and the burden of prophethood down the centuries. Hence the Qur'ān's narratives of those patriarchs and messengers through whom God summoned mankind to obedience, in anticipation of the culmination of their missions in Muhammad, 'the seal of the prophets'.

The long story of earlier prophethood, including that of Jesus, has its climax in the prophetic mission of Muhammad. Here the Qur'ān's own division into 'Meccan' and 'Medinan' chapters controls the sequence of my selection — the prophet-preacher and the prophet-ruler in the inclusive harmony, as Islam sees it, of faith and power, religion and rule.

Those twin movements of Muhammad's destiny inaugurate Islam as the definitive expression and establishment of what human religion was always meant to be and must yet become when aberrations are turned back into the way and misguidedness is at an end. It is natural, therefore, in making a thematic selection, to return to the content of the faith as 'religion' and of society under law as these derive from the prophethood accomplished. There will be some duplication here, in that these themes are articulate throughout the history which defined them. But there is point in gathering together those passages which embrace the convictions and the legal ordering of Islam. For the Qur'ān is the primary source and the sole final appeal of the *Sharī'ah*, or sacred law. Our final thematic heading, 'Unfaith, Judgement and the Last Things', is the Scripture's awesome conclusion.

It follows from the foregoing that a further section presses for inclusion in an Introductory Essay. It is the hardest of all to encompass. A Scripture whose acceptance as the very speech and word of God so long, so far, so deep, is a crucial fact of the contemporary world. We live in a perplexity of conscious pluralism, in what some have called 'an ecumene of religions'. Religion in some parts of the world and in some organs of society is clamant and self-assured, closed in mind and hard of heart. In other parts of the human scene it is in puzzled recession, constrained by secularity, beset by multiple indifference. In this ambiguous situation the Qur'ān cannot be isolated within Islam. Its sanctions of human behaviour, its criteria of social issues, its vistas of mystery and awe, have to be taken into the reckoning of all who pretend to realism in our age of change.

Whether *de fide* as for multitudes of Muslims, or *de facto* for the rest of humanity, the Islamic Scripture has to be to some degree a common mentor for us all. Education in multi-faith schools in Europe and the West has to discover its meanings and pursue them. The destinies of non-Muslim minorities within Muslim dominance hinge in part on its exegesis and reception. An inclusive reckoning with current technology can hardly dispense with it. What has authority for some of the human race must have relevance for all. As 'a mercy to the worlds', Muhammad and the Qur'ān cannot well be confined within Islam, nor their significance withheld from those who do not assent to its beliefs. For, in 'the world of all of us', the non-Muslim can no longer credibly be assigned to subjugation as *Dār al-Harb*, the household of inevitable (even mandatory) conflict. Even the diehards among us must in some sense be practising pluralists in today's world.

Response to the Qur'ān can only be from within the faith-context which inspires and informs the person responding: in my case, a Christian context. This calls for no apology. This translation of the Qur'ān stems from almost half a century of concern for its study and it has occupied many years of intermittent work. I began by sharing, in part, the frequently-met Christian attitude to the Book of Islam, which on several counts 'regretted' the way it was. The Qur'ān's disallowing of the crucial Christian understanding that 'God in Christ reconciled the world' made one unhappy. There was its failure to appreciate what Christians meant by 'the Word made flesh' and what they saw to be the Cross in the heart of God. These were weighty considerations, even though I never shared the instinct of some Christians to carry unhappiness with the Qur'ān into denigration or polemic. It seemed to me that what was evidently so precious and so final for so large a segment of humanity demanded an open, not to say also a generous reckoning. Furthermore initial and subsequent awareness of its Arabic quality would have given pause to any easy dismissiveness, had there been any inclination in that direction.

It rapidly became conclusively clear to me that the Qur'ān had dimensions of meaning that Christians ought to share fully and thankfully, and that it was their duty to counter the adverse judgements to which past attitudes had been prone. The Qur'ān's understanding of man in the world, of divine sovereignty undergirding our creaturely hospitality in nature *via* the sacramental character of all our experience, and much else, drew me — like the fascination of calligraphy — into a long, positive reckoning with the Qur'ān and a desire to get it more squarely into the consciousness of my fellow Christians and, indeed, of secular sceptics. These might still be deterred by the perplexities they encountered in responding or by the reservations they might wish to retain against the naivétiés (if they thought them so) of enthusiasm. In that event the proper course would be to meet those perplexities and reservations halfway. In four widely spaced books: *The Privilege of Man* (1967); *The Event of the Qur'ān* (1970); *The Mind of the Qur'ān* (1973) and *Muhammad and the Christian* (1982), I tried to present what might be called the Christian affinity with the Muslim Scripture and to argue spiritual community in some areas of its meaning. To prepare a selection of texts and a contemporary translation came to seem a logical step in this endeavour. But that was a long task that had to be pursued with diffidence in the midst of many pre-occupations.

Selection might well be seen as pretentious, an exercise in sheer temerity, tampering with the heavenly word. And were there not translations enough already? Could not would-be English readers rely sufficiently on one or other of them, or several in conjunction? They remain, anyway, in the field. Yet there seemed to me to be a case for a new version, which had the literary incentives discussed in the third section of the Introductory Essay, and which aimed to facilitate the lively presence of the Qur'ān within the religious issues belonging to our contemporary situation.

Let it be clear that selection and translation alike are wholly a Quranic activity. But they are attempted here in order to serve the inter-religious pluralism that obtains today, alongside a widespread secularisation. The Qur'ān is Arabic and defines Islam. There cannot then be a Buddhist, or a Jewish, or a Hindu, or a Christian, translation. But there may well be Buddhist, Jewish, Hindu, Christian reflections on the themes its translation makes available to those traditions, just as hopefully we look for Muslim reflections on the Greek New Testament based — if they are so minded — on a Muslim scholarship concerned for the nuances of the Greek in the languages of Islam.

It seemed necessary to set out these *raisons d'être* clearly in this Preface, in the hope that they may be taken in good faith. After centuries of suspicion and surmise (that *zann* which the Qur'ān so often condemns), Muslims may well have reservations about a Christian's concern with the sacred Scripture they so guard and cherish. Current events and tensions have done nothing to diminish postures of distrust and, for some, the time for the openness we long for may not be ripe. For others it is ripe indeed. Deep questions remain between us, as I tried to explore in *Jesus and the Muslim* (1985). But surely these can best be broached and faced within the confidence and honesty we may hope to come by through an awareness of the theism we hold, at least in part, in common in a world liable to suspect it in its pride of technology or fear of the absurd.

To repeat, readers who want only the Qur'ān for its own sake, are recommended to ignore these concerns which are developed in the Introductory Essay and take themselves promptly to the text.

While the first section of the Essay is for good reason free of footnotes, these have been indispensable in the other three sections. Normal transliteration of Arabic terms has been followed, though without the diacritical points below the letter that distinguish between Arabic consonants. The Glossary provides elucidation of terms: though usually the immediate context should sufficiently indicate their meaning. The English word 'God' has been used throughout for *Allāh* (and not the unhappy 'Englishing' of a resonant Arabic word). An Appendix lists the Chapters of the Qur'ān and provides a note on the naming of chapters. The Indices have to do both with subject matter, and with passages included and — equally important — the parallels to passages omitted. The verse numberings are those of the Royal Egyptian edition of the Qur'ān, now normally followed, published in 1342 A.H. in Cairo.

Sadly the book lacks the Foreword which His Excellency Dr. Allah Bukhsh K. Brohi of Karachi, Ambassador at large of Pakistan, a man of letters and eminent jurist, had graciously agreed to write. His illness and death in the autumn of the year intervened while he was preparing his assessment and review of the text. He had expressed lively interest in the enterprise and I had treasured his friendship since our first meeting in 1958. In honour of his memory I have sought no other commendation.

My thanks and appreciation go to the Editorial Director of Collins Liturgical, Mrs Suzanne R. Chapman, for her careful interest in this edition of the Qur'ān, and her hand in its format.

Oxford, England   Kenneth Cragg
Autumn, 1987

بسم الله الرحمن الرحيم

AN
INTRODUCTORY
ESSAY

بسم الله الرحمن الرحيم

1. The Qur'ān at First Meeting

Approaching the Qur'ān

Muslims down the centuries, scholars and mystics alike, have expressed their experience of the Qur'ān in a wealth of metaphor. Their Scripture is like a Damascus brocade. The patterned beauty of its true design bears an underside which the unwary may mistake, seeing what is there but not in its real fullness. Or the Book is like a veiled bride whose hidden face is only known in the intimacy of truth's consummation. It is like the pearl for which the diver must plunge to break the shell which both ensures and conceals the treasure. The Qur'ān, these images imply, yields itself only to those who rightly understand.

What, then, of newcomers? What hope for the uninitiated? Such analogies may well deter rather than excite them. Poetic imagery may suit the superb eloquence of the early Qur'ān, but beginnings for new readers are likely to be prosaic and pedestrian. There is much in a first encounter to daunt or perplex. Maybe the very title itself presents a problem: Qur'ān (no longer written 'Koran' — an alternative but inexact transliteration of the Arabic name) means 'reading' or 'recital'. The fact that you are reading a translation is another problem: for when the Scripture of Islam is no longer in Arabic it loses some of its vibrancy and power. Problems of sequence and continuity also loom large for the student who is liable to be left puzzling over why, by what logic of chronology or theme, the Qur'ān moves, as it frequently does, from one context to another. Chronology, Muslims say, is not a clue to the Qur'ān's significance since it is a timeless Scripture. Yet the fact that it had its formation during the twenty-three years of Muhammad's prophethood means that commentary has necessarily relied on these points in time known as 'occasions of the revelation'.

Our initial purpose here is with the broad implications rather than the technical details of these factors in the newcomer's situation. Obviously the first thing the reader needs is a degree of persistence and patience. Nothing can so well engender these as a lively sense of the Qur'ān's claim to attention beyond the confines of Islam and its relevance in the contemporary scene.

The Qur'ān is the definitive Scripture for multitudes of mankind. Like the Bible, the Dhammapada and the Bhagavad Gita in their communities,

14

familiarity with it is a primary requisite of inter-religious concern in the world of today. Liturgically, it is the most rehearsed and recited of all the Scriptures. Islam takes its documentation more explicitly, more emphatically, than any other household of worship. Received by Muslims in its Arabic form as the actual words or speech of God, the Qur'ān is memorised as the groundplan of all knowledge. So held in Muslim veneration and custody, it is the most decisive of the world's Scriptures in the regulation of law and of life. Its authority holds sway over vast populations in numerous lands, and has endured for fourteen centuries. Its nature and content are therefore of central significance for the future of humanity. It follows that the desire of the outsider to comprehend what the Qur'ān is to Muslims is much to be welcomed and urgently to be pursued.

It is as a positive service to such comprehension that the selection and translation in this volume are intended. It falls to parts 2 and 3 of the Introductory Essay to argue why and how. Here it suffices to underline that any English or other non-Arabic version of the Qur'ān is an attenuated thing, as every Arab and Arabist knows. The Book may be virtually untranslatable — as Muslim dogma holds. Yet it exists for all humanity and, in order to be accessible to all, must allow the surrender of identity which translation involves.

By whatever lights a translator proceeds — and issues here run deep — the reader must at least appreciate the diminution suffered by the change from one language to another. Translations do not convey the emotion, the fervour, the mystery the Qur'ān holds in the original. Reading the Book in the quiet of the study, perusing it with the eye, silences the force of the text which properly belongs with the ear and the soul. As its name indicates, the Qur'ān was from the beginning a vocal thing: *Recite in the Name of your Lord* was the initial summons to Muhammad when his mission began. Recital, utterance, have ever since been the heart of the Book's significance within Islam. To be able to recite by heart has been the first requisite of Muslim education. Ritual prayer, whatever the believer's native speech, must be in the Qur'ān's own tongue. However painstaking the translation, an English version can never aspire to the role of the original Arabic.

THE STRUCTURE OF THE QUR'ĀN: IN AT THE BEGINNING

The chapters of the Qur'ān are known as *sūrahs*. There are one hundred and fourteen *sūrahs*. The first is called 'The Opener' (*Al-Fātihah*) and contains seven verses (or *āyāt*). This *sūrah* is unique in being an inclusive hymn of praise and petition, recited in whole or in part throughout Islamic devotion and ritual prayer. It could well be described as the heart-beat of Muslim response to God, echoing His praise and sole Lordship and seeking aid, right guidance and the mercy which distinguishes the true believer from the false.

15

New readers will feel instinctively at home in The Opener. Surah 2, however, moves into a different idiom. With its 286 verses it is the longest chapter of all. After the invocation of 'the Name of God, the merciful Lord of mercy', (which precedes every chapter except Surah 9) and three mysterious letters (a, l, m), it affirms the indubitable character of the Book as a whole and then passes into a long and varied sequence of subjects. The reader is at once aware of the sharp contrast between belief and unbelief. We are ushered into a heavenly conclave of angels where God announces the dignity of man as the viceroy of the earth. Episodes in the history of Israel follow. Interweaving historical scenes in Moses' day are encounters between the Prophet Muhammad and the Jews of his day. It becomes clear that Christians too are involved in these exchanges, and we are introduced to the person of Abraham. What is contemporary to Muhammad and what is patriarchal fuse together. There follows mention of the rites and duties of the Islamic community as such — pilgrimage, the direction of prayer, laws relating to food, retaliation, enslavement, testamentary succession, fasting, warfare 'in the way of God' (or *Jihād*), orphanhood, marriage, divorce, divining, the duty of almsgiving (or *Zakāt*), usury and its prohibition and, finally, loans and contracts. Between these passages are brief references to Abraham and to Jesus. We sense an underlying current of resistance which Muhammad is facing. The whole concludes with a moving prayer for divine compassion, pardon and forbearance.

All these regulations and directives presuppose the community of faith. But Surah 2 has not put us in possession of the prophetic vocation which alone explains the emergence of the community. The confrontation we sense has its antecedents, as yet untold, in the life-story of Muhammad. For these we must turn far on into the Book, to Surah 96 for example, where the mandate to 'recite in the Name of the Lord' is found.

Clearly the beginning in the text is not the beginning of the story. But then the 'beginning' with Muhammad is not the beginning, because the patriarchs have been there before. Nor was their role an 'origin'. For all the prophets belong with a Book eternally pre-existent in heaven on 'a preserved tablet' (85.21-22). It becomes clear that the Qur'ān has a double approach to chronology. It does assign its own chapters to the two periods into which, as we will see, Muhammad's mission divides. But, for the sake of its eternal dimension, it does not organise its contents in line with those two periods. Neither the sequence of chapters nor, in many cases, their contents conform to that division. The reader has to be ready for a constant inter-penetration of times and themes within the whole.

Accordingly, one is well advised to begin from the end of the Book as it is and read forward from Surah 114 to Surah 2, since the chapters earliest in time are concentrated in the final third. Those in the long forepart of the Scripture are for the most part chronologically the latest. This situation corresponds with the fact that Muhammad's earliest deliverances as prophet were highly poetic in character, fervent and ecstatic. By contrast, the later legal and organisational provisions for the established community were prosaic and extended. Since length of chapters (though by no means uniformly) seems to have been a clue to their arrangement, the formula: 'shorter/earlier; longer/later', makes a rough rule of thumb. Intervening between these two 'sections' are the narrative pieces about patriarchal figures and prophetic precedents which linked the preaching of Islam with its establishment, and the calling of the messenger with a community's obedience. We see the relevance of those messengers of the past in the context of Muhammad's own vocation. Indeed, the circumstances of his vocation in its setting of Arabian paganism tend to induce a version or vision of the content and reception of all earlier revelation as arising in comparable circumstances. But, before exploring the theme of Muhammad in the Qur'ān, it will be well to set out the Islamic understanding of the Qur'ān as God's.

THE QUR'ĀN IN ITS DIVINE QUALITY

What sort of comprehension do Muslims expect of outsiders who would take the measure of the Qur'ān? In what does its Islamic standing consist? It is received in Islam as the *ipsissima verba* of God: in its Arabic syllables it is the very speech of 'the Lord of the worlds'. The formula with which to cite a quotation is: *Qāl Allāh*, 'God said', or *Qaul Allāh*, 'God's saying'. In Islam, Scripture is itself the heavenly words — the facsimile, or 'manifest' — of the volume *Umm al-Kitāb*, 'the mother of the Book', which is eternally preserved with God.

That conviction is self-warranting. Its authenticity does not, need not, stay for questioning. The Qur'ān is not a tribunal which is itself on trial: it is the divine words *per se*, a majestic summons to mankind, a divine imperative. It is not properly to be reckoned with on any other ground. The contrast with the New Testament underlines the point: the evangelists in the four Gospels are understood to be enabled in their writing by the Holy Spirit. Indeed, they are sometimes depicted, pen in hand, looking heavenward to transcribe a scroll unfolding there. But the content of their writing is the pre-existing 'Word' incarnate. The heart of Christian revelation is the 'event' of Jesus as the Christ, acknowledged as the disclosure, in human form, of the very nature of God. Hence, New Testament Scripture is a derivative from the prior and primary revelation of the living Word 'made flesh and dwelling among us'. Hence, the Gospels are held to be a reliable means of access to Christ, made adequate for that role by the Holy Spirit. This derivative character of New Testament writing is more evident still in respect of the Epistles, which clearly educate the faithful in the meaning of their faith, in pastoral concern for the new life of the community, and its nurture within the constraints of the great original: Jesus himself, teaching, suffering and risen.

By contrast, the Qur'ān does not present itself as documenting what is other than itself. It is not about the truth: it is the truth. It is not revelation by means of the description of a personality: it is revelation in mediation, as a book already existing eternally. Islam, to be sure, does have holy literature known as *Hadīth*, or 'tradition', drawn from the example and discourse of Muhammad and constituting a second source of the sacred law. But with rare exceptions this literature is essentially distinct from the Qur'ān both in form and status. The Qur'ān alone is the speech of God, and tradition derives its warrant from the fact that Muhammad was the Prophet and he, uniquely, received the Book from heaven.

To ask what such receiving might entail takes us to the concept of *tanzīl*, or 'sending down'. The content of the Scripture is understood as mediated to Muhammad during a period of some twenty-three years, by angelic or other means, so that he was enabled at successive intervals to utter its contents to his human hearers. These, as we shall see in the narrative, coincided with circumstances and episodes in his personal career. Their mediation to him from above is described as *wahy*, a term which includes both 'revelation' and 'inspiration', which — by virtue of the Qur'ān's character — are not distinguishable. In the state of *wahy*, *tanzīl* occurred. How the eternal partakes of the temporal, the divine with the human, must always remain mystery, but it is a mystery which is contained, not explained, within the meaning of these two terms. Instrumental to the incidence of *tanzīl* and the receiving of *wahy*, the identity of Muhammad is indispensable. It is his role which uniquely serves the one and experiences the other. What is *from* God is *through* Muhammad. The Qur'ān belongs within the formula which is the sum of Islamic faith, and occurs so frequently in its verses namely: 'God and His apostle'. Let us turn to the human side of that association.

THE QUR'ĀN IN ITS HUMAN QUALITY

Given the Islamic faith in the eternal 'original' (*Umm al-Kitāb*, the mother of the Book) with God, how do Muslims understand its incidence in the time and place of Muhammad's experience? How is its divine quality allied to his prophetic consciousness? The questions lead out into paradox and must not be curiously pursued. Muslim conviction sees divine communication and Muhammad's messengership as the two aspects of a single fact. The messenger has locale, circumstance, context and a history. The language is Arabic and the local setting is that of a commercial metropolis and a pilgrim shrine. The vocabulary reflects a range of influences and associations already current within the immediate society. Whatever enters into time must necessarily exist at a given time. Nor can an apostleship in God's Name be other than into a 'here and now' which in retrospect becomes a 'there and then'.

However, what is circumstantial to the Qur'ān is not what determines either its form or its contents. Nor is the Prophet's living engagement with its coming an initiative he makes in response to factors around him. The Book, to be sure, bears relevantly upon the situation, but only because *tanzīl* has it so. This is the firm conviction of Islamic faith, variously reconciled by individual thinkers with the evidently vivid and virile participation of Muhammad in the unfolding of the revelation. But he must not be assumed to inspire the genesis, nor to determine the content, of his preaching. The utterances on his part, which progressively comprise the Qur'ān in its earthly incidence, are believed to derive directly and exclusively from the divine mercy.

This sense of things underlies the long Muslim belief in the illiteracy of Muhammad. That he was — as this belief has it — unable to read or write means that his capacity for such eloquence as the Qur'ān displays must be miraculous. Had he been already gifted in poetic skill or book knowledge it would have been less manifestly a Book by God's gift. His very incapacity demonstrates the divine imparting. Non-Muslims need to appreciate this view for the clear implications it has within the faith-community.

The outsider may well see this as a means of securing authority and authorising security — those two perennial yearnings in religions. Yet it is by no means the only or the necessary way of viewing Muhammad's role in the Book. Indeed there has been a long tradition in Muslim devotion which, despite the view just noted, sees the 'illiterate' Muhammad a 'genius' of immaculate wisdom in whom prophethood means the irradiation of personality with the divine light.

Moreover, there are good Quranic reasons to question the Prophet's total illiteracy. As he was a prosperous merchant, we can assume his ability with accounts and bills of lading. When the Qur'ān states that he did not 'write' the text, it may mean that he used amanuenses — a fact otherwise attested in tradition. The verses which refer to his being: 'the apostle, the prophet, the unlettered' (Surah 7.157 and 159), and the term used (*ummī*), can most properly be understood, not in the sense of utter illiteracy, but of coming from among a people having no scripture. Arabs are contrasted with 'the people of the Book', i.e. Jews and Christians. Scriptures were crucial factors in the very identity of these 'people', whereas Muhammad's people were not yet blessed with scriptures in their own Arabic tongue. *Via* the Qur'ān they were to become so, through a man of their own kin and kind. This sense of the word *ummī* — 'unlettered' — as meaning 'not yet scriptured' coincides with the Qur'ān's frequent insistence on its being 'an Arabic (or Arab) Qur'ān'.

However, understanding his 'unletteredness' in this way leaves intact what the conviction about his 'illiteracy' intends to affirm, namely, that the Book was wholly bestowed upon Muhammad from above. What he receives in *wahy* is in no way explicable by natural talent or circumstantial occasion.

Thus the Muslim reception of the Qur'ān stands in the double fact of a transcendent source and the conscious activity of a human personality totally engaged. A message entirely from beyond is fulfilled in a mission within unfolding historical events. *Tanzīl* has a local history, and *wahy* a personal biography, in which the human agency is enlisted, educated and enlarged. The telling of that story belongs within those dimensions of faith.

MUHAMMAD WITH THE QUR'ĀN IN MECCA

The reader of the Qur'ān must repair imaginatively to Mecca, the city of Muhamamad's birth in the year 570 AD, and for thirteen years the locale of his prophethood. Set in a basin of hills flanking the trade routes that lay along the western littoral of Arabia linking the Yemen with the Levant, Mecca, in the decades prior to the rise of Islam, had been growing in commercial importance. As well as its merchandise, it had the greater asset of being a place of pilgrimage. At the heart of Mecca was the sacred *haram*, or enclosure, to which pagans came during the months of truce in tribal feuding — months vital to the prosperity of the shrine.

The control both of commerce and of the pagan pilgrims belonged to Meccas's rulers — the Quraish whose hegemony owed much to the acumen of Hāshim, Muhammad's great grandfather. Their power structure is graphically challenged in Surah 106:

'. . . the bringing to rendezvous of the Quraish, the gathering in convoy of their caravans, winter and summer. Let them serve the Lord of this house who gave them provision of food against hunger and security from fear.'

The 'house' was the *Ka'bah* in the centre of the sacred enclosure at the heart of Mecca. Built at the navel of the earth by the prototype of all true worship, Abraham, it had long been degraded by pagan rites the purging of which was to be the burden of Muhammad's call.

An orphan in the care first of his grandfather and then of his uncle, Muhammad emerged to manhood in those convoys of merchants and cameleers plying between south and north. The trade was highly organised, requiring expertise in loans and funding and resources to protect it from marauding tribes on the flanks. Hence the need for convoys, caravans serviced by giving would-be allies or enemies a stake in their success. This organisation helped to introduce into tribal loyalty a different nexus which could later displace the clan and serve to develop an economic, and in turn, a political awareness significant for the new faith.

History is not decisive as to what influences Muhammad encountered in his trading years, from the time of his marriage, aged twenty-five, to the widow Khadījah in whose caravans he served. Traditions and conjectures are many. His journeys certainly took him into Jewish and Christian contacts in the markets of Najran southward, the suqs of Jerusalem and Damascus northward, and the dispersion of the two monotheisms around the trade routes and at the poles of the cross traffic from Ethiopia to Lower Iraq. It may be that a kindling sense of 'Scriptures' possessed by peoples — and so of prophets as a means to scriptures — derived from those travels. Or the influences may have been more explicit. The Qur'ān refers to a heritage from Abraham by those known as *hunafā'* (s.*hanīf*) who, though 'neither Jews nor Christians', none the less believed in 'a pure worship' or monotheism. The nearly twenty years of Muhammad's journeyings as a merchant certainly served to arouse and deepen brooding thoughts about history's ruins, the vagaries of tribes, the clannishness of faiths and the mysteries beyond them.

A habit of meditation intensified around his fortieth year — a habit for which the hills and caves around Mecca afforded ample places of retreat, where the vocation supervened which was to transform him into a colossus on the stage of history. Vision and voice, in one, summoned him to 'recite in the Name of (thy) Lord'. As one 'wrapped in a mantle', he was called to 'arise and warn' (74.2-3, cf.73.2). The sense of prophetic destiny broke into his consciousness and was, first timorously, then decisively, obeyed. Imperatively commissioned, he began to urge his Meccan hearers to worship God alone, to repudiate their idols and to ready themselves for 'the day of judgement'. That public message was steadily renewed, primed one might almost say, by the recurrent instances of *tanzīl*, the 'coming down' of the heavenly words. At the outset there was an unnerving bewilderment about the whence and the whether of that *tanzīl*. Would each hiatus see the end? Was the sequence a delusion? Sustained by the succour of Khadījah, Muhammad gathered assurance. The deliverances became more reliable, their incidence no longer an anxiety. As misgivings passed, confidence became established. The content of the Book in heaven passed into a steady earthly accumulation in the human setting on the lips of its human mouthpiece. The consciousness of Muhammad fused with the meaning of *tanzīl*. From the inaugural date of 609 (approximately) the incidence of the Book and the destiny of Muhammad become one. His personal name, significantly, occurs only four times in the whole Qur'ān. Throughout he is *al-Rasūl*, the one sent with the *risālah* or message. Scripture and his prophethood are a unison of end and means.

Inevitably the place and the time, Mecca and the Quraish, reacted by their lights and interests. Muhammad's preaching of One sovereign Lord, *Allāh*, and the iniquitous folly of plural worship, struck at the heart — or so it seemed — of Mecca's stake in pilgrimage. It certainly collided with 'the traditions of our forebears' as the leading Meccans had it. The notion of

21

resurrection to judgement found little credence in their pagan ears. Muhammad's denunciation of usury, when this transpired, threatened their cherished trade. Commerce, privilege and pride alike conspired against the upstart prophet.

Controversy followed. It gathered inexorably around Muhammad's themes and so about the motives, the warrant, even the sanity, of the preacher. In their obduracy the Quraish stood for the *status quo*. Their interests and their gods were inseparable. They accused Muhammad of learning from strangers, ape-ing ecstatic poets, behaving as an enemy within. As he held firmly to his mission, animosity sharpened. The content of the Qur'ān passed more and more into contention, rebutting what 'they said', with what 'God said'. Here the precedent of earlier prophets became relevant. The narratives of their patriarchal experience with their perverse peoples served both to warn the gainsayers and to hearten Muhammad. For theirs were precedents of final vindication for steadfast messengers in the ruin and perdition of the heedless. The unbelieving folk of Mecca would do well to remember Pharaoh and the Red Sea, Haman and the gallows, the dire fate of the tribes of 'Ād and Thamūd, ancient dwellers by the trade-routes.

For thirteen years between 609 and 622 confrontation hardened into aggravated travail for Muhammad and the relatively few believers (some of whom found refuge in Ethiopia) and unrelenting hostility among the Meccan establishment. An unyielding power-structure and a steadfast messenger alike stood their ground. Eloquence and tenacity had not availed against the one, nor threat and ridicule against the other. The lengthening encounter stood in impasse, fraught with tragedy. Khadījāh — his wife — and Abū Tālib — his guardian-uncle — died in 619. Bereaved, Muhammad mused on the mystery of the incontrovertible message denied by entrenched perversity. It was, and is, the keenest of all issues that arouse religious perplexity. The key to the Qur'ān's significance is how it resolved the paradox implicit in the verbal non-success of a prophet bearing the indubitable truth by mandate of the omnipotent Name. Should not such prophethood be manifestly vindicated, achieve success, emerge authenticated from events? But how? If after sustained and costly effort words and preaching, exhortation and warning had not prevailed, what else might, or should, do so?

Given that the Meccan *haram* was a citadel of prestige, enjoying the immunity of a shrine and possessing economic sinews, perhaps it should literally be repudiated — for the time being — by a physical emigration with the intention of creating an alternative citadel of power, which might eventually bring the first to heel. It was later to become a doctrine of Muslim jurisprudence that a truly Muslim society could only subsist under its own polity and statehood and that the true Muslim should not willingly accept to be ruled by non-Muslims, but rather should emigrate into an Islamic rule. In the vital year 622, from which Islam's calendar begins, Muhammad and his small Meccan community enacted and so defined that principle by their departure to Yathrib, which was thus to become Medina — 'the city of the Prophet'.

This was the *Hijrah*, or 'emigration', the decisive event in the genesis of Islam, the transition from preaching to power, from warning to warring. It was the watershed in Muhammad's story and sets the categories of 'before' and 'after' for the Qur'ān itself. The transition from Mecca to Medina was as decisive for the whole future of Islam as the Exodus was for Jewry. Events in the two or three preceding years had paved the way for it, namely the abortive nature of Muhammad's foray to Tā'if, his own increasing jeopardy and, most important, the interest of a group of Yathribites in his message and their subsequent undertaking to defend him. Those 'pledges' meant that he had 'helpers' *(ansār)*, as they were called, in the northern city to facilitate the reception and safety of the emigrating Meccan Muslims called *Muhājirūn*, i.e. 'makers of *Hijrah*'.

Prior to this central event, the Qur'ān had always enjoined upon Muhammad that his sole duty was what it called *al-balāgh*, the communication of the word. This alone was his responsibility. After the *Hijrah* the message continues, but the burden of the Book is more and more the building of a power-community and military confrontation with the Quraish, and the politics of success. The Qur'ān leaves the reader in no doubt that it is out of the faith-issue that the force-issue arises — and legitimately so. There are many who assume that Muhammad had no practical alternative, in the given pattern of the time and place, unless his mission were to be left in permanent frustration.

MUHAMMAD AND THE QUR'ĀN AT MEDINA

The Qur'ān makes little actual reference to the event of the *Hijrah* in narrative terms. Surah 9.40 tells of how divine protecting peace, *Al-Sakīnah*, hovered over Muhammad and his closest associate, Abū Bakr, en route to Yathrib, and there may be an oblique reference in 36.9. But the content of the Book moves steadily into provisions for the liturgical life of the Muslims, their legal obligations, and the claims of campaigning against Mecca. The patterns of fivefold daily prayer had been emerging already but shortly after the *Hijrah* the *Qiblah*, or direction of prayer, was turned around from its earlier focus in Jerusalem to Mecca, clearly indicating that exile was not abandonment. The mother city was ever in view, politically as well as devotionally. Correspondingly, controversy against the Jews, who were numerous in the Yathrib area and beyond, intensified, apparently in response to Muhammad's fading hopes of recognition by them of his prophetic status.

The eight years of his sojourn in Medina culminated in the capitulation of Mecca after a long series of encounters — the battles of Badr, Uhud and the

23

Ditch in which, through varying fortunes, the Quraish were outmanoeuvred and outfought. By a treaty at Hudaibiyyah, Muhammad won the right to revisit Mecca as a pilgrim from which he gained in prestige and influence. Confiscations of Jewish property and distraint on tribes caught in would-be neutrality or actual subterfuge between the main combatants steadily strengthened his resources. When, finally, he advanced on Mecca to clinch his victory the Quraishī will was broken and their surrender complete. The credibility of their patron gods had been shattered by events and the obduracy which had stubbornly resisted the preacher readily yielded to the commander. What the Qur'ān calls 'manifest victory' had been attained. Some two years later, with Islam on the brink of further consolidations of allegiance, Muhammad died. With his passing the Qur'ān was complete.

The delineation of the life of the Muslim community, its religious law and social ethic, proceeded through the years of its active progress to victory. The reader, now abreast of the story, comes round again to Surah 2 with its long enumeration of duties and prescripts, many of them repeated and renewed through all the Medinan chapters. In the wake of Muhammad's achievement, the patriarchs and prophets give way to the climax for which their precedents were meant. The divine resolution of the issue between Muhammad and the unbelieving Quraish transpired within the energies of a bold leadership and the yearnings of an ardent faith. With a strong feel of immediacy and realism, Surah 4.101-102, for example, depicts how the prayer-rite was to cope with battle stations:

'When you are making an expedition anywhere, you will not be at fault in curtailing the act of prayer, if you have reason to suspect the unbelievers of some evil design against you. For that these deniers of the truth are at enmity with you is plain enough. When you (s.) are in the midst of engaging in the prayer-rite, let a number of them stand with you retaining their weapons by them. When these have performed the prayer let them make cover for you while the other part, who have yet to pray, come forward to pray with you, taking due precaution and retaining their arms. The unbelievers would dearly like you to be negligent about your weapons and your equipment in order to fall upon you in sudden attack'.

Thus the transcendent dimension of worship and the lively vigilance of the soldier marry together in the characteristic vigour of the later Qur'ān.

Its way with the sequence of events is not that of a chronicle. Rather it interprets the providences and underlines the lessons. Badr, the first encounter in the field, had been a signal victory, 'the day of the criterion' (Surah 8), when Muslim prowess pointed the way ahead. The battle of Uhud (Surah 3.102-175) proved less decisive, testing fidelity and tempering exuberance by partial defeat. Confrontation cannot well admit of neutrals and must either draw them into alliance or subject them to despoilation. Magnanimity must await the final victory when all *fitnah*, or seditious hostility, is unambiguously brought to an end. Until then warfare is a lesser evil than *fitnah*. The material fruits of battle have to be duly shared, force appropriately subdued to the cause. The casualties — widows and orphans — are to be compassionately tended with justice and provision. Gamblers, usurers and shirkers have no place in this disciplined society nor those who, pleading poverty, commit infanticide. The reader discovers how the laws of the Qur'ān belong squarely within the campaigning, how the incidence of *tanzīl* aligns with the activism of Medinan Islam.

It is in this context of political and military occasions that we come upon the rare references to matters marital and domestic within the Prophet's entourage. The living space of his immediate circle, of his wives, and access to his presence inevitably became areas of critical importance as his leadership assumed increasing stature and the range and cares of command intensified. Yet the Qur'ān never presents these in terms abstracted from the central authority of prophethood and the warrant it enjoyed. All came within the purview of divine revelation. It was not the nature of the Qur'ān to reserve the category of revelation to themes of purely spiritual import. That even the disciplining of insubordinate wives may afford an 'occasion of revelation' demonstrates that the Quranic message finds its relevance and states its claim in any and every context.

But, integral as they are in the Qur'ān, these features concerning the personal circle of the Prophet of Medina are significantly few. Tradition was needed in the years and centuries after his death to fill out details on which the Book itself is completely silent. Such data was also a vital necessity in the elaboration of Islamic law — by no means comprehensive within the Qur'ān. Though admitting us into privacies of Muhammad's ménage, the Scripture throughout holds firmly to the inclusive theme of the *Shahādah*, or confession of faith: 'There is no god but God: Muhammad is His apostle'. It is always in that nexus the reader finds him, the exclusive recipient of revelation, as final prophethood unfolds it, within the career it shapes and guides.

THE QUR'ĀN THROUGH THE CENTURIES

Islamic faith is confident that the death of Muhammad and the completion of the mediation of the Book coincided. Thus the passing of the sole recipient of the revelation did not mean any rupture in the process of *tanzīl*. The final deliverance of the Qur'ān is thought to be the words in Surah 5.3: 'Today I (God) have made perfect for you (pl.) your religion and fulfilled My grace upon you and have approved for you as religion "Islam".' Muhammad who had legitimate successors in rulership, needed no successor as prophet. At his demise the Scripture, through his instrumentality, was entire.

That demise, precisely because his stature was so towering and his status so unique, left a great gap needing to be filled so that the community might be guided in areas on which the revelation had been silent — areas of life and interpretation which the immediate and far-reaching expansion of the faith dramatically enlarged. The need was met by recruiting the dicta of Muhammad outside the Qur'ān, his habits of mind and conduct, as these were perpetuated and circulated in reverent memory. This was the source and elaboration of tradition, implementing but in no way displacing the Qur'ān itself, and ranking second to it in the definition of Islam.

But Muhammad's death, though finalising the contents of the Qur'ān, did not leave them in final shape. It is assumed that at the time of the trauma of his decease, the many utterances of the preceding twenty-three years were inscribed on a variety of fragments in a script which still lacked the diacritical points by which Arabic later differentiated many identically shaped letters, and which was not yet in serial or canonised form. If the sequences which the Qur'ān now possesses — the sequence of the chapters and the sequences inside them — were as Muhammad decided they should be, as Muslim devotion believes, it is hard to understand why there should have been any uncertainty afterwards or why any debate should have arisen. For it does appear that collections, or recensions, of what was authentically Quranic tended to vary. Variants also came to be sponsored by, or associated with, different centres such as Mecca, Medina, Basrah or Kufa — a process which could have endangered the unity both of the Book and of the faith-community. Accordingly, in the reign of the third Caliph, 'Uthmān (644-655), the second of two recensions was authorised and strong attempts made to suppress alternative versions, some of which were in the custody of Muhammad's widows. Though made in the interests of unity this authorisation of a definitive text was one of the factors in the disquiet attending 'Uthmān's rule.

There are several questions proper to scholarship about the text of the Qur'ān and tensions, certainly about interpretation, but also about readings, between the sects of both Sunnī and Shī'ah Islam. But these need not deter or pre-occupy the general reader. It is substantially agreed that the Qur'ān as we have it truly constitutes the deliverances of Muhammad in the distinctive state of *wahy* (as differentiated from what became tradition) and does so comprehensively and exclusively. That confident conviction turns on Muhammad's unique role and on the physical and psychic features which marked it. His hearers seem to have known when he was, so to speak, 'in Quranic capacity' and when not. For reasons both practical and historical the outside reader is well advised to share the Muslim assurance and leave more technical questions aside, though he may well regret that the recensions did not bequeath a more comprehensible form.

Given its sacrosanct source, its divine status and its decisive text, the

26

Qur'ān throughout the centuries has determined the law, the ethos, the culture and the mind of Islam. Classical commentary had to await the Arabicisation which followed Islamic expansion and the influences impinging on its readers from the intellectual and spiritual factors in its widening environment. These occasioned both a climate and a context in which its custodians had to respond to issues about God, and human will, creation and nature, reason and scripture, which had not arisen for its first reciters. Commentary became the mainstream of Islamic response, the Qur'ān, as it were, carrying in its margins the theology and ethics of Islam.

With all Scriptures, exegesis proceeds upon what pre-suppositions it brings to them, even though its intention is to submit to them. Given the concepts implicit in the Qur'ān's doctrine of itself as God's speech *verbatim*, the Islamic pre-suppositions understood the authority of the text — and their submission to it — in sharply literal terms. Grammar, syntax, parsing, became central duties. Though commentary did reflect theological controversies — not least in the middle centuries over the Qur'ān itself as 'created' or 'uncreated' — it tended to take to itself a derivative status and to become authoritarian in its own right. Then the margins acquired further margins outside themselves. The text itself, as the inner sanctum, came to be framed within a succession of custodial elaboration providing the lenses through which it should be read. One of the features of the present century and, by the Muslim calendar the previous one, has been the effort of some commentators to break through the classical margins as symbols of imprisonment and appeal directly to the perceived intention of the text.

In all such ventures, as with the traditional commentary, one central duty was recognised to be the 'occasions of the revelation', those circumstances and incidents of Muhammad's career with which the deliverances were linked. It was the work of tradition and of the early historians and chroniclers to determine and preserve the setting with which a passage should be associated, in order that the meaning could be rightly understood.

Such reading in the context was for the most part reverently elucidatory and no more. It sufficed to make the connection. More recently a critical reverence is invoked in order to wrestle with the deeper implications of 'there-and-then' in concern for 'here-and-now'. The passage of time becomes itself a question. Can radical pleas be made, maybe on the ground of the difference Islam itself has achieved, so that commentary is not merely set in time but translated out of 'time-then' into 'time-now'? For example, is the whole Medinan dimension somehow bound to time-then, leaving the Meccan dimension of a spiritual message all that contemporary Islam ought to be, ceasing to require statehood dominance and politically based expression? That would be a crucial translation which orthodox commentary stoutly rejects.

Nevertheless, some modern handling of the Qur'ān tends to relate to it in terms of *non*-repugnancy, rather than proven conformity, or it intends the latter by the freer criterion of the former. And what is, or is not, repugnant to the Book admits of various interpretation. Appealing as it must to some sort of consensus among Muslims, actual or implied, it liberates the Scripture, to a degree, from the purview of the rigorists and opens its exegesis to the insights or the predilections of 'lay' people. Scriptures are all in measure liable to be conformed to the mind of their communities so that the Qur'ān means what Muslims take it to mean. But even when classical readings of the Qur'ān, whether for faith or for law, are amended, revised or overturned, it is always the arbiter to which verdicts must appeal and whose support they will assume. We may say that if Muslims are to be assured on any and every issue, they will need to be Quranically persuaded, however variously they invoke it. It is this fact which makes intelligent reading of the Qur'ān outside Islam so necessary and desirable in today's world.

There is, finally, one rich vein of Qur'ān reading and savouring with a quality and fervour of its own. It is what Islamic mysticism, or Sufism, does with the Scripture. The habitual *dhikr*, or recital, is intensified into a technique of ecstacy, seeking the passing away of the ordinary self in an experience of unity with God. The salutation of the Prophet, enjoined on all in Surah 33.56, by which believers 'call down blessing upon him' at God's behest, becomes for the Sufis a veritable 'imitation' of Muhammad, seeking, by his example, to experience a mode of that same illumination which conveyed the Qur'ān itself. They thus become partakers of 'the light of Muhammad' and not simply students of the sacred words. This absorption into God gives voice to superb poetry which leaves far behind the laboured erudition of prosaic margins, and lyricises the text in an ardour of devotion. It gives rise also to those exhilarant metaphors about its beauty and wonder with which this chapter began. And in ways disconcerting to the prosaic faithful, it generates reproach of dry theology and spiritual detachment from the minutiae of religious duty. It writes a commentary all its own on the thrill and the themes of the Qur'ān, in irrepressible tribute to the Book's fecundity.

But it is wise to let mystic flights return us to the dogged fidelities of muezzin and preacher, reciter and scholar, whose lips and pens so imprinted the Qur'ān upon themselves as to require the attention of the rest of humanity.

بسم الله الرحمن الرحيم

2. The Qur'ān in Its Themes: The Logic of Selection

Is there something, at best inappropriate, at worst presumptuous, in making a selection from the Qur'ān? Even to look on the Scripture with the reverence of a true believer constitutes, for devout Muslims, an act of worship to God.[1] For the Book is His speech, His eternal attribute existing within His essence and thus sharing His uncreatedness. How then can human abridgement, however well-intentioned, be other than misguided? May it not imply some impatience with the whole as revelation left it? Can pruning somehow improve it? If readers are meant only to submit, have they any warrant to discriminate?

The misgivings are serious. Yet, on their own showing, there is a different case to be made. The conviction of an eternal Qur'ān belongs with an actual stage and an immediate scene. Revelation translates into a fabric of events and sequences and these necessarily take their character and have their incidence within a local context. Prolonged encounter between Muhammad and the Meccan leaders and populace meant urgent and sustained reiteration of his message in a situation of chronic *shirk*, or polytheism, and powerful vested interests for long years unyielding to his call. Thanks to Islam itself that situation has quite changed for many who read after the lapse of centuries and in a setting the Qur'ān — and other factors — have availed to alter. The case for translation, which we have yet to consider (see below, part 3), takes the Qur'ān out of its own arena in the Arabic and into the receiving culture in the prepossessions of its language. Selection is somewhat akin, as being also an enterprise of meaning in transit or migration. Just as idiom and grammar yield their treasures by being reminted in another language, so the strategy of the whole may require to undergo the sort of interpretation in reference to

---

1 See Muhammad Abul Quasem: *The Recitation and Interpretation of the Qur'ān*, Bagi, Selangor, Malaysia, 1979, p.59, citing Al-Ghazāli: *Ihyā' 'Ulūm al-Dīn*, 1, 279.

Cf also the comment: 'The sounds (of the Arabic) have become like the body and the dwelling-place for the divine wisdom and divine wisdom has become like the soul and spirit of the sounds.'

every new constituency or alien readership which selection by themes intends.

Properly reverent and alert, selection may free the resonance of the whole from impediments which — as experience has shown — hinder comprehension. Attention to meaning needs freedom from distraction. A mind for central themes may be a more sure service to the Book in general terms and for a wider audience. Muslims long initiated into the possession of their Scripture may not appreciate the puzzles of the uninitiated. When the frustration these perplexities arouse is recognised within Islam, selection in the Qur'ān may deserve approval as a right response. An edition such as the present one is no substitute for, and in no way displaces, the entire Qur'ān. But it may enable interest and study to take itself there more intelligently. The resolute tenacity with which Muhammad, in Meccan time and place, sustained an undeviating message through bitter adversity is not lost on readers who come to know it, not in its serial occasions but in the perspective of the whole.

'A HEART AND THE PRESENT MIND'

In Surah 50.37 the Qur'ān refers, characteristically, to the ruin of earlier generations who had been heedless to prophetic summons and whose deserted strongholds stood as grim reminders along the trade routes of Muhammad. The verse sees them as a vivid reminder for the wise passer-by, 'for him who has a heart and lends hearing with present mind'. The Scripture, recruiting these intimations from history, is the most eloquent 'reminder' of all, the *Dhikr* (as one of its titles goes) or active focus of memory. So it is fitting to borrow the same description for the attentiveness the Book itself must command.

'The attention of a present mind' for generations of faithful Muslims has meant, quite literally, the recitation of the Qur'ān from beginning to end. The retentive memory this necessitates is a primary form of devotion and also the prerequisite of religious education. It is the form of loyalty to the Qur'ān which corresponds with the theology of *tanzīl*, or celestial mediation, by which Muhammad received it. As a *verbatim* Scripture it must live *verbatim* on the tongues of its community. This memorising of the book *in toto* follows the division of the whole into sixty equal lengths without regard for chapter endings or phases of meaning. The sections are of equal quantity.

This duty of *Hifz*, as the term goes, of 'reciting by heart', in the art of *tajwīd*, or (lit.) 'conforming to the Qur'ān's beauty', would seem to call into doubt any selective reading, as distinct from reciting, of the Book. When *tajwīd* cherishes the Qur'ān on the lips, in vocal expression of its quality as Arabic, and does so in segments determined simply by length, the 'mind that is present' moves with the flow of the recital. It is *not* handling the text by themes. The thought is habituated to move with the juxtapositions of the text as it is spoken. Thanks to memorisation, many Muslims think with the Qur'ān by relying on running quotation rather than logical sequence. The content is rehearsed in its actual flow rather than in the point of its topics. What comes next textually, not what obtains logically, decides how the content informs the intelligence.

In the light of this obligatory pattern of Qur'ān-usage through all the Muslim centuries, the question must arise whether *any* proposal to select can be approved, disturbing as it must the movement of a textual and literal sequence. Selection by themes will mean a way of taking the Book to heart otherwise than by the traditional discipline of memory. But if there is disapproval on this ground two responses may be made. The first, not to be explored further here, would be to call in question the whole philosophy of Scriptures on which such disavowal hinged. The second, more immediately pertinent here, would be to urge the distinction between Muslims within, and non-Muslims outside, the familiar rubric. The case for theme-selection need imply no insensitivity to what *Hifz* means in Muslim piety. An outsider's search for understanding in the text may well allow that an insider's recital spells a personal participation in the documentary mystery of revelation. Recital can become for the believer a sacramental experience, as organs of speech, tongue, lips and vocal chord move with the vowels and consonants, as the Prophet's did, of what faith holds to be divine, Arabic utterance. On that view literal fidelity is the duty of faith, and achieving it is the believer's wonder.

The non-Muslim, the non-Arabist, leaves this intact for those who are minded to seek it. The stranger to these intimacies of Islamic practice brings a different tribute to the Qur'ān. 'A present mind' in his case will not be the art of *tajwīd* savouring an oral thing. It will be the will to comprehend the meaning of the whole. There runs a tradition that 'he who recites the Qur'ān thereby includes prophethood between the two sides of his body'.[2] If such be the reward of *Hifz*, it is not the only way of having the Qur'ān within the compass of the mind.

To be anxious for meaning is no less an obligation than to be meticulous about syllables and vowel stresses. Indeed the very care for exactitude in recital, which the memoriser takes, is arguably a reason for the different attention to the content which a student brings. The reciter then — and the careful calligrapher too — become a parable for the commitment the serious outsider has to attain. Muslim tradition is full of warnings against inadequate reading. Anas Ibn Malik declared: 'It often happens that the Qur'ān curses him that recites it'.[3] He could hardly be referring to some inferior quality of recital without also reproaching other forms of imperception. Whether

2   Cf. Quasem, *op. cit.* p.25.
3   *Ibid.* p.29.

cursed or not, a memorising which does not open the heart at least forfeits all blessing.

A right respect, then, for the Muslim habit of recital need in no way dissuade us from seeking out the Qur'ān's themes by selection. A further reason for selection is that chronological sequence does not serve us well; or, where it might do so, theme-selection ensures that it does. Though the emigration of Muslims from Mecca to Medina in 622 is the time-watershed of the Qur'ān, and, accordingly, the Book identifies its Meccan and Medinan chapters, it does not arrange them in time sequence. Many Surahs are composite and do not wholly conform to the period in which they are allocated, but ignore the principle of their title identification.

Another possible reason for the non-arrangement of Quranic material by chronology is the fact that some exegesis strongly urges the dissociation of the contents from their immediate time-context. It is held that the timeless relevance of the text is thereby more surely seen. Though challenged in other quarters as incompatible with the 'occasions of revelation' which the Qur'ān itself stresses, this view hardly encourages the non-Muslim to venture chronological re-arrangement in his quest for a right understanding of the whole.

An arrangement of the Qur'ān on the basis of style would be possible, perhaps with an exclusive interest in the poetical parts. If prose and narrative and law were also included, the sequence would be broadly chronological. Changes in the feel and texture of the language are important.[4] Clues of style do illuminate the Book's incidence and the transitions through which it passed, and are part of intelligent study. Yet, belonging to language, they are instrumental to what is more than they. The Qur'ān was not designed to be read as literature.

It seems clear, then, that theme-study provides the most satisfactory principle of comprehension of the Qur'ān for the outsider seriously reckoning with its place in Islam and, *via* Islam, its meaning for the world at large. Theme-study centres on what the Book is set to convey. It enables the reader to enter imaginatively into the heart of Muhammad's mission. Further, it directs attention to the vocabulary of the Qur'ān, to terms and concepts formative in Islamic faith and culture. It also serves to obviate partial or idiosyncratic readings liable to impose some special pleading on the text. Such readings arise from pseudo-scientific commentary, to be noted later in part 4 below, purporting to read into the Qur'ān meanings only now

4 They found an important place in Arberry's translation. See note 19. For other
   arrangements based on style or theme, see e.g. S. Lane Poole: *Selections from the
   Qur'ān and Hadīth*, London, 1979, pp.37-62. See also: Muhtar Katircioglu: *The
   Wisdom of the Qur'ān*, Lahore, n.d.; A. Gauhar: *Translations from the Qur'ān*,
   London, 1977; T.B. Irving, *et. al.*: *Basic Teachings, Anthology of Selected
   Passages*, Leicester, 1979.

discernible through modern, scientific progress or invention. Or they may derive from esoteric instincts long present in the Sufi, or mystical, tradition. All such readings, claiming some futurist or private sophistication, raise the basic question as to the 'intention' of the whole. Theme-study is the best corrective, being also the most open to the categories where the Qur'ān's 'intention' is most dependably found. The concept of *Niyyah*, or 'intention', has always been central to Muslim ritual and devotion, so that with deliberation to 'intend' the daily prayer, the fast of Ramadān, the pilgrimage, is crucial to a right performance. 'Intention' is no alien criterion to bring to the Scripture itself as far as reverent deliberation may hope to discern what it was, and what it continues to be. 'What is the reader intended to find, to learn, or to heed?' is the question at the heart of all study. To identify the inclusive themes of the Qur'ān will be the surest way to an answer.

There is one caveat. The themes of the Qur'ān cannot be too rigorously isolated from each other. Its recurrent refrains mingle and blend together. Its character, we might say, is orchestral: its notes reverberate. Reiteration, as noted above (p. 29), was the textual form of Muhammad's fidelity to his mission in the context of rejection. The Book has so many parallel passages precisely because that mission was all of one piece in its sustained devotion to a harmony of themes in a discordant world.

It follows that the eight groups of passages given here, while broad denominators of the whole Qur'ān, are in no way free of echoes of each other. Except perhaps in the legal area, to have tried to extricate all particulars would have been to fragment what is best understood in concert. The arrangement we have sought does not distort the sense of the whole. To the unity of its many elements, the Qur'ān's opening chapter, *Sūrat al-Fātihah*, is the surest witness. Its accents are: God and His praise; mercy; judgement; undiverted worship; the blessedness of right guidance and the abiding distinction between those who possess it and those who wander and err. If the opening Surah is the quintessence of the Book the groupings that follow may claim to be in its spirit.

'PRAISE BE TO GOD'

All things in the Quranic universe begin, continue and end in God. The praise of God is the first note of revelation and the perpetual duty of the heart. Praise moves with the two credal affirmations of the confession of faith, or *Shahādah*: 'There is no god but God; Muhammad is the apostle of God'. Praise is the due recognition of that inalienable sovereignty and the invocation of the one divine Name. It is also the register of gratitude for the final prophethood with which the confession of faith inseparably links the acknowledgement of God. 'God and His apostle' is the insistent formula of the Quranic demand for obedience. That 'God is most great' — *Allāhu akbar*

— is a truth of the mind: it must also be the abiding consent of the will. Praise alerts, voices and sustains the responsive will and so constitutes the orientation of the responsible self.

Celebration of the praise of God in the Qur'ān rings with 'the most excellent Names'. Some of these are adjectival, denoting divine attributes — power, mercy, wisdom, forbearance, vigilance, supremacy and the like. Others are nounal, referring to the divine activities within the attributes — provision, bestowal, direction, succour, permission, and decision. The Names are the theme of *Dhikr*, a profound Quranic concept, engaging and achieving that recollection, or mindfulness, by which the human spirit is educated into, and dominated by, a steady consciousness of God in the possession and exercise of those divine attributes. In this role the Qur'ān itself is called *Al-Dhikr*, 'the bringer-to-mind'. Akin to the Hebraic 'mention of the Name of the Lord', these celebratory predicates about God are for authentic currency among the faithful, not for the idle curiosity of theologians. They are for acts of adoration and thanksgiving, not items in speculation. Revelation affirms that these Names belong to God; therefore, 'call upon Him by them' is its summons to the heart. Doing so transcends conceptual definition. God's Names are ours in the using, not in the probing or exploring. Prayer is consciously placing ourselves within the exercise of the divine prerogative they characterise.

Foremost among them is the double attribute of mercy invoked in the *Bismillāh*: 'In the Name of the merciful Lord of mercy,' which prefaces every chapter in the Qur'ān except Surah 9. The Arabic: *Al-Rahmān al-Rahīm* is often translated by two English words of different origin, namely 'the compassionate, the merciful'. But there is a single root (R H M) in Arabic which it seems unhappy to disregard. There is a ripe distinction within the common meaning of 'mercy'. *Al-Rahmān* has to do with God as 'merciful' in His very essence, irrespective of occasions or aspects of mercy's actual exercise. It is to these that *Al-Rahīm* relates. Thus He who *is* ever merciful orders, regulates, rules and bestows in pursuance of that mercy. Hence the translation: 'the merciful (*Rahīm*) Lord of mercy (*Rahmān*)' making *Rahīm* adjectival to *Rahmān* as substantive (which it often is outside the *Bismillāh*).[5] The rendering: 'the compassionate, the merciful' might be mere tautology, which the *Bismillāh* emphatically is not. The progression in the Arabic is vital to the import of the phrase. The praise of God needs to be discerning.

From the Opening Surah onwards the twin terms in the invocation have in

5 As for example in Surahs 13.30; 17.110; 19.18,26,44,45,58,61,69 and nine other occasions in the narrative of Mary in that Surah with its strongly Hebraic assocations; 20.5; 21.26; 68.29 and several other passages, where *Al-Rahmān* stands as a noun and is not linked with *Allāh* or followed by *Al-Rahīm*. *Al-Rahīm* is consistently an adjective, usually paired, if not with *Al-Rahmān*, then with another of the divine Names denoting forgiveness and forbearance.

apposition the words: *Rabb al 'Ālamīn*, 'the Lord of the worlds', or 'the Lord of all being'. All the rich connotations of sovereignty, mastery, authority and disposal, with nurture too, are there in the Semitic word *Rabb*. The *'ālamīn* are the worlds within sentient knowledge, the fact and the arena of everything 'phenomenal', i.e. what enters into human ken. In the context of praise the phrase embraces all that transpires in the world within responsive to the world without. 'Of all being' incorporates that breadth of meaning. Acts of thanksgiving, of recognition of divine bounty, all cognisance of the God-given order of our experience, kindle the lively imagination which informs all due praise and celebration.

MAN THE CREATURE'S REALM IN GOD THE CREATOR'S ORDER

Praise of God leads into the Qur'ān's vivid and constant concern with the theme of creation and the divine/human relationship of which the created order is the stage and scene. It is here that the Qur'ān-reader meets with impressive frequency the dimension to which Christian faith gives the term 'sacramental', namely an awareness of the physical, material and temporal occasions of life as being points of encounter with the power, rule and goodness of God. All things are seen as deriving from, and returning to, 'the Lord of all being'. Events in the cycle of nature — day and night, winds, rains, oases, wells, harvests, sun, moon and stars in their courses — are all among the *āyāt*, or signs, of God. All that nature affords to human hand and brain is to be interpreted not only as a means to exploitation but also, as such, a focus of celebration and gratitude. What is 'natural' is never merely so: it is a tryst with divine mercy to be duly acknowledged as such by a perception that kindles to worship of the supreme Creator-Lord.

These innumerable 'signs of God' within experience are lost upon the inalert, the callous, the casual and the unbelieving who fail to recognise them for what they are. In their unperceiving, they bring no thanks. By contrast the mindful, the sensitive, the believers, do note and ponder God's 'signs', and are duly tuned to gratitude.

This understanding of creation as a divine trust given to mankind as our *khilāfah*, or 'dominion', is a vital element in Quranic theism. It means a theology holding together the transcendence of God and the dignity of man. It tempers faith in divine exaltedness with faith in human meaning. We may think only of the former if we focus only on Lordship and sovereignty. Such an emphasis was a necessity born of the circumstances of Islamic origins in the campaign against idolatry, when it was urgent to insist on 'dissociation' of God from the things of nature and of time insofar as these were 'divinised' by false and plural worship. But that proper repudiation of idolatrous 'association' (a favourite translation of *Shirk* for many writers) between God and things in no way argues any dissociation, or unrelatedness, of the divine

35

power and mercy in respect of our human experience. Quite the contrary. Plural worship supposes a chaos of deities in phenomena, tribes, events, whereas the *āyāt* disclose the wisdom, authority and beneficence of 'the Lord of all being'.

Wilful disregard of our trusteeship in the earth is part of what the Qur'ān means by one of its most significant terms, namely *kufr*, often translated simply as 'unbelief'. But with its antonym of *shukr*, or 'gratitude', it denotes not merely a 'denial' of God in what we say but a repudiation of God in how we act. In *kufr* there is not simply the God we doubt; there is the God we ignore. The latter is the more damnable atheism. The *āyāt* are both the sphere, and the test, of whether we reject or acknowledge the divine hospitality which our mortality enjoys.

Faith as to our human creaturehood in the Qur'ān means that a divine initiative lies behind all that is. God 'only says: "Be!" and it is'. There is this intendedness about all things with humanity as the crux. The vocation to be human in this sense of glad tenancy and trust runs the gauntlet of the 'accusation' against it which is the Quranic role of *Iblīs*, or *Al-Shaitān*, who in the heavenly conclave (Surah 2.30f) disputes the wisdom which entrusts the world to such fickle irresponsibility as ours. That Satanic disclaimer which gives the lie to mankind is overruled by God. It then becomes the aim of the 'accuser' so to misguide and corrupt mankind that the whole divine enterprise is discredited and God emerges as a foolish gambler whose risk miscarries. It is, then, the role of man to give the lie to the liar, and thus to vindicate God, by silencing 'the enemy' (cf. Psalm 8.2). The purpose of the revelation *via* the Book is to inform the human response and actualise that *islām*, or due obedience, which achieves the divine intention on the human plane. History is the realm to which the issue belongs.

It is important for the Qur'ān-reader to appreciate how central is this theme of the crisis of man, seeing that it is the matter of mankind on which divine sovereignty is staked, at least as it concerns the world we know. The Satanic defiance of God turns on his refusal, as Surah 2 has it, to 'worship' Adam, the creature-tenant, the 'viceroy' of the Lord. Divine Lordship confers human dignity as a free and gracious investment of purpose. There is an evil which disputes and disavows it — an evil to be itself disputed and disavowed as, in its positive ordering, the Scripture shows men how, with Islam as the resolution of the 'crisis'. Such a reading of history speaks a theology where divine greatness in no way precludes, but emphatically underwrites, the high significance of man.

The most tellings of the 'signs', or *āyāt*, is sexuality — the foremost privilege of the creature and the crux of the continuity of the rest of 'signs'. Repeatedly the Qur'ān ponders the mystery of procreation and sets between the sexes 'love and tenderness' (Surah 30.21). The progress of the embryo in the womb from conception to birth is traced in numerous passages which evoke awe and reverence. Man is a creature of clay yet carries the trust of the perpetuation of his own kind. The Quranic concept of man in nature undergirds its whole ethic of marriage and the family.

AND SO — THE PROPHET EMISSARIES

How logically they follow. God being so in Lordship: man being so in custodianship — respectively over the world in total sovereignty and obligated 'dominion': how appropriately prophethood intervenes at God's behest to fulfill divine ends by evoking human obedience. Faith in the sequence of divine messengers is explicit in the Qur'ān's theology. The confession of faith, or *Shahādah*, in Islam is: 'God and His apostle'. The Muslim does not confess the One without the other. The Creeds refer to 'the prophets, the books and the angels'. It is right then to bring together the Quranic narratives about the long succession of predecessors of Muhammad from Abraham to Jesus. For Jesus, too, is understood to be in that succession as 'only a messenger' preparatory to the final Qur'ān. These mentors sent by God to mankind are both biblical and extra-biblical. With the exception of a brief reference to Jonah they end — as far as the Hebrew Scriptures are concerned — with Elijah and Elisha. They do not include those greater prophetic figures, Amos, Hosea, Isaiah, Jeremiah and their kindred souls.

The shape of the Quranic accounts indicates a twofold purpose. The earlier messengers align with the situation of Muhammad in serving to warn the obdurate in his day by underlining the nemesis which overtook the heedless in theirs. Further these messengers proved exemplars of tenacity under the sort of persecution Muhammad also endured, and thus helped to hearten both him and his followers in the distresses that preceded the *Hijrah*.

This double relevance means that the portrayal approximates closely to the actual encounter faced by Muhammad in Mecca. The Joseph story is the great exception, though there also the sense of providential ordering is paramount. Elsewhere it is idolatry, judgement upon it, and the central theme of the oneness of God, which occupy them all. In its confidence that the messages were one and the same, the Qur'ān situates all the prophets in setting akin to its own. Abraham, for example, is a bold iconoclast among his people, rather than a pilgrim who became a great progenitor. More obscure figures like Hūd and Sālih preach, protest and endure among stubborn pagans. The narratives underscore the Qur'ān's emphasis that prophethood brought one and the same challenge and was thereby faced with one and the same adversity. The perspective of Mecca prevails throughout.

Conversely the burden of Muhammad's message is read as the clue to the burden of theirs. All messengers are understood as confronting the evil of pluralism rooted in hardness of heart. The test of whether mankind betrays the vocation of the 'viceroy' is that of plural worship. The Qur'ān does not

37

portray messengers in a context of already unitary worship beset by moral compromise, or amid exilic perplexity searching for a theodicy. Issues have to do with the demands of divine sovereignty, rather than its interrogation or its travail. There is thus a great simplification of the complexities of history. Nevertheless, implicit in the very succession of the prophet-messengers and the necessity for reiteration of their message is the human capacity for heedlessness. It is because mankind is so hostile, inattentive, negligent, that 'reminder', or *dhikr*, had to be steadily renewed. The prophets' cumulative story raises large questions about human nature and how adamant it can prove when summoned in God's Name. What of the paradox in a succession which does not succeed? Before, however, that question becomes — as we say — eschatological, we have to forward it into the finality of the succession in Muhammad himself, the prophethood in which all precedents culminate.

ON TO THE CLIMAX: MUHAMMAD AND THE QUR'ĀN

Messengers before Muhammad had varying range of audience and differing levels of responsibility. His comprehends 'the worlds' and embraces the human whole in the whole truth. The Qur'ān is understood to finalise all precedents within Islam and to seal thereby the entire future. It becomes the criterion of all that is authentic both prior and to come. It is conclusive of all revelation.

Its finality comprises the two dimensions of preaching and power which, in their inter-dependence, determine the familiar characterisation of the Book as Meccan and Medinan, with the emigration from the one city to the other as the watershed between. The travail of the word and the triumph of the political, within the Qur'ān, are together the fabric of Muhammad's prophethood. The one is the vindication of the other. The confident politics are the corollary of the indisputable message. The reader in this part of the Qur'ān senses the staunch assurance that faith is properly, even necessarily, sanctioned by the exercise of force. In the light of the sharpness of the confrontation which the Qur'ān conveys in the Medinan chapters, the militarisation of original Islam seems inevitable. It is certainly taken as the logical response to Meccan resistance once the die had been cast by the emigration. For then the Prophet was no longer under physical constraints on the part of the Quraish, other than those of open warfare with an alternative city power-base. The *Hijrah* could hardly have had any other sequel, especially as it was followed by a steady consolidation of authority in Medina and a growing identification of the citizens with the Muslim cause, despite the fact that initially only a small minority of Medinans had been party to the 'security' Muhammad had been pledged there.

Those 'guarantors', known as 'helpers', or *Ansār*, making common cause with the emigrants, the *Muhājirūn*, were the nucleus of Muhammad's 'establishment' in the host-city. The sequel to the *Hijrah*[6] amply justified the decision which prompted it. Commentary reads it as the principle of personal allegiance triumphing over tribal nexus. Those who broke both physically and emotionally with their traditional haunts of mind and locale were thereby the more ready to meet the claims which subsequent struggle and danger laid upon them. One striking feature of the Book in this context is the need the cause had to surmount the reluctance for risk among would-be non-combatants concerned for their families and their lives. These passages in the Medinan Qur'ān are eloquent testimony to the fact that the battles and campaigns of that period were not a belligerence for its own sake. They may have harnessed martial prowess eager for opportunity, but they also daunted and dismayed impulses of conscience and the yearning for peace — factors which had to be overcome by the skilful, insistent promotion of the 'cause' and its legitimacy as 'God's and the Apostle's'.

The power-equation always develops its own momentum, the ends authorising the means and the means validated by the ends. It is natural then to find, through the Medinan chapters, a resolute interpretation of the conflict through providential episodes, and a steadily growing solidarity in the definition and formulation of Islam, its ritual and its autonomy. Islam emerges in this part of the Qur'ān into clear identity and in independence of earlier factors in its making. Its success and its confirmation proceed together.

The logic of power finds warrant in the wily hostility of the obdurate Meccans. In a situation of conflict where secure neutrality became impossible, neutrals were caught either way and allies were prone to actual, or alleged, vacillation or duplicity. In the Medinan Surahs we meet for the first time the 'hypocrites', *al-munāfiqūn*, whom Muhammad's gathering success provoked to deception. Still unyielding religiously, they pretended to attitudes they did not genuinely hold. They feigned allegiance out of prudence or guile, while scheming against the Muslim cause in surreptitious ways. Suspicion of them only sharpened Muslim vigilance, so deepening evil machinations to elude it. The Qur'ān sees these risks as the unavoidable accompaniment of a power establishment ensuring its own triumph. It was a price to be paid for the sake of the result. The Qur'ān lives by a healthy realism.

But in these pre-occupations of politics and power the Qur'ān never loses sight of its spiritual mandate. One fascinating feature throughout the Medinan chapters, as of the Meccan ones earlier, is the wealth of metaphor and parable drawn from the local and social setting of the entire sequence. The

6 The Prophet and Abū Bakr, his father-in-law, made the journey hazardously to Yathrib after the main body had departed there. As they sheltered in a cave to elude their pursuers they were preserved, thanks to a spider weaving a web across the opening, from which the enemy concluded that no one had lately entered.

landscape of the Hijāz in western Arabia, and the merchandise of the markets of the cities, are the twin sources of imagery and allusion. The Qur'ān travels with the nomad and is at home with the ledgers of the merchant. In its world the swirling winds shift the contours of the sand-dunes. Precipices crumble into ravines. The sudden, copious rains carpet the earth with vivid green which fades again into the bleak and barren terrain it briefly adorned. Fickle water-courses disappear into the ground and cheat the unwary traveller. The sirocco scorches the wilderness. Nature's grim austerity relents in the laden orchards of the oases with their luscious vines and staple olives. The Book registers the night sky with the keen eye of the tribesman, who by day is undeceived by the shimmering mirage that fills the burning sands with mocking pools. Clouds rear and bank and lour before the breaking storm.[7]

By contrast the analogies from merchandise and market are mundane, but they are no less amenable to Quranic meanings than the sights and scenes of the nomad. The stark contrasts of the Scripture between the believers and the unbelievers are those of the good and the bad bargains, the gainers and the losers. Those ledgers of the Quraish which the illiterate cameleers feared, suspected, but could not gainsay, prefigure the books to be opened at the last assize. Like caravanners we are all 'forwarding' into eternity the 'product' of our existence, the deeds that tell our character. The bankers and accountants of Meccan trade yield similitudes for the final reckoning of all the living. God Himself is the supreme actuary, with His attendant angels. *Al-Kitāb*, 'the Book', denotes the Qur'ān itself, but the word is also used of the life-ledger of every soul, the register which infallibly accompanies us all into the great beyond. Faith and obedience are 'a goodly loan'. We do not do well to sell ourselves cheaply. The forceful activism of the Medinan Qur'ān is sobered throughout, and tempered, by the imagery of eternal destiny, with martyrdom in the cause underwriting all else.

---

7 S. Lane-Poole: *Studies in a Mosque*, London, 1893, wrote: 'Muhammad had not spent long solitary nights in vain, gazing at the silent heaven and watching the dawn break over the mountains. This earliest portion of the Koran is one long blazonry of nature's beauty . . . brilliant images of God's workings in creation' p.129. The Qur'ān's invocation of the natural order in appeal to moral man is constant. Cf. Surah 51.1-6:

> 'By the winnowing winds
> The rain-laden clouds,
> By the swift running courses,
> By all that disposes,
> Faithful is all that you are pledged.
> The judgement will indeed befall.'

and Surah 77.1-7. See below, pp.337.

The Qur'ān in Its Themes: the Logic of Selection

ISLAM IN THE ACHIEVING AND DEFINING

It is natural to move from the Meccan and Medinan sequence of the Qur'ān to the world of the Quranic faith and conduct as steadily fashioned in the course of the shaping years. With the conquest of Mecca from Medina in year 8 of the *Hijrah*, the bringing of the two cities into a single faith and sovereignty inaugurated the *Ummah* — community — whose Shari'ah — sacred law — had been in process through revelation even before the emigration — a process intensified by the Medinan developments. *Dīn* — the practice of religion — found increasing definition as the cause of the faithful progressed.

It is useful to divide these aspects of the Qur'ān into the themes 'Faith and Religion', followed by 'Society and Law'. By Islamic criteria all four belong in a single category. 'Religion' is not seen by Muslims as a separate compartment of life, a sphere of devotion and ritual apart from all else. Religion must pervade the whole in a sense that intends altogether to exclude the notion, or the fact, of the secular. 'Faith' and 'society' are to be coterminous, through the authority of the State and the writ of sacred law. Nevertheless, there is *Dīn*, 'religion', through a ritual of prayer, fasting and pilgrimage as the form of acknowledgement of God, informing but distinguished from the pursuit of human affairs within the community.

Creed, code, cult, community and culture are five 'c's in necessary inter-relation in every religion. The readings selected here which gather these aspects of Islam in the Qur'ān embody material which is present also in its historical parts. It could hardly not be so, since the achieving and the defining were one story. But earlier, the concern was with their incidence in the narrative: it now has to do with admonitory description and commendation.

All directives and precepts derive from divine will and command. Conformity to the will of God is the inclusive ground and motive of ethics, of the obligations of being Muslim, of the duties of prayer and piety, of the behaviour of the person in society and between the generations. The demand of the good, the diagnosis and shunning of evil, are sharply personal. Every human being pursues a destiny as the vice-regent of God. The revelation in enjoining and prohibiting is understood as the law of ideal human nature (Surah 30.30). The Five Pillars of *Dīn* (as they are called) — witness, prayer, alms, fasting and pilgrimage — become familiar habit in the recurrence of times of day and ritual seasons of the year, and draw strength and sanction from the solidarity of the *Ummah*, the entire community of Islam.

The laws of the Qur'ān are most complete in the realm of personal status law and matters of commercial and economic activity. On certain other areas the Qur'ān is almost silent, leaving the corpus of *Fiqh*, or jurisprudence, to be elaborated from other sources, tradition and consensus, but always assuming the criterion of non-repugnancy to the Qur'ān itself. The political

41

field is also one where the Book leaves formulation to the future. The historic Caliphate, for thirteen centuries the essential symbol, and through many of those centuries the effective means, of Islamic polity, finds no mention in the Scripture.[8] During the life-time of Muhammad and throughout the mediation to him of the text in *tanzīl*, the ruling dictum reiterated there: 'Obey God and obey the Apostle' sufficed. Debate about the right or the duty to withhold obedience from rulers judged to be unworthy Muslims only arose in the long aftermath to the founding days. Some commentators, however, ground that right and duty in an interpretation of Surah 5.44, branding those who do not 'judge' (or 'rule') 'according to what God has sent down'.[9] As long as the personal leadership of Muhammad was there, as a veritable tower of authority, the issues attending his demise lay below the horizon. Islam receives its corpus of law and obedience from 'the Book which has no doubtfulness about it' (2.2).[10] But it recognises the need for their enlargement after the life-span of the Prophet to whom, exclusively, heavenly mediation had been accorded. The fulfilment of its guidance through the changing context of the centuries has been the perennial concern in the custody of the Qur'ān by its people, its scholars and its exegetes. Central to the Qur'ān's doctrine of itself is the constant, insistent sense of a divine imperative, the summons to a moral and social order wherein and whereby 'God is most great'.

'TO GOD OUR RETURNING': DEATH AND DESTINY

No principle of selection in the Qur'ān can ignore the sharp and urgent contrast which runs through all its pages between believers and unbelievers, between the right-doers and the wrong-doers. This great divide is the theme

8 There are several references to mankind as a whole and to tribes, as being 'successors,' using the word *khalīfah* in its plural forms (*khulafā'* or *khalā'if*) to denote the passing of generations to be replaced by others. But the singular denoting one who 'fills the room' of, and so deputises for, another does not occur at all in the sense of political succession, which became the technical sense of the term in the successive Caliphates which continued in Islam from 632 to 1924. David is described as a *Khalīfah* in 38.26 and, more importantly, Adam in 2.30, where man, as creature, is deputy for God, in vice-regency over the earth.

9 Ibn Taimiyyah, for example, the redoubtable rigorist of the 13th century (1263-1328) held that this verse warranted Muslims in withholding allegiance from Muslims considered wanting in purity of faith or of life. The passage does not explicitly sustain that view and 'ruling by God's revelation' is a criterion open to various interpretation. But exegesis akin to that of Ibn Taimiyyah and his successors e.g. Ibn Kathir (1300-1372) has been invoked by recent and contemporary figures such as Sayyid Qutb. See note 45.

10 The phrase in 2.2. '*la raibā fīhi*' (cf. 10.37;32.2) may be read in two senses — '. . . the Book in which there is nothing to be doubted,' i.e. inerrancy of content: or 'the Book in which there is no cause for disquiet' i.e. fully trustworthy in its guidance to the God-fearing (cf. the following phrase).

of its most striking metaphors and preoccupies its fertile imagery. The reader meets it at the outset in the Opening Surah. It continues through all the confrontations of the prophetic histories. It is the central feature of the encounter of Muhammad with the Quraish and all they represented as pagans and usurers both before and after the emigration.

This radical faith and unfaith, this human 'doing' and 'undoing', come to their climax of glad or dire requital in the eschatology of the Qur'ān. Nothing is more 'certain' — *Al-Yaqīn* as the Book calls it — than 'the Day of judgement', the great and aweful assize which ushers mankind into the destiny of heaven or hell. Warnings ring through the entire text as the counterpart of the message of the divine unity. Through the whole sequence of the revelation runs the issue, stark and total, between guidance and error, well-being and evil-doing, hope and despair, eternal reward and eternal damnation.

An intense personalism characterises the apocalyptic matter of life and death. The emigrants from Mecca who took their way into uncertain exile with Muhammad's faith set the tie of faith above the tie of kin, their conviction above their family and tribe. The choice of cities was for them a choice of destinies and it was individuals who made it. In that story, ties of kin might re-assert themselves when they no longer sundered people of faith. But in the last great Day no tie of kin, nor appeal to tradition, nor invocation of the 'fathers' can avail. The allegiance into Islam is one that only individual persons can bring. The liability of the self for the self dominates the vision of the eternal beyond the temporal. Man's own limbs and members, hand and foot and tongue, will testify against him. No relationship of kin or clan can plead or be pleaded. There is no burden, the Qur'ān insists, that is not the bearer's own and that bearer's alone.[11] 'God does not call any soul to account save for what is its own' (Surahs 2.286 and 65.7). All send forward deeds to the reckoning, accumulating a finality which the justice of God will inexorably expose, judge and perpetuate.

None can presume on the issue of that Day. The reckoning is ours to incur: it is not ours to resolve. The imagery of the Qur'ān is vivid and awesome in its drama of the cataclysm of the end-time, the tribunal of the ages, and the everlasting haunts of bliss and doom. Vivid, too, is its mind for the incidence of personal death, the threshold of all that waits beyond. Eschatology finds the Book at its most stern and its most fervent in the poetry of overwhelming conviction.

11 See Surahs 6.164; 17.15; 39.7 and 53.38. Guilt is inalienable: there is no shifting away from the doer the liability for wrong done. The meaning, it must be assumed, cannot be extended to deny the actuality, the reality, of suffering incurred by 'bearers of evil' done by those who inflict injury and wrong. In the bundle of life there are certainly endless occasions of vicarious pain and tragedy, in which burdens are innocently and — hopefully — redemptively borne.

'*Al-Ākhirah*, 'the end', writes Fazlur Rahman, 'is the moment of truth . . . when all veils between the mental pre-occupations of man and the objective moral reality will be rent.'[12]

'The Hour', as the Qur'ān also names the great assize, means the public verdict on every private quality of deed and character. There is all the force of irony in the fact that the familiar vocabulary of the market and the counting house which Muhammad employed in his confrontation with the obdurate in Mecca serves also to tell the eschatological truth. The fearsome embrace of all time in that 'Hour' is the burden of the Islamic Scripture written into what is beyond time. It is the final meaning of the affirmation of divine unity. For some readers it opens more questions than it closes. But in the perspective of linear time it is the summation of all the themes of the Qur'ān.

A PATTERN OF READING

Eschatology completes the rationale of selection here. The preceding pages serve to argue and to introduce the sequence, leaving the Readings, without the interruption of 'prefaces', to speak for themselves. Topics might have been more numerously classified. But it may reasonably be claimed that the eight sections proposed do justice to the thrust and the diversity of the one Qur'ān and that the device of selection, suppressing no element, in fact enables comprehension of both thrust and fulness as they are.

A careful justification of the temerity (if such it be) that selects at all seemed necessary: but the reader may be relieved by the knowledge that many Muslims have themselves been evaluators in the same way. Many traditions hold, for example, that the Opening Surah *is* the whole Qur'ān, or that the Surah of *Ikhlās* (Surah 112) is equal to a third of it, although it is only four verses long. Perhaps then we may hold that two-thirds of the Book, as here presented, comprise a whole.

In the fifth century A.H., the most celebrated of all Muslim theologians, the great Al-Ghazālī, wrote his *Kitāb Jawāhir al-Qur'ān*, 'The Book of the Qur'ān's Jewels', in which he chose 1,504 verses, 763 of which he called 'the jewels' and 741 'the pearls'. The former were verses about the essence and attributes of God — jewels of the light of the knowledge of God. The latter described 'the straight path' of conduct and exhorted men to follow it. Together they were the cognitive and the practical aspects of the Qur'ān.[13] Al-Ghazālī conceded that in many places the two were almost inextricable, even dividing the Opening Surah between them.

12 Fazlur Rahman: *Major Themes of the Qur'ān*, Chicago, 1980, p.106. His identification of themes coincides closely with those here.
13 *Kitāb Jawāhir al-Qur'ān*, (The Jewels of the Qur'ān) trans. by Muhammad Abul-Quasem, Kuala Lampur, 1977.

We, too, are aware of the interpenetration of the themes we separate. It is the Qur'ān itself which holds them in one, while yet needing the discrimination which singles out the several features of its manifold unity. Without using the ornate similes congenial in Al-Ghazālīs's day, we have had the perspective of Islamic faith and piety in all the foregoing, as was fitting. In our final section (part 4 below) we raise issues proper to those who do not share that perspective. Meanwhile, 'jewels' and 'pearls' have a preciousness that deserve a careful cherishing — which, in our context, is the art of translation. To that we now turn.

بسم الله الرحمن الرحيم

3. The Qur'ān into English: A Translator's Apology

It is the firm conviction of Muslims that without its Arabic the Qur'ān ceases to be itself. A non-Arabic Qur'ān is a contradiction in terms. Since all literature is both form and content, and since translation — even if 'perfect' — brings alien form, only content survives and content reminted is not the reality. In the case of the Islamic Scripture the misgivings go deeper than this familiar problem. There is a religious disquiet arising from the Muslim understanding of the Qur'ān's quality as 'the speech of God'. When the original Arabic is forfeited, not only does the whole feel of the Scripture change, its very status is impugned.

'The Koran cannot be translated . . . that is the view of the present writer,' wrote Marmaduke Pickthall, an English Muslim, in 1930.[14] He wrote, however, in the Introduction to his own English rendering which, with an effort after consistency, he entitled *The Meaning of the Glorious Koran*. Only had he printed the Arabic in parallel columns with his English version would he have been justified in dispensing with the safeguard: 'Here is meaning only'. Even in translation with parallel Arabic text, titles like 'The Message of the Qur'ān' have cautiously been retained.[15]

So we find a situation in which translation is ruled out of court and yet translations are ventured and, judging by the titles, are ventured with success, 'meaning' and 'message' surviving. The Italian proverb: *traduttore, traditore*, 'translator means traitor', need not obtain. Yet it will be wise for any who take up the task anew to begin apologetically. 'Apology' has a three-fold meaning, each of which is needed here. It can denote 'a poor substitute':[16] any alert Arabist, or Arab, will know an English version to be that in respect of their Qur'ān. 'Apology' means also an act of self-blame, a desire for exoneration. But it has also an older sense, familiar from Justin

14 Marmaduke Pickthall: *The Meaning of the Glorious Qur'ān*, London, 1930, p.vii.
15 E.g. Muhammad Asad: *The Message of the Qur'ān*, translated and explained, Gibraltar, 1980.
16 In a colloquial sense — of something that hardly passes muster as what it purports to be.

Martyr to John Henry Newman, of response to suspicion, of vindication against false imputation.

All three senses come together for whoever outside formal Islam undertakes a de-Arabicising of the Qur'ān. The result will certainly be a poor substitute for the original. As such it will warrant some self-reproach countered, however, by a lively self-defence. A feeling of imprudence will be balanced by the conviction that the enterprise, if not the result, is justified. For, given a proper humility of mind, self-doubt should not deter the will or the work involved in English-ing the Qur'ān.

VIA THE ARABIC TO A WIDER WORLD

The Qur'ān exists to be understood. 'Do they not reflect on the Qur'ān?' asks Surah 4.82, and the question is repeated in 47.24 which adds: '. . . or is it that hearts have locks upon them?' 'Do you not apply your minds?' or 'Perhaps you will apply your minds' were a steady refrain in Muhammad's preaching. Frequently there comes the comment: 'Most are quite uncomprehending'. These reiterated calls for intelligent hearers — and now, readers — were, of course, addressed to pagans. That fact makes false any notion that the Book was, or is, a monopoly of Muslims or a document that only insiders can understand. The dictum of Surah 56.79: 'Let none touch it except the cleansed' need not be read in that sense.[17] At its first hearing in time and place there were none but pagans to heed. 'Muslims' — albeit exemplified from the days of Noah and Abraham in godly souls — were still in the future when Muhammad's mission began. They were slow to emerge through the long years of hostility and indifference which he experienced and against which the Scripture was strenuously directed. Even if outsiders are still to be regarded as the spiritual kin of those obdurate heathen in Mecca, there can be no denying that the Qur'ān wants them for an audience.

If there was a 'closed shop' at its incidence it was that of pagan tradition: the Arabic language, as the language there current and treasured, was the means to break it open. It was the adversaries, not the Prophet, who wanted the Qur'ān privatised within its own coterie of adherents, the Quraish not Muhammad who saw it fit only for those minded to own it. The Arabic which was then its sounding-board now handicaps it as 'a mercy for the worlds'. Existing to be understood, its cherished language then conveyed the Qur'ān home but now impedes its way. In the several passages where the Scripture stresses its being Arabic, the context makes clear that the purpose of this was to reach the local Arabs. Mecca, 'the mother of the villages', was

---

17   Clean hands and a pure intention seem the evident meaning. Some exegetes suggest that the verse has to do with a proper ritual purity or membership in the true faith. But it would clearly be contrary to the whole thrust of the Qur'ān to withhold its message from all but *muslimīn*.

'native' in that language.[18] But the Book, there and then a public event, a local manifesto, was also an urgent communication to all mankind (Surah 21.107). If comprehension be the crucial thing the Arabic which there ensured it must elsewhere be relinquished. Translation is not only proper but mandatory.

To be sure, the Qur'ān offered the Arabs the credential of a literary miracle, of a 'matchlessness' which its peerless literary excellence possessed. This concept of its *i'jāz* (as the term is), underwriting its status, explains the claim that it should never be translated. But that credential, however convincing for Arab hearers and Arabic readers, though enshrined in Islamic dogma, is quite inaccessible to non-Muslims. Outsiders must take it on trust. Any literary excellence is, by its nature, discernible of register only within the given culture. It is a claim not at all open to external dispute: it is a factor which simply does not avail externally. It cannot, then, be a ground for pleading any exclusive right of the Arabic language to the meanings of the Qur'ān.

Yet a proper external respect for the Arabic of the Qur'ān has to be harnessed to the translator's task, as well as a ready sense of the Book's authority in the custody of its own people. But it would be treachery to that very custody to withhold it, as non-translation would, from the open forum of debate.

DECISION IN TRANSLATION

Translations of the Qur'ān have multiplied in western languages this century, as non-Muslim scholarship offered them and as Muslims overcame their reservations about disengaging Quranic meanings from their Arabic form. The two processes have much in common. Either way translation has to resolve one perennial question: how far may, or does, the receiving language rather than the giving language control the end-result? There is a transaction between them, necessarily, a sort of negotiation in which the shape of one defers to the shape of the other. Vexed questions of vocabulary equivalence belong in this negotiation. The Arabic of the Qur'ān is rich in terms of multiple import. Not all nuances can go over in all their subtlety to the receiving language. Options in the layers of meaning which may be latent for interior interpretation by commentary have to become explicit in transla-

---

18 While the Qur'ān firmly declares itself a Scripture for all mankind (e.g. 21.107, 34.28) it equally firmly stresses its Arabic language (12.2, 13.37, 20.113, 41.3, 42.7, 43.3) in its setting of an Arab audience. 'No messenger is ever sent save with the tongue of his own people' (14.4). Muhammad is 'a warner to them from among them' (50.2).

tion. Simplification, loss, limitation, have all to be risked and, to borrow a nautical metaphor: 'ships are but boards, sailors but men . . .'. Channels into port are hazardous, and the cargo is highly sensitive and precious. It has a sacred quality which ensures that its faithful custodians suspect and resist not only the options translators must take but their making any decisions at all. These and other issues all return to the basic matter of which language — in a right sense — dominates. Attention to A.J. Arberry's *The Koran Interpreted* illuminates the point.[19] Its title could well have been 'The Qur'ān Rendered' for there is no commentary. 'Interpreted' denoted a worthy attempt to let the Arabic control the English. One critic characterised it as 'a bare (but palatable) translation which delicately conveys the obscurities of the original without resolving them'.[20] If we substitute 'nuances' for 'obscurities', Arberry, we may guess, would have found the comment welcome. He left his English full of Arabisms, sometimes to the point of oddity and unintelligibility.[21] It is evident that the claims of modern English did not determine his rendering.

The decision that they should not do so was deliberate. It was taken in the interests, as he saw them, of the prior claims of the Arabic diction, the metre and accentual stresses of the original. He was very properly conscious of the sheer poetry of the Book, the qualities of which he analysed in great detail in his introduction to the selections which preceded the full translation.[22] These, he argued, should decide his English at least in the poetic sections of the Qur'ān. Aware that this factor should not be pressed too far, he noted that it was impossible to know how Arabic speech was stressed in Muham-

19 2 vols. London, 1955. One vol. edit, Oxford, 1964. The bases of Arberry's 'interpretation' were argued in his *The Holy Qur'ān*, London, 1953, where he set out his analysis of the 'fives' and 'tens' in Quranic refrains, and paragraphed his English on the same rhythmic patterns. It was in these he detected what he called the 'original units of revelation.'
20 Michael Cook in: *Founders of Faith*, Oxford, 1986, p. 367.
21 Examples in Arberry: *The Koran Interpreted*, which, by other criteria than his, might be thought infelicitous include:
20.113: '. . . We have turned about in it something of . . .!:
36.68: 'To whomsoever We give long life We bend him over in his constitution.'
7.71: 'touching which God has sent down never authority.'
4.129: '. . . so that you leave her (a wife) as it were suspended' (for: 'in suspense.')
74.45: 'We plunge along with the plungers . . .'
102.2: '. . . even till you visit the tombs'
2.35: '. . . and brought them out of that they were in.'
46.8: 'He knows very well what you are pressing upon.' There should, however, be no queries about Arberry's text on the part of any who have not read and shared the emotion of his Preface in the 2 vol. 1955 edition.
22 *The Holy Qur'ān*, London, 1953. p.24.

mad's time. It is also obvious that rhyme defeats translation.[23] Nevertheless, *The Koran Interpreted* expresses in its English format the shape of the Arabic original. The auditory quality it possessed had to be the paramount concern of the translation. It was, he wrote, 'profitable to consider how far the excitative properties . . . correspond with the emotional effects of drum rhythms'.[24] Assonance if possible should be reproduced and attempt made to retain the lyricism. This was because the Qur'ān was oracle, not treatise, meant to be recited not perused, cherished as music not revered in silence. By such canons the exigencies of the Arabic, its syntax, sentence structure and idiom, had to make subordinate the claims and needs of the receptive English. Arberry felt, further, that sacred writing warranted certain archaisms like 'lo', 'deemest', 'whomsoever', 'haply', 'naught but', and 'to tarry'. A contemporary and idiomatic English would be dubiously proper.[25]

Within his own prescripts Arberry's version succeeded. The erudition and precision he brought to his task were surely vindicted. His place in Quranic readership has long been assured. His very success may be taken to justify the alternative approach, aiming to do for the thrust of the meaning what Arberry did for the form of the text. That alternative may plead that, despite the orthodox sense of the Qur'ān's literary matchlessness, Muhammad himself always passionately disclaimed poetic standing. To have been

23 Reproducing the rhyme of the Qur'ān is notoriously difficult and probably foolish. A passable attempt might be made to indicate the balance and the rhymes of Surah 94, where Muhammad is addressed. Arberry's version first:
'Did We not expand thy breast for thee
And lift from thee thy burden,
The burden that weighed down thy back?
Did We not exalt thy fame?
So truly with hardship comes ease (twice)
So when thou art empty, labour
And let thy Lord be thy quest.'
Or:
'Have We not lightened your heart,
Your shoulders now sparing
The load you were bearing
And lauding with honour your part?
For pain of grief there's gain of peace (twice)
(Arabic: *Fa innā ma' al-'usri yusran*)
When steadied, be readied anew,
And all your desire be your Lord's.
But the original defies the effort.

24 Arberry, *loc. cit.* p.24.

25 This despite his intention stated in the Preface in the 1964 edition p.12, to 'avoid the "Biblical" style favoured by some of my predecessors'. He explained his use of 'Thou' and 'Thy' for God to overcome the ambiguity of 'you' (sing. and pl.) — a point taken care of here by the device of the capitalised 'You', seeing that the English capital letter helps to connote precisely what Arabic has in the word *Allāh*.

thought merely a poet was to risk being disowned as a prophet. The two categories were not only distinguishable: they were opposed. We must assume that when his hearers were challenged to 'bring a surah like it' (2.23 and 10.38), the reference was to the content and authority, not merely or mainly to the diction and rhythm. If, then, we opt for a philosophy of translation that sets meaning in precedence over poetry will we not be in line with Muhammad's own priorities? And with meaning at stake comprehension in the mind addressed is the final test, where-ever literary factors obscure the force of the original through obtuseness in the English. Savoured, as far as possible, the native Qur'ān must surely be. But it is not, finally, a thing for admiration. Its rhetoric and its irony, its imagery and eloquence, are not ends in themselves. They were calculated to arouse, to convince, to warn and to educate. Peremptory, they demanded not patronage but obedience.

In the nature of things the outside reader cannot be expected to know those graces of the Arabic Qur'ān which Muslims find in their liturgical devotion, in recitation and calligraphy. The translation which has to forego these is the outsider's only route to experience of the meaning they enshrine and which must 'go' into any idiom if the Scripture is to make good its universal range. Nowhere has its content been better heralded than in Arberry's own introductory words:

> 'The Koran was the prime inspiration of a religious movement which gave rise to a civilisation of wide extent, vast power and profound vitality. The literature and fine arts of all Muslim peoples spring from this fountain head . . . No man seeking to live in the same world as Islam can afford to regard lightly, or to judge ignorantly, the Book that is called The Koran. It is among the greatest monuments of mankind. It surely deserves and demands to be more widely known and better comprehended in the West.'[26]

Arberry contributed superbly, yet not sufficiently, to such comprehension.

NEGOTIATING BETWEEN LANGUAGES

Concluding that translation which aims *not* to read like one is legitimate leads into a variety of other issues. Letting the receptive language decide means disapproving and avoiding the device — followed, for example, by Muhammad Asad in his *The Message of the Qur'ān* — of inserting phrases and sequences in brackets as 'words' not found in the Arabic but necessary to the English. Cumbersome and disconcerting in itself, this procedure indicates a *verbatim* approach to the Arabic text and can amount to an evasion of the translator's task. For it lacks the faith to achieve a true equivalence of

26 *The Holy Qur'ān.* p.33.

meaning or the freedom to house it in the constraints of the language required to 'take' it. Where there are ambiguities in the original which translation has necessarily to resolve, decisions must be taken in the stride, and not in the brackets, of the rendering. Sometimes a nice ambiguity can be retained.[27] The loyalty to meaning, which is paramount, cannot well be discharged by avoiding, as brackets do, the syntax and imagery of the recipient language. The poet Robert Browning, in respect of Greek translation, had a rule which ran: 'In as Greek a fashion as the English will bear.' What, not least from Arabic, 'the English will bear' will always be at issue. For in translation it is not only a text which is in trust but also an audience. The movement *of* a meaning is *into* a mind-reception. What is most vital in the one may well be most elusive in the other.

Not all, however, is difficulty. There is a tonic quality in the enterprise of translation as one of the finest of intellectual pursuits. We can reject John Dryden's hapless image of the translator as one 'dancing on ropes with fettered legs'. Receiving languages have sometimes given a new wealth to transmitted treasures.

'A phrase used by Dante not only contains and is illuminated by the meanings it derived from Virgil or the Vulgate, it gives new meaning to them. It not only passes on those meanings, supercharged with Dante's own meaning, to Tennyson and Landor, to . . . Yeats, Eliot and Pound: it receives back from them the reflected *splendore* of their own imaginative use of it'.[28]

Such literary transactions, it may be said, are more suited to poets than Scriptures, imbued as the latter are with a sacred aura and possessed by a vigilant dogmatism. Nevertheless, in any context language has to be seen, not as a coding device but as a communicative event. The translator serves a mediation where meaning cannot be taken from the one language except in a partaking by another. It cannot be an exercise in neutrality but requires a reciprocal relation for which idiom and vocabulary are never merely passive but active factors in a living exchange. Faiths have to be — to a degree — in communion, if their Scriptures are for translation. There are many instances in which the English Bible of the 17th century remints in the taking the

---

27 As, for example, in the refrain in Surah 55, repeated there thirty-one times:
    '. . . which of your (dual) Lord's blessings will you (dual) discount and deny?'
    The two English verbs embrace the Arabic verb *kadhdhaba*, i.e. refuse to
    recognise for what they are, give the lie to. The sense has to do with both verbal
    negation and actual disallowance. The context of serial enumeration of divine
    benefactions may be said to demand both senses.

28 D.L. Sayers: *The Poetry of Search and the Poetry of Statement*, London, 1963,
    p.272.

wealth of the original Hebrew.[29] Perhaps a receptive language can do likewise with the Arabic of the Qur'ān if its telling phrases are conveyed into an English which really savours them. How to prove so is the problem. Take the question in Surah 75.36: *A yahsibu-l-insān an yutraka sudan?* Arberry has 'Does man reckon that he will be left to roam at will?' The picture in the final word is of camels untethered or animals left unshepherded to wander where they will. Some take the verse as asking whether human life is all in vain or whether man is unaccountable to some last judgement. Others suggest that man must not think himself other than mortal. 'Does man imagine that he is left on the loose,' best captures the idea. By the 'tether' metaphor a contemporary reader discerns an apt analogy for current secularity — a cast of mind for which it is often supposed that Quranic Arabic has no precise term. For nothing is 'secular' in the sense of being outside the domain of God. But secular man does imagine that he wields an autonomy free from transcendent liability, the only constraints being those of economic forces and cultural conditioning. He thinks himself, otherwise, 'neither prohibited nor commanded'. He is left to his own devices in a universe devoid of God. *Sudan* in 75.36 exactly fits this stance, and is illuminated by it, though the image is from the scenes Muhammad knew. Formed as a question, the verse knows that secular notions *are* harboured. Hence, of course, the necessity of prophets and the central Islamic word of a divine imperative commanding the human world. The Qur'ān here has a strongly contemporary ring. English can well render it in the randomness that thinks itself 'left on the loose'.

In Surah 16.9 comes the observation: *Wa 'alā-Allāhi qasdu-l-sabīl*, 'the direction of the way is (lit.) upon God'. Ethical direction, that is, derives from divine command. But the word *qasd* has to do with more than 'direction', while *sabīl* is more than just a path or road. The verse, then, may be read as comprehending the whole 'course' of history and not merely the ordering of some particular situation. It may cover not only moral discernment of duty but also the providences of time. The verse goes on to say: 'and from it (lit.) there is what deviates', meaning either 'roads' or 'persons' with the second the likelier. When a variety of translations have been volunteered there remains a feel about the Arabic which eludes a single rendering. It is necessary to bring together both ethics and eschatology. Detached as it is from the context about natural phenomena — as pregnant phrases sometimes

29 See David Daiches: *The King James Version of the English Bible*, Chicago, 1941, and the same writer's: *Literary Essays*, London, 1956, 'Translating the Hebrew Bible', pp.191-205, where he illustrates how sensitive translation can yield enrichment to the original. But it must be 'sensitive', not the crudity which, for example, modernises 'Cast thy bread on the waters' into 'Send your goods overseas'.

are — the verse serves equally well the intricacies of politics, the vicissitudes of life, or the dialogue between religions, the whole whence and whither of faith and history.

And what should we make of the same word *'ala* ('upon') in the phrase in Surah 5.105: 'You who believe, upon you are your souls'? 'Look after your own souls', is Arberry's choice. Is there some kinship with Psalm 119.109: 'My soul is ever in my hand'? Certainly the ways in which we are in trust with ourselves comprise the very core of religion, not to say the gist of life. But how best is the cryptic Arabic translated? 'On you are your souls' can mean so much.

Or take the words in 6.91, repeated again in 22.74 and 39.67: *Mā qadarū Allāha haqqa qadrihi.*? ('They, i.e. the idolators, did not measure God by His true measure'.) The sentence uses the familiar absolute accusative, the verb supplying the object. 'They had no adequate sense of God' would be a loose rendering; or: 'they did not esteem God as He is truly to be esteemed'. The crisp force of the Arabic is hardly amenable to English equivalence though the meaning opens up vistas of theology and of devotion which over-simplify, distort or ill-serve the divine reality. It is uncanny how near the implications are to the Greek *doxa* which means 'glory' in the context of 'a right mind about . . .'.[30]

Inter-language negotiation in these ways has to keep a lively mind for nuances, keeping a faith which is watchful but not slavish with *both* the original and the new language. This means, among other things, a will *not* to be woodenly consistent in rendering rich single terms. These may well require variants in different contexts. *Taqwā* and *dhikr* are important examples. Both are highly significant terms and occur in differing senses. The former, noted by Fazlur Rahman in his *Major Themes of the Qur'ān*, as 'the central term in the Qur'ān's vision of man under God',[31] means 'awe' before God, 'God-fearingness' and 'utmost reverence'. It is somewhat akin to the Latin *pietas*. Derivatives from it, like *muttaqūn* take on the implied sense of 'warding off evil', because a true fear shuns what defiles and blasphemes. Such souls, in turn, preserve and protect society. To insist on a single English word betrays rather than fulfills loyalty to the original.

Dhikr, too, is rich in implication around the core sense of both 'recollection' and the 'reminding' which stirs it. The English 'mention' is too trite for this deep 'mindfulness'. But *dhikr*, for obvious reasons, is also a title of the Qur'ān itself — God's *Dhikr* to humanity. It is also used for the believers' discipline of prayer, both formal and mystical, and the recitation of the

30 For a full study of the term *qadar* and its uses in the Qur'ān see, Muhammad Daud Rahbar: *God of Justice: Ethical Doctrine of the Qur'ān*, Leiden, 1960. pp.108-119.
31 *Major Themes*, p.28.

Names of God. God, according to 38.2, is *Dhū-l-dhikr*, 'possessor of the renown that is ever due'. The word is also used of the Jewish Scriptures (21.7 and 105). 'Will you not hold in your thoughts?' is the reiterated plea of the verb *tadhakkara* relating either to the words of the Qur'ān or the 'signs' in nature. Underlying the term *dhikr* throughout is the concept of the cosmic pledge mankind gave to the Lord in response to the question: 'Am I not your Lord?' (Surah 7.172) — a response which needs to be steadily brought back to mind. 'Remember Me and I will remember you' (2.152) is one of the most loved of all Quranic verses. It is wise for a translator to let a range of English vocabulary serve such an inclusive theme.

Another term where this is imperative is *fitnah*. For the sense of this word changes significantly within the sequence of the Scripture. The root meaning has to do with what tests or tries and hence temptation or 'putting to the proof'. Thus children could be a *fitnah* to their fathers if pleaded as ground or excuse for evading the obligation to fight in the *Jihād* against the foes of Islam. *Fitnah* in the days when Islam was a harried minority, prey to the hostile establishment in Mecca, meant 'persecution'. As Muslims came to dominate the scene at Medina, *fitnah* was 'sedition' against them. That meaning of 'conspiracy' could not have obtained earlier. Warfare, the Qur'ān says, is a lesser evil than *fitnah* (Surah 2.217) and must be maintained until *fitnah* is at an end, i.e. warfare directed against the seditious, not against Muslims too timid, or too solicitous of family, to wage it. There is thus a *fitnah* within Muslim ranks as 'conspiracy', a *fitnah* against Muslims as 'oppression' and a *fitnah* for Muslims in their own cowardice, sloth or family ties. It is clear that no single English word handles this manifold adequately.

So it is well to emulate the scholars who toiled on the King James' Bible in the seventeenth century and who wrote in their Preface:

'Another thing we think good to admonish thee of, O gentle reader, that we have not tied ourselves to an uniformity of phrasing or to an identity of words, as some peradventure would wish that we had done . . . There be some words that be not of the same sense everywhere . . . That we should express the same notion in the same particular word: as, for example, if we translate the Hebrew or Greek word once by *purpose*, never to call it *intent*; if one were *journeying* never *travelling*: if one where *pain* never *ache*: if one where *joy*, never *gladness* etc. thus to mince the matter we thought to savour more of curiosity than wisdom.'[32]

When they went on to ask: 'Is the Kingdom of God become words and

32 Preface to the King James Bible, 1611.

syllables?' Quranic orthodoxy might feel uneasy. But there is obvious warrant in their attitude.[33]

There are occasions when it may be right to let an Arabic term stay in the English, inviting attention by the reader to the Glossary. One such is *Jāhiliyyah*, which is found frequently and denotes the state of 'ignorance' and those guilty of it, in the time before Muhammad. But with the lack of revelation there went a certain 'wildness' resulting from and abetting the state of ignorance. In such a context as 11.18 the meaning is 'having no mind for the truth', a wilfulness rather than a mere absence of information. A few words that are rare, or technical, may also be left in their Arabic form — *Hittah*, for example, in Surah 7.161, some password or salutation on entering a town. Consulting a Glossary in these cases — and in general — will be more satisfactory than a paraphrase which breaks the flow of the Qur'ān's diction or logic.

A very common usage calling for differing treatment in English is: *min dūni-Illāhi*. 'To the exclusion of God' gives the sense in many passages which rebuke the pagan pseudo-worships which have no place for God. This blatant 'mindlessness' or neglect of God on the part of unbelievers is in total antithesis to the *dhikr* in which He is truly acknowledged. The phrase is an accusation of life, a reproach of wilful, unconcern for the divine claim. To be oblivious of God's mercies and 'signs' — a chronic evil in Muhammad's day — is much the secular habit in ours. *Min dūni-Illāhi* has a very comprehensive and contemporary ring.

APPRECIATING THE TASK

A perceptive reader of the Qur'ān quickly realises that there is a kind of spiral character to its sequences. It circles around a theme, seems to leave it only to return to it again. When the pattern is recognised the import emerges through the thought-rhythms. Renewed reference, for example, to the fidelity of the patriarchal prophets is punctuated with reminders of calamity for all gainsayers who despise the messengers. Appeals for attentiveness to the 'signs' in nature are interspersed with recollection of the ruin of former generations denying them.

Through this spiral movement which recurs and progresses, reciter or reader enter into Muhammad's actual environment. For preaching, no less than poetry, has refrains. To arrest, convert and educate pagans takes a sustained venture in words. This encounter with the Prophet's vocation is

33 For Muhammad Asad's rationale of his sustained option for 'Sustainer' see his translation, pp.1-2. His invariable use of this English word for the Arabic *Rabb* makes the secondary sense of 'one who nurtures' or 'guides to maturity' total and leaves aside the central Semitic sense of divine sovereignty. But Asad required of himself a uniform rendering throughout.

captured in the very texture of the Book. It is no ordered treatise shaped in detached reflection, nor an academic essay in religious ideas. 'The sense of the word' is not just a register of meaning: it is a fabric of life and language combining to enshrine it.

It needs to be remembered also how the circumstances of the collection of the Qur'ān were responsible in part for how its sequences run.[34] To a degree, succession of contents followed the vicissitudes of the gathering process when the 'piecemeal' *tanzīl* (Surah 17.106) was complete. It is invidious to apply dissecting scissors to the chapters in an effort to formalise the whole and wiser to savour its actuality in life.[35] For the life within, then and now, is what the translator is in pledge to convey.

That life, allowed to pulsate in its own vigour, breathes through all the familiar arts of language — rhyme, assonance, stress and metre, harnessing sound to sense and serving meaning by the fascination of form. Refrain preoccupies anticipation and cadences are tuned to meaning. The ear's register rules the mind's grasp, with oral recitation to serve both as a vital duty of faith. Arabic grammar and syntax are well-suited to this end, with the various derivatives from the triliteral roots dependably conforming — for the most part — to the needs of rhyme and rhythm. English cannot match this quality with its vocabulary of diverse origins and variant forms. The Names of God, as many other adjectives, are in rhyming pattern: *wa huwa al-'azīz al-hakīm*, 'and He is the mighty, the wise',[36] with regular syllabic lengths, as is the case with the plural nouns — the *muslimūn* and the *kāfirūn*, the *mu'minūn* and the *mushrikūn*, the *muflihūn* and the *mujrimūn*. The 'broken plurals' also have a syllabic shape which yields readily to poetic form, while the verbs, in their variety, conform to rhythmic patterns. And linking all is the Arabic *waslah* or flowing letter (in shape like the comma of English hiatus but otherwise a total contrast), which merges before and after in a fluency of sound unmatched in translation. Conspiring with the *waslah*, of course, are the *'al*'s of the definite article, or the possessing 'construct', which vary their vowels sympathetically with case endings and which unite with solar letters to form the *shaddah* or explosive stress so characteristic of Arabic diction. Or if they do not unite they serve a liquid flow into the lunar letters — a flow nowhere more remarkable than in the first part of the *Shahādah* itself: with

34 See, for example, John Burton: *The Collection of the Qur'ān*, Cambridge, 1977, Part ii, and Richard Bell: *Introduction to the Qur'ān*, rev. ed. W.M. Watt, Edinburgh, 1972. Muhammad Asad sees the Qur'ān 'arranged in accordance with the inner requirements of its message as a whole.' *Op. cit.* p.i, in a comment on non-chronology. But he does not elaborate.

35 As, for example, in: Richard Bell: *The Qur'ān: Translated with a Critical Re-arrangement of the Surahs*, 2 vols., Edinburgh, 1977.

36 At times some liberty is appropriate in turning these rhyming pairs of adjectival Names into nouns in English, e.g. here: 'Lord of might and wisdom'.

its six 'l's *Lā ilāha illā-Allāh*, 'there is no god except God'. The English translates but is no substitute.

There is no case, however, for transliterating the word *Allāh*. The precise English equivalent in meaning is the word: 'God' (capitalised to distinguish *ilāhun* from *Allāh*, i.e. 'a god') denoting 'the One and the only'. To employ the Arabic word as if it were English implies a deliberate attempt to exclusify the word *Allāh* to Islam (for it is good Christian Arabic) or to imply that God/*Allāh* is not, eternally, the God of all peoples. The monosyllabic English word 'God' forfeits all the resonance but carries the theology. Variant as that theology is between usages, it is not rightly served by adopting *Allāh* into English where it will most likely be ill-pronounced. The poetry of words is the property of the languages where they belong.

The Qur'ān's poetry exults in almost untranslatable eloquence in the Prophet's earliest years with his mission. These passages, bewildering to the stranger, charm and captivate the Arab ear and splendidly fulfill the role of language in exciting the imagination. *Sūrat al-Mursalāt* (Surah 77) is a striking case in point:

> By the chartered winds in their familiar courses
> And tempests in their stormy pride,
> By the dispersing, fructifying rain-clouds,
> By all that deciphers and discerns
> And brings home a reminder as plea and as warning —
> All that you are promised will assuredly happen.

These seven opening verses, containing only sixteen words with linking particles, yield forty-four English words in an effort after poetic translation striving to comprise the range and force of the original, with its seven *an* terminations (known as 'nunation') and its five rhyming plurals in *-āt*. Arberry's rendering reads:

> By the loosed ones successively
> Storming tempestuously,
> By the scatterers scattering
> And the severally severing
> And those hurling a reminder
> Excusing or warning,
> Surely that which you are promised is about to fall.

There is a literal fidelity here and an effort after the original accentuations (which are hardly transferable if it is to be English). 'Loosed ones successively', 'scatterers scattering' have abandoned all trace of the poetic. 'Severally

58

severing' catches a refrain but strains to do so. Muhammad Asad, with his bracketed explications, has:

> Consider these (messages) sent forth in waves
> And then storming on with a tempest's force!
> Consider these (messages) that spread (the truth) far and wide,
> Thus separating (right and wrong) with all clarity,
> And then giving forth a reminder
> (promising) freedom from blame or (offering) a warning!
> Behold, all that you are told to expect will surely come to pass.

No poetry remains here and the wide perceptions the eloquence invites are confined in the single dimension of 'messages.' It is true that *mursalāt* belongs with the same root as *rasūl* (messenger) and *risālah* (the word he brings), but it is by no means clear that the gradual, step by step revelation of the Qur'ān' (Asad's words) is the sole intent of a powerful invocation of forces in the natural order to which, elsewhere, the Scripture passionately appeals in the Lord's 'controversies'. Do we not need a translation which keeps its moralising within the steady insistence of the Qur'ān on the significance of the *āyāt* of nature? 'Sent forth in waves' hardly captures the incisive social and moral encounters in which Muhammad's preaching had to engage in the context of Mecca.

Syed Abdul Latif resorts to natural themes but elaborates with free parentheses.

> By those sent forth breezes which first move gently
> Then gather force to move swiftly
> And spread rain-laden clouds far and wide
> And separate them from one another (to pour down rain at different places)
> By those who deliver the revelation,
> Condoning (the lapses of those who repent) or warning (against evil)
> Assuredly that which you are promised will come to pass.[37]

The French of Kasirmirski opts for 'angels' as *mursalāt*.

> Par les anges envoyées l'un après l'autre,
> Par ceux qui se meuvent avec rapidité,
> Par ceux qui dispersent au loin,
> Par ceux qui divisent et distinguent
> Par ceux qui font parvenir la parole
> D'excuse ou d'avertissement.
> Les peines dont on vous menace viendront.[38]

37 Syed Abdul-Latif: *Al-Qur'ān rendered into English*, Hyderabad, 1969, p.505.
38 Kasirmirski: *Le Coran traduit de l'Arabe*, Paris, 1970, p.465.

But the repetitiveness of 'par ceux qui' here is far from the cumulative eloquence of the original.

It will be clear from these efforts that the handling of the Arabic needs to be resourceful as well as loyal, ready to venture reflective rather than studiously literal English. 'Chartered' and 'familiar' in the above register implications of *'urfan*: 'dispersing' and 'fructifying' have in mind the double signficance in a single root used in two Arabic words. 'Deciphers' and 'discerns' keeps a certain assonance while exploring the twin meanings of one form in two derivatives. 'Bringing home' seems a better option than 'hurling' or 'giving forth' for a 'reminder', whether borne by winds or angels or messages. But merits or demerits apart (which experts must assess), the seven verses, followed as they are by natural portents of the last Day, illustrate the demands the Arabic makes on the translator and how diverse the discharge of them can be. The logic for the reader is not to rely on any one mentor and to know that none deserves an unquestioning confidence.

An awkwardness in English may well be a failure in rendition as the price of an honest perplexity: a facility in English may conceal a suggestive ambiguity in the original. The entire enterprise is for perfectionists who know they will never succeed and requires readers ready to appreciate both their struggle for perfection and their non-success. The option of mastering Arabic is not open to the vast majority of those with a serious religious and/or academic concern for the Qur'ān. Only as a necessary 'evil' can translation propose and attain its good intent. It is time to turn, made cautious by that warning, to a contemporary 'translation' of the Qur'ān and review what the Arabic yields to English in the relevance its themes and meanings hold in the exchanges of this late twentieth century.

بسم الله الرحمن الرحيم

4. The Qur'ān for Today: Contemporary Concerns

Issues that run deep for the translator run deeper still for the theologian. Problems of a text and a language draw solutions from grammars and lexicons in the quiet of the study. Those of the believer must be pursued in the clamour of the world. A lively imagination and a ready mind will equip either yet need to be differently alerted when the setting is no longer the sanctuary of the holy text but the scepticism of a secular time, and the confidences of faith have to be interpreted to anxieties and preoccupations which scout or ignore them.

That the Qur'ān is through and through theological is evident even to the most cursory reader. 'In the beginning and in the end — God.' Its theology is not discursive, nor speculative: it does not stem from a dialogue of logicians nor emerge from a philosophical conclusion. It is an absolute of revelation, a supreme imperative.[39] It summons mankind categorically to obedience and submission and, given those attitudes, warrants the obedient in mandates to determine the submission of others. It is thus, both in concept and in practice, a most assured theism. It would be fair to describe it as *the* most assured, in the light of all it has been understood to validate in history and of how far latent, rather than explicit within it, are the many spiritual and intellectual duties of any theism.

It is this uncomplicated absoluteness for God of the Qur'ān which stands in sharp contrast to the climate of today in the West and wherever the secular tide flows. So the purpose of this concluding part of An Introductory Essay is to situate present-day readership squarely within the encounter of the Islamic Scripture with the mood and mind of the general constituency into which English translation is calculated to bring it. Such readers may be broadly anticipated of two kinds — readers with a general interest in the

39 Fazlur Rahman: *Major Themes*, stresses this 'imperative' character of the Qur'ān by, surprisingly, dissociating it altogether from any sort of 'disclosure' about God. 'The Qur'ān,' he writes, 'is no treatise about God and His nature; His existence, for the Qur'ān, is strictly functional . . . the aim of the Qur'ān is man and his behaviour, not God' pp.1 and 3. To think of God as a 'function' of man is a strangely un-Islamic theism.

Qur'ān arising out of their fascination or involvement with Islam in all the diversity of current affairs — political, academic, economic or social, and readers with a mind for the themes and relevance of the Islamic Scripture in the growing care for inter-faith relationships. The two motivations no doubt interact but may be treated separately here as being the religiously indifferent, or even hostile, and the religiously committed. We will find the Qur'ān, as interrogated by the former affording much for the guidance of the latter. They deserve, however, to be explored independently.

There is no doubt which is the more strenuous in its demands. From the reflections on selection in Part 2 it will have been clear how much the common mind of theism shares with Islam. Those who go to the Qur'ān from within that common mind, and indeed from the instincts of the Hindu and the Buddhist, will find much for their education and recognition in the quest for what some envisage as the coming 'ecumene' of religions. It is the abiding quarry of all who search for the spirituality of Islam by their own faith-criteria with any will to find community of meaning. Where instincts and attitudes are 'religious', community of course will not be without tension and controversy. There is nothing so fertile as religious commitment in generating them. But they will be of a different order, and more tractable than many of the things at stake between a Qur'ān-orientated pattern of mind and current secularity.

'They did not reckon God the truth of His reckoning,' we noted earlier in a clumsily literal rendering of Surahs 6.91, 22.74, and 39.67, or, in freer paraphrase: 'They did not have a true or adequate esteem of God,' or: 'Their theology quite failed in concept and worship to do justly by God.' For they held God in a quite unworthy esteem. The form of words in the Arabic is pregnant with meanings. What are the right ideas about God? How can they be identified? The criteria must be those God Himself provides: where, then, do we come by them? How can what is not true in theology give way to what is? All these are arduous questions.

But what of those who do not 'reckon' at all? The Qur'ān's verdict on the pagan idolaters assumes a reality that those in Mecca originally addressed had distorted or decried. Can it indict those who assume no reality at all, who do not 'alienate' their worship as the Quraish did to plural deities, but for whom worship itself is 'alien'? What of Quranic theology and faith when they take their way into a mentality for which such imperative theism is both uncongenial and unproven? How should fidelity to the Qur'ān respond to radical dis-esteem of God today?

THE TEXT FROM THE MARGINS

We can, perhaps, usefully initiate reflection on the contemporary scrutiny of the Qur'ān and the challenge it brings by taking analogy from what all

Scriptures possess, namely broad margins hospitable to ample commentary. Traditionally the margins are very deferential, sometimes only embroidering what they hold sacrosanct, with further margins aslant the first in a closed framework of admiration and confidence.

Today's general reader is likely to extract the text from these enclosures of dogma and piety and bring it into margins of experience and uncertainty of such contrast that they may almost marginalise the text itself, reversing its authority and scrutinising it for commentary on the elusive text of life itself. Believers in the Scripture have the duty to acknowledge how suspect the whole field of revelatory authority may be to today's reader, how man has come to forfeit or renounce the sense of the transcendent. They will need to reckon patiently with how the whole course of things seems, for some among us, to leave us only to ourselves under an empty or a silent heaven. The claim of an absolute, total, even at times arbitrary, sovereignty of God, such as the Qur'ān makes, may not only fail to persuade but may sharply repel, the dubious mind. There will be no present fidelity to 'the Book in which there is no dubiety' (Surah 2.2) that does not recognise a duty to respond, and to search for the response that is right in this situation. To deplore or condemn it as *jāhiliyyah* will not suffice. For these are 'margins' that really search the 'text'.

It is necessary to say, in preface to an undertaking of this task, that it in no way implies some sinister depreciation of the Qur'ān or some veiled attack upon it. Quite the contrary. But Muslims do harbour strong suspicion of outsiders these days. With some reason, they feel they and their Scriptures to be roughly handled or falsely depicted by westerners. Sincerity of intention here can offer no other credential but its own integrity and hope to be accepted. In the present climate the right posture for us all is to forego distrust and together to face squarely the realities of life as people read them anywhere, and thus seek good faith through the positive interpretation of a heritage of holy writ authentically, not suspiciously, possessed. The Qur'ān can only be vindicated in its doctrine of a timelessness of meaning if it firmly confronts the ethos of present time and the unprecedented developments in current history.

We have first to review the factors which have brought contemporary minds where they are and then ask how far Muslim society itself experiences those same influences.

A pervasive contributor to doubt of God, in point of fact if not of logic, is modern technology in which all to varying degrees participate. Techniques of applied science, and the attitudes behind them, appear to locate society wholly within the purview of *human* authority and disposal. Whatever may be the role of prayer and ritual, we tend actually to put our trust in the processes: the skills of the engineer, the surgeon, the expert. The changes induced in daily living by speed, mobility, invention, drugs, amenities and facilities, as furnished and maintained by technology, are — it would seem — humanly contrived. They supervene, and the information-media most of all, unasked and without prior reckoning with, or intelligent consent to, their consequences. They off-load their results — managerial, organisational, sexual, cultural — without reference to human meaning and significance. Indeed they may end in questioning whether there is a dependable, constant *human* significance at all. Clearly it is the technicians who call the tune, who assign society to the behests, the vagaries, even the potential enslavements, of expertise. The present and the future are wards of technology operating as an end in itself. Effective means supplant verified ends.

Efforts, to be sure, exist to discipline the whole process and to hold it in control. But are not these somehow as liable to dispense with the divine as the processes themselves? So the bewildered or the cynical ask: Where does God belong here? And, for a theism as absolute as the Qur'ān's: Where does His writ run? Is it feasible, people enquire, to comprehend the contemporary scene within the providence and disposition of personal omnipotence? When the noted exegete of the Qur'ān in the 1960's in Cairo, Sayyid Qutb, deplored 'man under the domination of man and not of God', was he not in fact describing actuality, deplorable as it might be, yet irreversible? For every new competence of men is indeed a new power over mankind, atheism no longer needs preaching since theism is now so manifestly void.[40]

The behavioural sciences, psychology and sociology, contrive to suggest or assume a relativity about all things. Reason cannot be a dependable guide since it is so far ridden by motives. Religious conviction reduces to social conditioning. Rite and code and creed only minister to human pretension or neuroses and have no warrant as interpreters of mystery or truth. Sincerity is merely belief in one's own propaganda. There is nothing to ontology: there are only phenomena. Value judgements must be abandoned since all sociological observation has to be 'value-free'. The old certainties of Scripture, revelation, tradition and dogma have no purchase on reality.

Such a climate of mind has no assurance about scriptural accounts of God and man which require to be accepted on their own showing. The Qur'ān, by virtue of its brief temporal incidence of twenty-three years in one country through a single Muhammad, may have fewer textual issues than other older, wider Scriptures. But Scriptures *per se*? Does not a proper scrutiny uncover the context of fallibiity in which they were conceived, transmitted and

---

40 On Sayyid Qutb, executed in Cairo in 1966, a leader of strong conviction and courage within the Muslim Brotherhood, further detail may be found in Emmanual Sivan: *Radical Islam, Medieval Theology and Modern Politics*, Yale, 1985, and Kenneth Cragg: *The Pen and the Faith: Eight Modern Muslim Writers and the Qur'ān*, London, 1985, pp.53-71. His Qur'ān Commentary, *Fi Zilāl al-Qur'ān*, (In the Shade of the Qur'ān), Cairo, from 1964, and *Ma'ālim fi-l-Tarīq* (Signposts on the Road), Beirut, n.d., are his most influential works.

endowed with an inviolate status which made them sacrosanct? They are in fact tribunals which are themselves on trial.

The arts too, following the sciences, yield their full quota of religious disquiet. Novelists and poets in the nineteenth century sensed a 'receding tide of faith'. But at least they wrote in a world of accepted fidelities and feasible patterns. For many of their twentieth century counterparts, all the waymarks are gone. If literature can direct at all it is only by indirection, by hint and surmise. Too often, it is content — or discontent — only to describe the human condition, with pity often, but without conviction. The stream of consciousness makes for the anti-hero and the anti-saint. Much philosophy, meanwhile, dismays the empty places of the soul by its pre-occupation with linguistic analysis and its supine distrust of meaning.

In a paradoxical way, religious faith itself all too often confirms this fashion of our time by an evident apprehension which takes refuge in heightened dogmatism and confirms the darkness by cursing it so loudly. Too often, faith — *via* the faiths — entrenches itself behind its own assertions rather than going for the fallacies and indulgences of its detractors. Dogmatic reiteration of dogma, variously called 'fundamentalism', does duty for sober and steady witness that has no need of panic. The question-mark too often is answered by the exclamation-mark, the critic by the pundit, the dubious by the fanatic. The anxious faith begins to look like a contradiction in terms. An apologist impatient makes a witness flawed. The issues of faith then seem to dissolve into a match between raucous credulity and incredulous minds.

But, it may be protested, these paragraphs concern only one segment of humanity. The people of the Qur'ān are splendidly immune. But how so? The technology at least is ubiquitous and ardently desired. The techniques are universal. Many of the concomitants in education and assumption are also pervasive in Muslim society. The paradox of defensiveness we have just noted is emphatically in place around the margins of the Qur'ān. Nor is it wise to assume that any part of the human whole can now enjoy immunity. The timing may be different; but the incidence of things at stake is similar. Current history is one history: there are no exemptions where oceans no longer separate and mountains do not hide.

Indeed, it might be thought that Islam, precisely by the strength of its imperative theism, is more open than other systems to the painful shock of modernity. The Qur'ān's very finality as the quintessence of religion invests it with a more commanding assurance, and perhaps a more sanguine self-confidence, than other theisms. It would seem to have less readiness for gentleness and tragedy — those sure ministrants to resilient humility in face of perplexity. Or perplexity itself, being uncongenial, is more readily suppressed. Certainly the Islamic Scripture brings a 'categorical divine imperative' which may be thought to conflict more directly with the modern mood of 'uncommandedness'.

Before turning to how amply equipped the Qur'ān is to respond with great positives to these current perceptions of the predicament of man, it is useful to have in mind an aggravating feature of contemporary experience for Muslims. It has to do with the fact that tensions are complicated for them by the external sources from which in large measure the pressures arise. Much technology comes from the West (or from Japan, the eastern 'West'). It is the same West from which Islamic countries are in political and emotional 'liberation'. To be under a continuing and inescapable 'connection' (*via* techniques) with parties for whom one has persistent and legitimate feelings of resentment sharpens the emotions involved. Technology comes in western packaging, has often to be serviced by western personnel and brings intrusive consequences *via* the media, films, advertising, tourism and market forces. These threaten and disrupt the Islamic patterns of thought and ethos. Islam, it is true, is not without material assets in this encounter. But the issues in the spirit combine the irresistible with the unwanted. There is a mixed bargain of the means for development and the menace of change.

It is not that there is any inherent hostility to science, technology or development in the Islamic world-view. On the contrary. In the middle centuries Muslims were in the van of research in the physical sciences, in chemistry, medicine, optics, mathematics, philosophy and even sociology.[41] Part of the dilemma for Muslims today is that the European pupil has ascended the ladder of the Muslim tutor. This is galling not only for the foreign-ness it entails but because its antecedents were once domestic to Islam. On many counts, historical and political, the West has to be re-proached. Yet there is no eluding relationships of the most telling kind.

The intensity of these emotions about the West has to be sympathetically understood. Even our present venture with the Qur'ān will not escape the strictures. There is need of patience in the context of deep protests about alleged denigration or stereotyping of Islam and 'the East' in western writing.[42] Muslims, it is felt, have been subjected to inferiorisation, being

---

41   Conspicuous names are those of the polymath, Ibn Sīnā; Ibn Haitham (optics); Al-Fārābī (philosophy); Al-Bīrūnī (geography and culture); Al-Rāzī (medicine); and The Brethren of Purity — all in the ninth to the eleventh centuries (C.E). The prince of 'sociologists' came later in the person of Ibn Khaldūn (d.1406) whose famous work: *Al-Muqaddimah* was far from 'value free'. A devout Muslim, he was concerned to explore the factors in the rise and fall of peoples and powers as the proper business of historiography. English trans. by Franz Rosenthal, New York, 2 vols, 1958.

42   Notably in Edward Said: *Orientalism*, New York, 1979, and ed. Asaf Hussain, Robert Olson and Jamil Qureshi: *Orientalism, Islam and Islamists*, Vermont, 1984. The charge is that western writers habitually subject 'the East' and 'Islam' to

'imaged' by western prejudice as backward, resistant to change, or just strange and romantic. If we move from scholarship and literature to daily journalism the charge is intensified. Islam suffers distortion and misrepresentation in the reporting and the editorials of western media.[43]

These deep factors in the psyche must be in view in any sensitive reckoning, on the part of Muslims or of others, with the contemporary duties of the heirs of the Qur'ān. Any self-image reacts to what it perceives itself to suffer. Self-scrutiny may not free itself from self-vindication. Extenuation or exoneration may impede interior examination. In human relations there is always the *tu quoque* which externalises blame. These common hazards should in no way obscure the deep resources of the Qur'ān and its people in confronting present toils, if their authority is prepared to grapple with them, to emerge from its bastions and engage its truths with the time without first requiring capitulation. The sense of human competence — and confusion — generated by technology, and the resultant reduction, or elimination, of a divine dimension have to be met by more than denunciation and regret. Qur'ān-users need to note the Book's own realistic measure of the human capacity for unfaith and of how men live *min dūni-Illāhi*, i.e. 'to the exclusion of God'. The factors may be different as between pagan pluralism in Mecca and the idolatries of today's metropolis, but the reproof of the one may shed light on the other. Why not reverse the roles of text and margins? Let the time of the present be the text and the Qur'ān the commentary. What will we find?

THE QUR'ĀN IN COMMENTARY ON OUR TIME

Before coming to the great positives let us review two broad schools of approach to how the Qur'ān's 'commentary' might be heard. But first we may briefly note and exclude a pseudo-type of formulation which does not wisely assess either the dynamics of the situation or the nature of the Book. It consists in the notion that the Scripture is somehow abreast of all the details of new technology with a foresight that has always known them. Such pseudo-scientific reading follows a false scent. It has been sufficiently repudiated by Muslims themselves who see that the Qur'ān is neither

arbitrary image-drawing and do not allow the East and Islam to interpret themselves. It is perhaps significant that these strictures on 'orientalism' develop from within the securities of western academica. There is a sense in which the alleged 'image' sometimes coincides with what Muslim writers of the Sayyid Qutb school have to say of Muslim society, i.e. that it is 'backward', 'lethargic,' and the victim of a colonialist conspiracy.

43 On the journalism in the West about Islam, see, e.g.: Edward Said: *Covering Islam*, New York, 1981; and ed. Edmund Ghareeb: *Split Image: The Portrayal of Arabs in the American Media*, Washington, 1983.

commended by some modern 'prescience' nor compromised without it, since it is revelation whose *sine qua non* is religious.[44] Pseudo-science is no stock in trade of the strong traditionalists — our first school of Qur'ān-reading. Their anxieties and perceptions are far more radical. Represented by the Muslim Brotherhood among Arab Muslims and by the kindred movement of Abū-l-Alā al-Maudūdī in Indo-Pakistan,[45] this response to modernity with the Qur'ān pleads the Book's mandate for rigorous discipline, self-sufficiency, and — in some circumstances — the right of political revolt against inadequately Islamic rulers. It bitterly rejects western intrusion and excoriates the local shaikhs and pundits who connive with it and abet its compromise of authentic Islam. Yet, in minds like Sayyid Qutb, the martyred Muslim 'Brother' (d.1966), it is not un-intelligent or obscurantist. It accepts a legitimate recruitment of technology which it believes can be subdued to Islamic norms. It plans to bring all education into a true 'Islamisation', thus off-setting the menace of sociology and psychology as factors in the growth of religious indifferentism. All such studies must be retrieved from their western proneness to scepticism and irreligion.[46]

44 There are numerous examples of an instinct to find prescience in the Qur'ān making the Scripture abreast of modern technology. Thus Muhammad Asad writes in his Foreword to his translation (Chap. 2, note 3): 'The more our worldly knowledge and historical experience increase, the more meanings, hitherto unsuspected, reveal themselves.' For a 19th century writer, Karamat Ali Jaunpuri in *Ma'ākhadh al 'Ulūm*, Calcutta, 1867, 'The whole Qur'ān is full of passages containing information on physical and mathematical sciences.' p.29.
This whole stance is sharply rejected by writers insisting on the essentially spiritual message of the Qur'ān which does not need, and is not well served by, validation on grounds of its anticipating modern scientfic invention. See, for example: Fazlur Rahman: *Islam and Modernity*, Chicago, 1982, and Muhammad Kamil Husain: *Mutanawwi'āt*, (Miscellanies), Cairo, 1957, Vol.2, pp.29-37. He calls the 'scientific' exegesis of the Qur'ān, a 'stupid heresy.' Of a different order are those Muslim interpreters of the Qur'ān who find it anticipating Marxist theories of the class war and read a 'dialectical' struggle in the sharp confrontation in the Qur'ān between believers (seen as 'the poor') and unbelievers (seen as the rich and mighty). See, for example, the analysis, and refutation, of such exegesis in: Ayatullah Murtaza Mutahhari: *Social and Historical Change: an Islamic Perspective*, trans. by R. Campbell, Berkeley, 1986.
45 Founded in Egypt in the twenties of this century by Hasan al-Bannā, the *Ikhwān al-Muslimūn*, as the Brotherhood is known, have stood for a rigorous Islamic piety in fulfilment of the *Sharī'ah*, for a firm resistance to 'liberal' ideas (though ready to grapple with 'scientific' change) and, from time to time, for active political conspiracy against régimes considered 'compromised'. The Jamā'at-i-Islāmī, founded in Indo-Pakistan by Al-Maudūdī has a comparable theology and concern for strict Islamic loyalty of which they see themselves as the true custodians.
46 See the several Reports of Conferences held in Saudi Arabia in the last decade: e.g. Syed Sajjad Husain and Syed Ali Ashraf: *Crisis in Muslim Education*, Jiddah, 1979; G.N. Saqib: *Modernisation of Islamic Education*, London, 1977;

The Qur'ān for Today: Contemporary Concerns

How these sciences, and technology with them, are to be aligned with the interests of one single faith, given their religious 'neutrality', is not clear, but it is seen as a matter of great ideological urgency.

This mode of Qur'ān interpretation inculcates rigorous Islamic observance among the masses as a long-term strategy towards a truly Islamic state, whether or not implemented by direct political action. The remarkable feature of all such radical conservatism with the Qur'ān is its readiness to disqualify all other 'Islam' as spurious or effete. It sees 'liberal' thinkers as 'internal exiles' and moderate rulers as 'collaborators' with western misleading. It goes so far as to dub all such compromise as *jāhiliyyah*, the woeful state of ignorance preceding the advent of Islam. It thinks of *jāhiliyyah* not simply as a point of history but as a way of betrayal of which Muslims themselves are guilty after fourteen centuries of Islam's history. There could be no more striking token of the fundamentalist's monopoly of a true Islam than this diagnosis of a non-Islam within Islamic ranks. It underlies the vehemence with which such mentors exclusify their reading of the Scripture.

In the different idiom of Shī'ah Islam in its current Iranian form there are many of the same features, a sharp defiance of 'secular' history and a will to resolve all issues by a radical re-assertion of their own Islam. These mentors, with all their mental acumen and firm resolve, are not minded to see the Qur'ān as possessing, or being liable to offer, credentials addressed to modern scepticism or calculated to guide the perplexed who find the Qur'ān itself part of their perplexity.

What, then, of those Muslims who do register the stresses and distresses of mind besetting many modern folk? Such Muslims certainly exist, obscured as they may often be by the public image of belligerence which attaches to highly disputatious Muslims. The radical conservatives may malign the doubtful and despise the diffident. But these do express themselves, less perhaps in having the Qur'ān at the fingertips of assurance as in knowing on what they yearn to hear its mind. These may be amateur exegetes who comment by their interrogation of life.

Writers and poets within Arab, Persian, Turkish and Indo-Pakistani Islam are quite evidently familiar with the sentiments of western authors like Franz Kafka, Albert Camus, Bertolt Brecht, Samuel Beckett and other sceptics and absurdists. They share the existential reasons for questioning both the consolations and the commands of religion. Some are also desolated by the grim spectacle presented by religion in current Middle Eastern history. They have observed no less sardonically than their western counterparts the

Muhammad W. Khan: *Education and Society in the Muslim World*, Jiddah, 1981; and two works of Ziauddin Sardar: *The Future of Muslim Civilization*, London, 1979, and *Islamic Futures*, London, 1985. Also the writings of Isma'il Ragi al-Faruqi, *Islamisation of Knowledge: General Principles and Workplan*, Washington, 1982.

compromises and paradoxes of doctrine, the discrepancy between what faith is said, and what it is seen, to be. The credibility of revelation and the credulity of the scriptured are comparably suspect. One or two examples must suffice. The prince of Egyptian writers this half-century, Najīb Mahfūz, has a short story, *Al-Zalām*, (The Darkness) about a malevolent deity and a religious lordling who tyrannises the neighbourhood in His name and is opposed by young rebels demanding social justice. 'The big house' of the dubious deity in that story re-appears more mysteriously in the same author's large work *Children of Our Quarter*, presenting a panorama of human history in the framework of Cairo's suburbs. Moses, Jesus and Muhammad, in no-disguise pseudonyms, come one after the other, allegedly from Gabalāwī, 'the Lord of the big house', who resides enigmatically within, to whom all things belong, whose messengers such prophets are, but who is himself an elusive absentee. His prophets briefly ameliorate the human misery and strife but after their demise their quarrelling followers bring back the wretched *status quo*. Futility hangs over all, while mankind languishes under oppression. Society seems incorrigible and religious hope a forlorn dupe. Heaven is a broken myth. The final section of the novel brings us to the disaster of the nuclear age.[47]

Najīb Mahfūz is outstanding but not unique. It is clear on many counts in literature that the Qur'ān belongs to Muslim perspectives where 'the West' is not the vulgarity, the 'Satan', the predator anathematised by diehards but an index to universal dimensions of human experience. There are jurists and philosophers also, in different idiom, who bring a like scrutiny into their Muslim heritage. Theirs is not the facile search for the 'rationality' of revelation in the style of an earlier mentor, Muhammad Abduh.[48] It is rather a desire to get to the Qur'ān's authority in terms of a 'religious' guidance needing to be enjoined only in religious norms. Here the Scripture's own distinction between 'Meccan' and 'Medina' — so it is claimed — comes into its own.

47 The major novel, *Awlād Hāratinā*, is translated into English by Philip Stewart: *Children of Gabalawi*, London, 1981. *The Pen and the Faith* (note 40) assesses the significance of the work of Najīb Mahfūz. See also: Sasson Somekh: *The Changing Rhythm: A Study of Najīb Mahfūz's Novels*, Leiden, 1973; and Jareer Abu Haidar: *Awlād Hāratinā, An Event in the Arab World* in *Journal of Arabic Literature*, Vol. 16, 1985.

48 Muhammad Abduh (1849-1905), Grand Mufti of Egypt and a pioneer 'modernist', wrote *Risālat al-Tauhīd*, Cairo, 1874, (Eng. trans. by Kenneth Cragg: *The Theology of Unity*, London, 1965.) He relied strongly on a rational 'agreement' of the Qur'ān and 'sound' philosophy and personally inspired progressive attitudes by his legal *fatwas*. But after his death there were few who loyally developed his legacy. His career predated the impact of those factors reflected, for example, in Najīb Mahfūz.

To appreciate this line of Qur'ān reading, it is necessary to reckon with the issue of 'secularisation' as it relates to the form of a State. Radical conservatives, as in the Muslim Brotherhood, see state-nationalism displacing the *Ummah* of a whole Islamic 'nation', and strongly denounce it as false patriotism.[49] On a 'modern' view however, Islam, it is said, should be ready for statehoods in which Islam may well dominate religiously but should not monopolise politically. The rights and status of minorities, on this view, deserve and demand to be respected. Radicals would see minorities as compromising Islamicity: such should either islamise or emigrate, that Islam may be 'all in all'. By contrast, 'secularisers' say, the State and its laws should admit of religious diversity, suggesting a measure of detachment of any one religion (however major) from monopoly of truth, of society or of wisdom.

All of this suggests that Islam should find a self-understanding in which its 'religious' quality is made central and definitive, a thing of the faithful as such and not what defines citizens as such or nationals. The ideal of government by God, say these mentors, cannot be realised by state control or the authority of pundits. That would mean oppressive 'government by men'. God's régime, if at all, can only be by virtue of religious integrity informing secular democracy. Clearly the Qur'ān's distinction between a 'religious' call in Mecca and a 'political' régime in Medina serves to undergird this pleading. The former can be seen as enduring, apolitical, time-transcending: the latter belonged only to that time and place and has no enduring warrant in Islam.[50]

It has to be said that in present tribulations such pleas from the Qur'ān have little chance of being implemented. The mood is against them or, as in Lebanon, the time they might have availed has been overtaken from almost

---

49 The separate Arab 'nationalisms' since the First World War deeply offend the pan-Islamic commitment of those who see the solidarity of Islam as improperly fragmented by nation states. Moreover the latter have to concede common citizenship, in some sense, to non-Muslims (cf. the slogan of the 'new Régime' in Cairo in 1952: 'We are all — i.e. Muslims and Copts — Egyptians now.').

50 It is a differentiation hard to sustain in the light of the vital Muslim sense of the unity of the Qur'ān and of the *Sīrah*. Medina did not represent any change in the mission of Muhammad but only its fulfilment. Nevertheless the distinction convinces those who seek to 'spiritualise' the message of Islam and detach it from the necessity of statehood, seeing the latter as in no way indispensable since the 'essential' Islam of pre-*Hijrah* Mecca lacked it. See, for example: Muhammad Said al-'Ashmāwī: *Usūl al-Sharī'ah*, (Sources of the Law), Cairo, 1979. Also Hasan Askari: *Inter-Religion*, Aligarh, 1971 and *Society and State in Islam*, New Delhi, 1978. Similar views were held by the Republican Brothers in the Sudan. See *An Introduction to the Second Message of Islam*, Khartoum, 1981, *et al*. 'The Second Message' is, for them, the recovery of the original 'religion' detached from the specifics temporarily necessitated by the Medinan context and not to be perpetually sacrosanct.

every side by the tyranny and polarisation that hold them in anathema.[51] But they can hardly be extinguished. Nor can their authenticity be denied as a viable reading of the Qur'ān. If the finality of Muhammad as preacher is not to be displaced, there is no necessary finality in his political decisions. The *Hijrah* itself finally led back to Mecca. And a 'depoliticisation' of Islam, however remote in fact, is certainly more consonant with what the times suggest than its rigorous entrenchment in political form.

Adamant or conjectural as these two contrasted appeals from the Qur'ān may be, it is time to turn to certain great positives in the Scripture's text on which, hopefully, all might agree, both inside and outside the Islamic 'household'. Some review of these ruling themes now will conclude our 'general' concerns and carry forward the issues into what we earlier envisaged as an 'ecumene of religions' and the Qur'ān's relevance for it. What verdict does the Qur'ān have on the *superbia*, the irreligion, the bewildered malaise, of contemporary humanity?

If the reader may be referred back to the themes pondered in Part 2 earlier, the answer can be tersely given. It lies in the Qur'ān's summons to a reverent, grateful and sustained acknowledgement of God as the clue, within the natural order and on the stage of history, to the real dignity and destiny of mankind. It means a 'letting God be God' as the sure context of 'letting man be truly man'. The Qur'ān stands for religion as a divine imperative. To have observed here how this is so sharply antithetical to current moods is only to underline its urgent relevance.[52] There *are* issues for theists outside Islam about *Allāhu akbar* as a cry and a confession. To those we will come. But we can all celebrate how that divine sovereignty makes room for mankind in the dignity of real subordination. The greatness of God as Creator and Lawgiver rides with a magnanimity that has generously endowed mankind with authority, with 'dominion' or *khilāfah*, in an order of things amenable to responsible creaturehood. Only when we so conceive ourselves do we truly receive ourselves.

51 By 'secular state' in this context no necessary indifferentism to, or hostility against, religious conviction and practice is meant, but simply the free and full participation of all faith-communities in the rights and duties of citizenship and a national legal system. But, given the desperate trauma of Lebanon, and much else in the Middle East, adoption of secular statehoods would be a quantum leap indeed. Advocates like Sādiq al-'Azm in Syria are few, or they are émigrés. A case in point is the Egyptian writer Khālid Muhammad Khālid. In the fifties he ardently espoused a separation of religion and state. In 1980 in *The State and Islam* he repudiated his earlier view and called for a near identity between them.

52 One might cite, at random, Virginia Woolf's musing on a writer's creativity from which she concludes: 'The whole world is a work of art . . . we are parts of the work of art. *Hamlet* or a Beethoven quartet is the truth about the vast mass we call the world.' Then she adds, surprisingly: 'But there is no Shakespeare, there is no Beethoven, certainly and emphatically there is no God: we are the music, we are the thing itself.' *Moments of Hope*, London, 1978. p.72.

This, the central message of the Qur'ān, is the sure prescript for the understanding and the management of our technological domain. The history that has witnessed its awesome advance is not to be regretted or undone. Its works cannot be disinvented but they can be consecrated. Its competences are to be read and received, not as right but privilege, not as possession but entrustment, not as prerogative but gift. They stand in a mastery which constitutes us servants. An *imperium* over nature by dint of hand and brain is to be understood as a tenancy subdued to reverence. The Qur'ān requires us to interpret our human status as that of guests within a hospitality where theology might be likened to the art of courtesy.

Only so do we subdue the lusts of power, the attitudes of wilful self-sufficiency for which the Qur'ān has a word when it tells of *istighnā'* (as in the 'initial' chapter 96). The word conjures up those postures by which we preen ourselves, despise the servant-status and claim a self-sufficiency. There can be no doubt that, conceptually at least, this faith of the Qur'ān is the answer to the contemporary scene, to the death of the heart in the tyranny of things. It is where theology bears upon the 'sickness' or *marad*, of which the Qur'ān so often speaks, whose symptoms today are consumerism, blatant exploitation, pride, envy and callous self-sufficiency. 'The saving health', to borrow the psalmist's phrase, consists in that hallowing of the self and society, through the consecration of all creaturehood, within the sense of mystery and wonder, to which the perpetual *āyāt*, addressing our senses from within the world around us, unfailingly point our minds and wills. Those 'signs', engaging the attention of the inductive scientist to yield him the techniques, also prompt the religious gratitude of the observant soul. Thus, science and religion, so often crudely seen in discord, meet in the human spirit. The reverence which hallows, the artistry which celebrates and the techniques which harness, may be a single unity, a true 'dominion'.

Plainly this ethos of the Qur'ān bears directly on the concept of God. For it is all His beneficence. Just as our creaturehood is not enslavement, so His Lordship is not dictation. We could even say that our sense of 'being left to ourselves' (so far forward in our day), so long as it is not obtuse or defiant, tells the very manner of the divine presence — absolute, to be sure, but not oppressive, determining our obligation only as the form of our dignity.

These may not be the notions currently popular about Islam as seen by non-Muslims. But they are the witness of its Scripture. It is not sheer capitulation which revelation demands nor, properly conceived, what custodians of revelation should require, but rather the vocation to the truth of ourselves. That vocation does not react to contemporary history either in panic or despair. It lays to rest the spectre of absurdity but leaves no warrant for that *superbia* which, in Nietzschean fashion, might pretend to defy it. It instils a temper in religion minded for the humility proper to creative co-existence between cultures today. It is, in sum, a 'letting God be God' as the active pledge of a true humanity. 'Letting God be God', in all its implications, is a comprehending and comprehensive summary of the Qur'ān.

It is, to be sure, a comprehending which has critical obligations to face. These we can best consider, not in the open, uncommitted terms in which we have thus far moved, but within the explicit context of religious faith where we find ourselves arriving. If the Qur'ān is calling us to the spiritual awareness of our humanity, spiritual partners — or not partners — become significant in any further reckoning with the meanings to which it has brought us. How does this gist of the Islamic Scripture relate to other theism? What place does the Qur'ān fill in the actual, or coming, relation between religions?

THE QUR'ĀN IN A CONVERSE OF FAITHS

In the spirit of the preceding conclusion, readers with religious concern outside Islam will probably find themselves occupied with four related themes, where the content of the Book leaves them with open questions. But first, two general points are in order. The questions — and the will to pose them — only arise from within the shared conviction and for its sake. Thus Muslims should be assured that raising these questions implies no disrespect, still less any malignity. The instinct of Muslims to find ground for suspicion, to see even relationship as sinister, should be set at rest. There can hardly be any religious meeting without a mutual integrity of purpose. The other point has to do with non-Muslims who, out of their own structures or schemes of authority, demur about moving with, or from, the Qur'ān altogether. Such tentative minds may be re-assured that engaging with the Qur'ān, out of a will to engagement with Muslims in a common world, *need* not involve any formal appraisal of authority or thesis about final status. It is simply a matter of starting where others start in the hope that we may not end apart.

Only on both counts can the honesty we expect of each other be forthcoming. It is easy enough, and perhaps congenial, to salute what can readily be shared: it is another thing to grapple with the uncongenial and themes that cause unease. To cite, for example, with Surah 24.41, how every bird on wings of flight knows its praise takes us readily to Wiliam Blake's lines:

"How do you know but ev'ry Bird that cuts the airy way
Is an immense world of delight, clos'd by your senses five.'[53]

Other sentiments in the Qur'ān may suggest no such welcome parallels.

53 William Blake: *Poetry and Prose*, ed. G. Keynes, London, 1948, p.183. (From: 'The Marriage of Heaven and Hell.')

Integrity cannot leave out of account what is not congenial.

The four areas have to do with

(1) the Qur'ān's position that Islam is what all religion should be were it not distorted, because Islam tallies with human nature:

(2) the issue that follows, namely whether, in the light of the Qur'ān's own realism about human wrong and perversity, humanity is educable by word and exhortation alone:

(3) the further emerging question as to a moral, judicial 'ultimate' on the Last Day in which evil is requited and whether it can, consistently with divine sovereignty, be *only* judicial: and

(4) the power-dimension sanctioned in the Medinan Qur'ān in the interests of truth and faith.

These questions may not be in the foreground of those practical matters of inter-faith co-operation with which our relationships as citizens, ecologists, traders and technicians are concerned. Issues of world peace, of poverty, of justice, of population, and many others in the sphere of the United Nations or UNESCO on the global or the local level, or in the World Health Organisation or the International Labour Office, do not find solution in the discursive exchanges between faiths. Yet none of them can be actively undertaken in neglect of how faiths interpret the meat of them in the convictions which must guide and sustain the tasks such issues set.

Firstly, then, what of the claim that Islam is 'the final and ultimate religion, the quintessence of revelation, the ecumenical faith'?[54] Surah 30.30 is the passage which Muslims hold as warranting this confident belief. The crucial phrase there might be crudely translated: '. . . the nature on which He (God) natured men'. The Arabic word is *fitrah* with the cognate verb *fatara*. It is taken to mean both 'nature' and 'religion', as mutually fitted. So Islam is 'the religion of God in accord with which He made men religious'. It follows that historic Islam was no 'new religion but the renewal or revival of an eternal monotheism . . . born with the world. All truly pious and righteous men of the past, present and future are by definition Muslim.'[55] Thus the Qur'ān, we may say, epitomises the religion instinctive and proper to mankind, perfectly suited to the very soul and body of humanity. All the prophets were *alter egos* of Muhammad with the same message.

It follows that where revelations diverge from this norm, or religions diversify in essential particulars, they are misled or compromised. They do not tally with the norm: but the norm determines the conclusion. Faiths do not coincide with Islam: therefore they are misguided. Philosophers would say that the argument is circular: the proof and the proven connive. Other faiths, loyal to what they see as their significant divergence from the Qur'ān,

---

54 Tarif Khālidī: *Classical Arab Islam, The Cultural Heritage of the Golden Age*, Princeton, 1985, p.13.
55 *Ibid.*

may be left without a hearing. Their case is foreclosed. There cannot be ecumenical relationships on this showing. We need to concede the other's distinctiveness and to hear it on its own terms.

Furthermore, difference from Islam, on this basis, has to be attributed to the ignorant or malign agency of parenthood. Since all are born 'Muslims', it must be upbringing and nurture which are responsible for aberration. Yet any doctrine, like Islam's, of creation and providence, must surely find positive purpose, not negative consequence, in such a vital factor as the family and in the gift of procreation which the Qur'ān so reverently salutes in its frequent reference to the mystery of the womb and the embryo. Nurture would seem to have an honoured place in the economy of God. Must we deny that somehow His economy has an interest in pluralism and diversity? Diversity is in fact what the Qur'ān itself celebrates. God did not make us all of identical race or kind.

Parenthood apart, what of the concept of 'finality' in relation to faith-diversity? Muslims understand the Qur'ān to be historically final. Muhammad is 'the seal of the prophets'. 'In the Qur'ān man has finally encountered the word of God . . . God has finally become first person singular.'[56] Even where earlier revelations were consonant with Islam, they were partial. The Qur'ān is revelation's climax.

May this conviction hinge on the calendar? The Qur'ān postdates the Bible, the Vedas, the Upanishads, the Bhagavad Gita, the Dhammapada, indeed all major Scriptures save those of the Sikhs. But chronology apart, what other tests of 'finality' are appropriate? May aspects of 'finality' coincide both earlier and later? Should not themes be explored in mutual trust with reference to their content, not their timing? For in the things of faith what is to be counted 'final' cannot be identified by date. Many Muslims would certainly confirm that understanding. Nevertheless the image of the several caravans, en route to truth, which halted prematurely on the road, with only the caravan of Islam completing the trek and attaining the goal, looms large in Muslim thinking.

It is, of course, open to any faith to esteem the rest approximating to itself, if only duly corrected or matured. But to be truly ecumenical is to be honest and constructive about irreducible divergence and mutual contradiction. We have to learn how presently to disagree if we would wisely serve the hope of refining what we hold. There are emphases of contrast and controversy in the text of the Qur'ān which have stimulated, and still sustain, a vigorous rejectionism of what is not Islam, and an impatience with its persistence against the indubitable truth. That temper springs from the confrontational quality inseparable from the Meccan scene in Muhammad's time. But, happily, despite that circumstance in the Qur'ān's incidence in history, there

56 *Ibid.* pp.19 and 30.

are other passages which commend and warrant patience, a tolerance of diversity, and a will to comprehend.[57] Our present situation requires that these be paramount in the interests of an openness that is genuinely mutual, a temper that only witnesses in having listened.

Our second concern in inter-faith meeting has to do with the paradox within the Qur'ān's presentation of humanity. On the one hand is the confidence we have just reviewed of mankind 'naturally muslim', with the *fitrah* by which nature and 'religion' (Islam) are synonymous. On the other is the recurring theme of human perversity, the incorrigible character of mankind's capacity for unbelief, for *kufr* and *shirk*, its chronic will for idolatry, its repudiation of the wisdom and the warnings of the prophets. All such *kufr* is not merely verbal disbelief: it is a wilful resistance to truth and to God. It persists in the gracelessness which ignores the 'signs' of God. In the Qur'ān's accusation: 'Most of them give no thanks' (2.243, 10.60, 12.38, 27.73 and 40.61). Man is not merely dubious about God: he is woefully defiant. Unbelief is more than propositional: it is insurrectionary.

Further, it is a habit — as we have earlier noted — among recent radical Muslims to characterise other Muslims, of whom they disapprove, as in a contemporary *jāhiliyyah*.[58] They reproduce, these current miscreants, the very wilfulness and blindness which antedated the Qur'ān. There could be no more damning charge. Can it be that there are Muslims as perverse as the old heathen? If so, what of the efficacy of hortatory revelation? What of the congruence between human 'nature' and 'God's religion'? Yet on radical showing, it happens. There are Muslim rulers who default on Islam, Muslim societies which fail to conform, Muslims who conspire with western follies and deceits, even mosque personnel who smoothly connive with blandishments they should denounce. All these are as if Islam had never been. So the pure religion, both faith and practice, has to originate anew through the militant fidelity of its only loyal disciples. As some aver, there has been no authentic Islam since the first four 'rightly guided Caliphs' (632-661).

There is clearly, then, a paradox of evil. What is more important here, for all religions in their guilt, is not so much a theory to explain as a way to

---

57 Surah 22.67, for example, reads: 'To every people We have appointed a way of worship, which they have followed. So let them not wrangle with you (s.) over the matter.' 'For every people there has been a guide' (13.7) *may* be read as suggesting diversity, but 21.25 emphasises that all pre-Islamic prophets brought Islam's message (cf. Surah 109 where there is sharp repudiation by the true of the false). Yet God has created a whole diversity of peoples, has not willed they should be all alike, and has what they believe or disbelieve in His disposal. The true Muslim reasons and answers gently and fairly (3.64, 16.125, 29.46).

58 It is important to appreciate how heinous this characterisation is, and how frequently it comes, in accusation of one segment of Muslims by another. See, for example, Muhammad Qutb: *Jāhiliyyah al-Qarn al-'Ishrīn*, (The Jāhiliyyah of the 20th Century), Cairo, 1970.

overcome. Some 'ways' only aggravate the evils. Islam holds, broadly, that the revelation itself, 'reminder' of it, ritual habituation, solidarity in the *Ummah* and state power, together avail to accomplish man's vocation under God.

Is it not part of ecumenical encounter to deepen these categories, to explore the paradox more thoroughly? Is man educable by teaching and prophethood into conformity with the divine will? Despite the Qur'ān's realist sense of the human 'sickness' (*marad*) and its vista of the desolations of past history, there is a strange absence of the tragic dimension. Divine greatness certainly presides: may it also be in travail? Is there a dimension beyond prophethood, for prophethood's own sake, in the divine dealings with mankind?

The Qur'ān is full of a sense of the divine mercy. For its Christian readers that mercy achieves the forgiveness and reconciliation of sinful mankind in the meaning of the Cross. At least we all start from the same discovery of ourselves as 'falling short of the glory of God'.

A third theme around the Qur'ān for a sensitive reading by non-Muslims must be that enshrined in the final Section of the readings that follow this Essay: 'Unfaith, Judgement and the Last Things'. Humans individually 'forward' to an eternal reckoning the logic of their choices and their deeds. Merit and demerit accumulate to the reckoning. God is the supreme judiciary. Eternity inaugurates the great assize. When the firmament of all the living crumbles into dust, the books are opened. In its single life-span and its stark individuality this is not the *karma* of Hinduism. Yet to a degree it resembles karmic law in that assuredly 'sin will find us out'. In our volition there is cause and there is effect. The divine justice is the awesome, overwhelming witness of the Qur'ān. Neither the portrayal nor the theme will brook to be ignored.

Yet how should we who read respond to this burden so integral to the Qur'ān? Clearly there is a moral ultimacy in history which coincides with the imperative nature of the Islamic revelation. This assured ethicism demands a judicial culmination at the end of time. Judgement and time-end are one and the same. We are left in no doubt that the ultimate is judicial and the judicial is the ultimate.

But the question waits: will what is omnipotent be only judicial? Will a 'hell' of the remorseful not be somehow a divine defeat? Perhaps not — if the category be only justice. May we legitimately ask about what is ultimate *in* God in this awed Quranic setting of what is ultimate *from* God? Or, put differently, can the theme of 'being' take priority over the theme of 'judging', when we ponder what is final in divine sovereignty?

The issue here aligns, in part, with the distinction we make in grammar between the indicative and the imperative. Judgement concerns the latter: it is the reckoning about obedience and disobedience. But what is the ultimate reality which such judgement 'indicates'? What of divine reality in and beyond the incidence of judgement? Can the category of justice suffice as the clue to omnipotence? Or must it be love?

Such questions evidently bear on the second ecumenical theme for Qur'ān readers as explored already. We are not simply saying — though this may well be the case — that many outside readers find the eschatological passages in the Qur'ān desolating and disquieting. That might be readers' haste or prejudice. More deeply, we are saying that there are visions of hell which leave the sovereignty of God a darkly open question and set judgement itself under judgement.

The fourth area of the Qur'ān in any inter-faith reading must concern the force-factor involved in the transition from Mecca to Medina and the subsequent pattern of Muhammad's story and of Islamic expansion. External success became the proof of the mission and it was achieved by the invocation of power. The setting and circumstances of the Prophet's time and place, it may be argued, allowed no other option. The outwardly unavailing years in Mecca and the effective outcome of the policy in Medina may be read as total vindication of the decision taken. Those pleas, however vigorous, do not lay the issue to rest. In fact they sharpen it, inasmuch as the pattern of power was so clearly in the name of religious truth. The *Hijrah* and its sequel were no vulgar venture into belligerence for personal bravado or tribal gain. They were *fī sabīl illāhi*, 'on behalf of God'. In any dialogue of faiths Islam is not absolved, by historical pleading, from reckoning with the contrasts found elsewhere and with the compromises of coercive struggle pursued in God's Name. For coercion, sanctioned by such auspices, is rarely capable of knowing its own compromise. It may be true that unbelief and vested interest, resisting the call of religious truth, may be forcibly overcome and routed.

However, what they inwardly symbolise, the evil in the soul, is not thereby subdued. It persists within. It disguises itself in veiled conformity or pretence. It has dimensions force cannot reach. Coercion may, perhaps, secure and hold the field for the spiritual factors force itself abandons, for patience, suffering and compassion. But it may well, so doing, exclude or displace the different victory these might bring. However 'manifestly victorious' (to use the Qur'ān's phrase), there are remainders in every situation which are beyond its reach. There have been many militancies which only changed the form of evil.

These are reflections which certain passages in the Qur'ān stand to approve.[59] But they are not the consensus of the whole. A religious sense of

---

59 As, for example, Surah 36.30 which has been interpreted as a divine emotion of yearning over human waywardness akin to that in ;mated by the Prophet Hosea. 'O the pity of it about My servants.' See ed. A.H. Green: *In Quest of an Islamic*

the human situation as 'standing in the need of grace' may well be implied in the Qur'ān's panorama of history, of communities that perished in their pride. But Muslims, in their will to relation with other faiths, must allow themselves to be more fully drawn into awareness of the travail that inevitably belongs with the response of truth to error and of love to wrong.

Among clues in the Qur'ān to such an awareness perhaps the most telling is its frequent call to what it terms *istighfār*, or 'the seeking of forgiveness'. This is a central note in the mission of the prophets. Men are summoned to penitence, to a state of acknowledging the *need* to be forgiven as the condition of being so. The theme comes most strikingly in Surah 100:

'When God's help comes about, and conquest, and you have seen people come crowding into the religion of God, then sing the praise of your Lord and seek His forgiveness. To be merciful was ever His wont.'[60]

In that climax, as in every phase of our humanity, forgiveness is the very touchstone of religion. The 'why' and the 'how' of it are at the heart of theology. For, if there is to be forgiveness there must be a grace to bring it and a penitence to want it. Where evil is the question, these are what we mean by faith.

These four areas do not exhaust what transactions with the Qur'ān may be ours from the ground of other faiths. But they are paramount. And they underlie all those practical matters for action in the contemporary world which rightly take concerned readers to the Qur'ān. They are the stuff of ecumenical engagement across the boundaries of separate allegiance. To have them in view when we read will be the surest tribute to the Islamic status of the Qur'ān. It will be to take it in its own seriousness. To do less, to stay in a casual or only academic interest, to come to the Book simply out of curiosity, or for controversy, would be to forfeit the integrity it expects and requires. A right readership has need of a ready patience and a keen perception and, to inform these, the perspectives of hope. Wise readers will bring these steadily until the Book itself rewards them.

Humanism, Cairo, 1984, pp.191f. The exegete in question was Muhammad al-Nuwaihy of Cairo. Other exegesis takes the passage in the sense of 'Woe be to My Servants.' Another example might be the pre-Hijrah situation of Muhammad where he is warned that 'he may die' before his cause succeeds (10.46). Surahs 10.100 and 11.29 insist that there can be no compelling of faith.

60   See Glossary: *istighfār*. This Surah, significantly, is inscribed on the Mausoleum of Muhammad Ali Jinnah, the architect and first ruler of Pakistan, in Karachi.

بسم الله الرحمن الرحيم

THE READINGS

The Opening Chapter
Surat al-Fātihah

In the Name of God, the merciful Lord of mercy.
Praise be to God, the Lord of all being,
The merciful Lord of mercy,
Master of the Day of judgement.
You alone we serve and to You alone come we for aid.
Guide us in the straight path,
The path of those whom You have blessed,
Not of those against whom there is displeasure,
Nor of those who go astray.

The verse above is an English rendering of the seven
Arabic verses given on the facing page, which open the
Qur'ān and are understood to comprehend the whole
Book.

The first line of these verses is reproduced in this
publication above the Part Title, Chapter Titles and each
of the Themes. This is the invocation of the divine Name
and mercy which properly begins all Muslim acts.

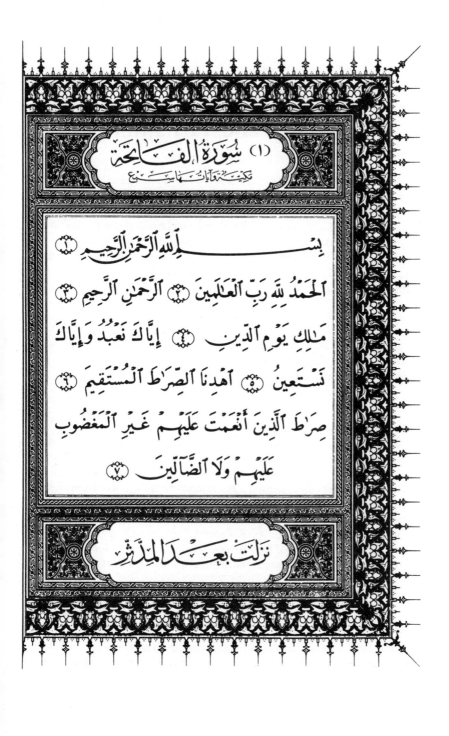

بِسْمِ اللَّهِ الرَّحْمَنِ الرَّحِيمِ ﴿١﴾

الْحَمْدُ لِلَّهِ رَبِّ الْعَالَمِينَ ﴿٢﴾ الرَّحْمَنِ الرَّحِيمِ ﴿٣﴾

مَالِكِ يَوْمِ الدِّينِ ﴿٤﴾ إِيَّاكَ نَعْبُدُ وَإِيَّاكَ

نَسْتَعِينُ ﴿٥﴾ اهْدِنَا الصِّرَاطَ الْمُسْتَقِيمَ ﴿٦﴾

صِرَاطَ الَّذِينَ أَنْعَمْتَ عَلَيْهِمْ غَيْرِ الْمَغْضُوبِ

عَلَيْهِمْ وَلَا الضَّالِّينَ ﴿٧﴾

نزلت بعد المدثر

بسم الله الرحمن الرحيم

A. God and His Praise

GOD, there is none but He, the alive, the ever real. Slumber takes Him not, nor sleep. Everything in the heavens and in the earth is His, and who — His leave apart — shall intercede with Him? He knows everything that mankind have presently in hand and everything about them that is yet to be. Of a knowledge like His they are entirely uncomprehending — unless He gives them leave to know. In the vastness of the heavens and the earth His Throne is established. Tirelessly He preserves them. So great is His majesty.   *Surah 2.255*

GOD is His own witness that there is no god but He. Angels bear witness also and those of discerning mind. He is the arbiter of justice. There is no god but He, infinite in power and wisdom.   *Surah 3.18*

THOSE who bear up the Throne and all around it celebrate the praise of their Lord. In Him is their trust and they seek forgiveness for the believers. O Lord, our Lord, You in mercy and in knowledge comprehend all things. Forgive those who turn in penitence and who follow Your way. Protect them from the retribution of Hell. Lord, bring them into the gardens of Eden which You promised to them and to those of their fathers, their wives and their offspring who lived righteously. Truly You are the strong and the wise. Protect them from evil. For whomsoever You protect on that Day from evil him You have assuredly taken into Your mercy. That is the great consummation.   *Surah 40.7-9*

HE is God. There is no god but He. He knows the hidden and the evident. He is the merciful Lord of mercy.

He is God, there is no god but He. He is the King, the holy One, the Lord of peace, the Keeper of faith, the watch-Keeper, the all-strong, the ever-powerful, the Self-aware in His greatness. Glory be to God above all that idolators conceive.

He is God, Creator, Maker, Fashioner. His are the most excellent Names. All that is in the heavens and in the earth magnifies Him, the Almighty, the all-wise.   *Surah 59.22-24*

ALL that is in the heavens and in the earth magnifies God. He is the all-strong, the all-wise. To Him belongs the kingdom of the heavens and of the earth. He gives life and He brings on death and He is omnipotent over all things. He is the first and the last, the manifest and the hidden, and has knowledge of all things. It is He who created the heavens and the earth in six days and then assumed His Throne. He knows all that permeates the ground and all that issues from it, what comes down from the heaven and what ascends thither. He is with you where-ever you are. God is aware of all you do.

His is the kingdom of the heavens and of the earth and to Him all things return. He makes the night to give way to the day and the day to the night and He knows the innermost heart.   *Surah 57.1-6*

SAY: 'O God, Lord of all sovereignty, to whom You will You give authority and whom You will You divest of it. Whom You will You exalt and whom You will You abase. Good is in Your hand and Your power extends over all things. You make the night to pass into day and day into night. You bring forth the living from the dead and from the dead You bring forth the living. Provision You bestow on whomsoever You will and that without measure.'   *Surah 3.26-27*

IN the Name of the merciful Lord of mercy. Say: 'He is God, One, God the ever self-sufficing, unbegetting, unbegotten. None is like to Him.'
                                                      Surah 112

TO God belongs the praise, Lord of the heavens and Lord of the earth, the Lord of all being. His is the dominion in the heavens and in the earth. He is the all-strong, the all-wise.   *Surah 45.36-37*

IT is God who made the earth for you as an abode and the heaven for a building. He fashioned you — and how admirably! — and with good things did He provide you.

Blessed, then, be God your Lord, this God, Lord of all being. He is the living God. There is none but He. Call upon Him in sincerity of worship. Praise be to God the Lord of all being. *Surah 40.64-65*

TO God belong the east and the west and wheresoever you turn there is the face of God. Truly God is all-pervading, all-knowing. *Surah 2.115*

EVERYTHING with Him has its measure, knower of the unseen and of the seen, all-great and ever-exalted. It is all the same with Him whether your word is furtive or open loud, whether you go stealthily in the night or fare forth in the open day . . . It is He who displays the lightning before your eyes, spelling fear and yearning, who brings up the heavy clouds. The very thunder speaks His praise and the angels stand in awe of Him . . . All things in the heavens and the earth bow in worship of God, whether of their own volition or volition apart, as do their shadows by morning and evening. *Surah 13.8b-10, 12-13a, 15*

BE patient (Muhammad), awaiting the judgement of your Lord. You have Our eyes upon you. Celebrate the praise of your Lord when you arise and by night also speak His praise and when the stars withdraw from sight. *Surah 52.48-49*

GOD is the light of the heavens and of the earth. Here is how we may conceive of His light — a lamp is set in a niche where, encased in glass which glistens with the very brilliance of a star, it is kindled from the oil of the olive, a blessed tree, which is confined neither to the east nor to the west. Its oil is almost luminous without the touch of fire. Light upon light. God guides to His light whom He wills and God, who knows all things, gives to mankind the thoughts by which to ponder His ways — in houses He has willed should be established in which His Name is remembered and where, glorifying Him morning and evening, are men whom neither trading nor merchandising divert from the remembrance of God, nor from the performance of the prayer-rite and the bringing of *Zakāt*. These all stand in awe of a Day when hearts and eyes alike will be in consternation, the Day when God's reward will bounteously exceed their utmost well-doing. God provides without measure for whom He so wills.

Do you not see how it is God whom all things praise in the heavens and in the earth and the birds also on wings of flight? Each truly knows its prayer and its praising and God knows their every deed. For to God belongs the kingdom of the heavens and of the earth. To Him their whole destiny moves.   *Surah 24.35-38 and 41-42*

SUCH is God your Lord. There is no God but He, Creator of all things. Then worship Him who is guardian over all there is. No human perception comprehends Him, while He comprehends all perception. He is beyond all conceiving, the One who is infinitely aware.
                                                        Surah 6.102-103

PRAISE be to God to whom all things belong in the heavens and in the earth. His be the praise in the hereafter. He is the all-wise, the ever aware. He knows what enters into the earth and what emerges from it, what descends from heaven and what ascends into it. He is the merciful, the forgiving.   *Surah 34.1-2*

GLORY be to God in the evening and in the morning of your days. His be the praise in the heavens and in the earth, alike in the day's decline and when high noon is upon you. It is He who brings forth the living from the dead and the dead from the living, who quickens the earth from its lifeless state. You, likewise, will be brought forth.   *Surah 30.17-19*

BLESSED be He in whose hand all sovereignty lies, He whose power extends over all. He it is who created death and life, putting you to the proof whose works would be the noblest. Strong and forgiving is He. It is He who created in array the seven heavens: in all the handiwork of the Lord of mercy you will find no discrepancy. Scrutinise as you will, what flaw do you find? Again and again your scanning may persist, only to yield up a weary search. We adorned the lowest heaven with lamps — the stars whereby the very devils are accused, devils for whom God has prepared the chastisement of the Fire.   *Surah 67.1-5*

GOD is He who created seven heavens and like aspects of the earth. The divine commanding word descends through them all, that you may know how God has power over all things and how His knowledge embraces all that is.   *Surah 65.12*

ALL that is in the heavens and in the earth gives praise to God. His is the kingdom and His the praise and His the will that has power over all things. He it is who has created you. There are both unbelievers and believers among you and God is watchful over all your actions.

With truth He created the heavens and the earth. He fashioned you and well He made your frame. To Him is your destiny. His knowledge encompasses everything in the heavens and the earth. He knows your hidden secrets and your manifest deeds. God knows the very heart within.   *Surah 64.1-4*

ALL in the heavens and the earth gives praise to God: He is the all-strong, the all-wise.   *Surah 61.1*

BLESSED be the name of your Lord, whose is the glory and the majesty.   *Surah 55.78*

SAY: 'Had the all-merciful a son I would be the very first to worship him. Glory be to the Lord of the heavens and of the earth, the Lord of the Throne, beyond all the attributes they ascribe. Let them persist in their inanities until they encounter the Day promised them. He it is who is God in heaven and God in the earth, the all-wise, the all-knowing. Blessed be He whose is the sovereignty of the heavens and of the earth and everything within them. His is the knowledge of the Hour and to Him again is your final returning.'   *Surah 43.81-85*

GLORY be to your (s.) Lord, the Lord of majesty above all they, describing, say of Him. Peace be upon those sent as messengers. Praise be to God, the Lord of all being.   *Surah 37.180-182*

PRAISE be to God, inaugurator of the heavens and of the earth, He who commissioned the angels as messengers with their double, triple, or fourfold pairs of wings. He amplifies His creation as He wills. For God has the mastery over all things. Whatever mercy God extends to mankind there is none to hold it back: what God withholds there is none can then dispense. He is the all-strong, the all-wise.

People! Have ever in mind God's grace towards you. Is there any creator other than God who provides for you from the heaven and from the earth? There is no god but He. How then are you so prone to deception? *Surah 35.1-3*

HE is God: there is no god but He. His be the praise from the first to the last. His is the governance and to Him is your final return. Say: 'Consider — how if God were to make the night around you perpetual until the Day of resurrection: what God else — Him apart — would give you light? Will you not hearken?' Say: 'Consider — how if God were to make the day around you perpetual until the Day of resurrection: what god else — Him apart — would bring night round again for your repose? Will you not realise? It is of His mercy that He has ordained the night wherein to rest and the day wherein to seek out His bounty and thus, perhaps, your gratitude.' *Surah 28.70-73*

HAVE you (s.) not seen that it is to God all that is in the heavens and the earth gives worship — sun, and moon, and stars, mountains and trees and beasts, and many of mankind? And many there are on whom retribution justly falls, and whom God abases there are none to honour. God does the thing He wills. *Surah 22.18*

TO Him belongs all that is, in the heavens and in the earth. Truly God is He who is infinitely rich, altogether to be praised. *Surah 22.64*

TO Him all belongs in the heavens and in the earth. Those who abide in His presence allow no pride to hold them from His worship, in which they are unwearied, praising Him night and day in praise unfailing. *Surah 21.19-20*

WE (the angels) come down only by command of your (s.) Lord. To Him belongs all that is before us and all behind us and all else between, and never is your Lord forgetful. He is Lord of the heavens and of the earth and all within them. So worship Him and be constant in His service. Do you know one worthy to be named with Him?

Surah 19.64-65

GLORY be to Him, exalted above all they say in transcendent greatness. The seven heavens and the earth and all within them glorify Him. There is nothing which does not celebrate His praise, though you (pl.) do not comprehend their praising. He is ever forbearing and forgiving.

Surah 17.43-44

HAVE they not observed all that God has created, how their shadows fall to the right and to the left in prostration to God in entire submission? To God all things bow in the heavens and in the earth, every living creature and the angels too. They are not self-conceited: they fear their Lord above them and they do what they are bidden. *Surah 16.48-50*

THEIR cry there (in Paradise) will be: 'Praise be to You, O God,' and their greeting: 'Peace.' 'Praise be to God, Lord of all being' will be the sum and end of their cry. *Surah 10.10*

WHO is there with a finer religion than he who surrenders himself wholly to God and does what is good, following in the faith-community of Abraham — a man of pure faith whom God chose for a beloved friend?

To God belongs all that is in the heavens and in the earth — God encircling, comprehending everything. *Surah 4.125-126*

بسم الله الرحمن الرحيم

B. God in Creation: Man and Nature

IN the Name of the merciful Lord of mercy. The Lord of mercy, He has taught the Qur'ān. He created man and taught him discernment and language (al-bayān). Sun and moon have their measured circuits, stars and trees bring their worship. He raised the heaven above and laid down the scale (al-mizān) in which all things are weighed — See that you do not play it false: weigh with justice and do not make the balance cheat — and the earth He established for all living creatures, with its fruits, its palm-trees and their fruiting dates, the grain in the blade and herbs of fragrance. Which of the blessings of your Lord will you discount and deny?

Man He created from a potter's clay while the jinn He created from flame of fire. Which of the blessings of your Lord will you discount and deny?

He is Lord of the points of the sunrise and Lord of the setting suns. Which of the blessings of your Lord will you discount and deny?

He made the confluence of the two waters and the bound between them which they may not pass. Which of the blessings of your Lord will you discount and deny?

From these come the pearl and the coral. Which of the blessings of your Lord will you discount and deny?

His also are the ships which stand out on the face of the waters like banners. Which of the blessings of your Lord will you discount and deny? All that is on earth is passing away. Only the face of your Lord abides, in majesty and glory all His own. Which, then, of the blessings of your Lord will you discount and deny?

All beings in the heavens and the earth are suppliants to Him. Every day He is at work. Which, then, of the blessings of your Lord will you discount and deny?   *Surah 55.1-30*

IT is We who have created you. How is it you do not recognise that truth? Have you considered what you do in intercourse? Is it you who do the creating, or We? We exercise the power of death among you and there is nothing that can forestall Us should We intend to alter the way you are and have you become what is beyond your comprehension. In what fashion you were first created is familiar enough to Us. How is it that you do not ruminate on all this?

Have you considered the soil you till? Is it you who bring the crop or are We the real agent of growth? Were it Our will We had turned it into chaff and that would have meant for you a sorry jest, as you say: 'The loss is heavy on us: we are left resourceless.'

Have you considered the water you drink? Was it you who made it fall from the rain-clouds or are We the rain-maker? Had We so willed bitter water had We sent. How is it that you have no gratitude?

Have you considered the fire you kindle? Was it you who made the tree to grow or are We the source of its being? We devised it to be a point of recollection and to provide solace for those who pass through desert ways.

Praise, then, each of you the Name of your great Lord.

Surah 56.57-74

WE created man from clay, from earthy substance duly fashioned, while the jinn We created aforetime from fiery winds. When your Lord said to the angels: 'I am creating a man from clay, moulded from earthy substance, you are to fall down before him in prostration, when I have given him form and breathed into him My spirit.' All the angels together made prostration, save for *Iblīs*, the devil, who refused to join them in prostration.

God said: '*Iblīs*, how is it that you are not among the prostrating angels?' He replied: 'Bow down to man! Not me! Him you created from mere clay: he was moulded from earthy substance.' God said: 'Begone from here, accursed one.' The curse is on you till the Day of judgement.' *Iblīs* pleaded: 'My Lord, reprieve me until the Day when men are raised again.' 'You will be among the reprieved until the Day of the appointed time.'

'My Lord,' responded *Iblīs*, 'because You have contrived my temptation and fall, I am going to contrive theirs by plausible blandishments, the whole lot of them, save for those among them who are honestly devout servants of Yours.'

'Such sincerity is a straight path due to Me. As for My servants, you have no authority over them, except for those who go your way, being beguiled. *Jahannam* shall be their destiny, all of them together.'

Surah 15.26-43

OF old, We made a covenant with Adam. But he proved forgetful and We found no firm purpose in him. When We said to the angels: 'Prostrate yourselves before Adam,' they did so prostrate, except for *Iblīs*, the devil, who refused. Then We said to Adam: 'Here is an enemy to you and to your wife. Do not let him expel the pair of you from the garden to your grievous loss. For, here, it is meant that you should know no hunger nor sense your nakedness, that here you should neither thirst nor endure the burning sun.'

Satan, however, whispered to him and said: 'Adam, shall I show you the way to the tree of eternity and to a kingdom that shall never pass away?' They both ate of it and became aware of shame in their naked state, and the two of them fell to sewing together leaves of the garden over themselves. Thus Adam violated his Lord's will and went astray.

Subsequently his Lord showed him favour and relented towards him and guided him, saying: 'Both of you go down from here. There is a state of mutual enmity between you. Nevertheless, guidance on My part will avail you and whoever follows My guidance will not go astray nor come to grief. Whoever turns away from the remembrance of Me shall find his life wretched and We will raise him sightless on the Day of resurrection.'

Adam said: 'My lord, have You brought me here, a blind man — I who have been possessed of sight?' To whom God replied: 'It is thus, in that when Our signs came into your ken you were oblivious of them. So on this Day you are forgotten too.'

It is thus that We reward everyone who has cast away restraint not believing in the signs of his Lord. Stern in the extreme and unremitting is the retribution of the world to come.   *Surah 20.115-127*

YOUR (s.) Lord said to the angels: 'Out of clay am I making a human being. When I have fashioned him and breathed My spirit into him, then fall down in prostration to him.' And all the angels together made prostration, except *Iblīs*, the devil. He asserted his arrogance and ranged himself with those who defy the truth.

'What is it, *Iblīs*,' God said, 'which stands in your way of acknowledging in prostration the creation of My own hands? Is it your arrogance or do you rank yourself a higher being?'

Iblīs replied: 'I am worthier than he. From fire You created me, while him You have made out of clay!' God's answer was: 'Accursed one, get you out from here. On you will My malediction rest until judgement Day.'

'Lord,' he said, 'reprieve me until the Day when men are raised again.' 'You are so reprieved until the Day of the appointed time,' God answered. The devil said: 'By Your might, I swear I will make the whole race of them to go wrong, except Your servants, sincere in their God-fearing.' And God said: 'The truth is — and the truth it is I speak — I will for sure fill *Jahannam* with you and with all, whoever they be, who take your way — the whole lot of them.' *Surah 38.71-85*

AND your (s.) Lord said to the angels: 'I am setting a viceregent in the earth.' They replied: 'Are You going to place there one who will deal corruptly and shed blood, while we celebrate Your praise and cry "Holy" before You?'

God said: 'I know what your knowledge does not comprehend.' He taught Adam all the names of things and then lay them before the angels, saying: 'Inform Me as to the names of all these, if you mean what you say.' To which they responded: 'Glory be to You: all we know is what You have taught us. You are all-knowing and all-wise.'

'Adam,' He said, 'you tell them what the names are.' Whereupon, after Adam's informing them as to the names, He said: 'Did I not tell you that I know the hidden secret of the heavens and of the earth, and that I know everything to do with you, whether you disclose it or have concealed it?'

When We told the angels to make prostration before Adam they did so, with the exception of *Iblis*. He refused in his arrogance, and took his place among the miscreants.

We said: 'Adam, have your dwelling-place, you and your wife, in the garden. Together feed there freely, where-ever you wish. But this tree, neither of you must approach, lest you commit gross violation.'

Satan, however, brought about their fall, causing them to be ousted from their state of life. For We said: 'Go out from here in mutual enmity. Out in the earth is a habitation and needful provision for a season.'

Adam was made aware of words that came to him from his Lord, who turned relenting towards him. For truly He is merciful in cognisance of penitence.

We said: 'Go down from here, all of you. Guidance will come to you from Me. There will be no fear for any who follow My guidance, nor any reason to grieve.' *Surah 2.30-38*

WE have set you (pl.) in dominion on the earth and appointed your livelihood in it. There is little gratitude in you! We have created you, then fashioned you, and thereupon commanded the angels to worship Adam. They all prostrated except *Iblīs* — no worshipper he! God said: 'What has prevented you that you have not prostrated when I commanded you to do so?' He replied: 'I am better than he! Of fire You created me; him You created from clay!' God said: 'Get out from here! There is no place here for vaunting arrogance from you! Go out! small beer is what you are!' *Iblīs* prayed: 'Reprieve me until the Day they are raised again.' 'Reprieved you are,' God said. Satan continued: 'Seeing You have contrived to make me sin, I will waylay them on the straight path of Yours, then come at them from before and behind, on the right hand and on the left. The most part of them You will find to be unthankful.'

God answered: 'Go out from here, disgraced and banished. Those of them who follow you — truly I will fill *Jahannam* with the lot of you!'

'Adam! dwell, you and your wife, in the garden: eat from whatever fruit either of you wish but do not come near this one tree, lest you become transgressors.' Satan whispered to them intending to make them perceive their nakedness, of which they had been unaware. He said: 'Your Lord only prohibited you from this tree to prevent you becoming angels or immortal.' He swore to them both: 'I am advising you as a genuine friend.' Guilefully he enticed them forward and when they had both tasted the tree their nakedness was evident to them and they began to conceal themselves with leaves of the garden. Their Lord called to them: 'Did I not forbid the tree to you? Did I not tell you that Satan is an open enemy to you?' They said: 'Our Lord, we have sinned against ourselves. If you do not forgive us and show us mercy we will surely be among the lost.' He said: 'Go down in mutual enmity between you and Satan. For a period you will have habitation and sustenance,' adding: 'There you will live and there you will die and from there you will be raised.'

'Children of Adam! We have bestowed clothing on you from on high to cover your nakedness and as pleasant array, but better far is the garment of true piety. Herein are the signs of God, of which perhaps mankind will be mindful.'

'Children of Adam! Do not let Satan seduce you in the way in which he occasioned the exit of your forebears from the garden, stripping their innocence from them to have both of them realise their nakedness. He and his ilk have you in their sights from where they are out of yours. We have made the satans to take into their patronage those who do not believe.' When these commit some indecency they say: 'We found our

fathers doing so, and God has commanded us so to do.' Say: 'He does
not command the committing of foul acts. Will you say of God things of
which you know nothing?' Say: 'My Lord commands what is right and
just. At every mosque set your face and pray to Him in sincerity of faith.
As He brought you into being to Him you will return. Some of you He
has guided and for others some error has become the ineluctable thing,
seeing they have taken the satans as their mentors, leaving God aside, and
assumed themselves rightly guided.'   *Surah 7.10-30*

HE it is who created you from a single soul, ordaining thence his wifely
partner that in her he might find rest. When in the veil of intercourse she
conceived, the burden first was light and she went about with it freely.
But when she was heavy with child they called upon God, their Lord:
'Grant us a goodly child and thankful indeed shall we be.' Yet, when He
duly gave them a sound boy, they made the gift an occasion to invoke the
idols over him.

God be exalted above all that men associate with Him. Will they
accord worship to what creates nothing and are themselves created?
                                                      Surah 7.189-191

AND when your (s.) Lord took the progeny of the sons of Adam from
their loins, He took them to witness on their own souls, saying: 'Am I
not your Lord?' They answered: 'Yes, indeed: we witness to it' — this,
lest you should say on the Day of resurrection: 'We had not known it to
be so,' or lest you should say: 'It was our forebears aforetime who went
after pseudo-gods, and we were only their subsequent descendants. Will
You then make us to perish for the deeds of those strangers to the truth?'

It is thus that We set forth the things that signify: it may be there will
be a turning back.   *Surah 7.172-174*

WE have created man from an emission, a thing of clay, as a sperm drop
for which We assigned a secure lodgement. The sperm drop We created
into a germ-cell, and the germ-cell We created into tissue, and the tissue
into bone, clothing bone with flesh, thus fashioning into being an
individual creature. Blessed be God, the finest Creator!

To be sure, in due course, death will be your lot and at the Day of
resurrection you will be raised again to life.

Away above you is Our creation of the seven spheres. In Our creation there is nothing We have left in neglect.

From heaven We cause the measured rain to fall — rain We house securely in the earth, though Our power can also make those waters fail — the waters from which We bring about your fertile gardens, your palm trees and vines, your haunts of ample fruits to eat and a tree of trees originating in Mount Sinai, yielding oil that is always there to hand at your meals.

Cattle, too, have much to teach you. We give you to drink of what they have within their bodies. You have in them many assets and they are food for you. Moreover, they provide you transport as the ships also do. *Surah 23.12-22*

THE night and the day, the sun and the moon, are some of His signs. Do not prostrate in worship to sun and moon. Worship God, He who made them — if it be He whose servants you are.

If men are too proud, in the presence of your (s.) Lord are those who prostrate before Him night and day in unwearied worship.

Among His signs is the sight of the parched earth quickened and bursting with growth when We send down the rains. He who quickens it into life is the one who raises the dead, having all things within His power. *Surah 41.37-39*

GOD created the heavens and the earth — a real creation. Let Him be exalted above all false worship.

He created man from a drop of sperm — man who is brazenly contentious: the live-stock also He created on your behalf, for the warmth and other uses, as well as the food, you have of them. Beautiful they are, too, in your sight as you bring them in to rest and when you take them out to pasture. Moreover, they carry your loads to places you could only reach otherwise by strenuous hardship. Your Lord is truly gracious and compassionate.

There are horses, too, and mules and donkeys for you to ride and to deck out in fine array. Things beyond your knowledge He has created also.

It is for God to indicate what the right path is: there are some that go astray. Had God willed He had surely guided all of you aright.

It is He who sends down rain from heaven for you to drink and to water the trees of your pasture — the rain by which He ensures the growth of your crops and olives, palms and vines, and every variety of fruits — all of which is surely a sign for those who are thoughtful.

The night and the day He has made to serve your ends. Sun, moon and stars are all recruited to His command and here, too, are signs for those who use their minds. There is a sign, too, for mindful folk, in the colours of rich diversity in the manifold things He has arrayed for you.

It is He who has made the sea to serve you for purposes of fresh food and the gems for which you dive there to use as ornament. There go the ships, breasting the waves, in pursuit of God's bounty. Perhaps you will be grateful people.

He has also set the mountains firm on the earth that it may be solid under you. There are rivers and tracks for you so that you may find your way, landmarks too, and the stars by which men are piloted.

Shall He, then, who created, be on a par with that which does not? Will you not realise? Were you set to count up the mercies of God you would not be able to number them. God is truly forgiving and merciful. *Surah 16.3-18*

GOD it is who created the heavens and the earth and gives the rain that comes down from heaven, bringing forth fruits in provision for you. His ordering makes possible the ships that at His command traverse the sea. He made the rivers also to serve you. Sun and moon, likewise, in their constant orbits He recruits to your service, and night and day as well.

Everything you desired of Him He has brought you. If you were to add up all God's grace you would not reach the sum of it. Man is perverse and thankless. *Surah 14.32-34*

IT is He who made the sun a glowing radiance and the moon a light, ordering the measure of its phases that you might reckon the years and tell their number. With truth alone did He create them, showing the signs distinctly for those who understand.

Truly there are signs for those who fear Him in the alternation of night and day, and in the whole of God's creation in the heavens and in the earth.

The life of this present world is like the water that We send down from heaven, mantling the earth with vegetation as food for man and beast. But then, when the earth is gay with golden splendour and people imagine that they own and rule it, Our command goes out over it and, whether by night or by day, We turn it all to stubble, as though yesterday's fertility had never been.

Even so do We make Our signs evident for people with a mind to ponder. *Surah 10.5-6 and 24*

BY the sun and the midday glory and the moon that follows after; by the day telling its splendour and the night that envelops it; by the heaven and its rearing; by the earth and its shaping; by the soul and its fashioning — the soul He has alerted alike to self-defilement and to true piety — true well-being is his who purifies his soul. But he who defiles his spirit assuredly comes to grief. *Surah 91.1-10*

HAVE they not beheld the heaven above them, how We established and adorned it in its unbroken reach? And the earth also We stretched out, setting thereon the mighty hills, where We made every kind of joyous thing to grow for insight and for token to every penitent servant. From heaven We have sent down the blessed rain whereby We make the gardens grow, and grain of harvest and tall palm trees laden with clustered dates, in provision for men, thereby bringing again to life a land that was dead — similitude of the coming forth.

We created man: We know the very whisperings within him and We are closer to him than his jugular vein. There are two attendant angels posted to his right and to his left and nothing passes his lips but the auditor is on the alert for it. *Surah 50.6-11 and 16-18*

WHICH was the harder task in His creating, you or the heaven He reared? He raised the canopy of heaven and set in it poise. He made the night a cover for it and He brought forth its high noon. And then He laid the expanse of the earth, bringing forth waters and pastures therein. He made the hills fast to be a joy to you and your flocks. *Surah 79.27-33*

IN the heaven We have set constellations, making them glorious to behold, and guarding them from every accursed satan save those who practice listening by stealth — on whom fiery flames attend — and the earth We have stretched out, whereon are borne great mountains and where We have caused everything to grow accordingly, providing there a livelihood for you and for those for whom you take no liability. There is nothing whose treasure sources are not Ours and all are constituted from above in their appointed measure. We send the fertilising winds and bring down the rain from heaven, giving you to drink of reservoirs that are not yours. It is We who give life and who make to die and We alone abide in the passing away of all else. *Surah 15.16-23*

BY the dawn and the ten nights, by the multiple and the individuated, by the night on its way — are not these what may be sworn to by a man of sense? *Surah 89.1-5*

O MAN, what has seduced you from your gracious Lord — He who created you and fashioned you, who proportioned you duly and in the form He desired contrived you? *Surah 82.6-8*

THE revelation of the Book is from God who is mighty and wise. There are signs for men of faith, in the heavens and in the earth, in your being created and in God's scattered throng of creatures — signs for people with a grasp on truth.

There are signs, too — for those with a mind to understand — in the alternation of night and day, and in the gracious rain God sends from heaven to renew the face of the parched earth, and in the veering of the winds.

These are the signs of God which truly We recite to you. Having God and His signs, in what else after that will you believe as a message? *Surah 45.1-6*

GOD has given you the sea for seamanship: by His leave the ships ply freely as you go after His good things. Perhaps you will be grateful.

Indeed, He has put to your service all things in the heavens and in the earth. All are His, and truly in all there are signs for reflective people.

Tell the believers, in forgiving those who do not set their hope on the days of God, to let Him decide how people get their deserts. Whoever acts righteously the gain is his alone and he who does evil suffers the consequences, and then to your Lord is your returning. *Surah 45.12-15*

HE it is who sends down the rain when men are in despair and dispenses His mercy. For He is the guardian, ever to be praised.

The creation of the heavens and the earth is one of His signs and the creatures, too, He has made to roam there, and whenever He wills He is able to gather them all again.

Whatever affliction comes upon you is to be traced to your own deeds. Many, many things God pardons. It is not in your power to frustrate Him in the earth and you have neither guardian nor helper other than God.

The ships that ride the sea and stand out like banners — they are among God's signs. At His will He makes the winds to drop and the ships are becalmed upon the waters — all of which will be significant to all who are of patient and grateful mind. Or, He makes the ships to founder because of men's ill deserts, though there is much that He does not exact.

Those who cavil at Our signs should know that there is no eluding them.   *Surah 42.28-35*

A SIGN for them is the dead land which We brought to life and made to bear the grain they eat — the land where We made gardens of palms and vines with copious flowing springs that they might have fruits for food and the produce for which they laboured with their own hands. Have they no gratitude?

Glory be to Him who, in pairs, created all that the earth brings forth, and themselves likewise, and so also in realms unknown to them.

Another sign for them is the night. We draw day to its close and all grows dark around them. There is the sun running its course to an appointed setting, by will of Him who is mighty and all-knowing.

The moon also with its phases We have ordained until it comes round again like the thin line of an old palm. The sun must not outstrip the moon nor night overtake the day. Each has its orbit through which it glides.

Another sign for them is that We carried their generations in the crowded ark and have made vessels like it in which they make voyages. If We so will, We let them drown with none to rescue them or hear their cry, unless it be through a mercy of Ours giving them respite for a season. When they are told to be watchful about their present affairs and future consequences that they may have mercy shown to them, they reject each and every sign of their Lord that comes their way.

When they are bidden to give to others in need, for the sake of God's bounty to them, what the unbelievers say in reply to those who have believed is to ask: 'Shall we feed those whom God would have fed had He wanted to?'

It is clear how sadly astray you all are.   *Surah 36.33-47*

IT is God who bursts open the grain and the date-stone. He brings forth the living from the dead: He it is who brings forth the dead from the living. This is the fact of God. How is it, then, that you are taken in by lies?

He makes the dawn to break and has appointed the night for repose and sun and moon for reckoning, by the disposing will of the Almighty who knows all. It is He who has ordained the stars whereby to guide yourselves in the darkness of land and sea. We have made these signs discernible to a people with perception.

He it is who has brought you into being from a single soul and afforded you a term of life and a place to lay your bones. We have made these signs discernible to a comprehending people.

He it is who sends down rain from heaven. Thereby We bring forth growing shoots of every kind, whence We bring forth green foliage, and whence again We bring forth clustering grain, and from the spathe of the palm-tree hanging bunches of dates, and gardens of vines and olives and pomegranates — all alike yet all incomparably different. Take stock of their fruit, when fruit they do, and as they ripen. In these things there are signs for a believing people.

They have ascribed invisible beings as partners to God, though He created them, and in their total ignorance they have attributed to Him sons and daughters. Glory to Him and exalted be He above what they allege. The very Creator of the heavens and of the earth, how could there be 'son' to Him there never having been a 'spouse' to Him — He who created everything and who is omniscient over all things?

Surah 6.95-101

TO God belongs the sovereignty of the heavens and of the earth and God has the disposal of everything within His power. Truly in the creation of the heavens and of the earth and in the alternation of night and day there are signs for those with perceptive minds — those who are mindful of God, when they stand and are seated and when they are lying down, and who ponder the creation of the heavens and the earth and who say: 'Our Lord, it was not in vain that You created all this. All praise be Yours. Keep us safe from the doom of the Fire.   *Surah 3.189-191*

THERE is sweet fresh water that is good to drink and sea-water, different altogether, salt and bitter. Yet both yield you fresh fish for food and ornaments to wear which you can bring up from them. Then you see the ships in which you seek out God's bounty, ploughing the waters. What of your thankfulness?

He makes night give way to day and day to night: the sun and the moon He has enlisted for His purposes and both have their fixed cycles. Such is God your Lord. Sovereignty is His. Those deities on whom you call instead of Him do not own so much as the husk of a date-stone. If you call on them they will not hear your prayer, or if they were to hear they would not answer you. On the Day of resurrection they will disown your having taken them for gods.

There is none who can tell you like one who really knows. O people, it is you who are in need of God. God is He who is all wealthy, ever to be praised. If He were so to will He would dispense with you and inaugurate a new creation. For God there would be no problem in that! *Surah 35.12-17*

To God belongs all that is in the heavens and in the earth. God is all-wealthy, ever to be praised.

Though all the trees on earth were pens and the sea were all ink, with seven seas more to add to it, they would be exhausted before ever the words of God were. For God is the Lord of might and wisdom.

Your coming to be and and your being raised to life are as individual souls. God is the One who hears and sees all.

You surely observe how God makes the night give way to the day and day to night, how He has enlisted the sun and the moon for His purposes, each having its fixed cycle, and how God is aware of your every deed?

These things are so because God is altogether real. All that you invoke instead of Him is vain. God most high — He is great.

You have seen, have you not? the ships at sea where God by His grace, in their passage, shows you His signs, signs for every forbearing and thankful soul. In all religious sincerity men call upon God when the waves break over them like heavy clouds. But when He has brought them safe to land some of them lapse into half-heartedness. It is only the graceless faith-breaker who denies Our signs altogether.

O people, be in awe before your Lord: dread the Day when no father shall make satisfaction in any way for his child, nor child for his parent. What God has pledged is real. Do not, then, let the life of this present world deceive you. Do not let the deceiver beguile you away from God.

With God, in truth, is the knowledge of the Hour. He sends down the rain: He knows what the wombs have within them. No soul knows what will be its lot on the morrow, and no soul knows in what land it will die. God knows all, is aware of all. *Surah 31.26-34*

THE very creation of the heavens and of the earth are signs of His, and the diversity of your languages and colour — signs, truly, for all that lives.

Other signs, again, are in the daily, nightly habit of sleep, and all your acquisitive pursuit of His good things — signs at least for people who give heed to them.

Again, there are signs from Him in the lightning you see, inspiring fear and yearning, and in the rain that pours from heaven with which He rouses the dead land into life — signs, that is, for people who use their minds.

There are signs, yet again, in the very stability of the heavens and of the earth, by His authority, and signs, too, in that when His summons calls you from the earth, forth you will come.

To Him belongs all that is, in the heavens and in the earth, each and all subservient to His will. He it is who initiates creation and continually renews it — a light task for Him! For supreme excellence is His, in the heavens and in the earth: He is the Lord of might and wisdom.

Surah 30.22-27

THERE are signs from God in the winds He sends as heralds of good things, making you to experience His mercy, and in the ships to sail at His command, in your pursuit of His bounty. Perhaps you will have a gratitude to show.

Before you (s.) We have sent messengers to their own people to whom they brought clear proofs of their mission. On the guilty We took vengeance: for clearly there was an obligation on Us to bring believers through to victory.

God is He who sends the winds to stir up the clouds till, as He wills, the heavens are overcast and then, when the clouds burst, you see the rain pouring down, gladdening the hearts of those of His servants on whom He wills the showers should fall, whereas before the onset of the rain they had been in utter despair.

Have regard, then, for the traces of God's mercy, how He quickens the earth out of death. He is truly the quickener of the dead and He has power over all things. Yet if We had sent a wind to wither their crops they would have persisted afterwards in their denial of faith.

You (s.) cannot make the dead to listen nor the deaf to hear the call, when they deliberately turn away. You are not a guide for the blind out of their delusion. Only those who believe in Our signs can you cause to listen, namely those who have surrendered to God. *Surah 30.46-53*

SAY: 'Praise be to God and peace to His servants whom He has chosen. God, or all that they falsely worship, which is better? Is not He who created the heavens and the earth and the rain from heaven upon you, whereby We have made orchards to flourish for your delight, the trees of which you have yourselves no power to bring to growth?'

'Is there any god beside God? Yet these are people who make gods equal!'

'Is He not God who established the earth as a sure dwelling place, inter-sected with rivers and girt with mountains, and who set the bar of land between waters salt and fresh?'

'Another god beside God! Yet most of men do not realise.'

'Is He not God who answers the distressed soul that cries to Him and relieves his affliction, the God who has made you custodians of the earth on His behalf? Is there, then, another god other than God Himself? How little do you have a mind to understand.'

'Is He not God who guides you in the darkness by land and by sea, who sends the winds as harbingers of His mercy? Another god beside God? Let God be exalted above all their false deities.'

'Is He not God who brought creation into being and who renews it, who provides for you from heaven and earth? Another god beside God?' Say: 'If what you hold is true, bring the evidence.'

Say, 'No one in the heavens and on earth knows things unseen except God.' They have no presentiment of when their resurrection will be. Indeed the hereafter altogether is beyond their comprehension. All they have is doubt and blindness about the last Day. *Surah 27.59-66*

To God all things unknown in the heavens and in the earth belong. As for the judgement Hour it will be as but the twinkling of an eye or even more sudden. God has all things in His competence.

God has brought you out of the wombs of your mothers when you were all unaware and He gave you hearing and sight and hearts to feel, that you might give Him thanks.

Do not men take stock of how the birds are schooled to fly in the air of heaven? It is only God who upholds them and for believing people this is truly a sign.

God also has given you a house to dwell in and animal skins for tent-dwellings, suited in their lightness both when you strike camp and when you encamp again. From their wool, hair and fur come furnishings and goods that give you pleasure while they last.

There is shade for you, too, provided in God's creation. The hills He has fashioned afford you refuge and you have, by His devising, garments to protect you from the sun and battle clothing to protect you in violent encounter. In these ways He makes good His benediction on you that you may submit yourselves devotedly to Him.

If they still reject what you (s.) say, your duty is simply to communicate the word plainly. They acknowledge the grace of God and then they deny it. Most of them are thankless unbelievers.　　　*Surah 16.77-83*

GOD is He who raised the heavens without pillars visible to you and then seated Himself upon the Throne, ordaining the appointed phases of the sun and moon in their courses. He it is whose writ runs everywhere. He sets forth His signs — it may be you will realise and know that it is your Lord whom you encounter.

He it is who has unrolled the earth's expanse with its mighty hills and flowing rivers. There are two kinds to all the fruits of the earth as He made them. He brings over the day the veil of night — in all of which there are signs for thoughtful people. The earth is dotted with adjacent fields and vineyards, with farms and clumps of palms or single trees — all watered from the same water, though some excel others in their yield, as We direct — all of which will be significant for those with minds alert.

Of all the things that might amaze you (s.) must be that question of theirs: 'When we have become dust are we going to find ourselves created over again?' Those are folk who deny their Lord. Denizens of the Fire they will be eternally, with fetters round their necks. Though there have been precedents enough as examples, they scout the good and tell you to get on quickly with those dire evils!

Your (s.) Lord is the Lord of forgiveness for the wrongs that men commit: yet your Lord is strict in retribution. Those who disbelieve say: 'Why was no sign given to him from above by his Lord?' Yours it is simply to be a warner. For every people there is a guide.

God knows the pregnancy in every womb and every foetus in miscarriage or in maturing.　　　*Surah 13.2-8a*

SAY: 'Who is Lord of the heavens and of the earth?' Say in answer: 'God.' Say: 'Have you then taken to yourselves other protectors instead of Him, who have no ability at all to benefit or harm even themselves?' Say: 'Are the blind and the seeing one and the same? Are the shadows and the light identical? Have they put deities in company with God, creating as He has created, as if in their view there could be any comparable creation?' Say: 'God is the Creator of all that is: He is the One and the only, the all-competent.'   *Surah 13.16*

YOUR Lord is God who created the heavens and the earth in six days. Then sovereign on the Throne, He makes the night overtake the day, pressing hard on its heels. Sun and moon and stars, His creation, bend to His command. Creation and authority are His prerogative: blessed be God, the Lord of the worlds.

Call upon your Lord in humble supplication and in heart privacy. He has no love for transgressors. Do not defile the good earth, hallowed as it has been. Call upon Him in fear and yearning. Truly the mercy of God draws near to those who do rightly.

It is He who sends the winds, harbingers of the mercy He holds ready, bearing heavy clouds of Our thrusting towards some dead land, where, in a copious rainfall, We bring forth a fulness of fruits. In the same way We bring the dead forth. It may be these things will be ever in your mind. For the good land brings forth crops by leave of your Lord, while the barren land yields next to nothing. It is thus We give a sense of things significant to people ready for gratitude.   *Surah 7.54-58*

WE offered the trust to the heavens and to the earth and the hills and they refused to undertake the burden of it, being apprehensive of the responsibility. Man assumed it. He is surely a creature of sinful folly. Wherefore, God punishes the hypocritical, the false worshippers, and relents towards the believers — men and women alike. For God is ever merciful and forgiving.   *Surah 33.72-73*

NAY! I swear by this land, this place of your security, by father and by fathered, surely We have created man in trouble. Does he reckon that there is no power over him? 'I have consumed abundant wealth,' he says, Does he think that goes unnoticed?

Have We not given him two eyes, a tongue and two lips? Have we not brought him where the two highways are? Yet he has not attempted the steep ascent.

Would that you knew what the steep is! It is the freeing of the slave or giving food in the hungry day to an orphan near of kin or to some needy soul in his distress. Such are believers indeed. Patience and mercy are their counsel, their counsel to each other. Such are the companions of the right hand. Those who disbelieve Our signs, they are the companions of the left hand. Over them there is a confining fire.   *Surah 90*

THEN will they not look well at the camel and the form with which it was created; at the heaven and how it was set on high; at the mountains and how they were established; at the earth with its wide expanses?

Call all these things to their mind, for that is your (s.) whole task. You are not appointed to rule over them. God will bring retribution, great retribution, on those who turn away and give the lie to what you say. It is to Us they are destined to present themselves and Ours is the accounting.   *Surah 88.17-26*

MAN — death take him! How thankless he is! From what has God created him? — from a drop of sperm He created him and ordered his being and made his way amenable. He brings him later to the experience of death and lays him in the grave. Thence, as He wills, He brings him anew to life. Yet, for all that, man does not fulfill what his Lord has commanded.

So let man look well at his sustenance. We have sent the rain in copious downpours and broken up channels in the ground, bringing forth grain there, grapes and vegetation, olives and date-palms, and orchards with dense foliage, fruits and pastures — glad provision for you and for your cattle.   *Surah 80.17-32*

HAS there ever passed over man a flux of mortal time when he was a thing of no importance? We created man from the sperm of sexual intercourse and We endowed him with hearing and sight and guided him in the way. Grateful, or thankless in unfaith? — that is what is at stake.

                    Surah 76.1-3

Do you (s.) not see that God knows all in the heavens and in the earth? There is no secret conference of three but He is the fourth with them, nor of five but He is the sixth, nor any conclave of less or more persons where He is not with them where-ever they be. Then on the Day of resurrection He will tell them of their doings. For God knows all things.   *Surah 58.7*

Have you (s.) not perceived how your Lord lengthens the evening shadow, whereas — had He willed — He could have made it halt and stay? We have made the sun its guiding principle and then gradually We take the shadow and draw it to Ourselves.

It is He who has ordained the night for you as a cloak and for the repose of slumber, and made the day for life's renewal. It is He who sends the winds as heralds borne by His mercy. We have sent down pure water from heaven that We may bring to life a dead land and by it to give drink to the many creatures of Our creation, both cattle and men.

We have reiterated it frequently in their midst with a view to their taking thought of it. But the most part of mankind reject and have only a sceptical ingratitude.

Had We so willed We might have sent a warning emissary into every community. Do not yield to the unbelievers: struggle with them to your (s.) utmost with the revelation.

It is He who has made the two waters to flow — the one sweet to quench the thirst, the other salt and bitter. He has set a barrier between them and made them for ever distinct. It is He who creates mortal man from water and gives him kinship by blood and by marriage. Your (s.) Lord is all-powerful. Yet, in place of God they worship what can neither benefit nor harm them. The unbeliever has taken sides against his Lord.   *Surah 25.45-55*

Your God is one God: there is no god but He, the merciful Lord of mercy.

For a people who think intelligently there are signs in the creation of the heavens and of the earth, in the alternation of night and day, in the ships which voyage on the seas to the profit of mankind, in the waters God sends down from the heaven giving life out of lifelessness to the earth, in the populating of the earth with every kind of living creature, in the hither and thither of winds and clouds harnessed to His purposes between sky and land.   *Surah 2.163-164*

MANKIND! Worship and serve your Lord who has created you and those who preceded you, that you may hold Him ever in godly awe. It is He who gave you the earth for a place of rest and set the sky for a canopy whence He sends the waters whereby He brings forth fruits for your sustenance.

Allow nothing whatever to be rivalling the place of God: that you know full well. *Surah 2.21-22*

بِسْمِ اللهِ الرَّحْمٰنِ الرَّحِيمِ

C. Prophets and Messengers from Adam to Jesus

TRULY God chose Adam and Noah and the house of Abraham and the house of 'Imrān above all sentient beings, in one line of descent. God hears and knows.   *Surah 3.33-34*

TELL them truly the story of the two sons of Adam — how each of them made an offering and how the offering of the one was accepted and that of the other not.

And Cain said: 'I will kill you, I will!' But his brother said: 'Only from those who truly fear Him does God accept an offering. If you lay your hands on me I will not lay hands on you. For I fear God, the Lord of all beings. My wish would be to let all my sins be on you as well as your own. The burden would number you among the denizens of the Fire. For that is the requital of those who commit a terrible deed.' But Cain was set on his brother's death. He murdered him and took his place among the lost.

And God sent a raven that scratched the ground to show him how to hide the vile deed, the corpse of his brother. 'Woe is me,' he said, 'am I so paralysed that I cannot be like this raven and hide the evil done to my brother?' And he was filled with remorse.

For that reason We decreed for the Children of Israel that anyone who kills a human being — if not in retaliation for a murder, nor for causing corruption in the land — must be accounted to have killed all mankind: and whoever saves a life it will be as if he had saved the life of all mankind.

Our messengers came to them with clear signs. Nevertheless many of them continue to commit their unbridled evils in the earth.

Surah 5.27-32

WE have granted revelation to you (s.) as We gave revelation to Noah and the prophets who came after him. To Abraham also We gave revelation, and to Ishmael, Isaac, Jacob and the tribes, to Jesus and to

Job, to Jonah, Aaron and Solomon. To David We brought the Psalms. There are messengers whose story We have already made known to you and there are others whose history We have not told you. With Moses God spoke face to face. These were all bearers of good tidings and of warning, messengers thanks to whose coming mankind could have no possible case against God, the God of infinite power and wisdom.

God Himself is witness that what He has sent down to you is indeed His sending with His full knowledge. To this the angels also bear witness. God's is all the witness we need.   *Surah 4.163-166*

WE sent Noah to his people, saying: 'I come to you with a clear warning. Worship none but God. I am afraid on your account of a day of grievous retribution.' The nobles of his people who were unbelieving said: 'As it seems to us you are just a human like ourselves. We do not see any following you except the most vulgar among us in their ill-considered haste. We do not regard you as having any superiority over us. Indeed, we think you a bunch of imposters!' He replied: 'My people, have you considered? What if I have a clear token from my Lord and a mercy has been granted me from Him, to which you have been rendered blind, can we compel you to it by duress when you are altogether averse to it? My people! I ask of you no wealth for myself from this: my reward is on God alone. I am in no mind to thrust away those who have believed — they have their encounter with their Lord. But I realise that you are people with no mind for the truth. My people! who would come to my help against God were I to repulse them? Will you not stop and think? I am not telling you that I have with me the treasuries of God, nor have I knowledge of the great unseen. Nor do I say that I am an angel. Nor do I say to those whom you regard with scornful contempt that God will never bring them good — God knows well what is in your hearts — for in that event I would certainly be doing wrong.'

They said: 'Noah! you have been in dispute with us and have gone on with your contention at great length. Bring on us what you threaten, if you are telling the truth.' He replied: 'God alone will bring it on you if He wills and there will be no frustrating it on your part. For my counsel will not benefit you — should I have a mind to go on with counsel to you — were God to will your persistent delusion. He is your Lord and to Him will your return be.'

Or are they saying: 'He has invented it all'? Tell them: 'If I have invented it my crime is on me: but of your crimes I am innocent.' And it was revealed to Noah that none of his people would come to believe who had not already believed. 'Do not be distressed at what they do. Construct the ark under Our eyes and by Our inspiration. Make no pleas to me about those wrong-doers: they will be drowned.'

As he was making the ark, every time the chiefs of his people went by they derided him. He told them: 'You may mock at us but we will have gibes for you to match yours, and you will know who is in for a humiliating punishment and over whom a lasting doom impends.'

So it was, until Our decree came to pass and the waters gushed forth from the surface of the earth. We said: 'Load into it two of every kind, of either sex, and your family also — except the one against whom sentence has already been passed — and those who are believers' — and they were only a few. And he said: 'Embark in it: in God's name be the course and the mooring. My Lord is forgiving and merciful.' It sailed with them through waves like mountains.

Noah called to his son who was standing away off from them: 'My dear son, embark with us: do not stay with the unbelievers.' He said: 'I will take shelter in a mountain which will protect me from the waters.' Noah cried back: 'This day there is no protection from the decree of God, save for those on whom He has mercy.' Waves came between them and he was drowned with the rest.

The word was spoken: 'Earth! swallow your waters! Heaven! hold!' The water subsided: the commandment was fulfilled, and the ark settled on Mount Jūdī. The word rang out: 'Away with the people who worked evil.'

Noah cried to his Lord and said: 'My son was a member of my family. Your promise is truth and you are the most just of judges.' He said: 'Noah! he was not of your family: what he did was unrighteous. So do not ask Me for that of which you have no comprehension. I admonish you, so that you may not be numbered among the wilful and ignorant.' Noah said: 'My Lord, I seek refuge with you from asking what I have no knowledge of. Unless You forgive me and have mercy on me I shall be with the lost.'

The word came: 'Noah! take your way down in peace from Us and blessings be upon you and upon the nations descending from those with you. Nations there are to whom We will give satisfactions and a painful retribution from Us will later afflict them. That represents an intimation from the unseen which We have inspired in you, unknown before this both to you and to your people. Be patient: the issue belongs to those who truly fear God.' *Surah 11.25-49*

WE sent Noah to his people saying: 'Give warning to your people before stern retribution overtakes them.' He said: 'O my people, I have come to warn you plainly, to tell you that you should serve God and hold Him in awe. Pay heed to me and He will forgive you your sins and grant you respite until the time appointed. God's time, when the moment is come, brooks no delay. If only you would realise!'

And Noah said: 'Lord, night and day I have pleaded with my people. But the only effect of my pleading has been that they have fled away from it. Each time I have called them to Your forgiveness they have put their fingers in their ears and wrapped their heads in their garments. They have persisted in arrogant stubbornness. At that I have gone on pleading with them publicly, making my point openly, and in private entreaty also, urging them: "Seek your Lord's forgiveness: He is always ready to forgive. He sends down copious rain from heaven and enriches you with wealth and sons. Your gardens and your flowing streams are all His doing. How can you fail to recognise the awesome majesty of God? — God who created you stage by stage? Do you not realise how He brought into being the seven heavens in their order, setting the moon there for a light and the sun for a lantern? God caused you to grow out of the earth as His planting. To the earth He will bring you back and from it bring you forth again. God has stretched out before you the wide reaches of the earth and there you tread your beaten tracks." '

'Lord,' said Noah, 'they have said No! to me and gone after the way of him whose wealth and family augment only to his ruin. They have put their heads together in a grand scheme, saying: "On no account abandon your gods. Do not abandon Wadd nor Suwā', nor Yaghūth, Ya'ūq and Nasr." They have led many astray. Only in error let such evil-doers increase!'

Because of their sins the flood overwhelmed them and they were made to enter the Fire. Without God they were destitute of all help. And Noah said: 'Lord, do not leave on earth a single unbeliever. For, if You spare them, they will lead your servants astray and all their offspring will be faithless, evil-living people.'

'Lord, forgive me and those who bare me and every believing person under my roof. Forgive all who believe, men and women alike. As for the wrongdoers, the more they gain the more their ruin.'   *Surah 71*

BEFORE them, the people of Noah said Our signs were lies, and lies the words of Our servant. They said of him: 'He is mad,' and they spurned him completely. Then he called upon his Lord and said: 'Lord, I am at the end of my tether. Come to my help.' Then We opened the gates of heaven with a torrential rain and made the springs of the earth to gush forth. The waters became one great flood to bring about what had been decreed.

Noah, the man they had maligned, We conveyed safely in a ship of wooden boards well caulked, which We kept steadily under Our gaze. Such was Noah's reward. All was a sign on Our part for posterity. But are there any to take it in? *Surah 54.9-15*

WE sent Noah and Abraham, and established prophethood and the Book, among their progeny, some of whom are well-guided, while many of them behave corruptly. *Surah 57.26*

ABRAHAM said: 'Lord, make this place (Mecca) secure: preserve me and my sons from the worship of idols. For idols, Lord, have led many men astray. Whoever sides with me shall be my kin. As for those who set themselves against me, it is Yours alone to forgive and to have mercy.'

'Our Lord, I have settled some of my family near Your sacred house, in a valley where there is no cultivation. There they will perform the prayer. Let the hearts of men be kindly toward them and provide them with fruits. They will, I trust, prove grateful people.'

'Lord, You know what we conceal, and what we disclose. Nothing in earth or heaven is hidden from God. Praise be to God who has given me Ishmael and Isaac, old man that I am. My Lord is truly the hearer of prayer.'

'Lord, make me one who performs the prayer, and my descendants also. Lord, receive my prayer. Forgive me, Lord, and those who bore me, with all the faithful, on the Day when the reckoning shall be.' *Surah 14.35-41*

RELATE to them the story of Abraham, how he said to his father and his people: 'What is it you worship?' They said: 'We worship idols and we are steadfast in our devotion to them.' 'And do they hear you when you call? Can they do anything for you good or bad?' 'Well,' they said, 'it is this we found our fathers doing.' Abraham said: 'Have you really considered what it is you are worshipping, you and your forebears of old? To me they are enemies. There is only the Lord of all creation, the One who created me and guides me, who gives me food and drink. When

I am sick, it is He who heals me. He determines my dying and my coming back into life. His forgiveness for my sin is what I long for eagerly on the Day of judgement.'

O Lord, be my vindication and join me with the righteous. Let me be honest in all I say to others and include me with the heirs of the paradise of bliss. Forgive my father, for he is among the erring. Let me not be confounded on the Day of resurrection when neither wealth nor sons can avail, but only he who comes to God with a pure heart.

The God-fearers shall have the garden spread before their eyes but the perverse shall have *Jahannam* gaping before them. It will be said to them: 'Where are your idols now, whom you worshipped instead of God? Can they help you — or themselves?' Into Hell they will be bundled, with those who led them falsely and all the legions of *Iblīs* together. They will wrangle bitterly among themselves saying: 'By God, we were surely in utter error when we equated you with the Lord of all being. Those who led us astray were guilty criminals and now we have none to intercede for us, nor any loyal friend. Would we could live our lives again and be believing.'

In all this there is truly a meaning to be read yet, for the most part, men do not believe. Your (s.) Lord is the Lord of all power and mercy.

Surah 26.69-104

ABRAHAM said to his father, Āzar: 'Do you take idols for gods? As I see it, you and your people are clearly in the wrong.'

So We showed Abraham the kingdom of the heavens and of the earth that he might be a man of convinced faith. When the night was dark about him he saw a star and said: 'This is my Lord.' But when it set, he said: 'I do not love what sets.' Then he saw the moon rising and exclaimed: 'This is my Lord.' But when the moon, too, waned, he said: 'Unless my Lord guides me aright I too will be among the people who have wandered into error.' Then when he saw the sun rising he said: 'This is my Lord, this is grander.' But when the sun, too, set he said: 'O my people, I am done with your idolatry. I have set my face toward Him who brought into being the heavens and the earth, to be His in pure faith. I repudiate idolaters.'

When his people remonstrated with him he said: 'Will you dispute with me about God — God who has guided me? I have no fear — please God — of the idols you worship. My Lord holds all things in the embrace of His knowledge. Will you not keep that in your thoughts? Why should I be afraid of what you falsely worship seeing you show no

fear in having ascribed to God what you have absolutely no warrant for?'
So which of the two sides — if you can tell — has the truer claim to feel
secure? Those who have come to faith and have not cloaked their faith by
evil-doing, theirs is the true security, they being the rightly guided.

Surah 6.74-82

IT was We who of old gave Abraham his rectitude. For well We knew his
quality. He said to his father and his people: 'What are these images to
which you are so devoted?' They said: 'We found our fathers worshipping them.' He replied: 'Then assuredly both you and your fathers are
clearly in error.' 'Are you bringing the truth to us,' they said, 'or are you
talking in jest?' Abraham said: 'Far from it. Your Lord is the Lord of the
heavens and the earth: He brought them into being. To that I am a
witness among others. And, by God, I will surely deal with your idols
when your backs are turned and you are not around.'

So he broke them all in bits, except for one big one they could turn to
and question.

'Who has done this to our gods?' they cried. 'What an outrage he has
committed!' Others said: 'We heard a youth named Abraham speaking
about them.' 'Fetch him,' they cried 'and let all the people set eyes on
him that they may be witnesses.'

'Was it you, Abraham,' they asked, 'who did this to our gods?' 'No!'
said Abraham, 'it was the big one here who did it. If they can talk to you,
question them.'

At this, they bethought themselves, saying to each other that it was
they who were doing wrong. But their mood changed and they retorted
to Abraham: 'You know full well that idols do not speak!' to which he
answered: 'So then, you worship in despite of God what can do nothing
for you, can neither help nor harm. Shame on you and on your
idolatrous worship! Have you no sense?'

'Rally to your gods,' they cried, 'and to the stake with him, if you
mean business.' And We said: 'Be cool, O fire, for Abraham, unharmed
in peace.'

They devised a plot against him but it was them We made the real
losers. Both Abraham and Lot with him We delivered and brought into
the land on which, for all humanity, We made a blessing rest. We gave
him Isaac and Jacob, his sons, and made them all righteous, appointing
them leaders, bringing men guidance according to Our command. We
inspired them to well-doing, to the activity of prayer and the bringing of
alms. It was Us they served.

Surah 21.51-73

A KINDRED soul (with Noah) was Abraham who came before his Lord
with a pure heart. To his father and his people he said: 'What are you
worshipping? Are you bent on false worship, taking deities to the
exclusion of God Himself? What idea have you got of the Lord of all
being?'

Looking up at the stars, he said: 'How your worship sickens me!' But
his people turned their backs on him and slunk away. Then, making his
way toward their gods, he said to them: 'Not eating your offerings?
What is the matter with you that you don't speak?' Then he set on them
and began striking at them with his right hand. When the people came
running up, he said to them: 'Are you worshipping what your own
hands have fashioned when it is God who created both you and your
handiwork itself?' They answered: 'Build a pyre for him and throw him
into the blaze.' They meant to get him in their clutches but We made
them bite the dust.

And Abraham said: 'I am going to my Lord: He will guide me. O my
Lord, grant me, I pray, an heir who will be numbered among the
righteous.' So We gave him good news of a gentle son. When the boy was
old enough to share in things with his father, Abraham said: 'My son, in
a dream I dreamt that I should offer you in sacrifice. What can your
thoughts be of that?' He said: 'Father, do what you are told: God
willing, you will find me patient.' So together they submitted to God's
will. Abraham laid his son down with his face to the ground. Whereupon
We called to him: 'Abraham, you have kept faith with the vision. Yours
is the reward We grant to those whose deeds are worthy.' It was as clear a
test as could be. We redeemed his son with a great sacrifice and through
the generations that followed We left for him the benediction: 'Peace be
upon Abraham.'

In such ways are the righteous rewarded. He was one of Our believing
servants. We gave him the good news of Isaac, one of the best of prophets
whom We blessed along with Abraham. Among their descendants there
were some who did good deeds, while others were blatant evil-doers
who sinned against themselves.   *Surah 37.83-113*

ABRAHAM said to his father and to his people: 'I will have nothing more
to do with the things you worship. For me there is only He who gave me
being. He will be my guide' — words he made an abiding precept for his
posterity, one to which they may turn their minds.

Thus I gave both them and their fathers life through the years until the
truth came and a messenger whom they could not mistake. But, when

the truth came they said it was witchcraft they could not believe. They said also: 'Why was not this Qur'ān revealed to someone of significance in the twin cities?'   *Surah 43.26-31*

YOU people of the Book, why are you so argumentative about Abraham, seeing that the Torah and the Gospel were only sent down after his time? Will you not use your reason? You are people much given to disputing about things within your comprehension: why insist on disputing about things of which you have no knowledge? Knowledge belongs to God and you lack it!

Abraham was not a Jew, nor was he a Christian. He was a man of pure worship (a *hanīf*) and a Muslim: he was not one of those pagan idolaters. The people nearest to Abraham are those who followed him and this prophet too and those who have believed. Believers are under God's care.   *Surah 3.65-68*

WHEN his Lord tested Abraham with words of command and he fulfilled them the Lord said: 'I will make you a leader of men.' And Abraham asked: 'What of my descendants?' 'My covenant' God replied, 'shall not hold for those who do evil.'

We made the house (at Mecca) a place of sanctuary and security for the people, saying: 'Make the place where Abraham prayed your house of prayer.' Thus We made Our covenant with Abraham and Ishmael, that they should cleanse My house as a sanctuary for pilgrims and men of devotion to make the pilgrim circuit and do acts of worship and prostration. And Abraham said: 'Lord, make this land secure and provide its people with fruits, those of them who believe in God and in the last Day.' 'But the man who does not believe,' said God, 'I will make to prosper for a while, until My inexorable doom overtakes him in fiery anguish, and how evil will his destiny be!'

Abraham and Ishmael built the foundations of the house, saying: 'Lord, accept it at our hands, You who hear and know our hearts. Make us ever submissive to You and make our descendants a community of obedience to You. Show us our forms of devotion and turn to us in mercy. For You are the merciful One who turns again to men. Send among our people after us a messenger of their own kin, who will recite to them Your revelations, teach them the Book and the wisdom and purge them from evil. For You are ever powerful and wise.'

Who but a fool would forsake the community of Abraham? We chose him in this present world: and in the world to come he will be among the righteous.

When his Lord said to him: 'Submit yourself wholly,' he said: 'I have surrendered to the Lord of all being.' Abraham charged his sons, as did Jacob also, saying: 'My sons, God has chosen for you the true religion. To your dying day be sure that you are among those who are wholly submitted to God.'

When death came to Jacob were you not witnesses of how he said to his sons: 'Whom will you worship when I am gone?' 'We will worship your God,' they replied, 'the God of your fathers, Abraham and Isaac, the One God. To Him will we submit ourselves.'

That community has passed away. They have in store ahead for them what they have earned, as you have yours. It is not about their deeds that you are going to be questioned.

To be rightly guided they say that you must be Jews or Christians. Say rather: 'Ours is the community of Abraham, a man of pure worship. No polytheist he! Let your word be: "We believe in God and in what has been revealed to us, and revealed to Abraham, Ishmael, Isaac, Jacob and the tribes, and we believe in what was brought to Moses, to Jesus and to the prophets, from their Lord. We do not distinguish between any of them and to God we make submission."' If they believe in accordance with this faith of yours, then are they truly guided. But if they turn away from it they are plainly in schism. God who hears and knows all will see you through in all your dealings with them.

The baptism of God — who could be better than God at truth-initiation? All our worship belongs to Him. Say: 'God is our Lord and your Lord. Do you want arguments with us about Him? We have our deeds and you have yours. It is Him, in sincerity, we serve. Do you want to say that Abraham, Ishmael, Isaac, Jacob and the tribes were all Jews or Christians? Let me ask you: "Who knows best, you or God?" Could there be a greater crime for a man to conceal a message he has received from God? God is not unmindful of all you are doing.'

That community has passed away. It has what it earned, as you have what you have earned. It is not about their deeds that you are going to be questioned.   *Surah 2.124-141*

HAVE you (s.) had word of the tradition about the honoured guests of Abraham who came into his tent, saying: 'Peace.'? He gave his peace in reply, thinking: 'These are strangers to me.' So he went in quietly to his family and laid on a fatted calf which he set before them, saying: 'Will you not eat?' He became apprehensive about them. But they said: 'Have no fear,' and they gave him the good news of a son, gifted with knowledge. His wife approached in great agitation, beating her face and saying: 'What! a barren old woman like me!' They told her. 'It is even so. Your Lord has said — He who is wise, who knows all.'

Abraham said: 'Messengers, what is your errand?' They answered: 'We have been sent to a guilty people: brickbats of clay we have to release against them, assigned on your Lord's part for those who live in wanton debauchery.'

We brought out those in the city who were believers, finding only one household of people surrendered (*muslimūn*) to God. We left behind in it a sign for those who dread the doom of pain.   *Surah 51.24-37*

ABRAHAM said to his people: 'Worship God and hold Him in reverent awe: that is the better thing, did you but realise. It is idols you are worshipping, to the exclusion of God. It is an outrage you are committing. Those you worship to the exclusion of God can afford you no sustenance at all. So seek sustenance from God and give Him thanks: it is to Him you will be brought again. If you call it lies nations before you have denied also. The messenger's only duty is to bring the clear word home.'

Do they not recognise how God initially gives being to the creation and then renews it? Effortlessly He does so.

Say: 'Go through the land and see how He originated the creation and then how God makes yet another growth to come forth. God has competence over all things. He brings retribution on whom He wills and has mercy on whom He wills. It is before Him you will be brought. There is no eluding Him on your part, neither in the earth nor in the heaven: apart from God you have neither friend nor protector. Those who disbelieve in the revelations of God and in the destiny to meet Him have no hope of My mercy. For such there is dire punishment.'

The only answer of Abraham's people was to cry: 'Slay him or burn him!' God saved him from the fire, and in that fact are signs for a believing people.

He said: 'You have adopted idols to worship instead of God only for the love-ties you have in the life of this present world. On the Day of resurrection, however, you will deny and curse one another. The Fire will be your abode and you will have none to help you.'

In Abraham Lot believed and said: 'I will go forth and repair to my Lord. He is the almighty, the ever-wise.' And We gave him Isaac and

123

Jacob, establishing prophethood and the Scripture in his progeny: We rewarded him in this world while in the world to come he will be among the righteous.

Lot said to his people: 'You are committing abomination unparalleled by any in the wide world hitherto. Do you not go lusting after men and violate the way of God with your perversities, doing forbidden things in your very assemblies?' But the only answer his people gave him was to say: 'If you are telling us the truth bring down on us the punishment of God.' Lot said: 'My Lord, give me help against these people who work abomination.'

When Our messengers brought Abraham the good news they added: 'We are going to destroy the people of this city. Its people are evil-doers.' He said: 'Lot is in there!' To which they replied: 'I know who is there. We will certainly rescue him and his family, save only his wife — she will be among those who stay behind.' When Our messengers came to Lot, he was troubled for them, it not being in his power to protect them. But they said: 'Have no fear: do not grieve: we are going to deliver you and your family — your wife excepted — she being among the laggards who remain there. We are about to visit the people of this city with a doom of wrath from heaven for all the foul deeds they have committed.'

We truly left therein a clear sign for comprehending people.

Surah 29.16-35

HAVE you (s.) not in mind that king who entered into an argument with Abraham concerning his Lord? God granted him kingly rule and when Abraham said to him: 'It is my Lord who gives life and who brings to death' he replied: 'I am the one who determines life and death.' Abraham responded: 'Well, God brings the sun from the east, you make it rise from the place of sunset.' The unbeliever was taken aback in confusion. God has no guidance for those who pervert the truth.

Or take stock of the likes of him who passed by a city all in ruins and remarked: 'How ever will God bring life to this place, dead as it is?' God caused him to die and brought him back to life after a hundred years. He asked him: 'How long have you been deceased?' To which he answered: 'I have remained so just a day or part of a day.' 'Not so,' He said, 'you have been dead one hundred years. Take a look at your food and drink: they have not spoiled. And look, there is your donkey. And look at these bones, how We bring them together and clothe them with flesh — making you yourself a sign to the people.' When all was clearly brought home to him he confessed: 'I know that God has all things in the disposal of His power.'

And Abraham said to his Lord: 'My Lord, show me how you give life to the dead.' He said: 'Is it then that there is no faith in you?' Abraham said: 'Not at all, but in order to have my heart at rest.' God said: 'Then take four birds and make them familiar with you. Then place them separately each of them atop each hill. Call them and they will come flying to you, and realise that God is strong and wise.' *Surah 2.258-260*

LOT, too, was among those who were sent as messengers. We rescued him and his entire family, except for one old woman who hung back. All the other inhabitants We destroyed. In your travels you pass by their ruins in the morning light or at nightfall. Do you not understand?
Surah 37.133-138

AND there was Lot who said to his people: 'What is this lewdness you are committing with open eyes? Are you going lustfully after men leaving the women folk aside? a people heedlessly perverse.' But the only answer he had from his people was: 'Throw the family of Lot out of your city — such puritan folk!' So We rescued Lot and his family — all but his wife who lingered behind with others. It was by Our decree. And We rained down upon them the rain that is the grim fate of those who have been warned. *Surah 27.54-58*

TO the tribe of 'Ād We sent their brother, Hūd, who said: 'My people, worship God: you have no other god but He. All you do is to put about your spurious notions. My people, I do not ask any wage from you for this mission. My reward belongs with Him who fashioned me. Will you not understand? My people, seek forgiveness from your Lord and then repent before Him. He will send heaven's copious rain upon you and make you go from strength to strength. Do not revert into evil ways.' They said: 'Hūd, you have brought us no clear sign, and we are not ones to abandon our gods at a word from you. We put no faith in you. All we say is that some of our gods have afflicted you with some delusion.' He replied: 'I call God — and you — to witness that I am guiltless of the pseudo worship you engage in, in denial of Him. Contrive what you will against me, all of you: do not give me any respite! My trust is in God, my Lord and your Lord. There is not a single thing that moves but He has it

125

under total control. Truly the path of my Lord is the straight one. But if you turn away, the message with which I am sent to you I have certainly communicated to you. My Lord will bring on another people in your place and no loss will you do to Him! For my Lord has watch over all things.'

When Our decree came to pass We delivered Hūd and those who believed with him by Our act of mercy and We saved them from dire suffering.

Such was the tribe of 'Ād. They belied the revelations of their Lord and rebelled against His messengers. They followed the command of any and every obstinate braggart. Malediction attended them in this present world and will pursue them on the Day of resurrection. For, of a truth, 'Ād denied their Lord. Cast utterly away were 'Ād, the people of Hūd. *Surah 11.50-60*

To the tribe of 'Ād We sent their brother, Hūd. He said: 'My people, worship God: you have no other god but He. Will you not stand in awe of Him?' The elders of his tribe, in their unbelief, said: 'We regard you as being a simpleton: our guess is that you are just a liar.' Hūd replied: 'My people, I am no simpleton but, in truth, an apostle from the Lord of all being. I bring to you the messages of my Lord. A faithful mentor I am to you. Are you taken by surprise that there should come to you a reminder from your Lord by means of a man from your own people, to warn you? Remember how He appointed you as successors after the people of Noah and made you to become increasingly strong. Remember, then, the blessings of God and it may be that all will go well with you.'

But they responded: 'Have you come to us demanding that we worship God alone and abandon the worship of our fathers? If you are an honest man, bring on us what you promise us.' Hūd answered: 'A foul evil and wrath have seized you. Are you contending with me about names you and your fathers have put about, for which God has sent down no authority? Wait, then, to see what follows: I will be waiting with you.' So We delivered him and his associates by an act of Our mercy and We cut off the last remnant of those who, in their unbelief, denied Our revelations. *Surah 7.65-72*

THE tribe of 'Ād held the messengers to be liars. For their brother, Hūd, said to them: 'Will you not have fear of God? I am a faithful messenger to you. Hold God in awe, then, and pay heed to me. I do not ask any wage of you, for my reward is wholly with the Lord of all being. Are you in your folly building a shrine on every high place and acquiring great building works with a prospect of being there for ever? You have been tyrannical in the exercise of your strong arm. Have fear of God and give heed to me. Fear Him who has freely bestowed on you all your knowledge and has furnished you with flocks and sons, with gardens and wells. I am fearful for you, fearful of the penalty of a great day.'

They said: 'It is all the same to us whether you preach or give up preaching. The way we are is none other than the firm custom of our forebears. We are not candidates for penalties!' Thus they rejected him as one who lied and We caused them to perish — wherein is a sign, though the majority do not believe. As for your (s.) Lord, he is strong and merciful.   *Surah 26.123-140*

AND We sent their brother, Sālih, to the tribe of Thamūd, calling on them to worship God. There were two contending parties of them. He said: 'My people, why do you hasten on the evil rather than the good? Why do you not seek pardon from God that you may find mercy?' They said: ' We find in you and in those with you an evil omen.' He said: 'Your destiny is in God's hands. Indeed, you are a people being put to the test.'

Now there were in the city nine incorrigible rogues who dealt corruptly in the land, who said: 'Swear by God a mutual oath to attack him and his family by night. We will protest to his next-of-kin that we had not witnessed the destruction of his family and that we are telling the truth.' So they entered into a plot and We devised a plan too, of which they were unaware. See (s.) then what the outcome of their conspiracy was. We utterly destroyed them and their people, one and all. Those are their deserted dwellings, in ruins for the wrongs they committed. Wherein is a sign for a knowing people. We saved those who believed and were God-fearing.   *Surah 27.45-53*

TO the tribe of Thamūd We sent their brother, Sālih, who said: 'My people, worship God: you have no other god but He. He brought you into being from the earth and established you as occupants there. Therefore, seek His forgiveness and turn to Him in penitence. For my Lord is near and ready to answer.' They said: 'Sālih, we had good hopes of you until now. Are you forbidding us to worship what our fathers worshipped? We are dubious about what you are calling us to, and suspicious.' He replied: 'My people, have you realised how it is with me? If I have a sign from my Lord, a mercy which has come to me from Him, what defence would I have before God were I to repudiate Him? To heed you would mean nothing for me but aggravated ruin. My people, here is a she-camel, God's camel and a sign for you. Let her graze in God's earth and do her no harm, lest punishment, near at hand, overtake you.' When they slaughtered her Sālih said: 'Three days regale yourselves in your houses; what surely threatens will not be found false.' When Our decree transpired We delivered Sālih and those with him who believed by an act of mercy on Our part, out of the shame of that day. For your (s.) Lord is mighty and strong. Catastrophe seized the evil-doers and when morning came there they lay, lifeless in their dwellings, as though they had never flourished there. Thamūd denied their Lord: Thamūd is cast away.

Surah 11.61-68

To the tribe of Thamūd We sent their brother, Sālih, who said: 'My people, worship God: you have no other god but He. A sign has come to you from your Lord. This is God's she-camel, a symbol for you. Let her be free to graze in God's earth and do her no harm, lest painful punishment take you. Remember how He made you successors to the tribe of 'Ād and gave you tenure in the land, so that you build castles on its plains and hew dwellings out of the hills. Remember God's blessings and do not deal corruptly, defiling the land.' The elders among his people in their arrogance said to those of their number who believed and whom they considered base: 'Do you really know that Sālih is a messenger from his Lord?' They replied: 'We do believe in the message with which he was commissioned.' To which the arrogant folk retorted: 'We deny what you believe in.' They slaughtered the she-camel and disdained the command of their Lord and they said to Sālih: 'If you are indeed a messenger, bring on us what you threaten.'

An earthquake overwhelmed them and in the morning they lay lifeless in their dwellings. Turning aside from them, Sālih said: 'O my people, I did bring to you the message of my Lord and counselled you. But you have no love for true counsellors!' *Surah 7.73-79*

THE tribe of Thamūd took the messengers for liars when Sālih, their brother, said to them: 'Have you no fear of God?' 'I am a faithful apostle to you. Fear God, then, and give me obedient heed. For this I ask no wage from you: my reward is from the Lord of all being, Him alone. Are you going to be left in security in your present case, with gardens and wells here and tilled fields and palm-trees bearing their slender sheaths? Will you hew houses from the hills with your skilled hands? Hold God in awe, give me heed, and do not follow the bidding of those who practise excess, behave corruptly in the land and make no amends.' They replied: 'You are just a crazy fellow: you are human as the likes of us! If you are truthful then bring some sign to pass.' He said: 'Here is this she-camel. Let her have her share of water as yours have on the day assigned and do her no harm, lest retribution should overtake you on a dread day.' They slaughtered her, only to be remorseful when retribution caught up with them — wherein is a sign, though the majority give it no credence. Truly your (s.) Lord is the mighty One and merciful.

Surah 26.141-159

THE sure reality! how aweful the sure reality! what comprehension have you of the sure reality? The tribes of 'Ād and Thamūd said the cry of impending doom was all lies. But as for Thamūd, they were destroyed by a violent earthquake and 'Ād were overwhelmed by a raging tempest in its fury which God called up against them ceaselessly for seven nights and eight days. See them you (s.) might — all flattened lifeless, strewn like stumps of hollow palm-trees. Is there any remnant left of them before your eyes? It was the same with Pharaoh and those before him and with the cities that were overthrown in their sins. They rejected the apostle of their Lord and He seized them in a grasp of sharpening intensity.　　　*Surah 69.1-10*

HAVE you not seen how your (s.) Lord dealt with the tribe of 'Ād, with Iram whose were the pillars the like of which had never been wrought in the land; and with the tribe of Thamūd who hollowed out rocks in the valley; and Pharaoh also, lord of the tent-poles — those who lorded it tyranically over the land and multiplied evil therein. Your (s.) Lord loosed on them a scourge of punishment. For your Lord is ever on the watch.　　　*Surah 89.6-14*

THE tribe of 'Ād said: 'Lies!' How dire was My chastisement in the wake of My warnings! We sent upon them a violent wind that raged in a day of unrelenting disaster, plucking men away as if they were stumps of uprooted palm-trees. How dire was My chastisement in the wake of My warnings! We have made the Qur'ān easy to remember: but is there anyone remembering?

The tribe of Thamūd belied the warnings. They said: 'Shall we follow a mere human, one of ourselves? To do so would be error and lunacy. Has the *Dhikr* been delivered to him alone among us? Nay! but he is an insolent liar.'

They will know on the morrow who is the insolent liar! We are sending the she-camel as a test for them. Keep watch on them and hold yourself in patience. Tell them that the water is to be shared between them, each in supervised turns. Then they summoned their leader, who caught and slaughtered her. How dire was My punishment in the wake of My warnings. We brought upon them a single blast and they were as discarded twigs left by one who builds a sheepfold.

Indeed We have made the Qur'ān easy to remember: but is there anyone remembering? *Surah 54.18-32*

RECALL Our servants Abraham, Isaac and Jacob, men of strength and vision, men We made altogether genuine in faith through their pure sense of the eternal world. Truly We count them the chosen and most excellent. *Surah 38.45-47*

ALIF, Lām, Rā' — the signs of the Book which illumines. We have sent it down a Qur'ān in Arabic so that you (pl.) may take it in intelligently. In Our revealing this Qur'ān to you (s.) We give you in narrative the finest of stories — one of which you, with others, were quite unaware previously.

Joseph said to his father: 'Father, I saw eleven stars and the sun and moon in a dream and they were prostrating themselves before me.' To this his father replied: 'My son, do not tell your brothers what you have dreamed. They may concoct some plot against you. Satan is an avowed enemy to man. Your Lord is making choice of you to teach you the interpretation of events and dreams, perfecting His grace upon you and upon the house of Jacob, as in the past He did for your fathers, Abraham and Isaac. Wise and all-knowing is your Lord.'

There are, to be sure, many significant things in the story of Joseph and his brothers for those who are of enquiring mind.

'Our father,' observed the brothers, 'is much fonder of Joseph and his brother than he is of us — the whole lot of us. Our father is clearly under an aberration. Let us kill Joseph or get rid of him somewhere.' In that way, they told themselves, they would have their father's favour to

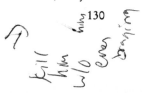

130

themselves. After the deed they could conduct themselves as right-dealing folk.

But one of them said: 'Do not kill Joseph. If you are really bent on action, find some pit and leave him there for some passing caravan to take him off.'

So they said to their father: 'Father, why not trust us with Joseph? In all honesty, we mean him well. Send him with us tomorrow for a jaunt and let him enjoy himself. We will take care of him.' Jacob answered: 'It distresses me to have you take him out with you. I fear some wolf may snatch him when you grow careless about protecting him.' To this the brothers said: 'If a wolf devours him — and we a whole band as we are — it would be over our dead bodies!'

They went off, and Joseph with them. They agreed on the plan to put him in a deep pit and there We revealed to Joseph that he would one day confront them with their deed when they had no idea who he was.

In the evening they came to his father with tears in their eyes and said: 'Father, we went off racing, leaving Joseph with our things. A wolf seized him. You will not believe us though we are telling you the very truth.' They showed him Joseph's shirt, stained with false blood. And Jacob said: 'I think it is not so: what you say has happened comes from the promptings of your own selves. Sweet fortitude, be mine! It is to God I turn for aid, faced with what you are telling me.'

Then there came a caravan whose water-carrier was sent with a bucket to draw. He cried: 'Bless us all! there is a lad in here!' They hid Joseph in their merchandise. God knew what they did. They sold him for a paltry price — a few dirhams counted out. For they set little store by him.

The man who purchased Joseph, an Egyptian, said to his wife: 'Give him a good lodging: maybe he will be useful to us and we may adopt him as a son.' So We gave Joseph a footing in the land in order to teach him the interpretation of storied happenings. God was working out His purpose, unaware of the fact as most people are. When Joseph reached manhood We conferred on him wisdom and knowledge, as Our way is with those whose lives are righteous.

The woman in whose house he lived schemed to entice him. She locked the doors and said: 'Come, I am yours.' But Joseph answered: 'God be my refuge. My master has been generous to me. Those who do evil will never prosper.' But she made for him madly and he would have taken her had he not seen a clear sign from his Lord, that We might keep him clear of evil and lust. He proved a loyal servant of Ours.

Both of them rushed to the door and she tore his tunic from behind. At the door, they met her husband. Whereupon she said: 'Is not imprisonment or some other dire punishment the due and proper way to deal with a fellow who tries to violate your own family?' Joseph said: 'It was she who tried to seduce me.' Then a witness from her own household commented: 'If his tunic is torn in the front, then she is speaking the truth and he is the one who is lying: but if it is torn from behind, she is the liar and he is telling the truth.'

When her husband saw that Joseph's tunic had been torn from behind, he said to her: 'This is some of your women's guile, and a pretty cunning one too! Joseph, keep clear of this kind of thing and you, madam, ask God's forgiveness for the sin you did, sinner that you are!'

Out in the city the women began to talk, putting the word around that the master's wife had fallen for her servant and had been soliciting him. 'She is a bad lot,' they were saying. When she had wind of their gossip, she sent to invite them to a banquet at her house. To every one of them she gave a knife and directed Joseph to present himself. Stunned with admiration when they saw him, they cut their hands, exclaiming: 'God preserve us! This is no mere human, this is some noble and angelic being.' 'Now you see,' she said, 'this is he you reproached me about. True, I tried to seduce him and he remained chaste. If he will not do as I require of him he will find himself in gaol, degraded.' To this Joseph responded: 'Lord, I would rather go to prison than submit to their advances. Unless You preserve me from their seductive snares, I will succumb and be numbered with the foolish.' His Lord heard his prayer and made him immune to their blandishments. For He hears and understands.

Nevertheless, in view of the signs given to them to that effect, they decided to put Joseph in prison for a while. With him there went to prison two young men, one of whom said to Joseph: 'I dreamed that I was pressing grapes,' while the other said: 'I dreamed that I was carrying bread on my head and the birds were eating it. Tell each of us the interpretation. It is evident to us that you are a man of parts and a good fellow.'

Joseph said: 'I will tell the meaning to each of you before the food arrives which is your daily sustenance. What I tell you is out of what my Lord has taught me. I have abandoned the community of those who do not believe in God and who, moreover, have no faith in the world to come. My community is that of the faith of our fathers, Abraham, Isaac and Jacob. It is our duty never to have other gods in the place of God in any form whatever. All this is the goodness of God to us and to all mankind. But most of humanity remain thankless. Tell me, fellow-prisoners, is a medley of gods better than God the One, the omnipotent?

132

Other objects of worship which you take instead of Him are nothing but names you have coined, you and your fathers. God has revealed no authority for them. Sovereignty belongs to none but God. He has commanded that you worship none but Him. That is true religion, even though most men do not know it.'

'My fellow-prisoners, one of you will again pour wine before his lord, while the other will be crucified and the birds will peck from off his head. That is the way the matter stands about which you enquired of me.'

To the one whom he expected to be freed Joseph said: 'Remember me when you stand before your lord.' But Satan caused him to forget to recall Joseph in mention to his lord. Thus Joseph remained in prison for a space of some years.

And the king said: 'I saw in a dream seven fat cattle and seven lean ones which ate them up; also seven green ears of corn and another seven which were dried up. Tell me, sages at my court, the meaning of what I have seen, if you can expound such dreams.' 'These are confusing dreams with no clues,' they answered, 'and, moreover, we have no skills to know what dreams mean.' It was then that the ex-prisoner, now freed, remembered Joseph after all the years, and he burst out: 'I will have the interpretation for you: give me leave to go.'

'Joseph,' he said, 'you are a man of truth; tell us about those seven fatted cattle which the seven lean ones devoured, and about the seven green ears of corn and the dried up ones, so that I can go back and report and the meaning will be known.' Joseph told him: 'For seven years running you will sow. At harvest time store the corn in the ear and eat only a little for your needs. For there will come seven barren years during which you will be consuming all that you have held in store, with little left. Then, following these years, there will come again a year when abundance will return and the vats will fill again.'

The king said: 'Bring the man into my presence.' But when the messenger came to summon him, Joseph said: 'Go back to your lord and ask him about the women who cut their hands. My master knows how crafty they were.' The king said to the women: 'Come clean about your action when you enticed Joseph: what about it?' 'God save us!' they said: 'we know nothing evil of him.' But the wife of his erstwhile master said: 'Now the truth is out at last: it was I who tried to seduce him. He is an upright man.' 'Hereby,' said Joseph, 'my master knows that I did not betray him behind his back. God does not guide the devices of tricksters. It is not that I want to justify myself. For the soul has an inward bias towards evil which would take over were it not for the mercy of my Lord, who indeed forgives and holds me in His mercy.'

active the passive [handwritten]

GOD [handwritten in left margin]

The king said: 'Bring him here to me: I will have him serving in my entourage.' After talking with Joseph he declared: 'From now on you are in our trust and favour.' Whereupon Joseph said: 'Put me in charge of the storehouses of the land: I will be an intelligent custodian.' Thus did We establish Joseph in the land with complete authority throughout it. For We confer Our mercy on whom We will and never let the wages of the good to fail. The reward of the world to come is better still and it belongs to those who believe and are devoted to God.

The brothers of Joseph came and entered into his presence. He recognised who they were but they had no idea who he was. When he had arranged for their supplies, he added: 'And bring that brother of yours from your father! Giving you full measure you can see what an excellent host I am. But if you do not bring him back with you, there will be no measure for you at all again. I will not have you in my presence.' 'We will try,' they said, 'to get our father to let him come. That, for sure, we will do.'

Joseph directed his attendants to put their money in their saddle-bags, saying: 'They may well know what is meant by it when they get back to their families and come back here again.'

When they were once more with their father they said to him: 'Father, there is a ban on our buying corn. You have to send our brother down with us if we are to get anything. We will take every care of him.' But Jacob said: 'Shall I entrust him into your hands as once I entrusted his brother to you? There is no more sure guardian than God. He is the Lord of utmost mercy.'

When they opened their goods they found their money returned to them. They said: 'Father what more can we desire? Here is our money given back to us. We can go and secure what we need for our families and look well after our brother. We shall have an extra camel-load. It was a light load before.'

But Jacob replied: 'I will never let him go with you, unless you take a solemn oath before God to bring him back to me, failing only something dire which engulfs you all.' They gave him that solemn pledge and he said: 'God take your oath into His keeping,' and he added: 'My sons, do not go in all of you by one gate, when you arrive: go in by different gates. But there is no point in my giving you such orders. The whole is in God's power to dispose. It is in Him that I put my trust, where all trusting men must put theirs.'

They came in as their father had directed them. Within God's disposal of events Jacob's precaution did not achieve anything. But it met a need in Jacob's soul. Moreover, Jacob had insight into a secret which We had

weak human vs. Gods will [handwritten]

indicated to him — the sort of knowledge which does not come to people in general.

When the brothers came into Joseph's presence, he embraced his own brother and said: 'I am your brother: do not grieve over what they did.' When he had provided them with provender he had his drinking-cup put into his own brother's saddle-bag.

Then the town-crier called out to them: 'Camel-drivers! you are surely thieves!' 'What is missing?' they asked, turning round to face those who spoke. 'The king's drinking-cup has gone,' was the reply: 'a camel-load of corn for the man who brings it back — my word for it!' 'In God's Name,' said the brothers, 'we did not come here to do evil in the land: we are no thieves.' 'And if you should be lying,' the men retorted, 'what then? What shall be done to the culprit?' They answered: 'Whoever is found with the cup in his saddle-bag will take the penalty. That is how we deal with criminals.'

Joseph went through all their saddle-bags coming finally to his brother's, from which he pulled out the cup. It was a design on Our part. Otherwise Joseph would have had no right, under the king's law, to detain his brother. Whom We will We exalt in honour: over every man of knowledge there is the One supreme Knower.

They said: 'If he has stolen it, a brother of his was a thief before him.' Still Joseph kept his secret and did not let them see anything. He said to them: 'Your own case is a worse evil: what you are referring to God knows well enough.' Then they said: 'O man of power, this brother here has a father who is a very old man. Take one of us in his place. You are a man of generous spirit — we can see that.' But Joseph replied: 'God forbid we should detain any man except the one with whom our property was found. For, otherwise, we would be doing a gross injustice.'

When they were in despair over him they went aside privately to confer. The eldest of them said: 'Your father, as you know full well, took from you a solemn pledge before God. Earlier you failed to keep faith with him over Joseph. Until I have my father's leave to do so I will on no account move from here — or until God gives me His verdict. There is no judgement to match His. You go back to your father and say to him: "Father, your son stole. We are only telling you what we know, being witnesses to it. Our power to stand guardians does not extend to things unseen. Ask in the city where we were and the camel-train in which we travelled. It is the truth we are telling you." '

'No!' cried Jacob, 'it is your doing in the evil of your hearts. Let me bear it with fortitude. It may be God will bring them all back to me. He is ever wise and knowing.' He went away from them, crying: 'Alas! alas! for Joseph.' From the grief pent up in his heart his eyes flooded with tears. They said to him: 'In God's Name! You go on for ever reminding yourself of Joseph: you will wear yourself into the grave.' Jacob said: 'My grief and anguish cry out to God for answer: God has made me to know things beyond your knowledge. Go, my sons, search for word of Joseph and his brother. Do not lose hope of God's spirit. It is only those who deny the faith who despair of the spirit of God.'

So they came again to Joseph. When they had entered in before him they said: 'O man of power, great ill has befallen us and our families. We have come with money that is worth little. But give to us out of your charity, allowing to us the measure of our need. God rewards those who give in charity.'

'Do you know,' he asked, 'what you did to Joseph and his brother in your obduracy?' 'Are you then Joseph?' they cried. 'I am Joseph,' he said, 'and this is my brother. God has been very good to us. Whoever fears Him and holds out patiently, God does not let him miss the reward of the well-doers.' 'In God's Name,' they cried, 'we were indeed sinners and God has set you in honour over us.'

'No reproach shall be held against you today. May God forgive you. He is the Lord of utmost mercy. Go, take this shirt of mine and place it over my father's face to recover his sight and come back here to me with all your people.'

As their caravan was setting out, their father said: 'The breath of Joseph! I can scent it! though you will think that what I say is the folly of an old man.' 'By God,' said those who heard him, 'this is just your old illusion.'

When the messengers came with the happy news and the shirt was laid on Jacob's face his sight came back to him and he said: 'Did I not tell that I was told from God things you knew nothing of?' They answered: 'Father, ask forgiveness for us for the wrongs we did. What sinners we have been.' 'I will indeed ask forgiveness for you from my Lord,' he replied, 'He is ever forgiving and merciful.'

So when they arrived in Joseph's presence he embraced his parents and said: 'Come in into Egypt and dwell here in safety, if God wills.' He brought his parents up on to the royal dais and they all prostrated before him and he said: 'Father, you see what that vision of mine long ago signified. My Lord has made it all true. How good He was to me, bringing me out of prison and bringing you out of the wilderness when Satan had sown enmity between me and my brothers. My Lord deals graciously according to His will: for He is ever wise and knowing.' 'My

Lord, you have brought me to power and made me learned in interpretation of storied things — You who gave being to the heavens and the earth, my trusted guardian in this world and in the next. Let me die in true submission and belong in the fellowship of the righteous.'

All the foregoing which We reveal to you (s.) brings you word of the world that is unseen. You were not there to see when Joseph's brothers resolved together on their evil scheme. However eagerly you desire it otherwise, most men are not believers. You are not asking them to give you any reward for your message: it is simply and solely a reminder to the worlds. Many a sign there is in the heavens and in the earth, yet men pass them by heedlessly. The majority will only believe in God while they stay polytheists as well! Are they so sure they will be immune from the overwhelming chastisement of God and the Hour which will suddenly overtake them unawares?

Say: 'This is the way for me. I call you to God with a clear mind, I and those who follow me. Glory be to God: I am no worshipper of idols.'

Those whom We sent before your time as messengers were simply men whom We inspired from among the people of the cities.

Have they not travelled in the earth to see how those ended up who lived before them? Truly the mansion of the world to come is the better reward of those who hold God in awe. Do you still not understand? The messengers despaired, thinking themselves taken for nothing but liars, until Our help came to their rescue, delivering whom We willed. Evil-doing people do not elude Our power. In their histories is a salutary lesson for those with minds to take it in. This is not some forged tale but a confirmation of previous scriptures, and inclusive explanation, and guidance and mercy to believing people.   *Surah 12.1-111*

JOSEPH came to you earlier with clear evidences but you did not desist from your scepticism about what he brought to you. Indeed, even when he died you said: 'God will send no messenger after him.' Even so God leads astray the spendthrift and the sceptic.   *Surah 40.34*

TO Madyan We sent their brother, Shu'aib, who said: 'My people, worship God and anticipate the last Day: do not behave perversely, working corruption in the land.' But they belied his words. An earthquake overwhelmed them and in the morning they lay lifeless in their dwellings.   *Surah 29.36-37*

137

THOSE who belonged to the forest of Madyan called the messengers liars, when Shu'aib said to them: 'Have you no fear of God? I am a faithful apostle to you: hold God in awe and give me obedient heed. I ask no wage of you on this account, for my reward is only from the Lord of all being. Pay in full measure: do not cheat by stinting: weigh with a true balance: do not defraud people of their due nor behave perversely in the land. Fear the One who created you and the generations of the men of old time.' But they said: 'You are one of those bewitched fellows. You are nothing but a mortal man, like us. Our guess is that you are just a liar. If you are speaking truth, have pieces of the sky fall down on us.' He said: 'My Lord knows well all your doings.'

Thus they denied his words and the retribution of the day of shadow overtook them — the anguish of a dreadful day.

Wherein is a sign, though most men are not believers. Your Lord is ever mighty, ever merciful. *Surah 26.176-191*

TO Madyan We sent Shu'aib, their brother, who said: 'My people, worship God: you have no other god but He. Do not give short measure nor short weight on the scales. Noting your prosperous condition, I fear for you the retribution of a day that will lay siege to you. My people, pay with a true measure and be honest on the scales. Do not defraud people of their goods and do not act corruptly and violently in the land. That which remains with God is better for you, if believers you be. It is not my duty to be your overseer.'

They said: 'Shu'aib, does your form of prayer require you to have us forsake what our fathers worshipped or no longer to do as we like with our possessions — you who are so gentle and right-minded?' 'My people,' he replied, 'Do you not see how it is? here as I am with a clear proof from my Lord who has given me ample provision. I have no desire to be at odds with you by doing the very thing I have forbidden you to do. My sole desire is to set things to rights, to the limit of my ability. In God alone is my fulfilment: in Him I have put my trust and to Him I turn in penitence. My people, on no account let your altercation with me bring down upon you what befell Noah's people, or Hūd's people, or Sālih's people. The people of Lot lived near enough to you! Ask your Lord's forgiveness and turn to Him in repentance. My Lord is merciful and loving.'

They said: 'Shu'aib, we do not get the point of much of what you are saying. We realise that you are a weak fellow in our midst: but for your family we would have stoned you. For you have no clout with us.' He

138

said: 'My people, is my family considered of more force with you than God? Do you cast Him contemptuously behind your backs? My Lord is there where-ever you turn in all you are doing. My people, do what you find within your power: I hold on to my task. You will yet know on whom condign punishment and disgrace will fall and who it is who is a liar. Watch out, then: I am watching with you.'

When Our decree came We delivered Shu'aib and those who believed with him by an act of Our mercy and those wrongdoers — a blast seized them and in the morning they lay lifeless in their dwellings as if they had never lived there. Away with Madyan even as Thamūd was done away!   *Surah 11.84-95*

SHU'AIB, their brother, said to them of Madyan: 'My people, worship God; there is no other god for you but He. A clear sign has come to you from your Lord. Pay full measure and full weight on the scale. Do not let what belongs to others be despoiled in your hands and do not work corruption in this earth, so finely ordered. If you are believers that is the good way for you.'

'Do not lie in wait on every road, threatening and impeding from the way of God those who have believed in Him, wanting to make it out to be a crooked way. Remember how, when you were few, He multiplied you: see what the end was of those who dealt corruptly. If there is a group of you who have believed in what I have been sent to bring you, and a group who have not believed, exercise patience until God shall judge between you, for He is the best of judges.'

The elders of his people in their arrogance said: 'Shu'aib, we will certainly expel you and those with you who have believed from our city, or else you will come back to our community and cult.' To which he replied: 'How so? seeing that we detest your *millah*. We would be making God into a liar were we to return to it after God has delivered us from it. It is not for us to return to it unless God our Lord were to will so. Our Lord embraces all things in His knowledge. In God have we trusted. Our Lord, disclose between us and our people where the truth lies. There is no truth disclosing to match Yours.'   *Surah 7.85-89*

WE will rehearse to you what is told of Moses and Pharaoh — the true account to a people who believe. Pharaoh lorded it over the earth. He made the people of the land into castes. He humiliated one section of the population, slaughtering their male children and letting only the females survive. Pharaoh was a man of evil. Our will was to do grace to the humiliated people in the land, to make them leaders and to bring them into a heritage and into the exercise of power in the land. It was to make Pharaoh and Haman experience, at their hand, the very thing against which their precautions were taken.

We inspired the mother of Moses in a revelation: 'Suckle him, and if you fear for him, lay him in the water: do not be afraid, nor grieve: We will bring him back to you and will make him to be one of the apostles.' The family of Pharaoh took him up—in the event, it was to be a foe and a sorrow to them, sinners as they were, Pharaoh and Haman and their armies. The wife of Pharaoh said: 'Do not put the child to death; he could well be the delight of our eyes, mine and yours. He may give promise of use to us or we might adopt him.' Little did they know what they were doing.

The next morning Moses' mother felt utterly bereft and, had We not fortified her in heart to trust, she could well have disclosed who he was. She said to his sister: 'Go and trail him.' So she watched from a distance, they being unaware she was there. We had already made him to reject the breasts of his nurses when his sister said: 'Shall I lead you to a household who will bring him up for you and take good care of him?' So We restored him to his mother to delight her eyes and banish her sorrows, that she might learn how true is the promise of God—though most men know it not.

When Moses had reached maturity and come to manhood We endued him with wisdom and knowledge. Even so We reward those who deal righteously. He came into the city on one occasion when the people were not noticing. He came across two men fighting each other, one being from his own separate community, the other from a hostile element. The man from his own community besought his help against the other fellow. Moses hit out at him and killed him on the spot. 'This is Satan's handiwork,' cried Moses, 'Satan, an enemy and an arrant deceiver.' And he prayed: 'Lord, I have done wrong against my own soul: forgive me.' Forgive him He did, for He is pardoning and merciful. Moses said: 'My Lord, seeing You have granted me grace I will never come to the help of those who are committing wrong.'

Next morning, when he was walking in the city warily and on the watch, the man who had asked his help the previous day cried out again to him. Whereupon Moses said: 'Quite evidently you are a belligerent fellow!' Moses had in mind to lay hands on the other antagonist, their mutual enemy who then broke in: 'Moses, do you intend to kill me like you killed a man yesterday? Is it your idea to become "big bully" in the

land? Have you no will to help to better things?' At that point there came
a man running from the far end of the city who said: 'Moses, the leading
men are deliberating together to kill you. Take my advice as one who
means you well, get away from here!' So in much apprehension he
departed from there, keeping cautious watch as he went, with the prayer:
'My Lord, keep me safe from these iniquitous people.'

Turning his face in the direction of Madyan, he said: 'Maybe my Lord
will direct me on the right way.' When he reached the waters of Madyan
he found there a large company of men drawing water. Alongside them
he found two women holding back. He said: 'What is the matter?' 'We
may not draw water,' they explained, 'until the herdsmen go off. Our
father is a very old man.' So he drew water for them both and then turned
aside into the shade, praying: 'My Lord, I am surely in need of any good
You may send me.' Then one of them came up to him bashfully and said:
'My father invites you in order to pay you the wage for drawing the
water for us.' When Moses came to him and told him his story the father
said: 'Have no fear: you have escaped from evil-doing folk.' One of the
women said: 'Father, take him as a hired servant: one who is strong and
loyal is the best man for you to have on hire.' The father said: 'It is my
wish to wed you to one of my two daughters on the understanding that
you bind yourself to me for eight years. If you complete ten years, that
will be of your own free will. I have no desire to be exacting with you.
You will find me — God willing — one who deals fairly.' Moses said:
'Let the matter be so between us: whichever of the two periods I fulfill,
there will be no ill-feeling towards me. God has in His trust what has
passed between us.'

When Moses had fulfilled the period and was travelling with his
family, he had sight of a fire on the side of the mountain of Tūr and he
said to his family: 'Stay here! I see a fire: perhaps I will bring you some
word from it or a firebrand for you to warm yourselves.' When he
reached there a voice called to him from the right side of the watercourse
and coming from the bush in the sacred valley: 'Moses, I am God, the
Lord of all being. Throw down your staff.' When he saw it, writhing like
a serpent he drew back and stayed out of reach. 'Moses, come near: do
not be afraid: you are safe enough. Put your hand into your bosom. It
will come out white and untainted. Draw your arm again to your side
unperturbed. For these are two signs from your Lord, to Pharaoh and
his nobles — evil-minded people that they are!' Moses said: 'My Lord, I
have killed a man of theirs and I fear they will kill me. My brother,
Aaron, is a better speaker than I am. Send him with me as an aide to attest
the truth I bring. For I am afraid they will hold me to be a purveyor of

lies.' God said: 'We will make you strong in arm through your brother and endue you both with authority. They will not get you into their clutches. With Our signs you two and those who follow you will be triumphant.' *Surah 28.3-35*

HAVE you had word of the things related to Moses? — he who saw the fire and said to his people: 'You stay here: I see a fire there, perhaps I will take a torch from it, or from the fire will find guidance.' When he came up to it, there was a voice calling him and saying: 'Moses! I am your Lord. Take off your sandals, for you are in the hallowed valley, the valley of Tūwā. I have chosen you: give careful heed to the revelation you receive. I am God: there is no god but Me. Therefore serve Me and be at prayer, celebrating My Name.' *Surah 20.9-14*

HAVE you heard the word of the things relating to Moses — he whose Lord called to him in the hallowed valley of Tūwā? 'Go to Pharaoh, that arch-renegade, and say: "Are you in any mind to be rid of your evil, that I might lead you to your Lord and to a true awe of Him?"' Moses showed him the great sign. But Pharaoh in his disobedience said it was all lies. With precipitate haste he assembled his people and said to them: 'I am your supreme lord.'

But God took hold of him and made him an example of retribution in the next world and in this — all of which is a salutary lesson for who-ever has a mind to fear. *Surah 79.15-26*

WHEN Moses said to his people: 'I see a fire and will bring you word of it, or a firebrand from it as fuel to warm you.' As he came near to it there was a voice saying to him: 'Blessed is He who dwells in the fire and encircles it. Praise be to God, the Lord of all realms of being. Moses, truly I am God, all-strong and all-wise. Throw down your staff.' When he saw it writhing as if it were a snake, he shrank away in retreat and kept well back. But the voice said: 'Moses, have no fear. In My presence those who are commissioned know no fears, only those who have been wrongdoers and after their wrongdoing have come round to the good. I am forgiving and merciful.'

Thrust your hand into your bosom and draw it out again white and cleansed. This will be one of nine signs to Pharaoh and his people — and what an ungodly people they are!'

When in due course Our signs were shown to them before their very eyes, their comment was: 'This is sheer sorcery.' Despite an inward conviction of their truth, they spurned Our signs out of arrogance and perversity. Mark the end which overtakes such workers of iniquity.

Surah 27.7-14

TRULY We sent Moses with Our signs to Pharaoh and his nobles. Moses said: 'I am the messenger of the Lord of all being.' When he did Our signs before them they greeted them with laughter. Every successive sign exceeded the one that preceded it. We afflicted them with chastisement to lead them to a change of heart. Whereupon they said to Moses: 'Magician, by the covenant you have with your Lord ask Him on our behalf and we will surely be dutifully guided.'

But when We gave them respite from affliction they went back on their word. And Pharaoh made a proclamation to his people, saying: 'People of mine, is not the sovereignty of Egypt mine, and the sovereignty of these rivers that flow beneath my feet, as you see with your own eyes? Am I no match for this contemptible fellow who cannot even speak plainly? Why have no braces of gold been lavished on him or any retinue of angels to attend on him?' So he cajoled his people into going along with him in the obduracy of their corrupt ways.

Thus roused to anger, We requited them with a vengeance, drowning the lot of them, so making them a precedent and a lesson to people in subsequent days.

Surah 43.46-56

AFTER them We set up other generations. There is no nation that can bring forward its appointed term nor yet defer it. We sent Our messengers in succession but the retort of each nation to its apostle was to call him a liar. So by Our decree the nations succeeded one another and passed into tales in history. Away, then, with people who do not believe!

Then We sent Moses and his brother, Aaron, with Our signs and a clear mandate to Pharaoh and his nobles. But they reacted with characteristic arrogance, saying: 'Are we to believe two fellows like you, whose tribes are slaves of ours?' So they rejected both of them as liars and passed into the ranks of the doomed. We gave Moses the Book that they might have guidance.

Surah 23.42-49

THERE was an occasion when Moses said to his young servant: 'I will not call a halt until I reach the confluence of the two seas, even if I go on for years on end.' When they reached where the two seas came together they both forgot their fish which got away into the sea through a conduit. After they had proceeded further, Moses said to his servant: 'Bring us our lunch: we are weary from our journey.' He said: 'What do you think! When we halted to rest at the rock, I forgot about the fish and it got away into the sea unaccountably. Only Satan could have made me forget like that!' 'That was the very place we were aiming for,' said Moses. So they went back together, retracing their steps.

There they came upon a servant of Ours, one who had received mercy from Us and whom We had Ourselves taught knowledge that was Ours. Moses addressed him, saying: 'Shall I follow you, on the understanding that you will teach me the right as it has been taught to you?' The other said: 'You will never be able to bear patiently with me. How, in fact, could you take patiently things that have not come within your comprehension?' Moses replied: 'If God wills, you will find me patient: I will not disobey you in anything.' He said: 'If you follow me, do not question me about anything until I myself bring it up in conversing with you.'

So Moses and 'the Lord's servant' journeyed until, embarking on a boat, the latter made a hole in it. Whereupon Moses asked: 'Why have you made a hole in it, as if to drown the people aboard it? It is a mad thing you have done.' To which answer came: 'Did I not say that you would never be able to bear patiently with me?' 'Pardon me for forgetting,' Moses replied. 'Do not be hard on me for interjecting as I did.' So they went on further until they encountered a youth. 'The Lord's servant' killed him. Moses cried: 'You have slain an innocent life and that not in any life-for-life retaliation. You have committed a terrible deed.' 'Did I not tell you,' came answer 'that you would never be able to bear patiently with me?' Moses said: 'If I question you from now on, stay no longer with me: you have every excuse.' They went on from there until they came to some townspeople from whom they asked food. The people refused to give them any hospitality. They found a wall there which was on the point of falling down. 'The Lord's servant' built it up again. Moses commented: 'Had you wanted to, you could have obtained a wage for that.' He said: 'This is where you and I go our separate ways! I will interpret for you the things you have had no patience for. As for the boat, it belonged to some poor men, working seafarers, for whom I wanted to make it unseaworthy because of a king who was on their track forcibly seizing all boats. As for the youth, his parents were believers and we had a fear that he would afflict them by wickedness and unbelief. We desired their Lord to give them in exchange a son purer than he and more tenderhearted. As for the wall — it belonged to two orphan boys in the town. Beneath it lay a treasure of theirs. Their father had been a godly man. Their Lord wanted them to come to full age and, by their Lord's mercy, take out their treasure. I did not act on my own orders. Such is the interpretation of things you were unable to take with patience.'

Surah 18.60-82

WE brought Moses the Book, an entire *Vade mecum* for the well-doer, an elucidation of all things, and guidance and mercy. It may be they will believe in the encounter with their Lord. *Surah 6.154*

AND to Moses We gave nine clear signs. Ask (s.) the people of Israel about Moses coming to them and how Pharaoh said to him: 'Moses, it is my opinion that you are bewitched.' To which Moses answered: 'You know very well that the signs you are seeing come from none other than the Lord of the heavens and of the earth and are entirely clear as evidences, and my opinion about you, Pharaoh, is that you are hellbound.'

Then Pharaoh set his heart on ridding the land of them. But We brought him and all who were with him into a watery grave. And to the people of Israel afterward We said: 'Dwell in the land and when the last Day comes as promised We will muster you to meet it.'

Surah 17.101-104

WE dealt graciously with Moses and Aaron and delivered both them and their people from great tribulation. By Our aid they emerged triumphant. We gave the two brothers the Book that makes things clear and We guided them in the path of right and left for them this greeting among posterity: 'Peace be on Moses and Aaron.' Even so do We reward the well-doers: the two of them were numbered among Our believing servants. *Surah 37.114-122*

THE Hour, truly, is coming — My choice is to keep its time hidden — that every soul may have reward of its efforts. Let no one who refuses belief in it and follows his own desires deter you (s.) from faith in it, lest you perish.

What is that, Moses, in your right hand? 'It is my staff,' he replied, 'on which I lean and with which I beat down leaves for my sheep, and I have many other uses for it too.' He said: 'Throw it down, Moses.' So he threw it down and it was a writhing serpent. He said: 'Take it up: do not fear. We will return it to its original state. Now place your hand inside your armpit: it will come out white and unblemished — yet another sign — to have you see some of Our supreme revelations. Go to Pharaoh, tyrant as he is.' Moses said: 'Lord, enlarge my heart and ease my task for me: loosen the knot in my tongue that they may understand what I say. Assign for me, from my own folk, one to share my burden — Aaron my brother: reinforce my strength through him and let him be my associate in the task before me, to the end we may multiply Your praise and our remembrance of You. For Your eye is upon us.'

He said: 'Moses, you are granted what you ask. Already on another occasion We have granted you Our good grace, when We inspired your mother in a revelation: "Lay him in the ark and place it in the water and the river will deposit it upon the bank and an enemy will pick him up — My enemy and his." I made you the object of My love, to have you reared under My eye. Your sister presented herself and said: "Shall I direct you to someone to be a nurse for him?" Thus We restored you to your mother, to gladden her eye and assuage her sorrow. You slew a man and We saved you in distress and tested you repeatedly. You spent years among the people of Madyan. And now, Moses, you have come to this juncture: for I have chosen you for Myself. Go — you and your brother — with Our signs and be unfaltering in recollection of Me. Go, both of you, to Pharaoh, the oppressor, though speak gently to him: it may be he will occupy his mind with what you say or register some fear.'

They said: 'Our Lord, we are afraid he will take prompt action against us or subject us to violence.' God said: 'Have no fear, you two: I am with you: I hear and I see. So go together to Pharaoh and say: "We are messengers of your Lord. Send the children of Israel with us: afflict them no longer. We have come to you with a sign from your Lord. Peace to him who follows the guidance. It has been revealed to us that retribution awaits those who count it false and turn away."' Pharaoh retorted: 'Who is this Lord, Moses?' He said: 'Our Lord is He who gave to everything that is its created form and then granted guidance.' Pharaoh said: 'What, then, of the former generations?' 'Knowledge of them is with my Lord in a book. My Lord never errs and never forgets. He has made the earth for you as a cradle, traced out roads there for you, and caused rain to come down from heaven. Thereby We have produced a variety of plants. So eat and pasture your cattle. For in these things are signs for those with intelligent perception. We created you from the earth, to the earth We bring you again and a second time bring you forth from it.' Thus did We show Pharaoh all Our signs. He denied they were true and rejected them all saying: 'Have you come, Moses, to drive us out of our land with your magic? We can present you with magic matching your own. Arrange an encounter between us, both of us pledged to it without fail, at a mutually convenient place.'

'Let the encounter you suggest be on Festival Day,' said Moses, 'and let the people be gathered at noon.' Whereupon Pharaoh withdrew and came back having resolved on what his magicians would do. Moses said to them: 'Woe be to you! Do not perpetrate some lie on God, lest He visit you with dire penalty. Every forger is confounded.' They fell into contention about their scheme but kept their counsel secret, saying: 'These two are magicians whose desire is to expel you from your land by their magic and to do away with your cherished way of life. Get your act together and proceed in concert. This day's success goes to those who get the mastery.' They said: 'Moses, either you throw first, or we will.' To which he replied: 'No! you be the first to throw.' Their ropes and their staves seemed to him to be conjured into motion by their wizardry and Moses became inwardly apprehensive. We said: 'Have no fear: you will have the upper hand. Throw what you have in your right hand. It will quickly swallow up their feat — a feat accomplished only by sorcerer's guile, such as never prospers anywhere.'

Their magicians were obliged to fall down in prostration saying: 'We believe in the Lord of Moses and Aaron.' Pharaoh broke in: 'You have believed in Him before you had leave from me? This man must be your supremo, the man who taught you magic! I will cut off your hands and feet on alternate sides and crucify you on the trunks of palm trees, and you will certainly discover whose punishment is the more fearsome and prolonged.' They replied: 'We will never set more store by you than by the clear evidences that have come to us and the One who fashioned us. Decree what you will decree: you will only be arbiter concerning the life of this present world. We have believed in our Lord that He may forgive us our sins and also the sorcery which you have compelled us to practise. God is the better Lord, eternally abiding.'

Whoever comes to his Lord in his sinfulness, his will be *Jahannam* where he will neither die nor live. Whoever comes to Him as a believer who has done righteously there await such the highest stations, the gardens of Eden where streams flow below and where they dwell eternally in the reward of those who attain to purity.

Moses We inspired, saying: ' Go forth with My servants by night and strike open for them a dry path in the sea: do not fear to be overtaken: have no fear at all.' Pharaoh pursued after them with his armies and they were overwhelmed by the sea. Far from guiding them, Pharaoh led his people astray.

Children of Israel! We rescued you from your enemy and made covenant with you on the right side of the mountain. We sent manna and quails down upon you, saying: 'Eat of the good things with which We have provided you. Do not do so to excess and My anger comes upon you. He is lost indeed on whom My wrath alights. To him who repents and believes, does righteously and then keeps to the right way, I am truly forgiving.'

'Moses, what has brought you in such haste away from your people?' He said: 'They are keeping to my way: I hastened to You my Lord for the sake of Your good pleasure.' God said: 'In your absence We have put your people to the test and *Al-Sāmirī* has led them astray.' Moses returned to his people in anger and sorrow of heart. 'My people,' he said, 'did not your Lord make a generous promise to you? Why have you broken pledge with me? Was I too long away from you, as it seemed to you, or did you intend to invite your Lord's wrath upon you?' They said: 'We have not broken pledge with you by our own will. The ornaments of the people weighed us down like a load, so we threw them into the fire, just as *Al-Sāmirī* did also.' He brought out to them a calf's effigy which made a lowing sound. Whereupon they said: 'This is your god, the erstwhile god of Moses whom he has forgotten.' Had they no eyes for the fact that it made no response to them, that it had no power at all to hurt or profit? Aaron had already said to them: 'My people you have been put to the test by this idol. But your Lord is the merciful One: follow me and do as I say.' But they said: 'Until Moses comes back to us we will never suspend our devotion to it.'

And Moses said: 'Aaron, what held you back from keeping loyally to me when you saw them going astray? Have you deliberately flouted my command?' Aaron said: 'Son of my mother, do not seize me by the beard, nor by the head! I was afraid that you would say I had caused division among the children of Israel and I had failed to keep your word.' 'And you, *Al-Sāmirī*,' Moses said, 'what have you to say for yourself?' 'I had seen,' he said, 'something unseen to them. At the prompting of my soul, I picked up a handful of dust from the pathway of the messenger and cast it away.' 'Begone,' Moses cried, 'all your life your fate will be to say: "Touch me not" and a tryst awaits you you cannot fail to keep. Look on that god of yours, whose devotee you have sedulously been! We will burn it to ashes and scatter them on the sea. God is God only:

there is no other god but He. Within His knowledge He embraces all things.'

Thus We relate to you (s.) histories of what happened in the past. We have given you from Our presence a *dhikr*.   *Surah 20.15-99*

BEFORE these We put to the test the people of Pharaoh. A kindly apostle came to them saying: 'Yield up to me God's servants: I am a faithful apostle to you. Do not set yourselves up over God. I come to you with clear authority. I have taken refuge with my Lord, and your Lord, should you think to stone me. If you do not believe me, at least let me be.' He called on his Lord saying: 'These are a sin-guilty people.'

'Set forth with My servants by night: you will be pursued hard. Leave the sea parted behind you: the host of them will be drowned.'

How many a garden, how many a fountain did they leave behind them, farm-fields and fine dwelling-places and that fine style of life in which they so delighted! So it befell and We made another people to inherit it. Neither heaven nor earth wept for them. For them there was no reprieve.   *Surah 44.17-29*

ONLY a few sons of his people believed in Moses, given the fear of Pharaoh and his nobles and the risk of persecution. For Pharaoh was in total dominance in the land and given to extreme measures.

Moses said: 'My people, if you have truly believed in God then put your trust in Him, if surrendered you are!' They said: 'In God have we trusted. Lord, do not let the evil people be incited against us by our presence: deliver us in Your mercy from those who reject faith.' We inspired Moses and his brother to set aside houses for their people in Egypt. 'Make your houses a *qiblah* for direction of prayer and perform the prayer-rite, and do you, Moses, give glad word to the believers.' Moses said: 'Our Lord, You have bestowed adornments and possessions on Pharaoh and his nobles in this present life. Lord, cause them to err from Your path: Lord, bring their wealth to nothing: harden their hearts so that they do not believe 'ere they see the pain of retribution.' He said: 'Answered is your prayer. Go on together in the straight path: follow not in the way of those who have no knowledge.'

We conveyed the children of Israel through the sea. Pharaoh and his armies followed after them in hot, impetuous pursuit until, on the point of drowning, Pharaoh cried: 'I believe that there is no god but He in whom the children of Israel believe. I, too, am with those who yield to Him.'

What? Now! you who were up to this point a rebel, one of the foul dealers? This day We will save your body to be a sign to those who come after you. Mankind for the most part takes no heed of the things We reveal.'

We settled the children of Israel in a secure abode and replenished them with good things. They did not fall into contention until knowledge came to them. Your (s.) Lord will judge between them on the Day of resurrection concerning the issues on which they differed.

Surah 10.83-93

WHEN Moses came to them with Our clear signs they said: 'This is nothing but contrived sorcery. We have never heard of such as this in the time of our fathers of old.' And Moses said: 'My Lord knows who it is who brings guidance from His presence and whose, eventually, will be the blest abode. Those who do wickedly will not come to good.'

Pharaoh said: 'Lords of the council, I did not know that you had any god but me. Haman, fire a kiln for me with clay and erect for me a very high tower in order that I may get a view of the god of Moses. I reckon he is just a liar!'

He and his armies lorded it proudly over the earth. Defying truth and right, they supposed that they would have no summons back to Us. We seized him and his forces and threw them into the sea. Look (s.) what the end was of the workers of evil. We made them *imāms*, leaders calling to the Fire. On the Day of resurrection there will be none to help them. In this world We had a curse following them and on the Day of resurrection they will be utterly disowned.

After We had destroyed the earlier generations We gave Moses the Book, scriptures to illuminate mankind, guidance and mercy. It may be they will give their minds to thinking.   *Surah 28.36-43*

THE chief men of Pharaoh's people said to him: 'Are you going to let Moses and his people spread their evil round the land? Will you let him flout you and your gods?' He said: 'We will kill their sons and spare their women folk. We have the mastery over them.'

To his people Moses said: 'Ask help of God: endure patiently. The earth is God's and whom He wills of His servants He makes to inherit it. The issue is with those who truly fear God.' The children of Israel said:

'Before you came to us we suffered oppression and it is the same since your arrival among us.' He said: 'It may be that your Lord is going to make your enemy perish and establish you in the land, with a view to seeing how you act.'

We afflicted Pharaoh with years of dearth and scarcity of fruits on the chance they might take thought. When things were good with them they said: 'This is our right.' But when bad times befell them they divined it was because of Moses and his companions, whereas the augury of the ill they divined was God's, though the majority of them had no realisation of that.

They said: 'Bring what sign you will to mesmerise us, we will in no case believe you.' We released the flood upon them, and the locusts, the lice, the frogs and the blood — signs evident enough. Overweening in their arrogance, they proved an iniquitous people. When disaster struck they called to Moses: 'Cry to your Lord for us by the covenant He has with you: if you turn back the plague from us we will believe in you and surely send the children of Israel away with you.' But when the calamity was lifted off them for a period in which they might attain to do so, they broke their word. We took revenge on them, drowning them in the sea, because they denied Our revelations and paid them no heed.

The people who were oppressed We made to inherit the land of Our benediction, from east to west of it, thus fulfilling the good word of your Lord to the people of Israel, after all the hardships they endured. The construction works of Pharaoh and his people We razed to the ground.

We brought the people of Israel across the sea, where they encountered a people who were devotees of idols. Whereupon they said to Moses: 'Make a god for us just as they have gods.' To which he replied: 'What witless folk you are! This kind of thing on their part has doom written all over it. What they do is utter futility.' And he went on: 'Shall I desire a god for you other than God Himself who has graced you above all peoples?'

It is We who delivered you from the people of Pharaoh when they were afflicting such tribulation upon you, putting your sons to death and letting only the girls live — all of which was a bitter affliction your Lord allowed.

We kept rendezvous with Moses through thirty nights. Then ten more We added to make forty nights in all — the appointed time of communion with his Lord. Moses said to his brother, Aaron: 'Deputise for me among my people with an honest heart: have no truck with evil ways.'

When Moses came to rendezvous with his Lord who talked with him, these were Moses's words: 'My Lord, let me see and look upon You.'

But He said: 'Me you will never see. Look upon the mountain: see Me you might were the mountain itself to stay firm in its place.' For when His Lord appeared in glory before the mountain it crumbled into dust and Moses collapsed in a swoon. When he came to, he cried: 'Glory be to You! In my penitence let me be the first to believe.' And He said: 'Moses, I have chosen you before all people by virtue of these words and directives of Mine. Receive, then, what I have imparted to you and be altogether grateful.'

On the tablets We inscribed for him an inclusive set of detailed precepts and said: 'Take it with both hands! Command your people to make its excellence their own. You will soon be made to realise where and what ungodliness is. Those who behave presumptuously in the land I will turn from My signs. For were they to register each one of them they would not believe them as signs. To see the way of true living is not, in their case, to adopt it, while readily enough they follow the path of evil, knowing it to be such. It is so with them because they call Our signs lies and pay them no heed. Those who repudiate Our signs and scout the judgement to come bring all their doings to futility. Can their fate be other than their own devising?'

While Moses was away his people adopted a calf, made out of their ornaments — a shape realistic enough to low! But never a word could it say to them, obviously. As for being any guidance to them, manifestly not. Yet in their hearts they made a god of it.

When, with much wringing of hands, they realised their wayward-ness, they cried out: 'Unless there is mercy for us from our Lord and He forgives us, we are surely lost.'

When Moses returned to his people in anger and sorrow he said to them: 'What wretched behaviour is this, while I was out of the way! Do you want to bring down upon yourselves the sudden doom of your Lord?' He threw down the tablets and, seizing his brother by the hair, dragged him to him, while Aaron shouted: 'Son of my mother, it was the people who forced my hand: they would have killed me. Do not give your enemies that satisfaction and treat me as an evil-doer like them.' And Moses prayed: 'Lord, forgive me, and forgive my brother and take us into Your mercy. For You are the very paragon of mercy.'

Those who took the calf for their worship, the wrath of their Lord will be upon them and in this present world they will bear the shame. For so do We requite those who work falsehood. But those who turned afterward from their evil deeds in repentance, and who believe, on them in the sequel your Lord is truly forgiving and merciful.

When Moses's anger cooled, he took up the tablets. Their text is guidance and mercy for those who stand in awe of their Lord. From among the people Moses chose seventy men to come with him to the time of meeting before God. When the mountain quaked around them Moses cried: 'My Lord, there have been occasions 'ere now for You to have caused them and me to perish, had You so willed. Will you destroy us now because of what has been done by some of our people in their folly? Surely, rather, You are putting us to the test and, according to Your will, some will go into error while others will be rightly guided. You are our guardian. Forgive us in Your mercy: there is no forgiveness like Yours.'

Appoint what is good for us in this world and in the hereafter. Truly we have turned to You. He said: 'Whom I will I strike with My retribution. My mercy embraces all things. I decree it upon those who are God-fearing, who bring the *Zakat* and give credence to Our signs.'

Surah 7.127-156

QĀRŪN (Korah) belonged to the people of Moses. The way he treated them was outrageous. We had brought him wealth such that even a band of ten or so strong men would have found his treasure-chests too heavy to carry. When his people said to him: 'Do not take such joy over what you own. God has no love for gloaters. Rather aim to possess what God has given you with a mind for the eternal mansion, not forgetting your lot in this present world. Be as generous as God has been to you, and not desirous of what corrupts the world. God is no lover of people given to corruption.'

He said: 'What I have come by stems from know-how of my own.' Did he not realise that God had made other generations before him to perish — people who were far stronger than he and who had amassed much greater wealth? Did he imagine that wicked doers would not be questioned about their sins?

He went out before his people in his splendid array. Those set on the life of this present world said: 'Would we had been given what Qārūn enjoys! He is a very lucky fellow.' Those, however, possessed with knowledge said: 'Woe to you! God's reward is better far for the believer, the well-doer. None but the patient will attain to it. We caused the earth to engulf both him and his house. There were none to come to his aid against God and he was powerless to aid himself. In the morning those who had longed to be in his shoes only the day before were saying: 'Ah well! God extends His provision to whom He wills among His servants or stints it. Had God not been gracious to us He would have engulfed us also. See! Those who deny the truth never come to good.'

Surah 28.76-82

QĀRŪN, Pharaoh and Haman — Moses came to them with clear proofs. Arrogantly they thought themselves the great of the earth, Us they could not elude. In their sin We seized each of them. There were those of them against whom We sent a mighty hurricane: others were overtaken by the cry of doom, others We engulfed in the earth, others again We drowned. It was not God who did them wrong: it was their own selves they wronged. *Surah 29.39-40*

MOSES said to his people: 'My people, remember the grace of God towards you, in ordaining prophets among you and in making kings for you, giving you what no others in the world have received. My people, enter into the holy land, which God has decreed for you. Give no thought to retreat, for then total loss would overtake you.'

But they said: 'Moses, there are mighty warriors there. We will never enter into the land unless they evacuate it. Only after departing will we venture in.' However, there were two of their numbers, God-fearers, on whom God's grace rested, who declared: 'Break in on them by the gate and, once inside, the victory will be yours. In God be your trust, if you be men of faith.'

The people still said: 'Moses, on no account will we enter as long as they are there inside. You go if you wish, and that Lord of yours, and do battle together. We stay sitting here!' Whereupon Moses said: 'My Lord, I can command only myself and my brother in this situation. You must decide the issue between me and this gutless people.' The Lord said: 'Very well, the land is proscribed to them for forty years, while they roam around in the earth. Do not distress yourself over this shiftless people.' *Surah 5.20-26*

FROM the people of Moses there has been a community giving guidance according to truth and in justice proceeding by it. We divided them into twelve tribes, or nations, and We inspired Moses when his people besought him for water: 'Strike the rock with your staff,' and twelve founts of water flowed out from it, and all the people knew the place where they should drink. We made the clouds to overshadow them and sent the manna down to them and the quails, saying: 'Eat of the good things wherewith We have provided you.' It was not Us they wronged; it was their own selves.

'Dwell in this city,' they were told, 'eat what you will there and Say: "*Hittatun!*" Go through the gate with prostration: We will forgive your sins and give the well-doers increase.' But the evil-bent among them changed the word they were told to say from the one they were given. We visited them with wrath from heaven for their evil doings.

Ask (s.) then about the city beside the sea and how its people used to break the Sabbath when their fish came easily detected in the water on their Sabbaths but did not present themselves on other than Sabbath days. By their own transgressions We made trial of them.

When an element among them said: 'Why are you (pl.) preaching to a people whom God is about to destroy or sternly to punish?' To which they replied: 'In order to be clear of guilt before your Lord and on the chance they may become God-fearing.' When they forgot the warning they had been reminded of, We delivered those who counselled against evil and We seized the wrong-doers with a fearful retribution on account of their foul ways and doings. When they remained proudly obdurate in forbidden things We pronounced them: 'Apes, detestable!'

Your (s.) Lord declared He would surely raise up against them those who, until the Day of resurrection, would afflict them cruelly. Your Lord is swift to retribution, yet He is forgiving and merciful.

We divided them into nations dispersed in the earth: some were righteous and some quite otherwise. We put them to the test with good and evil things in hope they would turn back from their ways. They were followed by other generations inheriting the Book, who regaled themselves with the things of this present world, saying: 'It will be forgiven us.' If a similar chance were to present itself they would take it. Was not the covenant of the Book binding on them that they should speak only the truth concerning God? They have studied its contents. The eternal mansion is better for those who fear God: will you not then see reason? As for those who hold firmly to the Book and fulfill the prayer, We will not let the reward of the righteous be lost.

We made the mount to shake over them, as if it had been a shadow, and they imagined it was falling on them. 'Take firm hold on what We have revealed to you and remember its contents, that you may prove truly God-fearing.'   *Surah 7.159-171*

MOSES said to his people: 'God commands you to sacrifice a cow.' They said: 'Are you having fun with us?' 'God forbid!' he replied, 'I seek refuge with God from such ignorant stupidity!' They said: 'Pray to your Lord for us to make clear to as what sort of cow.' Moses answered: 'He directs that the cow is to be neither old nor a heifer, but between. So do as you are commanded.' They said further: 'Pray to your Lord for us to

155

make clear what her colour has to be.' He replied: 'He indicates that she is to be a golden cow, of bright colour to delight the eyes.' They said: 'Pray to your Lord for us to make clear to us what else about her has to be. For to us cows are all much alike and — please God — we want to have it right!' Moses answered: 'He says she is to be a cow that has not been broken-in to plough the land nor to water the tillage, one fully sound and unblemished.' They replied: 'Now you have brought the full truth.' They sacrificed the cow though — with such equivocation — they had almost not done so.   *Surah 2.67-71*

HAVE you not thought on the elders of the sons of Israel after the time of Moses, who said to a prophet of theirs: 'A king is what we want from you, and we will go to war in the way of God.' He replied: 'May it well be that you would not in fact go out to fight were you ordered so to do?' They said: 'Should we not indeed fight in God's way when we have been driven from our homes and children?' When, however, they were enjoined to do battle, all but a few of them turned away. God knew well those with the wrong at their door. Their prophet said to them: 'God has given you Tālūt (Saul) as your king.' They responded: 'How can he have the kingship over us when we have more right to rule than he. He, moreover, has not come by any surfeit of wealth!' The prophet replied: 'God has chosen him to be over you and has given him excellent wisdom and a superb physique! God assigns dominion to whom He wills — God who embraces all things within His knowledge.' Their prophet said further: 'As a sign of his kingship, the ark will be brought to you in which resides a *Sakīnah* (presence) of your Lord, one of the surviving legacies of the families of Moses and Aaron, the ark the angels carry. It is indeed a sign for you — if believers you are.'

When Saul set out with his forces, he said: 'God puts you now to the test at a river. He who stops to drink at it does not belong with me, while he who does not take the water — unless it be a mere handful as he goes — he is my man.' All but a few did in fact take a real drink.

After he had crossed the river, he and those who kept faith with him, the others said: 'We have no strength to prevail against Goliath and his forces today.' But those with a sense of their rendezvous with God said: 'How often the few have overcome the many, by leave of God. God is with those who endure with patience.' When they were face to face with Goliath and his forces they prayed: 'Our Lord, give us resources of patience, make us to stand firm and aid us against those who deny the truth.' By leave of God they put them to rout. David slew Goliath and

God gave him the kingship and wisdom and taught him the things He willed. Had not God repulsed some by the might of others the earth would have been subject to corruption. But God is beneficent to all sentient beings.   *Surah 2.246-251*

BEAR patiently with what they say and remember Our servant David, a valorous man and a great penitent. In him We recruited to Our praise the very mountains at the fall of day and at the sunrising, and the birds also mustering in flight, each echoing his song.

We made his kingdom strong and gave him wisdom and forthrightness in word. Have you heard the story of the intruders who broke into his private sanctuary after climbing the wall? David was startled, but they said: 'Have no fear. We are two men with a quarrel about an injury one has done the other. Judge between us rightly and impartially: guide us to what is fair.'

'My brother here,' said the one, 'has ninety-nine ewes and I have only one. He demanded that I yield it up to him. He got the better of me in the quarrel.'

David said: 'He has surely done you wrong in demanding your one ewe to add to his own. How often it is so, where there are transactions between men and they wrong each other. Only believers and those who act righteously are not that way, and they are few indeed.'

Then it came to David as he thought that the incident was a test on Our part and he asked forgiveness from his Lord, falling down on his knees in penitence. We forgave him what he had done. Truly he has an honoured place before us and stands well in Our sight.

'David, We have appointed you as a viceroy in the earth. Therefore, judge rightly between men. Do not give way to passion, lest it divert you from the path of God. For those who stray from God's path, forgetting the Day of reckoning, incur a stern retribution.'   *Surah 38.17-26*

YOUR (s.) Lord knows all in the heavens and in the earth. We have graced some prophets above others. To David We gave the *Zabūr* (the Psalms).   *Surah 17.55*

WHEN David and Solomon gave judgement in the case of the cultivated field into which people had allowed their sheep to stray, We endorsed their verdict, Solomon resolving the matter with the fuller understanding

We gave him. Both David and Solomon We imbued with wisdom and knowledge. We recruited the mountains with David to celebrate praise, and the birds likewise. All was Our doing.   *Surah 21.78-79*

To David We gave Solomon — an excellent servant he! and a penitent too. For when one evening his prancing horses were paraded before him, he confessed: 'My love for good things is dear to me because of my remembrance of my Lord.' When the veil of darkness fell he said: 'Bring them back to me.' And he began to stroke their shanks and to pass his hand over their necks.

Solomon certainly We tested, placing on his throne a replica body. In penitence Solomon prayed: 'My Lord, pardon me and grant me a kingdom such as none after me will exercise. Yours it is to bestow.'

For Solomon We harnessed the winds to blow softly at his bidding and according to his direction. We pressed into his service demons, builders too and divers, and others fettered in chains. 'All this is Our gift to you — yours to disburse or to withhold unreservedly.' Truly he has an honoured place before Us and he stands well in Our sight.

                                                                        Surah 38.30-40

Upon David We bestowed Our bounty. 'Mountains, echo praises with him, and birds!' We made iron pliant to his hand, bidding it produce coats of mail, taking care to see the links were well proportioned. 'Make a sound job,' We said, 'there is a divine inspection!'

For Solomon We called the wind into service, its morning and its evening course each a month's journey. We made a fount of molten brass to flow for him and the jinn were put to work for him by leave of his Lord, while those who evaded Our commandment were made to taste the torment of *al-Sa'ir*. The jinn made for him whatever he pleased — sanctuaries, and images, bowls as big as watering-troughs, and cauldrons built into the ground. 'To the work, O house of David, thankfully!' Few are they of My servants who are thankful.   *Surah 34.10-13*

Knowledge We bestowed on David and Solomon. They said: 'Praise be to God who has dignified us above many of His believing servants.' Solomon was the heir of David. He told his people: 'We have been taught the language of the birds and everything has come our way — all quite evidently a signal favour!'

Solomon's armies of jinn and men and birds were mustered before him, proceeding in due order. When they came to the valley of the ants an ant cried: 'Ants! get into your anthills lest you be crushed, all unawares, by Solomon and his armies.' But Solomon broke into a smile, laughing over what she said and remarking: 'My Lord, give me a heart to be grateful for Your grace lavished on me and on my parents and to do what is good and well-pleasing to You. Let me, of Your mercy, come into the ranks of Your righteous servants.'

Then he inspected the birds, saying: 'How is it I do not see the *hudhud* (the lapwing). Is it not here? I will certainly punish him sternly or kill him outright, if he fails to bring me an excuse, clear and plain.' But the lapwing was not long in coming and he told Solomon: 'I have got to know something you have not yourself known. I have come to you from Sabā' with news on sure authority. There I found a woman, who rules as their queen, and who possesses everything. Hers is a superb throne. I found her and her people worshipping the sun instead of God. Satan has made them highly enamoured of what they do and so debarred them from the path of God. They are not rightly guided so that they fail to worship God — God who brings forth things hidden in the heavens and in the earth, who knows what you hide away and what you disclose. God: there is no god but He, the Lord of the great throne.'

Solomon said: 'We will see whether what you report is true or whether you have been a party to lies. Go with this letter of mine and deliver it to them. Then wait aside and see what reply they make.'

The queen said: 'My lords, an auspicious letter has been delivered to me. It is from Solomon and written "in the Name of God, the merciful Lord of mercy," who bids us: "Do not exalt yourselves against Me but come to Me, surrendering (as *muslims*)."' She said further: 'My lords, give a ruling in this issue before me: only on your evidence is it my wont to decide things.' They said: 'Powerful lords and men of prowess indeed we are, but the matter is in your hands. So consider what you are going to decree.' She replied: 'Kings have a way of entering into some city and despoiling it, humiliating its strongest citizens. They do that sort of thing. I will send a gift to them and wait to see what response the envoys bring back.'

Solomon said when the envoy came: 'Do you mean to offer wealth to me? — me to whom God has given what is better far than what He has granted you? Indeed, you even take delight in your present! Go back to them. We are coming on with forces they cannot resist. We will surely drive them out ignominiously and they will be made despicable.' He asked his nobles: 'Which of you will bring her throne to me before they come to me surrendering?'

An *'ifrīt* from among the jinn declared: 'I will bring it to you even before you rise up from where you sit. I am strong enough for the task and trustworthy.' One in his presence who was well-versed in the Book said: 'I will bring it to you in a twinkling.' When Solomon saw the throne before him he said: 'This is my Lord's goodness. He was testing me, whether I would give thanks or whether I would be a thankless unbeliever. He who gives thanks finds it to his soul's health: he who is thankless and unbelieving — God, my Lord, is altogether rich and bounteous.' Solomon said: 'Disguise the throne for her: let us see whether she is rightly led or not.' When she arrived she was asked: 'Is your throne like this one?' She replied: 'It seems the very one.' Solomon observed: 'Those other worships she practised apart from God impeded her, being among unbelieving people: we had knowledge brought to us before her and we were surrendered.'

She was told: 'Enter the palace.' But when she saw it, she supposed it to be a lake of water and she bared her legs. Solomon said: 'It is a palace paved with glass.' 'Lord,' she said, 'I have sinned against my own soul. With Solomon I have now surrendered to God, the Lord of all being.'

Surah 27.15-44

AND when We decreed that Solomon should die the only indication to them of his death was when he collapsed after worms had gnawed away at his staff. The jinn then realised that had they known what was concealed from them they would not have gone on toiling in the pain of abject humiliation. *Surah 34.14*

ELIJAH, too, was among those who were sent as messengers. He said to his people: 'Have you no fear of God? Would you call upon Baal and turn away your only and blessed Creator? God is your Lord, and the Lord of your fathers of old.' But they rejected his words as lies and were surely brought to book — as all are except the sincere worshippers of God.

In later generations We left to Elijah the tribute by which We reward those who do well, namely: 'Peace be on *Ilyāsīn*.' Truly he was one of Our believing servants. *Surah 37.123-132*

REMEMBER Ishmael and Elisha and *Dhū-l-Kifl* (he who pledged himself), each of them numbered among those who excel. *Surah 38.48*

REMEMBER Ishmael and Idrīs and *Dhū-l-Kifl*, each of them numbered among those who endure. We brought them into Our mercy. For they were numbered among the righteous. *Surah 21.85-86*

IF you (s.) are in doubt about what We have revealed to you, enquire of those who read the Book before you. The truth has indeed come to you from your Lord. So do not for a moment include yourself with the sceptical, nor with those who say nothing but 'No!' to the signs of their Lord, so as to lose all.

Those who do not believe, though there come to them every sign right up to the vision of their own doom, it is against them that the word of your Lord is fulfilled. One city alone there was which believed with a faith that availed to save them. This was the community of Jonah. When they believed We spared them the humiliation that would otherwise have requited them in this present world and We granted them a breathing space. If your Lord had so willed, all earth's people together would have believed. And you (s.), would you exert pressure to constrain people to faith? *Surah 10.94-99*

JONAH too was among those who were sent as messengers. He fled to the cargo vessel and, after the casting of lots, it was he — hapless one — on whom it fell. The great fish opened its mouth upon him, upon him who bore the blame. Had Jonah not been a man devoutly given to the praise of God, he would have stayed in its belly until resurrection Day.

But We cast him, in a sickly condition, upon a deserted beach where We caused a tree of gourds to grow over him. Then We sent him to a city with a population a hundred thousand strong, or more. They believed, and so We gave them respite for a while. *Surah 37.140-148*

BE patient under your (s.) Lord's disposing and do not be like the one who figured in the story of the great fish, who cried out in the pent-up emotions within himself. Had not his Lord's act of mercy supervened he would have been cast forth upon the desert shore with all his sins upon him. His Lord chose him and set him among the righteous. *Surah 68.48-50*

REMEMBER *Dhū-l-Nūn* (Jonah) who went away in anger supposing We were powerless concerning him. He cried out in the darkness: 'There is no god but You: glory be to You. I have been an evil-doer.' And so We hearkened to him and rescued him from his anguish. Even so do We save those who believe. *Surah 21.87-88*

WE brought Moses the Scripture, making it guidance for the sons of Israel, saying: 'Take none for your reliance other than Me, you who are the progeny of those whom We embarked with Noah — a grateful servant he!' In the Book We predicted to the sons of Israel: 'Twice over you will work corruption in the earth and indeed reach very high.' When on the first occasion this warning was fulfilled. We sent to you, in their fierce warlike prowess, a people in Our service who penetrated through all your habitations, and thus the prediction was realised. Afterwards We gave you once again the chance to prevail against them: We increased you in wealth and in offspring and gave you a larger army. If you act rightly it is for your own good that you do so: if you work evil you will be working it on yourselves.

When the second prediction came about, We sent others in Our service to shame your very faces, entering the house of worship, just as they did the first time, and utterly destroying everything they overran.

Your Lord may yet have mercy on you. If you revert to evil We will repeat the requital. *Jahannam* We have ordained to be a gaol for unbelievers. *Surah 17.2-8*

REMEMBER, too, Our servant *Ayyūb* (Job) and how he called to his Lord, saying: 'Satan has afflicted me with pain and tribulation.' And We said to him: 'Strike the ground hard with your foot. There is water here, cool water, for you to wash and drink.'

We granted him his new family comparably with the first as an act of Our mercy and an admonition to perceptive men. 'Take in your hand a bundle of rushes to strike with and do not go back upon your oath.' So We found Job a steadfast soul. How fine a servant he! — and a true penitent. *Surah 38.41-44*

HAVE in mind how *Ayyūb* called to his Lord: 'Calamity has befallen me and Yours is the mercy that transcends all others.' We heard his prayer and gave him relief from privation and We brought him his new family comparably with the first as an act of Our mercy and for worshipping people to keep in remembrance. *Surah 21.83-84*

IN succession to them by Our will Our messengers came and Jesus too, the son of Mary, We caused to come after them. To him We brought the Gospel (*al-Injīl*). In the hearts of those who became his disciples we set kindliness and mercy. *Surah 57.27a*

ONE who guarded her chastity, We breathed into her (Mary) of Our spirit and We made her and her son a sign to the worlds. *Surah 21.91*

GOD chose Adam, Noah, the house of Abraham, and the house of 'Imrān before all creatures in a continuous line of descent. God hears and knows.

When the wife of 'Imrān said: 'Lord, I vow to Your service my unborn child: accept my offering. For You see and know all things.'

When she gave birth to her daughter she said: 'Lord, a daughter is born to me.' God was well aware what the child was. A female birth is not the same as a male. 'I have named her Mary. I entrust her into Your protection and her seed after her from the malice of Satan.'

Her Lord received her with gracious favour and under His hand she grew into a goodly child. The Lord gave her into the care of Zachariah.

Every time Zachariah entered the sanctuary he found her supplied with food. 'Mary,' he said, 'how do you come to have this food?' 'It is God's providing,' she replied, 'for God gives without stint to whoever He wills.'

Then Zachariah prayed: 'Lord, hearer of prayer, grant me at Your hand a blessed offspring.' As he was standing in the sanctuary in the act of prayer, angels called to him and said: 'God, confirming His word, brings you happy news. It is about John, a prince of men and chaste, a prophet numbered with the righteous.' 'Lord,' said Zachariah, 'how shall I have a son when I am now an old man and my wife is barren?' 'God brings about what He wills: that is how it will be.'

Then Zachariah said: 'Lord, let me have a sign.' 'Your sign,' He said, 'will be that for three days you will speak to no one except by gestures. Celebrate the praise of your Lord evening and morning, and remember Him often.'

And the angels said: 'Mary, God has chosen you and made you pure.

Truly He has chosen you above all women everywhere. Mary, be obedient to your Lord, prostrate yourself in worship and join yourself with those who pray.'

This is a narrative of things concealed which We have given you (s.) to know. For you were not present when they cast their lots over who should have the care of Mary and you were not on hand to observe how they vied for the custody of her.

To Mary the angels said: 'Mary, God gives you glad news of a word from Him. His name is the Messiah Jesus, son of Mary. Eminent will he be in this world and in the age to come, and he will have his place among those who are brought near to God's Throne. He will speak to men in the cradle and in his mature years, and he will be among the righteous.'

Mary said: 'Lord, how shall I bear a son when no man has known me?' He replied: ' The will of God is so, for He creates as He wills. When His purpose is decreed He only says: "Be!" and it is. God will teach him the Scripture, the wisdom, the Torah and the Gospel, making him a messenger to the people of Israel, to whom he will say: "I have come to you with a sign from your Lord. Out of clay I will shape for you the form of a bird and as I breathe on it it will become one, by God's authority. Also I will heal the blind and the leper and bring the dead to life, by God's authority. I will bring you word of what to eat and what to hold in store in your houses. Truly that will constitute a sign for you, if you are minded to believe. I come confirming the truth that you have already in your possession, namely the Torah, and to authorise as lawful for you things that hitherto were forbidden. I am here among you with a sign from your Lord. Then hold God in awe and be obedient to me. God is my Lord and your Lord: therefore, serve Him. This is the straight path." '

When Jesus realised the unbelief in them he said: 'Who will be my helpers on behalf of God?' The disciples replied: 'We are the helpers of God. In God we have put our trust. Witness, O Jesus, our surrender. Lord, we believe in what You have revealed and we follow Your messenger. Write us down as loyal witnesses.'

Men schemed, but God, too, has His scheme of things and His prevails. Then God said: 'Jesus, I am causing you to die and I will exalt you to Myself, vindicating you from the people of unbelief over whom your followers will have victory at My hand and then, at the resurrection, is the homecoming of you all. I will be arbiter between you about all that is in contention among you. As for the unbelievers, I will afflict them sharply in this present world and in the world to come, and no aid will avail them.'

For those who have believed and done good works We will ensure their reward to the full. God has no love for doers of wrong. These verses as signs We thus recite to you (s.) and the *Dhikr* that brings wisdom. God would have you think of Jesus as you think of Adam, created by God from the dust, saying to him 'Be' and into being he came. This is the truth from your Lord, so do not be among those who are dubious.   *Surah 3.33-60*

KĀF, Hā', Yā', 'Ain, Sīn: the mercy of your(s.) Lord to His servant Zachariah is here recalled. In the secret of his heart he entreated his Lord, saying: 'My Lord, I am a feeble old man, with snow-white hair. Yet never, when I called on You, Lord, have I been left forlorn. I have a fear as to my kinsfolk after my decease and my wife is childless. Grant me, I pray, an heir at Your hand who will enter on my inheritance and that of Jacob's family also. Let him be a man to please You, Lord.'

'Zachariah,' came the answer, 'We give you glad word of a son, John his name, a name which We have not before now bestowed on any one.' He said: 'My Lord, how shall a son be mine when my wife is barren and I as old and decrepit as I am?' His Lord replied: 'It shall be so — your Lord's word for it. It is no hard thing. When you yourself long ago were non-existent, I brought you into being.' 'My Lord,' said Zachariah, 'grant me a sign.' 'The sign for you,' his Lord answered, 'is that for three whole nights you will not be able to speak.'

So he emerged from the sanctuary to his people and indicated to them that they should engage, morning and evening, in praise to God.

To John, when he was still a child, We gave authority saying: 'John, lay hold upon the Book with all your strength.' Tenderness, too, and purity, We granted him. He was devout and dutiful to his parents and never overbearing or contentious. Blessed be he on the day of his birth and the day of his death and the day when he is raised again to life.

Recall, too, in the Book, how it was with Mary when she withdrew from her family to a place eastward, where she was hidden from them behind a curtain. There We sent to her Our Spirit who came to her in comely form. 'I take refuge from you with the All-merciful,' she cried, 'if you are a man of honour . . .' But her words were lost in his as he said: 'I am the messenger of your Lord. "I will give you a son, a pure boy" is what he says to you.' Mary answered: 'How shall a son be mine when no man has ever known me, nor have I ever been unchaste?' 'So it shall be,' he said. 'Your Lord's word is: "It is easy for Me and We will make him a sign to humanity and a token of Our mercy." What is decreed is utterly sure.'

So she became pregnant and withdrew to a remote spot, where pangs of travail came upon her beside a palm tree, and she cried: 'Would I had died 'ere now, and gone without a trace!' There came a voice from below the tree: 'Be not sad. See, there is a stream beneath you — God's doing for you. Shake the trunk of the palm tree and fresh ripe dates will drop down around you. Eat and drink and take heart. If any one accosts you, all you have to say is: "I am under a vow to the All-merciful to fast and, this day, I hold converse with nobody."'

Then she brought the child in her arms to her family: they said to her: 'Mary! for shame! whatever have you done? Sister of Aaron, your father was no profligate, nor was your mother a loose woman!' Whereupon she simply turned their glances in the child's direction, and they retorted: 'How shall we address words to a child in the cradle?' And the child said: 'I am the servant of God. He has given me the Book and appointed me a prophet, and he has made me blessed where-ever I am. He has commanded me to pray and to do alms all my life long and to be duteous to my mother. What belongs to the arrogant and the wretched has no place in His will for me. Blessed am I in the day of my birth, my day of death and my day of resurrection to life.'

Such was Jesus, son of Mary — the true word about him which is a matter of doubt among them. It is not for God to adopt a son. All praise be His. When He decrees anything He only says: 'Be' and it is. Great is my Lord and your Lord. So worship and serve Him. For such is the straight path. *Surah 19.1-36*

WE commissioned Jesus, son of Mary, in the train of the prophets, attesting the truth of what is already in the Torah. We gave him the Gospel in which are guidance and light and which confirms what is already there in the Torah, as guidance and admonition to all who would be God-fearing.

So let the people of the Gospel judge according to what God has revealed in it. Those who do not judge in accordance with such divine revelation are surely ne'er-do-wells. *Surah 5.46-47*

THE Messiah, son of Mary, was simply an apostle. Apostles before him have passed away. His mother was a woman of truth. Both of them took food. *Surah 5.75*

WHEN the son of Mary's role as an example is put to your (s.) people they will have nothing to do with it. They say: 'Are our gods better, or he?' It is only in contentiousness that they bring him up anyway in arguing with you. They are a contentious lot! Jesus was none other than a servant on whom We bestowed grace and whom We made to be a symbol to the sons of Israel.

When Jesus came to them with clear thoughts, he said: Truly, I have come to you with wisdom and to make clear to you something of the things about which you were at odds. So hold God in awe and be obedient to me. God is my Lord and your Lord, so worship Him. That is an honest way.'   *Surah 43.57-59 and 62-64*

ON the day when God shall gather together the messengers He will say to them: 'What response did you have?' To which they will say: 'Of that we have no knowledge. Yours it is to know things that are hidden from us.'

And to Jesus He will say: 'Jesus, son of Mary, remember My grace towards your mother when I aided you with the holy spirit, so that in your cradle and in your mature years you spoke to men. Remember how I gave to you knowledge of the Book, and the wisdom, the Torah and the Gospel, and how by My leave you fashioned clay into the shape of the bird and when you breathed into it it became a bird by My leave, and how, by My leave too, you healed those born blind and the lepers and how, by My leave again, you brought the dead to life once more.'

'Remember, too, how when you came to the people of Israel with clear signs, I held back their antagonism against you, the unbelievers among them alleging that plainly it was all sorcery.'

'When I moved the disciples to put their trust in Me and in My messenger, their reply was: "We do so trust. Bear witness that we yield ourselves up to You."'

When the disciples said: 'Jesus, son of Mary, can your Lord bring down to us a table from heaven?' he said: 'Be in awe of God if you are true believers.' And they said: 'It is our desire to partake of that table, that our hearts may be at rest in the knowledge that you have indeed spoken truth to us and thus we too may be witnesses to it.'

So, Jesus, son of Mary, prayed, saying: 'O God, our Lord, send down for us a table from heaven that it may be to us for a festival through all our generations and a sign from You. Provide for us: for there is no provision like Yours.' And God said: 'Send it down to you I will. In time to come

167

whoever among you turns to unfaith will have retribution from Me such as none else incurred in all the world.'

God said to Jesus: 'Jesus, son of Mary, did you ever say to men: "Adopt me and my mother as two gods in disregard of God Himself"?' To which he replied: 'Glory be to You. It is not in me to say what I have no warrant for. If I had ever said such a thing You would have known it. For You know my innermost being. Knowedge of what is within You I do not possess. It is You who know altogether things unknown to us. I said to them only what You commanded me to say, namely: "Worship and serve God, my Lord and your Lord." As long as I was among them I bore witness to them and when You took me to Yourself it was You who were watcher over them. For all things are within Your scrutiny. If You submit them to chastisement they are Your servants, and if You forgive them it is because power and wisdom are yours.'

God said: 'The truth of those who deal truthfully this day avails them well. Theirs are gardens watered with flowing streams, where immortality is theirs, God being well-pleased with them and they with Him, where all is highest bliss.'

God's is the sovereignty of the heavens and of the earth and of all that is within them. His is the power that rules over all.   *Surah 5.109-120*

THEY have denied the truth who say: 'God, He is the Christ, son of Mary.' The Messiah said: 'Sons of Israel, worship God, my Lord and your Lord. God has prohibited Paradise to every one who alienates worship from God. Their dwelling will be the Fire. Doers of evil assuredly have none to come to their rescue.'   *Surah 5.72*

WE brought Jesus, son of Mary, the clear truths and upheld him with the holy spirit. Every time there came to you an apostle for whose message you had no appetite within you, you reacted in proud disdain. Some of the messengers you said were liars and some you put to death.

Surah 2.87b

WE brought Jesus, son of Mary, the clear truths and upheld him with the holy spirit. Had God willed, those who came after him would not have fallen into strife with one another, seeing that the clear signs had been brought to them. But they did differ one with the other. There were those who believed and those who denied. Had God so willed they would not have contended with each other. But God does as He wills.

Surah 2.253b

JESUS, son of Mary, said: 'People of Israel, I am the messenger of God to you, confirming the truth of the Torah which you have already and giving you glad word of a messenger who will come after me, whose name (*ahmad*) is more highly praised.'

When, however, he brought clear signs to them they said: 'All this is obviously sorcery.' Is anything more heinous than for someone to attribute falsehood to God when there comes to him the very call of God Himself to come into *islām*? God's guidance will never avail for such who flout the truth.

You who believe, be true allies of God, as Jesus, Mary's son, said to the disciples: 'Who will stand with me in the behalf of God?' and the disciples said: 'We will be the helpers of God.' One group of the people of Israel believed, while another body of them denied the faith. Those who believed We sustained against their adversaries and they became the victors. *Surah 61.6-7 and 14*

TRULY they have lied against the truth who say: 'God, He is the Messiah, son of Mary.' Say: 'Who can arrogate sovereignty from God in anything? If God but wills it His power could annihilate the Messiah and his mother and every one else in the world. To God belongs the sovereignty of the heavens and of the earth and all that is within them and He is omnipotent over all.' *Surah 5.17*

PEOPLE of the Book, do not go to unwarranted lengths in your religion and get involved in false utterances relating to God. Truly, Jesus, Mary's son, was the messenger of God and His word — the word which He imparted to Mary — and a spirit from Him. Believe, then, in God and His messengers and do not talk of three gods. You are well advised to abandon such ideas. Truly God is one God. Glory be to Him and no 'son' to Him whose are all things in the heavens and the earth, their one and only guardian.

That he should be servant to God will never be disdained by the Messiah as beneath his dignity, nor indeed by the angels who dwell in the divine presence. Servants of His who take on arrogant airs and think themselves above serving — well, God will have them all summoned to answer for it. *Surah 4.171-172*

As for their claim that they killed the Messiah Jesus, son of Mary, the messenger of God, the truth is they did not kill him nor did they crucify him. They were under the illusion that they had. There is a lot of doubt about this matter among those who are at odds over it. They have no real knowledge but follow only surmise. Assuredly, they did not kill him. On the contrary, God raised him to Himself — God whose are all wisdom and power. And before they come to die, the people of the Book, to a man, will surely believe on him. On the Day of resurrection he will be a witness against them.   *Surah 4.157-159*

A PARABLE for you (s.) to cite to them concerns a city-community to whose people the messengers came on their errand. There were two (Paul and Barnabas?) whom We sent to them but they rejected them as liars. So We sent a third to give further weight to their message. 'We are messengers to you,' they said. To which the people responded: 'You are just mortals like ourselves. Moreover the Merciful has revealed nothing. You are nothing but liars.' To which they answered: 'Our Lord knows that we are truly His messengers to you. Our one responsibility is to bring you the message — clear as it is.' The people said: 'For our part the auguries bode no good from you. Quit! or else we will certainly stone you: it will be dire punishment you will get at our hands!' To which they replied: 'The auguries you get from your birds are what you go by. What if this has been your call from God to remember? But you are people who wantonly go your own way.'

Then from the farthest part of the town there came a man running who said: 'My people, follow the messengers. Follow those who seek no reward from you, for they are rightly guided. My sole resolve is to serve the One to whom is our returning, all of us. Shall I take gods other than Him? Their intercession could avail me nothing, nor could they deliver me, if the Merciful Himself wills my affliction. Were I to do so I would be plainly deluded and wrong. Apostles, my faith is in your Lord. Townsmen, listen to me.'

The word to him was: 'Enter Paradise.' And he said: 'Would that my people knew how my Lord has forgiven me and made me to be among the honoured blest.' After what happened to him it was not any host out of heaven that We sent down against his people. Visitations from heaven were not Our method. Just one single blast there was, and they were lifeless and still.

The pity of it in respect of My servants! Never does a messenger come but derision is what people have for him. Have they not realised how many generations before them We have destroyed and these have never come back? It is before Us that all — each and everyone — will be arraigned. *Surah 36.13-32*

WE made the son of Mary and his mother a sign and gave them secure shelter on a hillside where there was a spring.

You who are messengers, let the good things of nature be your food and continue in well-doing. I am aware of your every deed.

The community to which you belong is one community and I am the Lord of you all. Hold Me in awe. But breaking up into sects is their doing, each party taking delight in their own thing. So let them be awhile, in their confusion. *Surah 23.50-54*

AS for monasticism, it was an invention of theirs, for which We gave no directive. Our only injunction was that men should desire God's good pleasure. Nor was their observance of it what it should have been. The believing among them We rewarded with recompense but many of them were actively corrupt. *Surah 57.27b*

ALL this retelling on Our part of the stories of the messengers is in order to put firm resolve in your (s.) heart. In them the truth is brought home to you, and admonition and recollection for all who believe. Say to those who believe not: 'Do whatever lies within your power. We are at work too. Wait on events: We have expectations too!' Things unseen in heaven and earth are God's alone. What He has decreed comes back to Him full circle. Make Him your (s.) worship. Let your trust be in Him. Your Lord is not one to have no mind for what all you (pl.) are doing. *Surah 11.120-123*

FOR We exacted from the prophets pledges on their part — from you (s.) and from Noah, Abraham and Moses, from Jesus, son of Mary. The solemn pledge We took from them was so that God might question these truth-speakers about how their truth fared and He has made ready a painful retribution for those who do not believe. *Surah 33.7-8*

HAS not word come to you (pl.) of those who were before your time —
the people of Noah, the tribes of 'Ad and Thamūd, and those of the time
after them? None but God knows them now. Their messengers came to
them with clear evidences but they rejected them out of hand saying: 'We
deny what you have been sent with: we are in sharp doubt about what
you are inviting us into, suspect as it is!' Their messengers replied: 'Is
there doubt as to God, the Originator of the heavens and of the earth,
who calls you in order to pardon your transgressions and grant you
respite until a time appointed?' To which the reply came: 'You are
humans just like ourselves. You want to divert us from the worship our
fathers followed. Bring us some clear warrant.' Their messengers said to
them: 'We are indeed only humans like yourselves, but God grants grace
to whom He wills among His servants. It is not for us to bring you any
warrant except by leave of God. Let believers put their trust simply in
God. How should we not trust in God, for He has guided us in our
paths. We will endure patiently whatever harm you do to us. Let it be in
God that trust is placed by those who will to trust.'

Those who disbelieved said to their messengers: 'We will surely expel
you from our land or else you return to our community and cult.' Their
Lord then revealed to the messengers: 'We will certainly cause the
workers of evil to perish and We will cause you to occupy the land after
them. So it will be for him who holds My tribunal in awe and who is in
awe of My warning.'

The messengers prayed for a way through to victory and each stubborn power-monger was foiled — beyond whom *Jahannam* lies, where
he is given fetid water to drink. He gulps but can hardly swallow. Death
besieges him on every side though die he cannot. Beyond lies a grim
torment. Thence is a parable of those who denied their Lord, whose
deeds are like ashes when the wind blows fiercely on a day of storm. Of
all that they have acquired there is nothing that remains within their
power. Such is the utmost in the world of lostness.   *Surah 14.9-18*

TELL (s.) them the word about the one to whom We brought Our
revelations and he abandoned them. Satan got after him and he was led
astray. Had We willed We might have brought him to high estate by
those revelations but he clung to his earthbound state and followed his
own desires. He could be likened to a dog who will pant with lolling
tongue whether you bear down on him or whether you leave him alone.
That is how people are who belie Our revelations.

Tell them the story: perhaps they may ponder it. People who give the lie to Our revelations make an evil example. It is themselves they wrong. He whom God guides is truly guided and those whom He leads astray are indeed the losers.   *Surah 7.175-178*

BEFORE your (s.) time, We have sent to the nations, visiting them with hardship and adversity that they might humble themselves. If only they had turned humbly when Our calamity fell upon them, but their hearts grew hardened and Satan made their doings seem fine to them.

When they forgot the things of which they had been reminded, We opened out to them doors of every sort and kind, until — when they were joyous over what had come their way — We seized them suddenly and they were brought to despair. The last remnant of the people who had committed evil was cut off. Praise be to God, the Lord of all being.

Surah 6.42-45

ALIF, Lām, Mīm: the Byzantines have been defeated in the near-by land but, following their defeat, they will be victorious within a few years. God's is the disposal of things, before and after, and on that day believers will rejoice in the help of God. For He aids whom He wills: He is the almighty, the merciful. Such is God's promise. God does not default on His promise though most people do not realise that. They know only the outward aspects of the life of this present world and are mindless of the hereafter.

Have they not taken thoughtful stock of themselves and of how with truth God created the heavens and the earth and all within them, and only for an allotted span? Most of mankind, though, altogether deny the coming encounter with their Lord. Have they not travelled in the world and seen the manner of the end of those before them who were of stronger mettle than they, who cultivated the land and civilised it to a greater degree than they have themselves? Moreover, their messengers, too, came to them with clear revelations and it was not God who did them wrong: it was they who wronged themselves. Evil was the doom that followed of those who committed evil in giving the lie to the revelations of God and in holding them in derision.   *Surah 30:1-10*

THE story of the companions in the cave and of the *Raqīm* — have you (s.) taken it into account as a wonderful thing among Our signs? The young men took refuge in the cave, praying: 'Our Lord, give us mercy from Your presence and let us have right guidance in our situation.' For a number of years We closed their ears with sleep and subsequently We brought them round again to ascertain which of the two parties would better reckon the span of time they had passed in that state. We will tell you (s.) the story exactly as it happened.

They were young men who believed in their Lord and We advanced them in guidance, strengthening their hearts as they stood forth and said: 'Our Lord is Lord of the heavens and of the earth: we will never invoke any but He as God. For to do so would be an outrageous thing. Our people here have taken for themselves deities other than He despite showing no clear authority for them. And who commits a greater evil than he who perpetrates a lie against God?'

They were told: 'When you have separated yourselves from them and from what, ousting God, they worship, take refuge in the cave. Your Lord will open to you His mercy and in your situation will accord you all you need.'

While they were in the hollow of the cave you (s.) might have followed the sun with your eyes, inclining away from the cave as it rose on the right, and turning away from them as it set on the left. That was one of God's signs. He whom God guides is well guided but he whom God leads astray for him you will never find a guiding friend.

As they lay asleep you would have thought them to be awake. We had them turning in their sleep to right and left as their dog lay with paws outstretched on the threshold. Had you watched them you would surely have turned away from them to flee, being filled with fright at the sight of them.

Finally We brought them out of sleep. They began questioning one another. One said: 'How long have you been here?' They said: 'We have passed a day or part of a day.' They said, further: 'Your Lord knows how long you have stayed here. Send one of your number with this silver coin of yours and let him look for the finest food and bring some provender here for you. Let him go discretely and on no account inform anyone about you. For if they have word of you they will stone you or make you come back into their religion — and, in that event, you will never come to good!'

We have in this way brought their story to mind so that men may know that the promise of God is true and that there is no doubt of the Hour.

There were contentions among the people concernng the story of the sleepers. They said: 'Erect an edifice over them: they are well known to their Lord.' Those who finally prevailed in the matter said: 'We must indeed establish a place of worship in their memory.'

There was also altercation about the number of the sleepers. 'Three,' it was said, 'and four with the dog.' 'Five with the dog making six' — all conjecturing, as if throwing stones at an object out of sight. 'Seven, with the dog for eight.' Say: 'It is my Lord who knows what the number was, and few others. So do not engage in dispute about it, unless it be on a plain point, and do not ask anyone for a verdict about them.'

'On no account say, in any matter: "Tomorrow I will do so and so . . . unless you add: "If God will." Remember your Lord, if you have forgotten to say that, and add: "May my Lord direct me to a better sense of things than that!"'

The sleepers remained in their cave for three hundred years with nine more added. Say: 'God knows best how long they stayed. To Him belong the things unseen of heaven and earth. Well He sees and hears. Apart from Him they have no protector and there are none with whom He associates His governance.' *Surah 18.9-26*

THEY question you (s.) about *Dhū-al-Qarnain* (the Two-Horned One). Say: 'I will relate to you an account of him. We established him powerfully in the land and bestowed on him the capacity to attain every objective. He made his way until he came to the place of the sun's setting. He found it setting in murky waters where, close by, he came upon a people there. We said: "*Dhū-al-Qarnain*, either inflict punishment on them or treat them kindly." To which he replied: "He who has committed wrong, him will we subject to punishment and afterwards he will be taken back to his Lord who will punish him with the utmost severity. But he who believes and does what is right will receive the most goodly reward and, in our command, we will require of him what is readily done."

Then *Dhū-al-Qarnain* took another road until he reached the place of the sun's rising, where he found it rising on a people for whom We had provided nothing to cover them. Thus it was: We had fully within Our knowledge the situation he was in.

Then he took a road until he arrived between two mountain-barriers where, at the foot of them, he found a people who could hardly understand anything said to them. They said: "*Dhū-al-Qarnain*, Gog and Magog are running riot in the land. Shall we pay a tax to you for you to erect a rampart between us and them?" He replied: "The power in which my Lord has set me up is more adequate. Give me your help in manual strength and I will set a rampart between you and them. Bring me pieces of iron!" When he had levelled the area between the two mountain sides he said: "Ply the bellows." When he had made it a glowing fire he cried: "Bring me molten copper to pour on it." The rampart was one they were unable to scale or to break through. He said: "This is a mercy from my Lord. But when the time promised by my Lord comes He will turn it to dust. My Lord's promise is true."

On that Day We will have Gog and Magog trampling in waves upon each other. The trumpet will be sounded and We will gather them in one throng and on that Day We will set *Jahannam* in place in full view for the unbelievers — those whose eyes were veiled from any remembrance of my Lord and who were incapable of hearing. Do those who do not believe reckon that they can take servants of Mine as protectors — Me apart? *Jahannam* have We made ready for the reception of the unbelievers.'   *Surah 18.83-102*

بسم الله الرحمن الرحيم

D. Muhammad:
The Prophet-Preacher and the
Meccan Years

TRULY We revealed it on the night of power.
Would that you knew what the night of power means!
Better than a thousand months is the night of power.
Thereon come the angels and the Spirit down by leave of their Lord
  with all-inclusive directive.
It is a night of peace till the breaking of the day.   *Surah 97*

RECITE, in the Name of your Lord who created,
Created man from a sperm-cell.
Recite, how altogether gracious is your Lord,
who taught by the pen, taught man what he knows not,
But No! man is perversely assertive, thinking himself his own lord.
Yet to your Lord is where all things return.

Have you taken count of him who puts a ban on a praying servant in
his devotions? Do you see him as rightly guided or enjoining the fear of
God? Is he not rather, in your sight, repudiating truth and acting
perversely? Does he not realise that God is all-seeing?

Mark! unless he stops in his tracks, We will take him by the forelock,
the forelock of his lies and sin. Then let him call up his cohorts. We will
call up the *Zabāniyah*. No! never yield to him. Worship and draw near to
God.   *Surah 96*

NO! I swear by the planets in their revolving and declining courses, by
the brooding night and the breathing dawn. This is truly the utterance of
a gracious bringer of truth, one imbued with strength and authenticated
before the Lord of the Throne, demanding obedience and worthy of
trust. Your kinsman, then, is not out of his mind. He saw truly, saw the

vision on the bright horizon. He is not one to keep jealously to himself the transcendent mystery. This is not the word of some accursed Satan. So, where are you heading? This is a word addressing and alerting all sentient beings, everyone of you who is willing for the straight path. Only will you so will, if God, the Lord of all being, wills it.

Surah 81.15-29

BY the star and its setting, your kinsman (Muhammad) has not been led astray, nor is he under delusion. He does not speak by some whim of his own. This is nothing else than a revelation imparted to him. One of awesome power has taught it him, a being of supreme strength, who stood on the height of the horizon and then approached, coming down to within two bows' lengths, even nearer, and then revealed to his servant the revelation he brought.

The vision he saw his heart did not deny. So will you take issue with him over what his vision is?

In truth, he saw him in another visitation by the Sidrah tree — the garden of refuge is close by — when the Sidrah tree was wrapped in a covering. His gaze was transfixed, never turning from the sight. Truly he saw the greatest of the signs of his Lord.   *Surah 53.1-18*

O YOU who are enwrapped, watch throughout the night with a little respite, or through half the night, or thereabouts, be it less or more. Recite the Qur'ān as it should be recited. We will charge you with a profound message.

Truly in the watches of the night impressions are weightiest and words most telling. By day you have pressing business. Remember the Name of your Lord and devote yourself altogether to Him. He is the Lord of the east and of the west. There is no god save He. Take Him for your trust. What they say bear patiently and go out from among them courteously.   *Surah 73.1-10*

YOU who are enfolded, arise and warn.
Your Lord magnify, your garments purify, and shun defilement.
Give not with a view to self-increase and turn patiently to your Lord.

Surah 74.1-7

BY high noon and by the deep silence of the night, your Lord has not abandoned you nor disowned you. What ends will be better for you than what comes first. In truth your Lord will yet grant it you and your satisfaction will be complete.
Did He not find you an orphan and gave you shelter?
Did He not find you lost on your way and guided you?
Did He not find you destitute and enrich you?
So then, do no wrong to the orphan,
the suppliant do not turn empty away
and make the grace of your Lord your constant theme.   *Surah 93*

HAVE We not made you to be open of heart?
Have We not lifted from you the burden that was breaking your back and have We not established your reputation?
Truly, with hardship there comes ease, with hardship there comes ease.
So then, having found the burden gone, pursue your task.
Make the Lord your heart's desire.   *Surah 94*

IT is We who have communicated the Qur'ān to you from above in gradual sequence. So await with patience what your Lord determines. Do not yield to any among them who is an evil-doer or an unbeliever. Remember the Name of your Lord morning and evening: prostrate yourself to Him by night and celebrate His praise all the long night.

These men are in love with this fleeting world and put behind them the harsh reality of doom's day.

We have created them and made them strong of limb. If We will We can exchange them for others like them in their place. This is a reminder. Whoever so wills let him make his way to his Lord. He will not so will, however, apart from God's willing so — God who is all-knowing and all-wise and who brings into His mercy whomever He wills, while for the evil-doers He has prepared painful retribution.   *Surah 76.23-31*

PRAISE the Name of the Lord, the most High, He who created all things and duly fashioned them, He who has determined their order and guided them, He who has brought forth the green pastures and then made them rotted, ashen waste.

We will give you to speak the Qur'ān and you will not forget — other than God has willed. He knows all that is in open evidence and all that is concealed. We will take you gently where rest shall be yours.

Make your summons to give heed — if calling them to heed may profit them. He who fears God will take the summons to heart and the evil wretch will evade it. He it is whose lot will be the raging Fire. There he shall neither die nor live. The man who cleanses himself and has in remembrance the Name of his Lord and prays, he it is who finds well-being. Your preference, though, is the life of this lower world, whereas the world to come is better and more lasting.

All this is to be found in the earlier pages of Scripture, the Scriptures of Abraham and Moses. *Surah 87*

SAY: 'You who reject faith, I do not worship what you worship, nor do you worship what I worship. Never shall I be a worshipper of what you have worshipped, nor will you be worshippers of what I worship. To you your religion, and to me mine. *Surah 109*

TRULY We have given you (s.) abundance. Pray then to your Lord and offer sacrifice. It is the one who hates you who will be without an heir. *Surah 108*

BY the snorting war-horses that strike fire with their hoofs as they storm forward at dawn, a single host in the midst of their dust cloud, man is indeed ungrateful to his Lord. He himself is the surest witness to the fact. He is violent in his passion for wealth. Is he not aware that their Lord knows them through and through on that Day when the tombs yield up their dead and all men's hidden thoughts are open knowledge? *Surah 100*

FOR the bringing to rendezvous of the Quraish, the gathering in convoy of their caravans winter and summer. Let them serve the Lord of this house, who gave them provision of food against hunger and security from fear. *Surah 106*

BY the pen and the Scripture they set down. In the grace of your Lord, you are not jinn-possessed. Truly yours is a rightful reward and you have in hand a great undertaking. You will see — as they will too — which of you it is who is demented. It is your Lord who surely knows the ones who have gone astray from His path and knows those who are rightly guided.

So then, do not obey those who call it all lies. Were you to be ingratiating with them they would like it well and be the same with you. Have no truck with a despicable maker of oaths, a slandering backbiter, a hinderer of the good, an evil aggressor, a man of violence and a bastard. Though such a one has wealth and sons, when Our revelations are rehearsed to him he dubs them: 'Fables of the ancients!' We will lay on him an evident stigma.

With affliction We have tested them as We did those orchard-keepers who vowed that they would definitely gather fruit in the morning, ignoring the proviso proper to their action. While they were sleeping someone from their Lord made a circuit around the orchard and in the morning it resembled an orchard that had been completely ransacked. When morning came, they summoned one another: 'If you are minded for harvesting, be sure to go out in good time to your field.' So they went off, remarking to each other in low voices: 'No destitute fellow is going to get a look-in today, if we can help it!' With this fixed purpose they went out early. But when they saw what a state the orchard was in, they said: 'We were in the wrong, that's certain. It is we who have been forestalled.' It was the most apt in mind among them who added: 'Did I not say to you: "How is it you give no glory to God?"' They replied: 'Glory to our Lord God. We were indeed greatly in the wrong.' They fell to blaming each other, crying: 'Woe to us! we were very presumptuous. Our Lord, maybe, will give us another orchard, a better one. To our Lord we look in aspiration.' *Surah 68.1-32*

BY the night with its veiling dark, by the day in radiant light, by male and female of His creating, truly your (pl.) strivings are to different ends. Whoever gives out of fear of God, who holds with the good as the true, We will make ready his way to ease. Whowever behaves as a miser and lives to himself, who gives the lie to the good, We will pave his way to hardship and when he comes to die his wealth will avail him nothing.

Ours it is to give guidance. The last Day is Ours as the first was. *Surah 92.1-13*

BY the fig and the olive, by the mount of Sinai and this inviolate land, We created man in the finest form of creaturehood and then We relegated him to the lowest of the low, excepting those who hold the faith and who do what is righteous. Theirs rightly is an unfailing reward.

Who then, after this, will have you (s.) deny the judgement? Is not God the supreme, conclusive judge?   *Surah 95*

THE incidence of the Book is from God, the mighty, the wise. In truth alone have We created the heavens and the earth and everything within them, and for a time that has a term. Those who deny the faith repudiate what the warning tells them.

Say: 'Have you any real comprehension of what is in those invocations of yours which oust God Himself? Show me what they have created in this earth: or have they any share in the heavens? Bring to me a scripture before this one or any vestige of knowledge, if you are right.'

Who could be in greater error than one who invokes, to the exclusion of God, what will not answer him even if he waits until the Day of resurrection. Those he invokes are quite unconscious of it and when mankind are assembled to the judgement will have for them a sharp enmity and will deny they ever had their worship.   *Surah 46.1-6*

THOSE who adopt to themselves guardian deities, to the exclusion of God Himself, resemble the spider with that frailest of all houses, a cobweb of her own making. If only they would take it in! God knows what they invoke — anything whatever — ignoring Him who is all-strong and all-wise.

These parables We propound to mankind. Only those who have knowledge take the point of them. God created the heavens and the earth in truth. In that fact there is a clear index for believing people.

Recite what is being inspired within you from the Book and perform the prayer-rite. The act of prayer restrains from what is indecent and reprehensible. The supreme thing is the remembrance of God who knows what you are all doing. Argue (pl.) with the people of the Book only in courteous terms, except in the case of those among them who have acted falsely, and tell them: 'We believe in what has been sent down to us and sent down to you. Our God and your God is One, and we are muslims, surrendered to Him.'

We have, in this way, sent down to you the Book, and those to whom We have brought the Book believe in it, as do some of these others too. Only those who are set in unbelief reject Our revelations. Prior to this you did not recite any Book nor set down any scripture in writing by your own hand. Had you done either, those bent on discredit would have had their suspicions.

But No! In the hearts of those to whom knowledge has come it constitutes clear revelations which are their own evidence. Only those who are wrong-doers reject Our revelations. They said: 'Why have no attesting signs been enacted for him from above by his Lord?' Say: 'Such signs are in God's hand. As for me, I am simply a bringer of plain warning.' Has it not been enough for them that We have sent down upon you the Book read to them? That fact is indeed an act of mercy and a reminder for believing people.

Say: 'God is all the witness I need between me and you. He knows all that is in the heavens and in the earth. Those who have put their faith in what is vain and have denied God they it is who are the losers.'

Surah 29.41-52

HAVE you (pl.) thoughts about Allāt, Al-'Uzzā, and the third, Manāt, the other goddess? Do you have male children and He the females? That would be a very unfair allotment! They are nothing but names: you have coined them yourselves and your fathers with no warrant at all from God. They are merely following supposition and their own wishful thinking, though guidance from their Lord has truly come to them.

Is it man's lot to have whatever he wishes? The last and the first are God's.

How many an angel there is in the heavens whose intercession avails nothing, unless it be after God has given leave for it to whomever He wills and approves.

Those who have no faith in the last Day give the angels female names, though they have no knowledge in the matter and merely follow surmise — and surmise has no place where truth is concerned.

Turn (s.) away from the man who repudiates Our *Dhikr* and wants only the life of this present world — which is all their knowledge comprehends. Your (s.) Lord knows who is in error and out of His way, and He knows who is rightly guided.

To God belong all things in the heavens and in the earth, to requite evil-doers according to their deeds and to reward well-doers with the goodliest recompense.

For those who shun heinous sins and abominations — occasional faults notwithstanding — your (s.) Lord has a wide forgiveness. He had knowledge of you (pl.) when He brought you into being from the earth, when you were in your mothers' wombs yet unborn. Do not count yourselves pure: He knows those who truly fear Him.

What is your (s.) thought of him who turns away, who stints his giving and that, grudgingly? Has he some comprehension of things unseen that he sees? Or has he had no word of what is there in the pages of Moses and of Abraham who did what was demanded of him? Has he no word about the soul's burden being no one else's and that no man has anything he has not himself striven for? that his efforts will be evident and paid in full finally and that the final end is with your Lord? that it is He who makes some to laugh and others to weep, He who brings to death and makes to live, that the two sexes — male and female — are His creation from the act of intercourse, that the other life is in His hands to bring about, that He enriches with wealth and possessions, and that He is the Lord of Sirius?   *Surah 53.19-49*

GIVE them to know that you (s.) are no soothsayer, no crazy fellow. Or are they saying: 'He is a poet! We expect some chance of fate will see to him!' Tell them: 'Wait as you may: I have my anticipations no less than yours.'

Is it their sagacity that constrains them this way or are they pernicious people? Are they putting it around that he has concocted it — this Qur'ān? They are not minded to believe. If they mean what they say, let them come out with a discourse like it!

Were they created out of the empty air? Or are they self-creators? Did they bring into being the heavens and the earth? Strangers to sure convictions they are! Are they in possession of your Lord's treasuries? Custodians in charge of them? Or have they some ladder from which to eavesdrop in heaven? If so, let some listener of theirs promulgate clearly!

Is He to have daughters and you sons?

Are you (s.) asking some fee from them, burdening them with insolvency? Do they have the unseen realm within their purview, putting it all down in writing?

Or is it that they aim to trap you (s.)? The ones who get caught in traps are those who deny the faith.

Have they a god other than God? Glory be to God from all their false worships.

Were they to see a piece of heaven falling down, they would say: 'It is just a heap of clouds.'

Let them alone till they come up to their day — the Day when they will be thunder-struck, the Day when their scheming will avail them nothing and they will be without all succour. There is a punishment besides that for those who do evil, though most of them have no realisation of it.

Surah 52.29-47

THEY had almost beguiled you (s.) away from what We had revealed to you with the temptation to invent something else against Us. On that score they would have taken you up as a friend. Had We not rallied you, you had almost conceded to them a little. Then We would have made you experience double retribution, in life and in death, when you would have found none to succour you against Us. They were on the point of frightening you out of the land, in order to expel you from it. In that event they would have remained only briefly there themselves. This is the way of things for those whom We have sent before you as Our apostles. No change will you find in Our *Sunnah*.

Surah 17.73-77

GIVE answer to your (pl.) Lord before there comes upon you from God a Day which there is no averting. On that Day there will be no refuge for you and no pleading innocence.

But if they reject We have not sent you (s.) to be responsible for their security. Your sole duty is to bring home the message. When We give man to taste Our mercy he rejoices in it: if We subject them to anything untoward because of their doings earlier, well, mankind foreswears faith. To God belongs the kingdom of the heavens and of the earth. What He wills He creates. To whom He wills He gives female offspring and to whom He wills males, or to whom He wills He gives both daughters and sons and makes whom He wills to be childless. All-wise and all-powerful is He.

Surah 42.47-50

YOUR God is One — on the word of witnesses in their ordered ranks, on the word of those who take the fight to the evil-doers, of the reciters with their voicing of Qur'ān. He is the Lord of the heavens and of the earth and of all within them, Lord of the sun-risings.

We have adorned the lower heaven with the stars in glorious array, guarding it from each evil Satan, lest they listen to the heavenly council. On every side they are attacked and repulsed, and consigned to abiding retribution, and should any overhear by stealth a searing flame is on his track.

So ask them, your hearers, to tell you (s.): Was their creation a harder

task than those others We created? Them We created from miry clay.
You (s.) have been surprised when they simply scoff and pay no heed.
When they have a visual sign before them they go in for mockery, saying:
'This is nothing but plain trickery! What! when we have died and become
dust and bones are we to be brought to life again and our fathers of
aforetime also?' Say: 'Yes! indeed, and to your utter humiliation.'

Surah 37.1-18

AND when Our revelations — clear as they are — are rehearsed to them,
those who disbelieve say of the truth when it has come to them: 'This is
plain sorcery.' Or do they say: 'It is a forgery on his part?' Say: 'If I had
forged it there is nothing you could do that would avail me against God.
He knows well enough how you multiply comment about it. He is a
sufficient witness between me and you concerning it. He is forgiving and
merciful.'

Say: 'I am not a new phenomenon among apostles, nor have I any
forward knowledge of my destiny nor of yours. I follow only what is
inspired within me by revelation. I am nothing but a warner — and a
clear one.'

Say: 'Have you taken thought? What if this be from God and you have
denied it, while witness is borne to what is comparable among Jewish
folk and believed as such, and you in your pride have thought it beneath
you? God does not guide people who deal in falsehood.'

Unbelieving people say of those who believe: 'Were there any good in
all this they would not have got it ahead of us.' Not having taken it as
guidance for them, they will indeed say: 'Old hat and false!' Yet
preceding it is the Book of Moses, both a model and a mercy, and this is a
Book in the Arabic language in confirmation, with a view to warning
those who pervert truth, and to be good news for those who do rightly.'

Those who say: 'God is our Lord' and who follow the straight path
have nothing to fear. Nor will they have cause to sorrow. For they are
the ones to whom Paradise belongs, where immortality is theirs, rewarding their deeds.

Surah 46.7-14

MUHAMMAD frowned and turned away, when the blind man
approached him. For all you knew he might have been bringing alms for
cleansing. Or he had taken the reminder to heart and was bent on putting
it to use? To anyone who has all he needs, you pay ready attention,

though you take no responsibility for his not being purified by alms. But one who comes to you eagerly in godly fear, him you disregard.

This is a revelation, a calling to mind. Let him who will keep it in mind. It is there on hallowed pages, pages that are extolled and purified by the hands of noble, virtuous scribes. *Surah 80.1-16*

SAY: 'People, I am the apostle of God to you all, of God who is sovereign over the heavens and the earth. There is no god save He. He gives life and He brings to death. So then, believe in God and in His apostle, the unlettered, *Ummī* prophet who believes in God and in His Word. Follow him and so find guidance. *Surah 7.158*

'MAKE haste, then, to take refuge in God. I am clear warner to you from Him. Do not set up any other god along with Him. I am clearly warning you from Him. Comparably no previous messenger ever came to those in earlier times of whom they did not say: "He is either a sorcerer, or he is mad." ' Is this a habit they have passed down to each other? In any event, they are a wilful and wicked people.

So turn away from them and be free of reproach. Keep on reminding, for those who believe will be profited by that re-iteration. *Surah 51.50-55*

DO not fall over yourself to give it voice as if to bring it on faster. It is We on Our part who see to its serial increase. So, as We recite, do you follow its recital. Then it is Our work to make its meaning clear. *Surah 75.16-19*

THOSE who refuse faith in the Reminder (the Qur'ān) when it reaches them — it is, nevertheless, a Book of inviolate worth. As a disclosure from on high by One who is all-wise and all-worthy, it is secured against all that is false whether from within or from without.

Nothing is being said to you (s.) differently from what was said to the messengers preceding you. Your Lord is truly the Lord who forgives and the Lord who exacts painful retribution.

Had we caused it to be a Qur'ān in an alien, non-Arabic language, they would surely have said: 'Why were its revelations not made intelligible? What! foreign, non-Arabic, and you are an Arab!' Say: 'To those who believe it is guidance and healing. As for those who do not believe, it falls, as it were, on deaf ears or as though it were offered to blind eyes. They are like people being called to from a long way off.

Surah 41.41-44

TRULY, revelation from above on the part of the Lord of all being. The faithful Spirit has come down with it upon your heart, that you might be among the warners, in a clear Arabic speech. In the psalms of those of old it is found. Is there not evidence for them in the fact that the learned among the children of Israel knew it so?

Had We sent it down upon some non-Arab stranger and he had recited it, they would not have believed it.

It is not by satans that it has been brought down from on high. Such was neither in their mandate nor their competence. Indeed, they are debarred from ever hearing it.

Do not invoke any god but God alone, lest you should find yourself among those who come to painful retribution. Give warning to your nearest kin: behave with gentle carefulness towards your believing followers. If they disobey you, say that you dissociate yourself from any liability for their actions. Trust in Him who is all-powerful, all merciful, who sees you where you stand and in your deportment as you participate in the prostrations. For truly, He sees and knows.

As for the satans — shall I tell you on whom they come down? They descend on every sinful liar. What they hear they impart and most of them are false informers.

As for the poets, it is the beguiled who follow them. Do you not see them around in every valley, wandering in their trances? Words not matched by deeds!

It is otherwise with those who believe and do what is righteous, who remember God often and, when subjected to wrong, defend themselves. And those who do the evil will know bye and bye the catastrophe that is going to overwhelm them. *Surah 26.192-199 and 210-227*

IT was not given to any mortal man to have God address him except by revelatory inspiration, or from behind a veil, or by His sending a messenger inspired by His leave with the revelation He wills. He is the most high, the all-wise.

It is thus We have inspired you by a Spirit from Our command. What the Book was, or the faith, you did not know, but We have now made it a light by which We guide whomsoever We will among Our servants. You, for your part, will be guide into the straight path — the path of God, whose are all things in the heavens and in the earth.

Is it not to God that all things move as their goal?   *Surah 42.51-53*

BLESSED be He who from above has sent the Criterion (the Qur'ān) to His servant that he may be a warner to all sentient beings — He whose is the kingdom of the heavens and the earth. He has adopted to Himself no progeny. In His sovereignty He has no associate. He created everything and established the order within which everything exists. Yet, ignoring Him, men have taken to themselves gods who create nothing but are themselves created and who in themselves are powerless either for hurt or for profit, and who have no authority over death, or life, or resurrection.

'This Qur'ān' say those who reject belief 'is nothing but a fraud he has perpetrated with the aid of others.' Evil and slanderous is the charge they have brought. 'Legends of the ancient peoples', they say. 'He has had them written as they were rehearsed to him morning and evening.'

Say: 'He who knows the secrets of the heavens and of the earth has sent it down — He who is all-forgiving and all-merciful.'

They said: 'What sort of a messenger is this who takes food and walks about in the sūqs? Why was no angel sent down to keep him company in his warnings? Why no treasure as a windfall for him? Why no gardens for him as his provender?' The perverse folk said: 'All you (pl.) are doing is going after a bewitched fellow!'

See what notions they bandy about to describe you, lost in error as they are, and unable to get on the right way. Blessed be He who will indeed bestow on you, as He wills, much better gardens than their idea — with running streams and palaces that He will confer.   *Surah 25.1-10*

HĀ, *Mīm*, the incidence of the Book is from God, the all-strong, the all-wise, who forgives transgression and accepts repentance, who is stern in retribution and of long forbearance. There is no god but He and He is the goal of all becoming. Only those who deny the faith dispute the revelations of God. Do not let their fluctuating fortunes in the land disquiet you (s.)   *Surah 40.1-4*

BE patient: the promise of God is true, Seek the forgiveness of your (s.) Lord for your sin. Celebrate the praise of your Lord at evening time and at the dawn.

Those who argue about the revelations of God, having no warrant bestowed on them for so doing, have nothing but pretentious pride in their hearts — a pride they have no chance of satisfying. Seek refuge with God; it is He who hears and sees.

The creation of the heavens and of the earth is a greater thing than the creation of mankind, though most of mankind does not comprehend.

The blind man and the sighted person are in no way equivalent, nor are those who believe and do what is righteous on a par with the evil-doer. Yet you give little thought to the fact.

The Hour is coming: of that there is no doubt, though most people give it no credence. Your Lord says: 'Call upon Me: I will answer you. Those whose pride scorns to serve Me will enter *Jahannam* in abject humiliation.' It is God who has appointed the night for your repose and the day to give you light. God is munificent to mankind, though most of humanity remains ungrateful. Such is God your Lord, the Creator of all things. There is no god but He. Why then are you set on falsehood? Such perversity is the way of those who repudiate God's revelations.

Surah 40.55-63

SAY: 'I am forbidden to worship the deities you invoke instead of God Himself. The clear evidences having come to me from my Lord, I am commanded to surrender to the Lord of all being — He who has created you from the dust by the sequence of semen, germ-cell and child, your inauguration at His hands, in order that you may go on to attain your full strength and then grow old, though there are some of you who die earlier. There is a stated term you reach, could you but comprehend these things. It is He who gives life and makes to die. If He decrees anything He only says: "Be" and it is.' *Surah 40.66-68*

THE incidence of the Book is from God, the all-strong, the all-wise. With truth have We sent down the Book upon you (s.). Worship God, sincere before Him in your religion. Is there sincere religion save to God alone? Those who adopt patrons other than He suggest that they only offer these their worship as acting to bring them close to God Himself. God will give His verdict about them in respect of their contending views. God gives no guidance to unbelieving people indulging in lies.

Had God willed to adopt a son He could have chosen as He wished from His creation. Glory be to Him: He is God, the One, the all-mastering One. He created the heavens and the earth in truth, enfolding the day with night and the night with day. He pressed sun and moon into His service, each with its appointed course to run. Is not He the all-strong, the One who practices forgiveness?

He created you from one single soul, from which He formed its counterpart. He has bestowed upon you four kinds of cattle in their pairs. He creates you in the wombs of your mothers, one act of creation, moving into a second and a third within the darkness there. That is the way God, your Lord, uses. The kingdom is His: there is no god but He. Why, then, are you alienated? Though you deny the faith, God is altogether rich without you. Yet He takes no pleasure in unfaith, ingratitude, on the part of His servants. He delights in you in your gratitude.

The soul in its burden of responsibility has no one else's added. To your Lord is your final returning and He will tell you of your deeds. For He knows the very secrets of the heart.

When some evil event touches man he calls upon his Lord in penitence but readily forgets the One he earlier invoked as soon as He graciously relieves him. He sets up rivals to God, leading others astray from the way. Say: 'Indulge your unbelief awhile: you are one of the denizens of the Fire. Are you to be taken for the man who devoutly keeps the watches of the night, prostrate and erect as he worships, in awe of the last Day and in hope of his Lord's mercy?' Say: 'Are they one and the same — those who know and those who think not?' Only men of understanding give their minds to think.

Say: 'My servants — you who have believed — have true fear of your Lord. It is well for those who do good in this world, and wide is God's earth. Those who endure patiently will be rewarded beyond all reckoning.'

Say: 'I am commanded to worship God as one who is sincere in his religion. I am commanded to be the first of those who surrender to God (*muslimūn*).'   *Surah 39.1-12*

ON the Qur'ān! — the Reminder itself ever to be in mind — those who disbelieve vaunt of their strength and create division. Many a generation before them have We destroyed. They called out when time allowed of no escape.

They are astounded that a warner has come to them from among themselves. The unbelievers say: 'This is a lying sorcerer. Has he indeed made the gods into one God? — a marvellous thing to do!' The leading men among them withdrew advising their people: 'Move off from him and hold staunchly to your gods. That is what is wanted. We have heard nothing of this sort of thing in religion to date: it is sheer invention.'

'Has the word that reminds been sent down only to him among us?' The fact is that they are in doubt about My *Dhikr*: they have not yet tasted My retribution. Are they in possession of your (s.) Lord's treasure houses of mercy — the all-strong, who disposes His own gifts? Do they own the sovereignty of the heavens and of the earth and all that they contain? If so, let them mount on high by any ascension in their reach! They are nothing but an army of factions on the run.   *Surah 38.1-11*

WHEN We bring a man in length of days to old age We cause him to decline in his physical powers. How is it that they do not comprehend?

We have not taught him poetry: it would not be fitting for him. For this is solely a *Dhikr* and a luminous Qur'ān, for warning on his part to the living and to authenticate what is spoken against the unbelievers.

Do they not realise how We have created cattle on their behalf, the work of Our own hands, over which they have the mastery, We having subjected the cattle to their will both for riding and for food, whence they derive both profitable uses and drink also? Will they register no gratitude?

They have adopted gods to the exclusion of God Himself, on the chance of finding succour. Yet such deities have no power to aid them: it is rather their devotees who fill the role of defending them like an army drawn up on fighting stations.

Do not let (s.) what they say grieve you. We are well aware of the things they conceal and what they show openly.

Does not man realise that We have created him from a sperm-drop? Yet he is evidently given to contention and devises comparison to apply to Us, forgetting his creature-status and querying: 'Who is going to revitalise bones when they have rotted?' Say: 'He will give them life again who, the first time, brought them into being. His knowledge takes in all creation — He who made the fire for you from the green tree — the fire you yourselves kindle. Is not He who created the heavens and the earth competent to create the like of them? To be sure, He can — all-wise Creator as He is. When He desires a thing He only says: "Be!" and it is. Glory be to Him in whose hand is the sovereignty over everything. To Him you are to be brought at last.'   *Surah 36.68-83*

Do you not see how God has brought into your service things in the heavens and in the earth and has liberally graced you with His mercies, without and within? Yet there are people who ignorantly dispute about God, having neither guidance nor a book to enlighten. When they are bidden to follow what God has sent down they say: 'Indeed not! we follow the traditions of our fathers.' What! though it were the very Satan calling them to the doom of *al-Sa'ir*?

He who surrenders his face to God, being a doer of good, he truly has grasped the firmest of bonds. With God is the issue of all things. He who denies the faith — have no grief about his unbelief. To us is their returning and We will tell them of their deeds. God knows the very thoughts within the heart. We will allow them some brief satisfaction and then harry them to grim retribution.

If you (s.) asked them who created the heavens and the earth, they would surely say: 'God.'

Say: 'Praise be to God. But most of them have no comprehension.'

Surah 31.20-25

THEY say: 'Were we to follow the guidance along with you we would be torn from our roots in the land.' Have We not in fact established a secure sanctuary for them, whither are gathered fruits of every kind of Our providing? But most of them do not realise it!

How many a city/community have We destroyed which luxuriated in its rich amenities! There lie their dwellings, scarcely inhabited since their day, the heritage of them falling to Us. Yet never did your (s.) Lord destroy those cities before We had sent an apostle to their mother-city to recite Our revelations to them and no city/community or its people did We destroy unless they were implicated in evil-doing.

Whatever has come your (pl.) way materially belongs to the servicing and delectation of this present life. That which is with God is better and more enduring. Will you not comprehend? *Surah 28.57-60*

THE life of this present world is nothing but play and a game. The abode hereafter is the place of life indeed — did they but know.

When they embark on ships they call upon God with a sincere intention towards Him in their religious practice, yet when He brings them safe to land, there they are — ascribing it to plural gods, repudiating gratitude for what We had done for them and yet enjoying its effects. The time is coming when they will know!

193

Have they not realised that We have established a secure sanctuary while all around them men are subject to violent seizure? Will they go on believing what is vain and giving the lie to the grace of God?

Who does a greater wrong than he who foists on God what is false or denies the truth when it has come to him? Is there in *Jahannam* no last destination for the unbelievers? Those who strive for Us We will surely guide in Our paths. For God is with those who do what is good and right. *Surah 29.64-69*

WHEN they see you (s.) they take you for a joke. 'Is this the fellow God has sent for an apostle? He would have led us astray from our gods, had we not held staunchly to them.' They will know, anon, when they see the retribution, who it is who is the more astray from the path! The man who makes a god of his vain desires — what is your conclusion about such as he? Can you think to be a guardian over him? Or do you reckon that most of them listen and think intelligently? They are just like cattle. No! farther off than that from the true path.

We have sent you only as a herald and as one who brings warning. Say: 'For this I seek no reward from you, save that who-ever wills shall take his way to his Lord.' Put your trust in the living One who dies not, and celebrate His praise. He is full well aware of His servants' sin — He who created the heavens and the earth in six days and then seated Himself on the Throne, the merciful One. Concerning Him, question a source that knows. When they are told: 'Worship the merciful One,' they say: 'What is the *Rahmān*? Are we to worship whatever you bid us?' and their aversion grows. *Surah 25.41-44 and 56-60*

THEIR hearts are perplexed by this Qur'ān and, furthermore, there are things they are doing which they will continue to do until they cry out in pleading, after We have seized those of them who revel in opulence with retribution. 'Do not cry out today: there is no help coming to you from Us! My revelations were constantly read to you but you turned on your heels in recoil and disdain, talking glibly like some chatterer after nightfall.'

Have they in no way reflected on what was said? Or has there come to them a message never brought to their fathers of old? Or is it that they do not know their messenger and so deny him? Or are they saying of him: 'He is possessed'? No! the fact is that the truth has come to them and most of them have a hatred of the truth.

Were the truth to tally with their desires the heavens and the earth and all within them would have fallen into corruption. We have brought them their *Dhikr* and from their *Dhikr* they turn away.

Say: 'To whom does the earth and those within it belong — if you have knowledge?' They will say: 'To God.' Say: 'Do you not then remember and consider?' Say: 'Who is the Lord of the seven heavens and the Lord of the great Throne?' They will say: 'God.' Say: 'Do you not fear Him then?' Say: 'In whose hand is the sovereignty over all things, who protects and who Himself needs no protector — if you have knowledge?' They will say: 'In God's.' Say: 'How then are you given to sorcery?' We have brought them the truth and they are giving the lie to it. God has adopted no son and there is no god with Him. For in that event each god would certainly have taken up his own creation and some would have got the better over others. Glory be to God immune from all they attribute, knowing the unseen and the visible, exalted in majesty above all they ascribe as associate to Him. *Surah 23.63-71 and 84-92*

To no human have We ever, before your time, granted immortality. So, when you (s.) come to die, will they be immortal? Indeed, every soul has to taste death. We test and try you (pl.) with the evil and with the good. To Us you will be brought again.

When those who deny see you (s.) they take you as altogether a joke: 'Is this the fellow who makes reference to your gods?' whereas they repudiate all mention of the One ever merciful.

Man was created a creature of haste. I will show to you (pl.) My signs, but do not practice your haste on Me! — as they are asking: 'When will this be that is promised, if you are telling the truth?' If the unbelievers did but know the time when they will be powerless to keep the Fire off their faces and their backs, when there will be no help for them! Suddenly will it come upon them and stupefy them and they will have no strength to ward it off, and they will have no reprieve.

Messengers before you (s.) have undergone ridicule and the thing they mocked at overtook those deriders.

Say: 'Who will protect you, by night and by day, from the Merciful?' But no! they turn aside from the remembrance of their Lord. Or do they have gods who can shield them from Us? These cannot even save themselves and, against Us, can take no part with their protégés. We have indeed granted these people and their fathers life's enjoyments through length of years. But do they not perceive how We bring curtailment upon the land and its borders? Are they going to win out? Say: 'It is by revelation that I warn you.' But the deaf, when they are warned, do not hear the summons. *Surah 21.34-45*

THOSE who reject faith said: 'What! when we and our forebears are dust of the earth are we going to be brought forth again? This was promised us and our forebears in the past. It is nothing but fables from old time!' Say: 'Go out and about in the world and see how it was with wicked doers in their painful end.' Do not sorrow over them nor be oppressed because of their intrigues.

They ask: 'If you are dealing honestly, when shall this promise come to pass?' Tell them: 'It could well be that something of what you want expedited is already riding hard on your heels!'

Your (s.) Lord is rich in grace toward mankind, but most of humanity give no thanks. Your Lord knows the secrets of their hearts as well as everything they openly reveal. There is not a hidden thing in heaven or on earth which is not within a Book where all is crystal clear.

This Qur'ān presents to the children of Israel many of the themes about which they are in dispute. To those who believe, it is guidance and mercy. In His wisdom your Lord will judge between them — He the all-strong, the all-knowing. Put your trust in God. You have the warrant of plain truth.

You will not avail to make dead folk hear, nor the deaf heed, the preaching: they turn their backs and slip away. You will not lead the blind away from their misguidedness, nor gain a hearing except from such as believe in Our revelations — those who are *muslimūn* surrendered to God.

When sentence is spoken against them, a beast We will bring forth out of the earth to arraign them, telling how mankind had no faith in Our revelations. On that day We will assemble from every people a multitude of whose who denied the truth of Our revelations. When, in their several categories they come forward He will say: 'Did you deny the truth of My revelations, without ever giving your mind to take in what they were? What were you doing then?' Sentence shall go against them on account of their wrong-doing and they will be speechless. . . .

I am commanded to serve the Lord of this place (Mecca) which He has sanctified. All things are His. I am commanded to be *muslim* with all those who are surrendered to God, and to be voice to this Qur'ān. He who receives guidance does so of and for himself. As for him who goes into error, well say: 'I gave you warning!'

Say: 'Praise be to God: He will show you (pl.) His revelations and you will recognise them for what they are.' Your (s.) Lord is not unmindful of what you are all doing.   *Surah 27.67-85 and 91-93*

THE apostle said: 'Lord, my people have been altogether dismissive of this Qur'ān.' It has been Our way in the case of every prophet to have him experience enmity from those who are evil-bent. But in your Lord there is all you need to guide and sustain you.

Those who asserted it was false said: 'How come the Qur'ān was not sent down upon him as one whole?' It is as it is with a view to Our re-assuring your heart. We have recited it in due order. For any notion they may have for you in the things they say We will give you the truth of the matter in better explanation.

Rounded up for *Jahannam*, crestfallen, those unbelievers will be in evil case and altogether out of the true way.   *Surah 25.30-34*

ACCORDINGLY We have sent it down as an Arabic Qur'ān, in which We have set out sundry warnings: it may be they will come to a godly fear or that right remembrance may be brought to life within them. Let God be exalted — the true and real Sovereign.

Do not be precipitate in respect of the Qur'ān before its revelation is determined for you, and say: 'Lord, increase me in knowledge.'
             Surah 20.113-114

HĀ, Mīm, 'Ain, Sīn, Qāf. Even so has God, the all-strong, the all-wise, made revelation to you and to those who came before you. All is His in the heavens and in the earth. He is the most high, the great. The heavens above come near to bursting open when the angels celebrate the praise of their Lord and pray forgiveness for earth's people. Truly God is all-forgiving and all-merciful.

As for those who adopt patron deities to the exclusion of God, well God has them under watch. It is not your job to be responsible for them.

Moreover, We have revealed to you an Arabic Qur'ān so that you may warn the mother-city (Mecca) and those in her environs — warn them of the Day of Gathering, that undoubted Day, when the garden of paradise will have its denizens and *al-Saʿīr* hers.   *Surah 42.1-7*

HĀ, Mīm. By the Book that throws light. We have constituted it an Arabic Qur'ān, so that perhaps you may comprehend. It is there in the Mother of the Book in Our presence, truly exalted, the definitive wisdom.

Ought We to take back the Reminder from you (pl.) altogether, seeing that you are such wanton people? How many a prophet have We sent to people in earlier times. But never was there a prophet who did not incur their mockery when he came. We brought ruin on people far more formidable in their power than these, and those of olden time are a parable that has gone into history.

If you asked them who it is who created the heavens and the earth, they would say: 'The Almighty, who is all-wise, He created them.' — He who formed the earth as a cradle for you and made it such as to afford route-ways for you on which to find direction, He who sends down water from heaven in due measure whereby We bring dead land to life. You will be brought likewise into resurrection. It is He who created all complementary pairs of things and gave you both ships and animals for transport so that, on deck or in saddle, you might call to mind the grace of your Lord in the mastery you have of them and say: 'Praise be to Him who has given this into our hand to control in this way, when we ourselves were inadequate for it. It is to our Lord we are always coming back in the end.'

Yet, here they are — setting on a par with Him the very things that serve Him! Patently man is an ungrateful creature!

Has God adopted daughters from His own creation while He blessed you with sons? You glower darkly in angry irritation, any of you, when he gets word of that befalling him which he pictures for the all-merciful. 'What! a girl-child to be reared for decking out in finery and be tediously argumentative!'

In their book the angels too — the servants of the all-merciful — are feminine. Have they been witnesses at their creation? This verdict of theirs will be recorded and they will be interrogated about it.

They say also: 'Had the all-merciful so willed we would not have worshipped them.' As to that they have no knowledge at all: they are merely guessing. Have We, previous to this, brought them a book to which they are now adhering? On the contrary. What they say is: 'We found our fathers following a community tradition and we are simply being guided by their precedents.'

So it is that, before you We never sent a warner to a city but those who lived there comfortably did not say: 'We found our fathers following a community tradition and we are simply doing as they did.' 'What if I have brought you better guidance than that which you found your fathers following?' each messenger would say. Their reply runs: 'We have no faith in what you are sent with.'

So We took vengeance on them. Look well how it ended for those who said it was all lies.   *Surah 43.1-25*

THEY say: 'Why was this Qur'ān not sent down to some man of great standing in the two cities?' Is it they who allot where your Lord's mercy goes? It is We who apportion among them what livelihood they have in respect of the things of this life. Some We have raised above others in standing: some can make others do them service. The mercy of your (s.) Lord is worth more than all their accumulated wealth. But for the fact that then all mankind would have become of one such persuasion, We would have seen to it that those who denied faith in the all-merciful possessed silver roofing for their houses, stairs to get up to them, and silver doors for their dwellings and reclining couches and ornaments of gold! Yet all these would be mere enjoyments of this present life. The life to come is with your Lord for those who fear Him.

For him who lets himself be blind to the remembrance of the all-merciful We assign a satan to be his *qarīn*. These shadowers of the self bar the way to the path of truth, their counterparts thinking meanwhile that they are being rightly guided, until — when they reach Our Presence — they say: 'Would you had been as far away from me as the east from the west — wretched *qarīn*!' It will be no profit to you on that day that, having been partners in evil-doing, you are also partners in doom.

Can you (s.) make the deaf hear or guide the blind and those who are patently misguided? Whether We remove you from the scene or let you see what We have forewarned them of, We will surely take vengeance on them. We have them totally in Our power.

You, for your part, hold fast to what has been revealed to you. You are on a straight path. This is truly a Reminder to you and to your people. You will all be questioned. Ask those of Our messengers whom We sent prior to you: Did We prescribe deities to be worshipped, and not the all-merciful?   *Surah 43.31-45*

HĀ, Mīm. A revelation from above from the merciful Lord of mercy, a Book whose verses have been clearly set forth as an Arabic Qur'ān, for a perceptive people, bringing good news and warning. Most of them turn aside and pay no heed. 'Our hearts,' they say, 'are impregnable to any message like yours. Our ears are deaf. Between us there is a curtain. Do as you will: what we do is our business.'

Say: 'I am a mortal man as you are. It is revealed to me that your God is one God. Take the straight path to Him and seek His forgiveness. Woe to those who worship other gods, who bring no alms and have no faith in the world to come. To those who believe and do good works is a reward that never fails.'   *Surah 41.1-8*

TĀ, HĀ. We have not caused the Qur'ān to come down to you to make you dismayed but as a reminder to the godly, a revelation from Him who created the earth and the highest heavens. The all-merciful regnant on the eternal Throne — His are all things in the heavens and in the earth, in the realms between, and beneath the ground. Irrespective of how loud your (s.) words, He knows the whole secret and more. God — there is no god but He. His are the beautiful Names. *Surah 20.1-8*

DOES it not come home to them how many generations before them We have caused to perish? They are walking in the very places they inhabited. Surely that constitutes a telling sign to any who are possessed of intelligence. But for a decree of your Lord already in being, with its time appointed, the judgement on them was necessarily immediate.

Bear, then, patiently with what they say: celebrate the praise of your Lord before the rising of the sun and before its setting, and at the watches of the night. Give praise to God at the opening and decline of day and be well-pleasing to Him. Do not cast longing eyes at the flourishing benefits of this present world which We have afforded some of them in order to put them to the test. Your Lord's provision for you is better and more lasting.

Lay the duty of prayer on your household and be diligent in it yourself. It is not as if We were asking you to provide for Us: it is We who provide for you. All that matters in the end is true godliness.

They ask: 'Why does he not bring us some sign from his Lord?' Have they not had sufficient clear proof in the earlier scriptures? Had We destroyed them in retribution prior to this (Qur'ān) they would have said: 'Our Lord, if only You had sent us a messenger we would have followed Your revelations before we were humiliated and put to shame.'

Say: 'Everyone is in anticipation. Be on the look-out, then, and you will yet know who they are who tread the right path and have been surely guided.' *Surah 20.128-135*

HOW many a generation of stronger mettle than they have We brought to ruin before them! They went over the land in frantic search for possible refuge. Surely there is point to ponder here for whoever has a heart or who heeds with alert perception?

We created the heavens and the earth and the realms between in six days with no touch of weariness.

Be patient, then, with what they say and celebrate the praise of your

Lord before the rising of the sun and before its setting, and by night, and praise Him, too, when you conclude the prostrations. Be on the alert to listen for the Day when, from close at hand shall come the herald's call — the Day men hear the cry in reality, the Day of exodus. We bring to life and We bring to death. It is to Us that all things move as their climax. We know full well what they are saying. You have no power of compulsion over them. So by the Qur'ān admonish any who will fear My warning. *Surah 50.36-45*

SAY: 'I do not ask of you any wage for it. I do not take upon myself to be more than I am. This is no more than a reminder to all sentient beings. Undoubtedly you will learn its import bye and bye.' *Surah 38.86-88*

THEY say: 'If you are dealing truthfully, when is the promise to be fulfilled?' Say: 'It is only God who knows that. I am just a clear warner. When they realise that it is imminent the faces of those who reject faith will darken with fear at the words: "This is what you were promised!"'
Say: 'Have you realised — whether God makes an end of me and my companions or whether He shows us mercy — who is there to safeguard the rejectors of faith from painful punishment?'
Say: 'He is the all-merciful. In Him we have believed: in Him we have placed our trust. In due course you will know who it is who is manifestly in the wrong.' Say: 'Have you realised — who is there to bring you gushing water were your water supply to retreat far underground?'
Surah 67.25-30

IN the very place of their habitation there was a sign for the people of Sabā' (Sheba) — gardens on either hand. 'Eat', We said, 'of your Lord's provision and give Him thanks.' Truly a goodly land and a forgiving Lord.
But they gave no heed. We sent against them the flood of 'Arim, replacing their gardens on right and left with others which brought forth bitter fruits and tamarisk shrubs and a scattering of *sidr* trees. Thus We requited them for their unbelief. For is Our retribution ever visited except on deniers of the truth?
Between the people of Sābā and the cities of Our benediction (Mecca and Jerusalem) We set a chain of villages readily accessible, to facilitate their journeys, saying: 'Go safely by night and by day.' But they

complained: 'Our Lord made the distances long between our staging posts.' They were involved in wrongdoing against themselves. We consigned them to the story-tellers and brought on them total disintegration — in all of which there is significance for everyone who is capable of patience and gratitude. *Iblīs* proved his conjecture about them to be true. For they followed him — all but a group who did believe. He had no authority of his own over them. It was only that We might know those who believed in the last Day from those who doubted. Your (s.) Lord is One who watches over all things.   *Surah 34.15-21*

BY the heaven with its starry spheres, and the promised Day, by witness seeing and witness borne, death to the perpetrators of *Al-Ukhdūd*, that trench of burning fire, where they sat surveying the scene of their handiwork against believers. They laid violent hands on them for the sole reason that their victims were believers in God, the mighty One, ever to be praised, to whom belongs the sovereignty of the heavens and of the earth, the God who is witness to everything.

Those who persecute believers, men and women, and do not later repent the torment of *Jahannam* awaits them, the retribution of the burning Fire. Those who hold the faith and do righteous deeds, theirs is the reward of gardens where streams flow — the supreme, saving climax. Relentless indeed is your (s.) Lord's power. He it is who brings into being and brings again anew. He is the One who forgives and who loves, the glorious Lord of the Throne, accomplishing all that He wills.

Surah 85.1-16

ARE you (s.) not aware of what your Lord did with that army of elephant riders? Did He not turn their stratagem awry? He sent against them swarms of creatures borne on the air, which showered on them the very stones of fate (*sijjīl*), leaving them like cropped-off stubble.   *Surah 105*

NO! I swear by all that you can see and by all that is unseen by you, that it is in truth the word of a gracious envoy. It is not the word of a poet, however little you find that credible. It is not what some diviner would be saying, however little you take it to heart. It is a revelation sent down from the Lord of all being. Had he (the messenger) foisted utterances on to Us We would have seized him by the right hand and cut his jugular vein, and not one of you could have restrained Us.

'It is a Reminder to those who are God-fearing. We are fully aware that there are those of you who deny its truth. It is repining grief to those who are set on unbelief. It is truth, certain truth. So praise the Name of your (s.) Lord most mighty. *Surah 69.38-52*

WHEN Our revelations are rehearsed to them — clear evidence that they are — the cry is: 'This fellow is simply wanting to dissuade you from the worship which your fathers followed. It is all a fraud and a fabrication.' When the truth comes to them those who reject faith say of it: 'This is plain sorcery.'

Yet We have not brought them any scriptures for them to have taken into their reckoning, nor — prior to you — have We sent anyone to them with admonition.

Peoples before them treated the truth as lies, although having less than a tenth of what We have here brought them. They gave a lie to My messengers and how intensely I disavowed them!

Say: 'I (Muhammad) have just one thing to press upon you — namely that you stand before God, whether accompanied or alone. Take stock, then, of your thoughts and realise that your kinsman is not mad. All he is doing is warning you of impending and sharp affliction.' Say: 'I have sought no wage from you. That is yours. My reward is from God alone: He is witness of everything.'

Say: 'It is with the truth that my Lord makes you His target. He knows all hidden things.' Say: 'The truth has come. Falsehood is a spent force, put to silence.' Say: 'If I am in error, I go astray to my own loss, and if I have been rightly guided, it is of my Lord's doing in revelation to me. He hears all and is ever at hand.' *Surah 34.43-50*

WHEN they hear the Reminder those who reject the faith look daggers at you (s.) and they say: 'He is surely demented!'

A Reminder to all sentient beings — that is the whole truth of the matter. *Surah 68.51-52*

ALIF, Lām, Rā. A Book We have sent down to you by leave of their Lord, so that you may bring men out of the shadows of darkness into the light, into the path of Him who is all strong, to whom all praise belongs — to God whose are all things in the heavens and in the earth. Woe be to those who reject faith: a terrible punishment is theirs — those who set their love on the life of this lower world rather than of the world to come and who turn others away from the path of God, eagerly making it out to be crooked. All such have gone very far wrong.

We have not sent any messenger except in the speech of his own people, in order to make everything clear to them. Whom He wills God leads astray and whom He wills He guides. For He is all-strong and all-wise.   *Surah 14.1-4*

GLORY to Him who by night took His servant journeying from the sacred mosque to the distant mosque, *Al-Aqsā*, whose precincts We have blessed, in order to show him Our revelations. He is the One who hears and sees all.   *Surah 17.1*

THIS Qur'ān is guide to what is fully upright. To believers who do righteous deeds it is good news of a great reward. Those who do not believe in the last Day it tells of painful punishment We have made ready.

In his prayer of petition for what is good man may be praying for what is evil, impetuous as man is. We have ordained night and day as two signs. We extinguish the night-sign and bring on the day-sign which gives occasion to sight, so that you may seek good things from your Lord and learn to compute the seasons and the years. All things We have given into intelligible analysis.

Every man's omen (*lit.* bird) of destiny We have attached to his neck. On the Day of resurrection We will take out a book which he will find opened wide before him: 'Read your record! you are this day a sufficient assessor against yourself.' Whoever has been rightly guided it has been only on his own account and whoever has gone astray his misguidedness is upon him alone. Of burdens there is no vicarious bearing by one for another. We have never inflicted chastisement without first sending a messenger. If it be Our will to destroy some community, We do so only after laying Our command on its fast-living people and the verdict is justified by their base conduct. In that event We bring it to total ruin.

How many generations of those after Noah have We destroyed. Your (s.) Lord is completely aware of the transgressions of His servitors, all-seeing as He is. Whoever is enamoured of this hasting life on him We will hasten what Our will holds for him. Then We assign *Jahannam*, for him, where, condemned and disowned, he will be in fire. Whoever has desired the life to come and strived earnestly towards it, being believers, their yearning will receive a ready welcome.

To all such — these here, those there — We extend the bounty of your
(s.) Lord. Giving on your Lord's part is not stinted. Observe how We
have here given preference to some over others, while the life to come is
of a greater quality and has larger measures of worth.   *Surah 17.9-21*

WHEN you give voice to the Qur'ān We have caused a curtain to be
drawn between you and those who do not believe in the last Day. We
cloak their hearts so that they do not take it in. Their ears are sluggish. So
it is that when you have named your Lord's Name in the Qur'ān — and
His alone — they promptly turn their backs in distaste. We know well
what they are listening for from it when they give you hearing, and how
they go aside to put their heads together with the evil-doers saying: 'You
are following a man who is nothing but a victim of sorcery.' See what
images of you they have coined, going far wrong, in total incomprehen-
sion of the true way. They say: 'When we have become bones and specks
of dust are we really going to the raised again, a new creation?' Say:
'Indeed — even were you stones and iron, or any other thing that seems
to your inmost thoughts still more grotesque.' 'Who?' they query, 'will
bring us back to life?' Tell them: 'The One who formed you the first
time.' Shaking their heads incredulously at you, they say: 'Then when
will this be?' Say: 'It may well be quite soon, on a day when He summons
you and you will respond by praising Him, thinking all the time that you
have spent only a brief stay.'
Tell My servants to speak kindly. Satan stirs up strife among them:
Satan has ever been an avowed enemy to mankind. Your Lord knows
you through and through. As He wills He has mercy on you, and as He
wills He afflicts you. We have not sent you to take over responsibility for
them.   *Surah 17.45-54*

SAY: 'Make your pleas to those whom you claim to invoke in the place of
God. They are powerless to relieve you of distress or to change anything.
The very ones to whom they make their pleas themselves take recourse to
their Lord, competing to be the nearest. They hope for His mercy and
they fear His punishment. Your Lord's chastisement merits a cautious
wariness.'   *Surah 17.56-57*

WITH the truth We have sent it down, with the truth it came from above.
We have only sent you as a bringer of good news and of warning. It is a

Qur'ān We have made serial so that you might announce it to mankind at intervals. We have made its revelation gradual.

Say: 'Believe it, or believe it not.' Those to whom knowledge of it has previously come fall down on their faces in prostration when it is recited to them, saying: 'Glory to our Lord. Truly the promise of our Lord is fulfilled.' They fall prostrate with their faces to the earth, in tears, in deepening humility.

Say: 'Call on God (*Allāh*), or call upon the all-merciful (*Al-Rahmān*) — whichever Name your prayer takes. For He is the possessor of the beautiful Names. Do not pray in a loud voice, nor in too low a voice, but cultivate what is well modulated.'

Say: 'Praise to God — He who takes none to Himself for a son, He who has no partner in sovereignty, He who needs no champion lest He should be worsted.'

Magnify Him, and again, magnify Him.   *Surah 17.105-111*

GOD'S enactment (*Amr*) is under way: do not seek to hasten it. Glory be to Him, transcendent beyond all that idolaters conceive. With the Spirit of His command (*Amr*) He sends the angels upon those of His servants whom He wills, to give warning that 'There is no god but I'. 'Hold Me then in awe.'   *Surah 16.1-2*

AND God said: 'Do not adopt dual deities. For He is one God. It is I whom you have to fear.' To Him belong all things in the heavens and in the earth. It is to Him that religious devotion must be unceasing. Will you bring God's fear to some other than He? There is no grace that comes your way which is not from God. When ill befalls you it is to Him you repair. Thereafter, when the evil is relieved, some among you revert to idolatrous associations against their Lord, giving the lie to all that We have afforded them. Alright! take your full delight: you will be wiser at the end.

They attribute part and lot in Our provision to figments of their own ignorance. By God! you will certainly be interrogated about your fabrications. They ascribe daughters to God — glory be to Him — and they get the coveted sons! For when any of them has word of a female child he glowers darkly in angry irritation. He keeps out of people's way in ill humour over the news of the child. Is he to keep it and stomach the loss of face or is he to hide it in the ground? How vile is the way their minds work.

Evil indeed is the character of those who do not believe in the last Day. God — the all-strong, the all-wise — He is the supreme theme of all man can characterise. *Surah 16.51-60*

WHEN you recite the Qur'ān seek refuge with God against the accursed Satan. He has no authority over those who have believed and who put their trust in their Lord. His authority is only over those who align themselves with him and who thereby practise idolatry.

When We exchange one verse in place of another — and God knows well what He sends in revelation — they say: 'You are just making it up yourself.' Most of them are quite without understanding. Say: 'The Spirit of holiness has revealed it from your Lord in truth, to establish in faith those who have believed and as guidance and good news to those who have surrendered.' We know well what they are saying, namely: 'It is some man or other who is teaching him.' The language of the one they are alluding to is a foreign tongue, whereas this Qur'ān is in clear Arabic.

Those who do not believe in God's revelations God will not guide. Theirs is a painful punishment. Falsehood is fabricated by those who do not believe in God's revelations — it is such as these who go about with lies. *Surah 16.98-105*

God has laid down for you the religion He ordained for Noah, the one We have revealed to you (s.) just as We charged Abraham with it also, and Moses, and Jesus, saying: 'Be doers of this religion and do not let yourselves become divided about it.' But those who indulge in false worships, to them your message is too onerous. God draws to Himself whom He wills and guides to Himself those who repent.

Divisions occurred among men only after knowledge had come to them — and that, because of their self-conceit. Had the word of your Lord not already decreed deferment of their reckoning, judgement would by now have been pronounced between them. Even those who have become heirs of the Book since their day are in grave doubts about it.

Accordingly, give your message steadfastly as you have been commanded. Do not follow their desires. Say: 'I believe in the Scripture God has sent down. I am commanded to deal justly with you. God is our Lord and your Lord. We have our deeds and you have yours. There is no argument between us; God will bring us together and to Him is the journey of our destiny.' Those who want to argue about God after they have pledged their faith in Him will find all they say pointless in the presence of their Lord. For such people there is anger and a stern requital.

God has sent down the Book with the truth, the balance that decides. Who can tell? It may be that the Hour is near. Those who have no faith in it would have it come as soon as it likes! But the real believers hold its approach in deep reverence and know it is the truth. It is a grave error to be sceptical about the Hour that is to come.

God is gentle with His servants. His bounty He bestows on whom he will. He is the Lord of might and power.   *Surah 42.13-19*

W HEN they see that which they are promised then they will know whose are the weaker allies and who the fewer number. Say: 'Whether that which you have been promised is imminent or whether my Lord has set for it a distant time, I do not know. He knows the realm unseen and to none does He disclose that unseen of His except to apostles of His choosing, for whom He commissions before and behind them an observant watch, ascertaining that they have duly delivered the messages of their Lord. He has within His grasp all they have in hand and He has count of everything.   *Surah 72.24-28*

W HAT possesses the unbelievers, jostling about in front of you (s.) all agog and crowding in from right and left? Are they aspiring, to a man, to enter into a garden of delight?

Hardly so! They know well enough from what We created them. No! I swear by the Lord of the place, east and west, of the sun's rising and its setting, We are able to replace them with others better than they and none will avail to stay Our hand. So let them chatter and amuse themselves until they reach that promised Day of theirs — the Day when they will scurry from the tombs as if racing to a rallying flag. Their eyes will be downcast on that Day in the onset of humiliation — the Day that they were promised.   *Surah 70.36-44*

Yā, Sīn: by the Qur'ān with its wisdom, you (s.) are among the apostles, sent upon a straight path. It is the revelation from above given by the all-strong, the all-merciful, for you to warn a people whose fathers were not warned before them and who have lived in unconcern.

Against most of them the word has been all too truly spoken: for they are unbelieving. Indeed, We have put shackles round their necks, up to their chins and that is how they are stiff-necked! We have set a bar in front of them and a bar in their rear and shrouded them so that they cannot see.

It is all the same to them whether you give them warning or you warn them not — either way they disbelieve. Effectively you only warn those who follow the *Dhikr* and who fear the all-merciful in the great unseen. Give glad word to such of forgiveness and ample reward. It is We who give life to the dead, We who record the deeds accumulated from the past and the effects they left behind. All is there by Our accounting in a clear register. *Surah 36.1-12*

ALIF, Lām, Mīm, Sad. A Book sent down to you (s.). Let there be no anxiety in your heart because of it, so that through it you may give warning: it is a mentor for the minds of believers. Follow obediently what has been sent down to you (pl.) from your Lord: do not adhere to guardian powers, displacing God alone. Scant is the place you give this in your thoughts.

How many a city-community have We made to perish when Our power seized them by night or while they were in noonday repose! The only plea they had when Our power came upon them was to acknowledge: 'We were indeed wrongdoers.'

We will surely interrogate those to whom a message was sent and We will interrogate the messengers themselves, recounting their deeds to them in full knowledge — We were not absentees at the time!

The weighing that Day is right and true. They whose scales are heavy are the ones to come to good, while those whose scales are light are the ones who forfeit their souls, having done violence to Our revelations. *Surah 7.1-9*

NOT a single revelation comes to them from their Lord but they turn away from it. The truth when it came to them they have alleged to be lies. Soon, however, the things they have been deriding will be brought home to them. Have they not realised how many a generation before them We have caused to perish whom We had set in power in the earth more amply than We established you — people on whom We sent copious rains from heaven and for whom We made rivers flow at their feet, but whom, nevertheless, We brought to ruin because of their transgressions. After them We gave rise to another generation.

Had We sent down to you (s.) a book on parchment they could

themselves handle those who disbelieved would have said: 'This is nothing but obvious trickery.' 'Why has not some angel been sent down to him?' Yet had an angel been sent down, that would have been the doom of judgement, with no chance of respite. Moreover, had We made it an angelic mission We would have had a human for angel and thus left them with the same confused ideas as they have now.

Long before your time messengers have been met with derision. But those who taunted them were overtaken by the very thing they had laughed out of court.

Say: 'Go through the world and see what happened in the end to those who said it was all lies.' Say: 'To whom belongs all that the heavens and the earth enfold?' Say: 'To God: He has made mercy His obligation. He will surely assemble you together on the Day of resurrection — the indubitable Day. Those who forfeit their own souls are those who do not believe.'

All that dwells in night and day belongs to Him — He the all-hearing, the all-knowing. Say: 'Shall I adopt any guardian but God, the One who fashioned the heavens and the earth — He who gives food and receives none?'

Say: 'I am commanded to be first of those who surrender.' The command to me was: 'On no account be among those polytheists.' Say: 'I stand in fear of the punishment of the great day were I to rebel against my Lord.' On that day whoever stands acquitted God's mercy has come to him and that is to attain the ultimate goal.

If God touches you (s.) with distress none but He can remove it: if with good all is within His omnipotent hand. He is sovereign over His servants — He the all-wise, the all-comprehending.

Say: 'What carries the greatest weight in bearing out a witness given?' Say: 'God is witness between me and you. This Qur'ān has been given to me by inspiration so that through it I might warn you and whomever it may reach. Are you (pl.) indeed saying as witnesses that there are other gods as well as God?' Say: 'That is no witness of mine. For my part I say that He is one God. I have nothing to do with your plural worship.' Those to whom We have brought the Book recognise it just as they recognise their own sons. Those who forfeit their own souls are those who do not believe. *Surah 6.4-20*

WE know well that what they are saying grieves you. It is not you whom they are making out a liar. It is the very revelations of God that wrongdoers repudiate. Other messengers before you have been subjected to such denials. They endured all the calumnies and the wrongs done to them patiently until We came to their aid. There is nothing that can alter the words of God. You are in possession of information about those emissaries. Their aversion to you is a great distress but had you the capacity to delve deep into the earth or take a ladder into heaven in order to constitute a sign for them, God — had He so willed — could have brought them all together to the true way. So, on your part, on no account fail to understand. It is only those who listen who can respond. As for the dead, God will raise them again and to Him will their returning be. *Surah 6.33-36*

SAY: 'I am forbidden to serve those you are invoking to the exclusion of God.' Say: 'I do not follow your appetites. For then I would have gone into error and ceased to be with the rightly guided.' Say: 'I take my stand on clear evidence from my Lord and you have alleged it to be false. What you want to bring quickly to issue is not in my hands. Decision is God's alone, who declares the truth. There is no better discriminator between true and false than He.' Say: 'If what you are in such haste to have were in my power no doubt there would be a clear decision about what is at stake between us. God knows well who are the evil-doers. With Him are the keys of the unseen: none knows them but Himself. He knows all things on land and sea. There is no grain in the dark earth, nothing green with moisture nor withered dry but that its record is in a book where all is plain. It is He who by night calls you from yourselves in sleep and who knows what you earn by day. He delegates you until a stated term is fulfilled, and then it is to Him your cycle finally returns. Then He will give you to know all your deeds. He is sovereign over all His servants. He sends over you those who stand watch. Then when death singles you out Our messengers call him to his account — and they are never lax in their arrest. Afterwards they are recalled to God, the rightful Master. Is not decision entirely His? — the swiftest of all who make reckoning.' *Surah 6.56-62*

THEY say: 'The Merciful has adopted a son.' It is an appalling assertion you have made! The heavens would almost break up and the earth disintegrate at it and the mountains collapse into ruin — they claiming a son to the Merciful! It is entirely unbefitting to the Merciful to adopt a child. Every being in the heavens and the earth comes to the Merciful only as a servant. Truly He has counted them and He has numbered them exactly. Every one of them will come to Him on the Day of

resurrection individually. To those who have believed and done righteously the Merciful will extend love.

We have made the Scripture to be readily in your (s.) utterance in order
that you may bring good news by it to the God-fearing and warn by it a
contentious people. How many a generation before them have We made
to perish. Can you (s.) find a trace of any one of them or hear even a
whisper of them?   *Surah 19.88-98*

THEY say: 'We will never believe you (s.) until you make a spring of
water gush forth from the ground for us; or you own a garden of
date-palms and grapes in which you have rivers flowing forth copiously;
or you make the sky to fall on us in fragments as you have claimed; or
you bring here God and His angels to make your point; or until you
possess a house of gold or you ascend into heaven. Even then we will
never credit your ascension unless you bring back from on high for us a
book which we can read.'

Say: 'Praise be to my Lord. What am I if not a mortal messenger?
Nothing has prevented people from believing when guidance came to
them except their own attitude in saying: "Would it be a mortal man God
sent as a messenger?"'

Say: 'Had it been angels walking around serenely on the earth We
would have sent them an angel out of heaven as messenger.'

Say: 'God is sufficient witness between me and you. He is altogether
aware of His servants and sees them through and through. He whom
God guides is well guided and whom He leads astray for them you will
find no protector apart from Him. On the Day of resurrection We will
assemble them all, prone on their faces, blind, dumb and deaf, and
Jahannam their abode. Every time the Fire abates We will increase the
blaze. That is their requital for their unbelief in Our revelations and their
saying: "When we are mere bones and broken debris shall we indeed be
raised again to a new creation?" Have they not realised that God who
created the heavens and the earth is well able to create their like again? He
has set their allotted term — of that there is no doubt. The unbelievers
reject everything save their unbelief.'

Say: 'Did you own the treasuries of your Lord's mercy you would still
hold back, fearing to expend. Man was ever miserly.'   *Surah 17.90-100*

WHEN Our clear revelations are recited to them those who have no mind
for their destiny to meet Us say: 'Bring some other Qur'ān than this or
change it.' Say: 'It is no right of mine to change it of my own accord. I

follow only what is revealed to me. I stand in fear of the retribution of a dread Day were I to go counter to my Lord.'

Say: 'Had God's will been so, I would not have recited it to you nor made it known to you. I have lived among you a life-time before it came to me. Will you not understand?'

Who does greater wrong than he who invents a lie against God or gives the lie to His revelations. Guilty wrong-doers will never come to good. They give worship — to the exclusion of God — to what can neither harm nor benefit them and they say: 'These are our intercessors with God.' Say: 'Are you in the business of informing God of what He does not know in the heavens and in the earth? Praise be to Him, exalted may He be beyond all their false ascriptions!'

Mankind were originally one single community and they fell into discord. The things about which they were at variance would have been decisively settled had it not been for a previous decree from your (s.) Lord.

They say: 'Why has no sign been sent down to him from his Lord?' Say: 'The unseen is with God. So wait: I will be waiting with you.'

No sooner have We let mankind taste mercy after some hardship has come their way than they conspire against Our revelations. Say: 'God has more rapid schemes! Messengers of Ours are recording your devious plots.'

It is He who sends you journeying by land and sea. When you are aboard ship sailing with a fair wind, seamen are glad. Then there comes on them a tempestuous wind, waves beating on every side, and they think themselves in dire straits and cry out to God in genuine sincerity: 'Would You but deliver us now we would truly be thankful men.' Yet when He has delivered them they behave iniquitously in the land and violate the right. 'Men! it is your own selves you are violating, thinking only of what this present life affords. To Us is your returning — anon, and We will confront you with your deeds.' *Surah 10.15-23*

IT is not for any soul to believe except by leave of God and on those who do not bring their minds to think He assigns the things that defile. Say: 'Look well at the heavens and the earth and what is in them. Revelations and warnings, however, are of no avail to unbelieving people. Have they in prospect anything other than the like of the days of their predecessors who passed away before them?' Say: 'Indulge your hopes: I, with you, am in expectation!' Our apostles and those who believe We in due time deliver. For so have We laid upon Ourselves to deliver believers.'

Say: 'People! if you are in doubt about my religion, well — I do not worship what you worship, to the exclusion of God. But I worship God alone, God who determines your mortal span. I am commanded to be among those who believe.'

'Set your (s.) face to the true religion as a *hanīf*, and on no account be among those who hold with plural gods. Make no prayer to other than God, no prayer to what can neither profit nor harm you. Were you to do so you would align yourself with those who are given to evil. If God brings on you some affliction, only He can remove it, and if he wills good for you none can turn away His goodness. He lets affliction befall whom-ever of His servants He wills. He is the forgiving and merciful One.'

Say: 'People! The truth has come to you from your Lord. Whoever is guided is so for his own soul's good and whoever goes astray does so to his own soul's loss. I am not a guardian over you.'

Follow what is inspired in you (s.). Be patient, until God judges. He is of judges the best.   *Surah 10.100-109*

CREDENTIALS to see by have come to you (pl.) from your Lord: he, then, who sees clearly does so to his soul's well-being, while the man who remains blind incriminates himself, and I am not on guard for you. In this way We set Our revelations out, so that they say to you (s.): 'You have studied.' So We elucidate them to a people who comprehend.

Follow what is revealed to you (s.) from your Lord — there is no god but He — and give wide berth to the pagan pluralists. Had God willed they would not have been idolaters. We have not appointed you to be a guardian over them and you do not hold responsibility for them. Do not (pl.) revile the objects on which they call, in their exclusion of God, lest these, retorting, revile God in their ignorance. To every nation We have made what they do seem fair in their sight: then their destiny is to be brought back to their Lord who will confront them with their deeds.

They have said on solemn oath that if a sign had been brought to them they would certainly have believed it. Say: 'Signs are in God's hands,' and what He means you (pl.) to understand is that were a sign to come to them they would not believe. We turn away their hearts and their sight since they did not believe in it at the first, and We leave them wandering blindly in their defiant pride. Were We to send angels down to them and had the dead speak to them and if We were to confront them with all things gathered to the proof, they would not become believers, unless God so willed. Most of them are sunk in ignorance.

To every prophet We have assigned an enemy — satans, men and jinn, who inspire in one another fair-sounding talk intended to delude. Had your (s.) Lord willed, they would not act so. Be quit of them and their devising to deceive, so that the hearts of those who do not believe in the hereafter may stay that way and take satisfaction in it and earn what they are earning.

Shall I desire any judge but God? — He who has sent down the Book to you (pl.) by stages, and those on whom We have bestowed the Book know that with truth it is sent down by your (s.) Lord. So on no account be a doubter. The word of your Lord has been fulfilled as true and just. There is no power that can alter His word. He is the One who hears and knows all. If you (s.) were to follow with the majority of earth's people they would lead you astray from the path of God. For they follow only surmise and indulge in mere conjecture. Your Lord — He knows who errs from His path and He best knows who are rightly guided.

Surah 6.104-117

THIS (Qur'ān) is a blessed Book which We have given from above. Follow it, in due fear of God. Thus it leaves no occasion for you to say that only to two communities prior to you has Scripture been sent down, or to add that you have not been occupied in any studying in them. There is no point in saying: 'Had the Book been sent down to us we would have followed its guidance much better than they!' For there has come to you a clear revelation from your Lord as both a mercy and guidance. Is there anything more heinous than the attitude of one who denies the signs of God and rejects them? Such renegades from Our signs We will requite with condign punishment for their refusal of them.

Is it that they are expecting angels to come down to them or for your Lord to come, or some of your Lord's signs? On the day when your Lord's signs do arrive no man's faith will then profit him who had not believed earlier or, while believing, acquired no good works. Say: 'Wait (all of you) for what is coming! We will wait also.'

As for those who have separated from each other in their religion and become sects, you (s.) have nothing to do with them: God will deal with them. He will show them anon what their deeds were. Whoever has done what is good will have the like ten times over and he who does what is evil will be repaid only the equivalent. None will be treated unjustly.

Say: 'As for me, my Lord has guided me into a straight path, a right religion, the faith-community of Abraham who was a *hanif*, a man of pure faith. He was no idolater.'

215

Say: 'My prayer, my rite of sacrifice, my living and my dying all belong to God, the Lord of the worlds. Of His Lordship there is no partnering. Even so I was commanded: I am the first among those surrendering to Him.'

Say: 'Shall I desire as Lord any but God who is Lord over all things? Every soul shall acquire only that for which he has responsibility: no liability of one soul can be transferred to another. It is to your Lord that finally your return will be. He will put you wise about everything that was in dispute among you.'

'It is He who appointed you to be entrusted with dominion in the earth. Some He has ranked above others in order to put you to the test in what He bestows upon you. Your (s.) Lord is swift in retribution and He is truly forgiving and merciful.   *Surah 6.155-165*

SPEAK what is revealed to you in the Book of your Lord: there is no altering His words on the part of anyone. You will never find a place of refuge except in Him. Possess your soul in patience in company with those who call upon their Lord at morning time and in the evening, desiring His face. Do not let your eyes be diverted from them in search of the gaudy things of this lower world. Do not give any deference to the man whose heart We have made lax in his recollection of Our Name — the man following his own lusts and far gone in profligacy. Say: 'The truth from your (pl.) Lord: — then let him who will, believe and let him who will, say No to faith. For those who are set on evil We have made ready a Fire which will envelop them like an awning on every side. Should they ask for water, water like molten metal will be theirs to scald their faces — a terrible drink and a wretched haunt in which to lie! As for those who believe and have done righteous deeds — the reward of such We do not let go by default. Theirs are gardens of bliss where rivers flow and where they will be arrayed with golden bracelets and robed in green garments of silk, of satin and brocade, and seated on couches. How excellent a reward, how delightsome a haven in which to lie!

Tell them as a parable the story of the two men, one of whom We made possessor of two vineyards surrounded by date-palms with a cultivated area between them. Each of the vineyards gave its yield in unstinted supply. Between them We sent a stream flowing in copious measure. The man who had this ample fruitage said to his friend in conversation: 'I have more wealth than you, and a larger establishment.' He went into his garden and — playing false with his own soul — he said: 'I can't think that this will ever come to perish: I can't imagine that last Hour happening. But if it does and I am ushered before my Lord I will surely have something better in its place.'

His friend said to him as they exchanged words: 'Have you denied the One who created you from dust, via a drop of sperm, and thus fashioned you into a man? As for me, He is God, my Lord. I will not have anyone usurp the place of my Lord. When you went into your garden, if only you had said: "What God's will may be — there is no power except in God." As you see, I am inferior to you in respect of property and family. Yet maybe my Lord will give me what is better than your garden. On that He may well let loose a thunderbolt from heaven and it will become a barren stretch of dust, or by morning its water recedes so far down into the ground that you will never be able to reach it.' His fruits were indeed completely destroyed. In the morning he was wringing his hands over all his investment in it, its grapevines lying ruined. His words were: 'Would I had not let anything take the place of my Lord!' He had nothing to turn to for help, apart from God and he was in no shape to help himself. For it is the fact of the matter that only in God, the God of truth, have we any sure reliance. In reward and in the final issue He is best.

Give them an analogy from this present life. Liken it to when We send rain from heaven which the earth's vegetation absorbs but then becomes mere dried out stalks which the winds blow around. God is the disposer of all things. Wealth and children grace this present life, but deeds of righteousness, the enduring things, are a better reward in the sight of your Lord and give better ground for hope, on the Day when We agitate the mountains and you behold the earth upheaving and We gather mankind in array and none is allowed to elude Us. Thus drawn up before your Lord, He will say to them: 'You have come before Us just as We created you at the first, for all your maintaining that We would never set for you an appointed time.' And the Book will be placed in position and you (s.) will see the sinful in their alarm at its contents. 'Woe to us! what a Book is this which omits nothing, small or great, with which it has not reckoned!' They will find, all there, the deeds they did, and your Lord will deal with none unjustly.   *Surah 18.27-49*

SAY: 'Shall we tell you who are the greatest losers in all they do, those whose entire effort goes awry in this present life, though they consider that they are on to a good thing? It is those who deny the revelations of their Lord and deny the encounter with Him. All their activities come to nought and on the Day of resurrection We will adjudge them of no weight. Their retribution — *Jahannam*, because of their denial of faith and the mocking way they treated My revelations and My messengers. Those who have believed and done righteous deeds, theirs will be the gardens of Paradise, an abode wherein to dwell eternally, with never a wish to be away.'

Say: 'If the sea were nothing but ink for the words of my Lord, truly the sea would run dry before the words of my Lord were exhausted, though He made available a like ocean again!'

Say: 'I am a mortal man, like all of you. It has been revealed to me that your God is one God. Let whoever has hope in the encounter with his Lord do righteously and in no way admit another to share the worship of his Lord.'   *Surah 18.103-110*

A LIF, Lām, Rā — These are the signs of the Book and of a lucid Qur'ān. Perhaps it will transpire that those who have rejected faith will wish they were muslims. Leave them: let them eat and enjoy life. Let their hope distract them: they will know in due course! We have not caused any community to perish without a record known to it beforehand. No nation can ever advance its decreed term, nor can they defer it.

They said: 'You, to whom the Reminder has been sent down, for sure, you are demented! If you are dealing truthfully why not bring the angels to us?' We send down the angels only for judgement, and in that event they would be beyond reprieve. We have sent down the Reminder and We Ourselves watch over it.

Before you (s.) We have sent messengers to various groups in earlier times but no apostle came to them they did not deride. Though the way of life of the old-time people has passed away, We let this have its way in the hearts of the sinful now who do not believe. Were We to open for them a gate in heaven and they ascended higher and higher through it, they would say: 'We are surely seeing as if we were drunken: we are folk under a spell!'   *Surah 15.1-15*

IT was with the truth alone that We created the heavens and the earth and everything within them. The Hour is indeed coming. Practise (s.) forgiveness with grace in your dealings. Your Lord is the all-knowing Creator. We have brought you the sevenfold verses (the *Fātihah*?) and the magnificent Qur'ān. Do not be looking enviously on the things We have given certain groups of them to enjoy: do not grieve over them. Relate with humble concern towards those who are believers. Say: 'I am simply a warner who speaks plainly.'

Your Lord will certainly interrogate for their doings all those, to a man, who have made out the Qur'ān to be subject to picking and choosing, just as those schismatics did with Our revelation to them. Proclaim boldly what you are bidden and steer clear of the polytheists. On your behalf We will take good care of the scoffers, those who put some god or other alongside God. They will know bye and bye. We know well how your heart is distressed by all they are saying. Celebrate the praise of your Lord and be one with other worshippers in prostration. Serve your Lord until the one sure thing comes to you.

Surah 15.85-99

IT may be that you are leaving out part of what is revealed to you, out of distress of heart at what they are saying, namely: 'Why has no treasure been given him from above? Or why has no angel come with him?' whereas you are simply a warner and God has everything within His charge. Or are they saying? 'It is a forgery on his part.'? Say: 'Then you bring ten comparable surahs, your own concoctions, and call on whatever you can — God apart — if you are talking honestly. If they give you no answer, know that it has been sent down with God's knowledge and that there is no God but He. Will you, then surrender to Him?'

Surah 11.12-14

THIS Qur'ān could not have been fraudulently produced without God knowing. It is in fact verifying what is already revealed and it is the elucidation, from the Lord of all being, of the Book containing nothing that is dubious.

Or are they saying: 'He has invented it.'? Well, tell them to bring a surah that is comparable. 'Call on whatever you can — God apart — if you are speaking honestly.' What their comprehension could in no way grasp they declared to be lies, while its interpretation was still lacking to them. It was likewise with their predecessors in their denials. See (s.) what happened to the evil-doers in the end. There are those of their number who will believe in it, and those who will not. Your Lord knows well enough those who are the corrupting element.

If they belie you, say to them: 'I have my responsibility and you have yours. You are not held liable for my actions, nor I for yours.' And though some of them let you have your say, can you make the deaf hear as long as they lack all comprehension? Though some of them will look to you, can you guide the blind as long as they cannot see? God does not wrong men at all: it is themselves that people wrong.

On the Day when He gathers them before Him it will seem as if their stay in the world had been but a single hour of the day. They will recognise each other. They are the lost who refused to believe in the encounter with God and did not let themselves be guided aright. Whether We show you (s.) something of what We have promised them, or whether We call you to die, it is to Us they must return and God is witness to their every deed.

To every nation there is an apostle. When their apostle comes, what is at issue between them is justly joined and no injustice is done to them.

They ask: 'When will this promised thing be, if your words are true?' Tell them: 'I have no power even over myself for harm or for advantage: it is only as God wills.' For every nation there is a time prescribed and when their time is ripe they can neither postpone it for a single hour, nor advance it.

Say: 'Have you considered that, night or day, the retribution might be upon you? What is it, then, about it that sinners want to bring on quickly? When it overtakes you, will you then believe in it?' "Ah! you believe it now! you who used to bid it come on fast!" ' Then it will be said to those wrong-doers: 'Taste the punishment which is eternal. Are you being requited for anything you had not been garnering for yourselves before?'

Some of them are wanting to know from you: 'Is this true?' Say: 'Yes. By my Lord it is assuredly true: nothing you can do can obviate it.' Any and every one who has done wrong, if he were possessed of the whole earth would redeem himself with it. They will be gripped with a secret remorse when they see the punishment. The verdict against them will be entirely just and they shall not be wronged. It is to God that all things indeed belong in the heavens and in the earth. God's promise is indeed true, though most men do not take it in. He gives life and He brings to death and to Him shall your returning be.

People! there has come a message from your Lord, healing for your hearts within you, and guidance and mercy, for those who believe.

Say: 'The goodness and mercy of God — in these let them rejoice. Better far these than their accumulation of wealth.' Say: 'Have you considered all the provision God has sent down for you and have you nominated some things prohibited and some others as lawful?' Say: 'Has God given you any warrant for this, or are you foisting things on God?' What will they think on the Day of resurrection who have indulged in lying against God? God is certainly rich in goodness toward mankind, but most of them bring no gratitude.

There is nothing you are actively about (s.), nor any recital by you (s.)

of Qur'ān, nor any activity in which you (pl.) are engaged, of which We are not witness as you pursue it. Not one atom's weight in earth or heaven escapes your (s.) Lord's knowing: there is nothing smaller than that — or larger — which is not recorded in a manifest.

The friends of God — no fear shall be theirs, nor sorrow. Those who believe and hold God in awe — theirs are glad tidings in this present world and in the life to come. There is no altering the words of God. That is the supreme victory.

Do not let what they say grieve you. All might is wholly God's: He is all-hearing and all-wise. Everyone in the heavens and on the earth belongs to God. Those who invoke pseudo-deities are following nothing but supposition: they are only fabricating falsehoods. He it is who has ordained the night for your repose and the day as light for your sight. There are signs in these things for people who heed.

They say: 'God has adopted a son.' Praise be to Him. He is altogether rich, possessing everything in the heavens and in the earth. You have no authority at all for this calumny. Will you go on saying about God what you do not know? Say? 'Those who devise falsehood about God will come to no good.'

Some enjoyment in this present world and then — their cycle of life returns back to Us. Then We will make them taste the heavy retribution on account of their denying the truth.   *Surah 10.37-70*

Are they counting as God what has actually created nothing — things that are themselves created? — things utterly powerless to aid them, being in fact unable to aid themselves? and whom, if you call them to guidance, they will not follow you? It would be all the same whether you invoke them or whether you stay silent. These whom you invoke, to the exclusion of God, are simply servitors like you. Call on them if you will, and let them respond, if what you say is true! Have they feet to walk with? Have they hands to grasp with? Have they eyes to see with? Have they ears to hear with? Say: 'Call on your pseudo-deities: plot against me and give me no quarter! Gód is my protector, who has revealed the Book from above. He takes into His protection those who deal righteously. Those you invoke, ignoring Him, are powerless to aid you: they cannot even aid themselves. They cannot hear if you call them to guidance. You (s.) will see them looking your way, but quite sightless.'

Be ready (s.) to forbear, enjoin fair play, turn away from the wilful and ignorant. If Satan provokes you in any way, seek refuge with God, for He hears and knows all. When those who are truly God-fearing experience some Satanic insinuation, they call Him to mind and, so doing, see things clearly, whereas their brethren satans lead on further and further into unremitting evil.

Should you (s.) not be bringing them any verse of revelation, they say: 'Why not invent one?' Say: 'I only follow what my Lord inspires within me. This (Qur'ān) is sent for your discernment from your Lord and as guidance and mercy for believing people. When the Qur'ān is recited listen to it and attend to it in silence: you may find mercy.'

Remember your Lord in your soul with humility and godly fear morning and evening: let your voice be subdued. Do not be negligent. Those who are in your Lord's presence do not disdain to serve Him. Celebrate His praise and prostrate in worship.   *Surah 7.191-206*

HE who has laid the Qur'ān upon you as a task will assuredly bring you back again to what you left. Say: 'My Lord knows well who brings guidance and who is manifestly misguided.' It was only as a mercy from your Lord that you hoped to be the recipient of the Book. So give no aid and comfort to those who disbelieve. Do not let them counter you in your Lord's revelations once they have been sent down to you. Call upon your Lord and have no part with the idolators.

Invoke no other god side by side with God. There is no god but He. Everything is passing away except His countenance. The judgement is His, and to Him you (pl.) will be brought.   *Surah 28.85-88*

ABRAHAM was the model progenitor of a community, devoted to God, a *hanīf*: he was not one of those who associate other deities with God. He was thankful for His acts of grace who chose him and guided him to a straight path. He bestowed good things on him in this present world and in the world to come he will be numbered among the righteous.

Afterwards We inspired you (s.): 'Follow the faith-community of Abraham as a *hanīf*.' He was no worshipper of false gods. The Sabbath was appointed upon those only who differed from him. Your (s.) Lord will judge between them on the Day of resurrection as to the issue of their disputes.

Call to the way of your (s.) Lord with wisdom and good exhortation and take up issues with them in a worthy fashion. Your Lord knows well those who have strayed from the path and He knows well those who are rightly guided. When you (pl.) retaliate, respond proportionately to what has been inflicted on you, yet if you endure patiently that is the better course for those who do exercise patience. So be (s.) patient: your (s.) patient endurance derives only from God. Do not grieve over them or be distressed by their devices. God is with those who devoutly fear Him and those who do what is good. *Surah 16.120-28*

THUS have We sent you (s.) to a nation, before whose time other nations have passed away, to recite to them what We have revealed to you, disbelievers — as they are — in the all-merciful One. Say: 'He is my Lord: there is no god but He. In Him have I trusted and to Him do I turn in penitence.'

Were there a Qur'ān by which the mountains might be moved or the earth cut through or the dead made to speak, would unbelief yield? Yet the sole authority is with God entirely. Have not believers yet come to realise that had God so willed He had guided all nations together? As for the unbelievers, calamity continues to come upon them for their deeds or hovers close to their dwellings, pending the fulfilment of what God has promised them. For God never fails to keep tryst.

Messengers before you (s.) have been treated with derision. I bore with those who denied the faith and afterwards seized on them — and with what retribution!

Who is He who stands watch over every soul concerning the sum of its deeds? They have made associates with God. Say: 'Give them names! Or would you inform Him of anything in the earth He does not know? Or are they so much verbiage?' Even so, their deception has been made attractive to the unbelieving and they have been deterred from the path of God. Whom God sends astray have none to guide. *Surah 13.30-33*

THOSE to whom We brought the Book rejoice in what is sent down to you (s.) but there are sects some of whom deny it in part. Say: 'I have been commanded only to worship God and not to set up any other god associate with Him. To Him do I call and to Him I repair.'

We have in this way sent it down as a divine decretal (*Hukm*) in the Arabic language. Were you (s.) to follow their wishes after knowledge has come to you you would indeed have no one to protect or defend you from God.

Before your time We have sent messengers for whom We have appointed wives and offspring. To no messenger was it given to bring any sign unless by leave of God. For every era there is a book. God annuls and confirms what He wills and with Him is *Umm al-Kitāb*.

Whether We allow you (s.) to witness in part the things We have promised them or whether We call you to die before then, your sole task is the communication: upon Us lies the reckoning.   *Surah 13.36-40*

TRULY God knows the hidden mysteries of the heavens and of the earth. He it is who knows the very hearts of men. It is He who has deputed you to exercise the trust of authority in the earth. Whoever violates that trust the wrong he does will recoil upon himself. Such gross disavowal of their Lord only intensifies the heinousness of all such rejectors of the truth. Their rank unbelief will mean the greater ruin for these God-deniers.

Say: 'Have you considered those pseudo-gods of yours whom you invoke to the exclusion of God? Show me anything on earth that they have created. Have they any part or lot in the governance of the heavens? Have We brought any Book to them, whereby clear revelations would be theirs? On the contrary, those who violate the truth can promise themselves nothing but mutual delusion.'

Truly God upholds the heavens and the earth so that they do not come to nought. Were they to fail no one, after Him, could assume their management and sustain them — He the ever-forbearing, the forgiving.

They have sworn an oath, a most solemn oath, by God that if a warner were ever to come their way they would follow the guidance more effectively than any other community. Yet when a warner has come to them the only result is their intensified disgust, their arrogance in the land and their evil scheming. Such evil devices only entrap their perpetrators. Do they anticipate anything different for them than the way it was with those of old? You (s.) will never find any change in the way of God's will, you will never find any deviance in the way God disposes things.

What! have they not travelled about in the land and seen how it was in the retribution of those before their time, who were more powerful than they? There is nothing in the heavens or the earth that can be any match for God — God who is all-knowing and infinite in power. Were God to hold mankind to their deserts for what they have wrought He would not leave a single living creature on the surface of the earth. But He defers them until the time prescribed and, when their time is ripe, God has all those servants under His scrutiny.   *Surah 35.38-45*

THOSE deniers of the faith plotted against you to detain you, or to kill you, or to expel you. While they conspired, God had His scheme also and God's is the more competent planning! When Our revelations were rehearsed to them their response was: 'We have heard it all before. Had we wanted we could have said the like of it. It is nothing but hoary tales from old times.' They said, too: 'O God, if this is the truth from You, rain stones down on us from heaven or subject us to dire chastisement.' God, however, was not set to inflict punishment on them as long as you (s.) were in their midst, Nor would He afflict them were they to seek His forgiveness. What is there left now for them but punishment from God, seeing that they block the way to the sacred mosque and are in no way its rightful guardians? Only those who truly revere God are its rightful custodians, though most of them have no sense of this. Their praying at the sacred house is nothing but whistling and hand-clapping. Taste, then, the sharp retribution, the deserts of your unbelief.   *Surah 8.30-35*

بسم الله الرحمن الرحيم

E. Muhammad:
The Prophet-Ruler and the
Medinan Climax

THOUGH you help him not, God came to his aid (Muhammad) when the unbelievers drove him out with only one companion (Abū Bakr). When they two were together in the cave, he said to his companion: 'Sorrow not. God is with us.' And God caused His peace (Sakīnah) to come over him and aided him with legions unseen. Thus did He utterly humble the words of the unbelievers and exalt the divine word to supremacy. For God is almighty and wise.   *Surah 9.40*

ALL that is in the heavens and the earth celebrates the praise of God, the King, the holy One, almighty and all-wise. He it is who has sent among the unlettered (*ummiyyūn*) people a messenger of their own number to rehearse to them His revelations, to cleanse them and to teach them the Book and wisdom, though earlier they were plainly far astray, and thus, in turn, among others when they have made contact with them. He is all-great and all-wise. Such is the goodness of God which He bestows on whom He wills. For God abounds in great goodness.   *Surah 62.1-4*

ALL that they are doing who refuse to believe and who impede people from the way of God, He will bring to nought. Those who believe and do righteous deeds and have faith in what has been sent down to Muhammad — being the truth from your Lord — God will absolve from their iniquities and He will prosper their condition.

God uses such expression of His ways in view of the fact that the unbelievers have gone after that which is vain, while those who hold the faith have followed the truth of their Lord.

When you come up against the unbelievers in conflict carry the war to the death until you have defeated them. Then take prisoners for subsequent release, either freely or for ransom, until the toils of war are ended. Had God's will been so, He would certainly have got His own victory over them. But His purpose is to put you mutually to the test. Those who are killed in the pursuit of God's way will never find what they have done cast aside. He will guide them and prosper their condition and He will bring them into the garden of which already He has given them to know.

You who have believed, if you serve God's victory He will serve yours, and make all your steps sure, while those who deny the faith — wretched is their case. All they have done is dissipated because they have detested God's revelation and all they have done He makes to fail.

Have they not travelled the earth and observed what happened in the end to those who lived before them, whom God utterly destroyed? It will be the same for the unbelievers. God is the guardian of believers while those who deny the faith have none to protect them. Believers and those who do righteously God will admit into gardens with flowing streams: but unbelievers, though they have their mead of pleasure and their fodder like cattle, will find the Fire their last abode.

Many a city of greater power than your city — the city which has expelled you — have We caused to perish, destitute of all help.

Surah 47.1-13

THOSE who have believed enquire: 'Why has no related Surah been sent down?' Yet when a decisive Surah has been sent down and the making of war is sanctioned there, you (s.) see those with sick hearts looking at you with the look of men aghast and faint at the prospect of death. Far better for them would be obedience and brave words in all honour. It will be for their good if they are loyal to God — the decision to fight having been taken. Were you to be renegades now, could it be that you meant to violate your ties of kin, working havoc in the land? Such people as those are under the curse of God: He makes their ears deaf and their eyes blind.

Do they not reflect upon the Qur'ān or are there locks on their hearts?

Those who revert once guidance has been shown to them are duped victims of Satan and what he instigates in them. This is on account of their having said to those who were averse to what God had sent down: 'We will go along with you in part in this matter.' God, however, knows their secret thoughts. How will it be when the angels take them in death, smiting them on the face and beating them on the back, inasmuch as they have gone after the things that incur God's wrath and have held His good pleasure in aversion? All they do He makes abortive. Did those with sick hearts assume that God would never expose their malice?

Were We to will so, We would let you (s.) know who they are and you would identify them by the marks they carry. Indeed, you surely know them already by their tone of speech. God knows your (pl.) deeds and We will test you by what is heard of you, and from you.

Those who do not believe, who debar others from the path of God and have broken away from the apostle after guidance has been made clear to them, do not inflict the least injury on God: He will bring to nothing their activities.

Believers! Obey God and obey the apostle: do not nullify your work. Those who disbelieve and deter others from God's way and die in their unbelief, God will never forgive.

Do not (pl.) lose heart and call for peace: you are the ones to prevail, God being with you. He will never cheat you of what you wrought.

Surah 47.20-35

GOD comes to the defence of those who have believed. God has no love for any who betray their trust and deny the faith.

Those who have been involved in fighting because they have been wronged have authorisation for it. God is well able to aid them to victory, namely those who have been unjustly expelled from their dwelling places simply for their words, in saying: 'Our Lord is God.' But for God's defence of people — some by means of others — certainly monasteries, churches, synagogues and mosques, where God's Name is oft remembered, would all have been demolished. God will assuredly make victorious those who come to His aid — God is all-powerful and great — those, that is, who, if We establish them firmly in the land, perform the prayer-rite, bring the *Zakāt*, enjoin the doing of what is right and forbid what is wrong. The end of all things is with God.

If they say you are a liar, before their time the people of Noah, of 'Ād and of Thamūd, the people of Abraham and the people of Lot, and the tribe of Madyan, all made the same charge — lies! Moses also was so accused. For a while I (God) bore with the truth-resisters but then I took hold of them and how stern was My repugnance!

How many a city, given to evil, have We made to perish and it is fallen on its own towers, how many an abandoned well, how many a fine palace! Have they not travelled the earth to take to heart these things? Have they no ears to give heed? It is not their sighted eyes that are blind but the hearts within them. So they taunt you (s.) to bring on fast their punishment! God never fails in what He promises, and a day with your Lord is like a thousand years as you (pl.) reckon.

How many a city, given to evil, have I borne with and then taken hold of and Mine was the destiny awaiting it!

Say: 'People! It is clear warning that I bring you. For those who have believed and done righteously there is forgiveness and kindly provision. Those who have endeavoured to make Our revelations null and void — in *Jahannam* they will find their kin.'   *Surah 22.38-51*

FIGHT in pursuit of the way of God those who fight against you but do not provoke hostility. God has no love for those who embark on aggression. Slay them where-ever you encounter them and drive them out from places whence they have driven you. Subversion is a worse thing than slaughter. Do not do battle with them however, in the vicinity of the sacred mosque unless they are warring with you there. If they fight you, slay them: such are the deserts of those who deny the faith. But if they desist God is certainly forgiving and merciful.

Fight them until there is no more subversion and religion is wholly God's. If they desist, hostility is at an end save for those who commit evil. Things sacrosanct allow of retaliation, so if in the sacred month let it be in the sacred month. Who-ever makes aggression against you, take up hostilities in the same measure against them, fearing God. Know that God is with those who fear Him.

In the path of God, be ready for what it will take and do not, by the work of your own hands, contrive your own destruction, but accomplish what is good. For God loves those who do so.

Going to war is prescribed for you, though it is to you a hateful thing. Yet it may well be that something you hate is nevertheless good for you, just as it can happen that you set your heart on what is bad for you. Knowledge in these things is God's, not yours.

They put questions to you about going to war in the sacred month. Say: 'To go to war in that month is a serious matter, but — in God's sight — it is an even graver thing to forbid entry to the path of God, to deny the faith, to ban the sacred mosque and to throw out its people. Subversion is more heinous than slaughter. They will not cease waging war against you until — if you are able — they make you turn back from your religion. Should any of you in fact turn back from his religion and die as a recreant from faith — the doings of all such will come to nought in this present world and in the next they will be denizens of the Fire eternally. Those who have believed, who have emigrated and striven in the path of God, can anticipate the mercy of God, who is ever forgiving and merciful. *Surah 2.190-195,216-218*

O PROPHET! Be devoted to God in true piety. Do not let the unbelievers and the hypocrites sway you. God in His wisdom knows all. Follow what is revealed to you from your Lord. God is aware of everything you do. Put all your trust in God — you need no other guardian. *Surah 33.1-3*

YOU (pl.) who have believed, when — on the day of assembly — the call to prayer is sounded, come eagerly to the remembrance of God and leave commerce aside. This is your well-being, as you should know. Then when the prayer-rite concludes disperse abroad and seek out God's bounty and remember God frequently that prosperity may be yours.

When they have seen a chance of trading or amusement they have gone off after it and left you (s.) standing there! Say: 'The things of God are better than amusement and commerce. God is the best of all suppliers of our need.' *Surah 62.9-11*

THE simpletons among the people will be saying: 'What has turned them from the prayer-direction they were observing?' Say: 'To God belong alike the east and the west. He guides whom He wills into a straight path.' Thus We have made you a central community that you might be witnesses to mankind as the prophet is witness to you. The prayer-direction which you (s.) hitherto observed We ordained so, only to identify those who would loyally follow the messenger in contrast to those who would turn tail. The matter has been a big issue, but not for such as keep to God's guidance. God is not one to let you down in your faith. God deals gently and mercifully with mankind.

We see you (s.) turning your face upward to heaven. We now definitely turn you to a prayer-direction of real satisfaction to you. The command is: 'Set your face toward the sacred mosque. Where-ever you (pl.) find yourselves set your face in its direction.' Those to whom the Book is brought know for sure that it is the truth from their Lord. God is not neglectful of what they do.

Those to whom the Book has been given would not follow your prayer-direction even if you (s.) were to bring them every evidential sign. You are not praying on their prayer-direction. Nor are they on each other's. You would certainly be numbered an evil-doer if you were to follow their capricious ideas once knowledge has become yours. Those to whom We have given the Book know it as well as they know their own sons. A group among them deliberately conceals the truth — the truth from your Lord. Do not yourself be a doubter. Every rite has a prayer-direction to which it turns. Try to excel each other in what is good. Where-ever you are God will have you all in His ordering. For God has the disposal of everything within His power.

Turn your (s.) face, then, to the place from which you have departed, in the direction of the sacred mosque. This is the very truth from your Lord. God is not neglectful about your actions. Turn your face to the place from which you have come out, in the direction of the sacred mosque. Where-ever all of you may be, turn your faces in its direction, that people may have no case against you, unless it be those among them who are just perverse. Have no dread of them: fear Me only, so that I may fulfill My grace toward you and that you may find guidance.

Thus it is that We have sent among you an apostle of your own kin to announce to you Our revelations, to cleanse you, to teach you the Book and the wisdom, and to bring to you the knowledge that you lacked.

Remember Me: I will be mindful of you. Be thankful to Me and have no room for ingratitude.   *Surah 2.142-152*

ONLY when the clear evidence (the Qur'ān) had been given them were those among the people of the Book who rejected the truth, and the idolaters, abandoned in their unfaith — the clear evidence of an apostle from God, reciting from pages of pure Scriptures which contain books of supreme value. It was only after the clear evidence became available to them that the people on whom the Book was bestowed fell into disagreement among themselves. Yet nothing was commanded them to do except to worship God in sincerity of devotion, to be *hanīfs* of pure faith, to perform the prayer-rite and to bring the *Zakāt*. All that is true religion.

Those of the people of the Book who disbelieved, together with the polytheists — for them is *Jahannam* eternally. They are the dregs of all creation. Those who have believed and done righteous deeds — they are the best of all creation. Their reward is with their Lord — the gardens of Paradise, beneath which are flowing streams, where they will for ever abide, God being well-pleased with them and they in Him. Thus it will be for him who fears his Lord.   *Surah 98*

THEY ask you about the spoils of war. Say: 'Spoils of war are God's and His apostle's.' Devote yourselves to God in true fear of Him and deal equitably with one another. Obey God and His apostle, if you would be true believers. They are believers whose hearts kindle at the mention of the Name of God, whose faith increases when His revelations are rehearsed to them, whose entire confidence is in their Lord, who perform the prayer-rite and who give to others out of the substance with which We have provided them. Such are, in truth, believers. Their station, severally, is with their Lord: in Him they have forgiveness and provident grace.

So it was that your (s.) Lord had you go forth from your house in truth's name (to Badr). Some among the believers had great reluctance concerning it, contending with you as to the true situation when it was clear enough — as though they were being driven to their death before their very eyes. God gave you His word that one of the two enemy detachments (caravans) would fall to you. Your (pl.) preference was to gain possession of the one which had no armed escort. God, however, meant to verify the truth of His words by the total rout of the truth-rejectors, demonstrating how true the truth is and how vain the false-hood, however much the sinners might detest it.

When you (pl.) were making supplication to your Lord He answered you, saying: 'I am aiding you with a thousand serried angels.' God brought all this about solely to be a gladdening piece of news and to set your hearts at rest. There is no victory save from God — God who is all-strong and all-wise.

As a means to your security He caused you to be overtaken by sleep and sent down a timely rain-shower whereby polluting thoughts from Satan were put away from you and God made you free of them. He meant in this way to make you stout-hearted and to set your feet firmly. It was then that your (s.) Lord revealed to the angels: 'I am with you: strengthen the believers.' 'Strike them hip and thigh' (*lit.* neck and finger). For they opposed God and His messenger. Whoever crosses swords with God and His messenger finds God terrible in retribution. 'So much for you! Savour what you get!' The anguish of the Fire is the portion of those who reject the faith.

Believers! When you face the unbelievers coming in battle array, do not turn your backs on them. Anyone who does so on that day — unless it be in battle tactics, or to join another troop of men — will incur the wrath of God and will end up in *Jahannam*, which is a terrible destiny.

It was not you who slew them: it was God who slew them. When you (s.) made your throw, it was not yours but God's, whose purpose was to confer on the believers a mark of special favour — God sees and knows all — and further to demonstrate how He nullifies the machinations of those who reject the faith. Victory was what you sought (O Quraish)! and victory has overtaken you! If you break off now it will be better for you but if you return again We will return too and your army — however numerous — will avail you nothing. For God is with those who believe.

Surah 8.1-19

TELL those who reject the faith that if they desist all that has passed will be forgiven them. If they persist, well — the byegone pattern of things with their forebears is warning enough!

Go on taking the fight to them until there is no more subversion and religion is wholly God's. If they desist, God will have all their actions under surveillance and if they turn back, know that God your defender is the finest of defenders and the best architect of victory.

Take note that a fifth of any booty you capture belongs to God and His apostle, to the next of kin and orphans, to the destitute and the wayfarer. The day when the two armies met in battle was the day of the criterion (*al-furqān*) when your whole reliance was on God and on what We sent Our servant in revelation from above. God has the disposal of all things within His power. That day you were encamped on the near side of the valley and they were on the further side, while the approaching caravan was on the lower ground away from you. Had there been a common intention among you to seek out a battle, you would have pulled back from it. What ensued was something God brought to pass, accomplishing His purpose so that, through what was proof-plain, there were those who perished and those who survived. God hears and knows all.

God showed them to you in a dream as being few in number. Had He disclosed them to you as a numerous host, you would have lost heart and fallen into dispute among yourselves about the situation — from all of which God saved you. God knows full well what goes on in your innermost thoughts. When the battle was joined, He made them seem to you as few and you, in their eyes, He made to seem few. Thus God brought about the issue He had decreed. All things are to be traced back to God.

So, believers, when you confront an army in battle, stand firm and be occupied with the remembrance of God, so that you may prosper in your cause. Obey God and His apostle and do not fall out among yourselves lest you falter and your resolution fails. Endure patiently: for

God is with those of steadfast patience. Do not be like those who sallied forth from their quarters (the Quraish), swaggering and making a brave show, intent on blocking the way to God. God has all they do within His vigilance. What they were doing was all very fine — so Satan had them think, saying to them: 'Nobody is going to get the better of you today: I will have you under my wing.' However, when the two armies met, Satan took to his heels, as he said: 'I have done with you! Seeing what is invisible to you, I am in fear of God! — God who is strong in retribution.'

The hypocrites and those with sickly hearts say: 'Their religion has thrown these people into a state of delusion.' But to anyone who trusts in God, God is all-strong and all-wise. *Surah 8.38-49*

O PROPHET! Stir up the believers to fight. Were there but twenty of you, and they truly steadfast, they would overcome two hundred: were there a hundred of you they would overcome a thousand of those who reject the faith. They are a people who comprehend nothing! Now God has made your task easier. He knew how weak you were. A hundred of you, of steadfast heart, will subdue two hundred, and a thousand of you two thousand, by God's leave. For God is with the steadfast.

It is no part of a prophet's business to hold prisoners until he has the land under rigorous control. You (pl.) had in view what this present world might afford whereas God looks to the world to come. He is almighty and all-wise. But for an earlier ordinance from God you would have incurred a very severe punishment for what you seized. Of legitimate and proper booty acquired by you take your fill and be in due fear of God. God is ever forgiving and merciful.

O Prophet! Say to the prisoners who are in your hands: 'If God knows any good in your hearts, he will give you something better than what has been taken from you. He will forgive you. For God is ever forgiving and merciful.' If, however, they will some act of treachery against you (s.) their treason is already against God. So He has given you power over them. God is all-knowing and all-wise.

Those who have believed, who have emigrated and strived in their persons and property in the path of God and those who have given them sanctuary and aided them — all these are protecting friends to one another. To those believers who have not emigrated you have no obligation of protection in any way until they do come into this exile. Yet, if they seek help from you in things appertaining to faith and religion, it is your duty to help them — but not to the detriment of any people with whom you have a treaty arrangement. God watches over all you do.

Those who have rejected the faith mutually befriend and protect each other and, unless you act likewise, subversion and great corruption will prevail in the land. Those who have believed and have emigrated and striven in the path of God and those who gave them asylum and help — these are believers indeed and in truth. Forgiveness and provident grace are theirs. Those who believed subsequently, emigrated and strove with you, these are party with you and, by God's ordering, those with ties of blood are in closer mutual bond. God has perfect knowledge of all things. *Surah 8.65-75*

THERE was a real sign for you in the encounter of the opposing forces, the one fighting in the path of God, the other anti-faith — how, as the eye saw it, the latter were twice the strength of the former, God lending His victorious aid as He wills, in which there is a clear lesson for the perceptive. *Surah 3.13*

IF you have suffered wounds, wounds have befallen other folk too! That is how it goes in days of battle that We make to fluctuate among men, so that God knows who are believers and that He may take martyr-witnesses from among you. God has no love for those who work evil. His purpose is to purify those who believe and to put away the evil-doers. Did you count on entering Paradise without God knowing whom they were who had struggled in *Jihad* and endured with patience? Prior to actually meeting it, you were eager to court death: now you have seen it before your own eyes.

Muhammad is only a messenger. Messengers before him have passed away. Were he to die or be killed, would you turn tail and take to your heels? Anyone who does so — he will be doing God no harm. God's reward is for the thankful. It is only by permission of God that any soul dies. It is all down in a book, a register. The reward of this world will be given to him who wants it and on him who seeks the reward of the world to come We bestow it, recompensing the thankful.

Many a prophet has there been of old with whom bands of godly men have gone forth in battle, without faltering in the face of adversities in the path of God and without weakening or accepting humiliation. God loves those who steadfastly endure. What they said was simply: 'Lord, forgive us our trespasses, forgive us where we have exceeded our brief. Make us to stand firm and grant us victory over the unbelieving people.'

Thus God rewarded them in this present world and gave them the more excellent reward of the world to come. For God loves the well-doers. Believers! If you obey those who are unbelievers they will make you revert back altogether and so come to total ruin. But God is your guardian-Lord: there is no better helper than He. We will strike terror into the hearts of the unbelievers. For they have done what no revealed mandate allows — they have violated the divine unity. The Fire is their abode, the wretched haunt of the wrong-doers.

God faithfully kept His word to you when, by His leave, you put them to the sword. The trouble was that you faltered and fell to quarrelling among yourselves about the situation. Thus you broke discipline just when God set before your very eyes the thing you longed to see. There are some among you who crave after this present world and there are some who yearn for the world to come. So it was that He tested you in letting them drive you back. He has pardoned you. God is a gracious Lord to those who believe.   *Surah 3.140-152*

CALL to mind when you were going uphill, impetuous and heedless, and the apostle was calling out to you from the rear. God brought double distress upon you, teaching you not to be in sorrow either for what had eluded you or for the calamity that befell you. For God is fully aware of all your deeds.

Then succeeding the sorrows, He sent down upon you a feeling of security. Some of you were overcome by sleep, while other some were in agitation of mind through their false thoughts about God — those pagan-style notions of the *Jāhiliyyah* — when they said: 'Had we anything to do with what happened?' Tell them: 'What happened was entirely in God's hands.' What they were secretly thinking to themselves and hiding from you (s.) was: 'If the issue had been in our hands we would not have had so many dead.' Say to them: 'Had you been at home in your dwellings those for whom death was decreed would have fared forth to lie in their last resting places.' All this came to pass that God might put to the test your inmost thoughts and sift the very contents of your hearts. God knows the inward selves of men through and through. As for those of you who turned back on the day when the two armies met, it was Satan who caused them to falter on account of their own past deeds. God has pardoned them: God is ever forgiving and forbearing.

Believers! Do not be like those unbelievers who said of their brethren who have been on expeditions in the land or have made raids: 'Had they remained with us they would not have died or been slain.' God will make such thoughts a source of deep anguish in their hearts. It is God who gives life and who brings to death. God is watchful over all your doings.

What if you are killed or you die in the cause of God? Forgiveness from God and mercy are better than all that men accumulate. Though you die or are killed, it is to God your ingathering will be.

It was out of God's mercy that you (s.) dealt leniently with them. Had you been harsh and madly angry in your heart, they would have dispersed and left you. Remit their fault and seek forgiveness for them. Take counsel with them in the situation and when you (s.) have reached a decision, put your trust in God. God has love for those who put their trust in Him.

If God comes to your (pl.) aid no one can vanquish you and if He abandons you who then could succour you? Let those who believe put their trust in God. *Surah 3.153-160*

Do not ever think of those who are killed in the cause of God as being dead — rather as living in the presence of their Lord and in His providence, rejoicing in the blessing God has brought them and made glad in those who have not yet joined their ranks but remain behind that no fear besets them nor should they grieve. They are made glad at the grace and goodness of God, seeing that God never lets the reward of believers fail — those believers who answered the call of God and His apostle after they experienced a reverse. A great reward belongs to those of them who performed well and who were truly God-fearing, those who had been told by people: 'Men are in array against you, so beware!' Their faith grew only the greater as they said: 'God is all we need: He is the best trust to have.' By the grace and goodness of God they came through unscathed. For to be pleasing to God was their one motive — God the Lord of supreme good.

It is only Satan who puts fright into the hearts of his adherents. Have no fear of them: fear Me, if believers you be! Let not those grieve you (s.) who rival one another in their impetuous unbelief: they can never do God any harm. They incur painful doom upon themselves.

Let not those who have denied the faith imagine that the leeway We allow them bodes them any good. We only give them latitude to have them fill up their iniquity. Theirs is a dreadful retribution. It is not the purpose of God to leave the believers in your present condition until He separates the evil from the good. Nor is it God's way to give you insight into the unseen. But God chooses whom He will from His messengers. So believe in God and in His messengers. If you believe and hold God in reverent fear yours is a great reward. *Surah 3.169-179*

YOU (s.) went out from your people at dawn to set the believers in battle order — God hearing and knowing all. Two contingents of yours were on the verge of losing heart, though God was guardian-Lord to both of them: it is on God that believers must place their trust. God truly helped you to victory at Badr contemptible as you then were. So hold God in reverence and maybe you will be grateful. What you (s.) said to the believers was: 'Is it not enough for you to know that your Lord will support you with three thousand angels sent down from above? Indeed, if you remain steadfast and devote yourselves to God, as the foe suddenly bears down upon you, your Lord will aid you with five thousand angels descending.' God had him say this only to bring you a heartening word whereby to set you at rest. Victory comes only from God, who is all-strong and all-wise. He meant also to make an end of one force of unbelievers, or to check them by making them beat a retreat. It is no part of yours (s.) whether God relents towards them or whether He brings retribution on them. For evil-doers they are. To God belong all things in the heavens and in the earth. Whom He wills He forgives and whom He wills He punishes. God is ever forgiving and merciful.

Surah 3.121-129

NO calamity occurs except by leave of God. God guides the heart of any man who believes in Him: God knows everything. Obey God and obey the messenger. If you turn aside, Our apostle has but one duty — the bringing of the clear word. God — there is no god but He. Let the believers trust wholly in Him.

Believers! Beware of certain among your wives and families who are inimical to you. If you are so minded, pardon them and be ready to bear with them forgivingly. God is forgiving and merciful. It is true that possessions and children of yours are a factor which may compromise your commitment. God rewards munificently. Then do your utmost to be devoted to God in true piety, give heed and obedience, and expend your resources: this will be to your own good. For it is those who are restrained from their own avarice who are the ones who truly prosper. If you lend to God generously He will multiply it to you and forgive you. God, in His forbearance, takes note of gratitude. The knower of the unseen and of things evident, He is ever mighty and wise.

Surah 64.11-18

WHEN the dissemblers come to you (s.) saying: 'We bear witness that you are the messenger of God,' God knows well enough that you are indeed His apostle and — about the dissemblers — God bears witness that they are liars. They have taken their pledges only as a cover and they have barricaded the way to God. Their actions are evil in that they make profession of faith and then deny the faith. Their hearts are sealed and they understand nothing. When you see them you feel admiration for their physique and you listen to what they say. But they are really like a pile of shored-up timber. Every clamour there is they think they must make their business. They are the enemy. So beware of them. May God fight them to the death, perverts that they are! If it is said to them: 'Come! the apostle of God will ask God's forgiveness for you,' they turn themselves away. In brushing you aside you can see how arrogant they are. With them it is all the same whether you ask for forgiveness on their behalf or whether you do not. God will never forgive them. God does not guide people so perverse.

These are the ones who tell Medinans not to make any outlay for the men who are with the apostle of God, thus obliging them to disband. God has the treasuries of the heavens and the earth, though the hypocrites have no idea of that. What they say is: 'When we return to Medina the people with the whip-hand will evict that contemptible lot!' Power belongs to God and to His messenger and the faithful. But the dissemblers know it not.   *Surah 63.1-8*

FOR every community We have ordained a rite of worship for them to observe. On this score do not let them take issue with you (s.). Call upon your Lord: you are following right guidance. If they contend with you, say: 'What you do is known to God.' God will judge between you on the Day of resurrection concerning what was at issue in your disagreements.

Have you (s.) not realised that God knows all in heaven and earth. All is noted in a book, which — for God — is perfectly easy. To the exclusion of God they are worshipping in ways for which no warrant has been sent down, a worship of which they have no real knowledge. There will be none to take up the cause of the evil-doers. When Our clear revelations are rehearsed to them you (s.) read their detestation on the faces of those deniers of the truth. It is almost a look of fierce venom against the very readers of the revelations. Say: 'Shall I tell you what is worse than all? — the Fire, which God has vowed for those who reject the faith. It is the most wretched of all destinies!'

People! Listen, here's a way of putting it for you. Those deities you

239

invoke, crowding God out of your worship, will never create even a fly, even if they were all to team together for the purpose. If that mere fly were to turn thief and steal something of theirs, they would never retrieve it from him. And the seeker is as feeble as the sought. They have in no way thought rightly of God and His power. God is truly powerful and strong. He chooses messengers from among angels and men. God hears and sees all things: He knows men's present concerns and what they have behind them in the past. To God all things are finally referred.

Believers! Kneel, make your prostration and worship your Lord: do good that well-being may be yours. Give yourselves in God's *Jihād* in a manner true to it. He has chosen you. In what has to do with religion He lays no onerous demand on you in the faith-community of your father Abraham. He named you 'the muslims', both in the early time and also here and now. The apostle is witness to you and you in turn are witnesses to mankind. He is your gracious Sovereign and the best of auspices.

Surah 22.67-78

BELIEVERS! Remember the grace of God on you when the armies came against you and We sent against them a storm-wind and hosts invisible to you. God was watchful over all your actions. Remember when they attacked you from the high ground and on the plain below. You turned your eyes away and were in great suspense, with wild supposition in your hearts about God. The believers were deeply agitated in a severe test of their morale. The dissemblers and those of sickly hearts were saying: 'What God and His messenger pledged to us is nothing but delusion.' A faction of them said: 'You people of Yathrib, this is no place for you to make a stand. Retreat!' Another group of them sought leave from the prophet to decamp, saying: 'Our houses are exposed to attack,' when it was not so. They simply wanted to run away.

Had the attackers broken through all around the city and the dissemblers had then been faced with a demand that they apostacise, it would not have taken them any time to do so. Yet they had earlier covenanted with God that they would never turn back. Covenant with God admits of no breach without reckoning: tell them: 'Running away will avail you nothing if it is your idea to escape death and slaughter. In any event you have only brief satisfaction to savour.' Tell them, further: 'Who or what is going to make you immune from God, whether His will for you is either evil or mercy?' Apart from God they will find there is no protector and no sponsor for them.

God knows well those of you who hold others back and those who say to their brothers: 'Come over to us,' and then show little stomach for the fight and stint their efforts for you. Yet when fear takes hold of them you (pl.) see how they look at you (s.), their eyes rolling like those of a man in a deathly swoon. When the fear has passed they are vociferous in stinting you of the good spoils that result. Such as these have not truly believed. God will bring all their activities to nothing — an easy enough thing for God to do.

The dissemblers are of the opinion that the confederate-clans have not finally withdrawn. Should the clans in fact come on again the dissemblers would prefer to be out in the desert among the *I'rāb*, the bedouin, asking how things go with you! Even if they were in fact in your ranks it would be scant combat they would share.

In God's apostle you have an excellent example of one whose hope is in God and the last Day and who lives in the practice of the remembrance of God.

When the believers saw the confederate-clans on the march again they said: 'This is exactly what God and His messenger promised us. God and His messenger had it right!' The experience only intensified their faith and their will to be surrendered to God. In the ranks of believers are men who have made good what they pledged in covenant to God and those also who have fulfilled their pledge by death in battle and those who will yet do so — as they expect. Their steadfastness is unflinching. God rewards those who fulfill the word they have vowed. The dissemblers He will requite, or He will relent — if it be His will. For God is ever forgiving and merciful. God repulsed the unbelievers, enraged at having gained no advantage. God spared the believers further combat, God who is all-powerful and strong. Those of the people of the Book who had sided with the confederate-clans He dislodged from their strongholds, striking terror into their hearts. A group of these you put to the sword and others were taken captive. He gave you the heritage of their land, their dwellings and their property and land, too, on which you had not as yet set foot. God has the disposal of all things in His power.

Surah 33.9-27

ALL that is in the heavens and in the earth magnifies God. He is the mighty and the wise. It is He who expelled the unbelievers among the people of the Book from their dwellings at the first rounding-up. You had not imagined that they would depart, while they took it for granted that their bastions would protect them against God. However, God got at them from an unexpected quarter, striking such terror into their hearts that they wrecked their houses with their own hands, apart from what the believers did. So let those who have eyes, use them. Had not expulsion been God's decree against them He would certainly have visited them with punishment in some other way in this present world, and in the world to come there awaits them the doom of the Fire. It was so because they resisted God and His apostle. God has sharp punishment for those who resist Him. You had God's leave for the cutting down of the palm-trees, leaving some of them, as you did, still standing with their roots. It was that He might confound the miscreants. As for what God has allotted to His Messenger from these spoils — for they were not won by horse or camel that you spurred into battle — He empowers His messenger over whomsoever He wills, since over all things God is sovereign. What God has assigned to His messenger from the property of the people of the towns belongs of right to God and His messenger and also to near kinsmen, to orphans and those who are desolate and to the wayfarer, so that it may not just circulate among you that are rich. So accept what the messenger gives you and accept as withheld what he withholds from you. Keep God reverently in all your thoughts. God is strict in retribution. The spoils go also to the impoverished, i.e. the *Muhājirūn* (those who left Mecca in the *Hijrah*) who were expelled from their homes and their possessions through their desire for the good hand of God and His good pleasure, and in support of the cause of God and His apostle. These are men of good faith, as are those (the *Ansār*) who, having their homes intact and coming already to the faith, love those who have emigrated into their midst and in their hearts disclaim any acquisitive interest in what they receive, giving others precedence over themselves even when their circumstances are straitened. It is such who, being preserved from inward greed for themselves, are the ones who flourish. As for those who were later emigrants, their prayer is: 'Our Lord, forgive us and those of our brethren who have preceded us in the faith. Let there be no ill-will in our hearts towards those who have believed. Lord you are gentle in mercy.'

Have you (s.) not noted those who acted hypocritically, saying to the unbelieving among the people of the Book: 'In the event of your being expelled we, too, will definitely go out with you as well and, in what relates to you, we will have no truck with anyone. If you are involved in battle we will certainly come to your aid.' God is witness what deceivers they are! If they are expelled, they will not go out with them nor take part with them when battle is joined. Even if they did, they would surely turn tail, and that will be the end of any aid! Truly you yourselves (the

Muslims) arouse more fear in their hearts than God Himself, for the simple reason that they are a people who are quite witless.

They will not join battle with you in total encounter but only in fortified places and from the cover of ramparts. Were you to take them as one force their fighting power would be formidable, but they are at odds among themselves. They are a people who lack understanding. Like those who, a while back, tasted the dire results of their doings, so these, too, are heading for condign punishment. Their case resembles Satan saying to man: 'Repudiate God!' When man did so, Satan said: 'I have nothing to do with you. For my part I fear God, the Lord of the worlds.' That is how it is with these people too. The end of both is the Fire, eternally. That is the retribution of wrong-doers.

Believers! Hold God in awe. Let every soul look to what he has forwarded for a morrow. Hold God in awe. God is aware of all you do. Do not be like those who forgot God and God caused them to forget themselves. Depraved they are. The denizens of the Fire are not like the denizens of the garden. The denizens of the garden — theirs is the state of triumph.

Had We caused this Qur'ān to come down upon a mountain you (s.) would have seen it crumbling away in very humility and awe before God. We employ these similitudes for mankind's sake. It may be they will ponder them. *Surah 59.1-21*

PROPHET! Why do you put a ban, as unlawful, on what God has made legitimate for you, with a view to pleasing your wives? God is ever forgiving and merciful. God has laid upon you (pl.) the duty of release from your oaths. God has entire authority over you: He is all-knowing and all-wise.

There was an occasion when the Prophet told one of his wives in confidence what she then divulged. God made him aware she had done so. Whereupon he let the matter be generally known — in part, while concealing the rest. On being informed she asked him: 'Who was it told you of this?' He answered: 'The One who knows all and is aware of all, He told me.' If you both (the two wives in question) are repentant before God — since both of you are implicated — it will be well; but if you connive with each other against him (Muhammad) God is His great custodian with Gabriel and the righteous believers and, furthermore, the angels will come to his aid.

Were he to divorce you (pl.) his Lord would give him other wives instead better than you — Muslim women, believers who are devout, penitent and true worshippers, who keep the fast faithfully, whether they be women previously married or virgins.

Believers! Guard yourselves and your households from that Fire whose fuel is mankind and stones, presided over by angels of stern and wrathful mien who are undeviating and relentless in their execution of God's commands.

You deniers of the faith! do not offer excuses on the Day you are being requited for your own past deeds.

Believers! Turn to God in sincere repentance. Your Lord may absolve you of your evil doings and bring you into gardens where streams flow, on the Day when God will not confound the prophet nor the believers with him. On that Day, their light resplendent around them, they will say: 'Lord, bring our light to its fullness and grant us forgiveness. For You have all things in the disposal of Your power.'

Prophet! 'Take up the *Jihād* against the deniers of the faith and the dissemblers: be ruthless with them. Their abode is *Jahannam* — a wretched destiny.'

There is an example God has given for those who deny the faith — the wife of Noah and the wife of Lot, who were under the charge of two of Our righteous servants whom they betrayed. It availed them nothing before God having devout husbands. The sentence was: 'Enter the Fire, both of you, with all who come there.'

In Pharaoh's wife God has afforded an example for believers. She prayed: 'Lord, build me a house in the garden: deliver me from Pharaoh and his doings: deliver me from men of evil.' Mary, too, the daughter of 'Imrān was one who guarded her virginity. We breathed of Our spirit into her womb. She credited her Lord's words to her and His Scriptures and was numbered among the godly.   *Surah 66*

PROPHET! Tell your wives: 'If your hearts are set on the life of this present world with its blandishments, come, I will give you maintenance and generously release you: but if your real desire is for God and His apostle and the life hereafter, God has in truth prepared a great reward for those of you who do what is good and right. Wives of the Prophet! there will readily be, from God, double punishment for any of you found to be guilty of flagrantly gross conduct. But for any of you chastely devoted to God and to His apostle and occupied in good works We will have double recompense and will make ready a rich provision.

Wives of the Prophet! you are not as other women are. In due piety before God, do not use ingratiating language so that some man of depraved mind has his desire kindled. Speak with due decorum, stay in your quarters and do not flaunt your beauty after the manner of the times of ignorance (*Al-Jāhiliyyah*), perform the prayer-rite and bring the *Zakāt*. Obey God and His apostle. God wills to rid you of all that is unworthy, as people of the house, and to have you altogether pure. Remember the revelations of God which are recited in your dwellings and the wisdom. God is the ever-kind, the ever-aware.

God has made ready His forgiveness and a great reward for all those, men and women alike, who have surrendered to Him, believers of both sexes, persons of deep piety, keeping faith, patient, lowly men and women who give alms and observe fasting, who keep their sexuality chaste and who practise the recollection of God.

It is no right of a believer, man or woman, to retain any option of their own in any matter on which God and His apostle have ruled by decree. Whoever goes counter to God and His apostle is in grievous error.

You (Muhammad) said to him whom God had granted blessing, and you had too (Zaid ibn Hàrithah, adopted son): 'Keep your wife as your own and live in fear of God.' You said this out of apprehension about popular gossip and keeping the actual situation to yourself. God allowed it to come out. It is God who is properly to be one's pre-occupying fear. Then, when Zaid renounced his bond with her, We united you and her in marriage, in order that there would be no reproach for believing men taking to wife the wives of their adopted sons when these had released them formally. Thus what God commanded was brought to pass. No reproach attaches to the prophet in a context where God has laid an obligation on him. Such was God's tradition aforetime with those who have left the scene — God's ordainment is absolute and final — those, namely, who brought home the messages of God and, in fearing Him, feared none other. There is no more comprehensive reckoning than that which God makes.

Muhammad is not the father of any man among you. He is the apostle of God and the seal of the prophets. God's knowledge embraces everything.   *Surah 33.28-40*

THE Jews affirm that 'Uzair is the son of God while the Christians affirm that the Christ is the son of God. Such is the talk of their mouths: it is the kind of thing that unbelievers have alleged in earlier times. May they perish at God's hand: perverse are all their thoughts! They take their priests and monks as lords and the Christ, son of Mary also, displacing the worship of God. This — when they were commanded to worship one God only — there is no other God but He. May He be glorified from all that they falsely associate with Him. They seek to extinguish the very light of God with their utterances. But this God will frustrate. For He wills only the perfecting of His light, however hateful the unbelievers find it. It is He who has sent His messenger with guidance and the religion of truth, making it victorious over all religion, notwithstanding the hatred of those who worship plural gods.

Believers! There are numerous priests and monks who purloin and squander the property of the people and debar them from the way of God. They are the ones who hoard gold and silver putting it to no use in the way of God. Let them have the news that a dire torment awaits them!   *Surah 9.30-34*

GOD made a covenant with the children of Israel. We commissioned twelve of their number as tribal leaders, to whom God said: 'I am with you. If you perform the prayer-rite and bring the *Zakāt*, if you believe in My messengers and rally to their cause, and if you lend liberally to God, then I will surely acquit you of your evil doings and bring you into gardens with flowing streams. Whoever of your number thereafter who denies the faith is indeed far gone from the right path.'

However, on account of their breach of the covenant We laid them under a curse and hardened their hearts. They distort the meanings of the words and have forgotten part of what had been committed to them to have ever in mind. All but a few of them you (s.) will find constantly engaged in treachery. Pardon them and forgive: God loves those who behave with magnanimity.

With those who say: 'We are Christians' We also entered into covenant. They too forgot in part what had been committed to them to keep ever in mind. So We have kindled enmity and hatred among them until the Day of resurrection. God will assuredly make them realise how they have behaved.

People of the Book! Our apostle has come to bring into clear light for you what, in large measure, you have been obscuring from yourselves within the Book, and to free you from much misconception. There has come to you from God a light and a Book of utmost clarity, whereby God guides those who seek His good pleasure into the ways of peace, bringing them out from the shadows into the light by His act of will and guiding them into a straight path.

Jews and Christians say: 'We are children of God and beloved of Him.' Say: 'Why then does He punish you for your transgressions?' No!

You are human beings, His creatures along with the rest. Whom He wills He pardons and whom He wills He punishes. To God belongs the sovereignty of the heavens and of the earth and all that is within them, and with Him is the final issue.

People of the Book! Our apostle has come to you, bringing a clear revelation, following an abeyance in the sequence of messengers. This leaves you no ground to say: 'Neither messenger nor warner has come to us.' A messenger and a warner has in truth come to you. God has all things in the disposal of His power.   *Surah 5.12-16, 18-19*

GOD has sent down to you a *Dhikr*, a messenger reciting to you the revelations of God as clear signs, that He may bring those who believe and do righteously out of the shades of darkness into the light. Whoever believes in God and does what is right He will usher into gardens where streams flow, to abide there for ever. Excellent for him has God made His provision.   *Surah 65.10b-11*

THOSE who were called to bear the trust of the Torah and then failed to carry it are to be likened to a donkey laden with books. It is a sorry metaphor of how those people are who denied the revelations of God. God does not guide aright recalcitrant wrong-doers.

Say: 'Those of you who are Jewish people, if you claim that you are uniquely befriended by God to the exclusion of mankind at large, then, if you really mean it, you should be longing for death.' Yet they do not long for it at all — thanks to all they have been doing which is accruing for hereafter. God knows transgressors through and through.

Say: 'The death you evade will meet you and then you will be brought back to the One who knows the unseen and the evident. He will inform you of your deeds.'   *Surah 62.5-8*

HAVE you (s.) not noted those who were forbidden to hold secret meetings and have gone back to doing so, and whose conspiratorial aims are iniquitous, in enmity and rebellion against the apostle? When they come to greet you, it is not with the greeting God has for you. For they are inwardly saying: 'Why does not God take it out of us for what we think and say of him (Muhammad)?' *Jahannam* will do well enough for them. They will burn there — a wretched enough climax!

Believers! When you confer with each other do not let it be conspiracy to evil-doing, hostility and disobedience towards the apostle. Concert together for righteousness and devotion to God. Hold God in awe, for it is to Him you will be gathered.

Conspiracy is Satan's way, for the grief of believers. However, only by leave of God can he do them any hurt. So let believers trust wholly in God.

Believers! When the request comes to make room in your assemblies, do so: God affords room for you. When the word is: 'Go up higher' then do so. God will elevate to higher estate believers among you who have received knowledge. God is aware of all your actions.

Believers! When you come to confer with the apostle make a free gift of alms before your conference. That will be the better course of action for you and will make for purer intention. If you lack the means, God in His mercy forgives. Are you embarrassed about an act of free almsgiving, prior to your meeting to confer? In that case of omitting it — given that God has relented towards you — fulfill the prayer-rite and bring the obligatory *Zakāt*. Obey God and obey the apostle. God is aware of all your actions.

Have you (s.) not noted those who take into their friendship people on whom God's anger rests? They have no part with you, nor indeed with those allies. Their oath is falsely sworn — and they know it! God has made ready for them a stern retribution. What they were perpetrating was evil indeed. They have made their oaths a cover and debarred others from the way of God, incurring shameful punishment. Their property and their offspring will avail them nothing against God. Companions of the Fire they are, and there will they be for ever. On the Day when God raises them all again they will profess their pledges to Him as they do now to you and they will reckon that they win their point.' But are they not, in fact, strangers to the truth? Satan has got the better of them and made them forsake the remembrance of God. They are partisans of Satan — and is not Satan's party on the losing side?

Those who resist God and His apostle are the ones bound for total humiliation. God's writ reads: 'I will indeed conquer — I and my apostles!' God is mighty and strong.

You (s.) will not find people who believe in God and in the last Day having any fondness for those who oppose God and His apostle, even though these are their fathers, their sons, their brothers or their clan.

God has engraved faith on the hearts of such believers and strengthened them with a spirit from Himself. He will bring them into gardens where streams flow where they will abide evermore. God delights in them and they in Him. It is these who are the partisans of God and is not the party of God in true *falāh*? *Surah 58.8-22*

Is it not time that the hearts of believers should be bowed in reverent humility at the remembrance of God and the truth He has sent down, that they be not like those who earlier received the Book but whose hearts, as time lengthened, became hardened, many of whom are now living evil lives?

Be alive to how God brings the earth to life out of its deadness. We have made Our revelations manifest to you (pl.): perhaps you (pl.) will use your intelligence.

Those who give voluntary alms, men and women alike, and who lend a good loan to God will find it multiplied to them. Theirs is a generous reward.

Those who believe in God and His apostle are the ones who keep faith and are witnesses in the sight of their Lord: they receive their reward and the light is theirs. Those who deny the faith and belie Our revelations are companions of *Al-Jahīm*.

You (pl.) must realise that the life of this present world is only play and diversion and passing show, a vie-ing for glory and rivalry over flaunted wealth and offspring. After a shower of rain there is vegetation over which unbelievers enthuse until, by and by, it withers away, grows yellow before your eyes and ends up like straw. That is how it is with the vanities of this life, and — in the last Day — both stern retribution and forgiveness from God and satisfaction.

The life of this present world is nothing but indulgence in delusion. Compete, instead, with one another in ardour for pardon from your Lord and to attain the garden whose reach is as wide as the heaven and the earth, prepared for those who believe in God and His apostles, bestowed of His goodness by God on whom He wills. For God is the Lord of magnanimous grace.

There is no calamity occurring on earth or in your own selves that is not already written in a book before We cause it to happen — all of which is easy with God. So then do not be disheartened about what has passed you by, nor enthuse with joy over what has come to you. God has no love for any proud boaster — those who are themselves miserly and call mankind to avarice. Whoever is a renegade, God is all-sufficient and ever to be praised.

We have sent Our messengers with clear evidences and with them We have sent down the Book and the criterion by which to weigh, so that men might act with equity. We have sent down iron, with its mighty potential and its diverse utility to man, that God may know those who are for Him and His messengers, siding with the hidden mystery. God is ever strong and mighty. *Surah 57.16-26-5*

BUT for the goodness and mercy of God over you and the fact that God, the all-wise, welcomes penitence — how would it have been? They are a faction among you who have brought a slanderous charge: do not hold it a bad thing in your respect. Indeed it is to your advantage: every man-jack of them will have the consequence of the sin he has done and he who played the foremost part in the business will incur heavy punishment. Why did the believers, both men and women, when they heard of it, not inwardly conjecture the best and conclude: 'The story is plainly a calumny.'? How is it they did not produce four witnesses? Seeing they have brought no witnesses then in God's sight those vilifiers speak falsehood. But for the goodness and mercy of God upon you in this present world and in the world to come a heavy punishment would have taken you for all your fulsome gossip about it, in getting your tongues around matters of which you had no knowledge and mouthing them about, on the assumption that it was a frivolous matter, when in God's sight it was truly serious.

Why, when you heard about it, did you not say: 'It is not for us to bandy words about this. Glory be to You: this is complete slander.'? God admonishes you never to repeat the like of it again, if believers you be. God makes His signs clear to you — God who is all-wise and knows all.

Those who relish spreading foul slander around about believers are in for painful retribution both in the present world and in the life to come. God knows, while you have no knowledge. But for the goodness and mercy of God — for God is compassionate and merciful — how would it have been? *Surah 24.10-20*

WE have sent, before you, no messenger and no prophet into whose intentions as he was proceeding in them Satan did not cast insinuations. But God annuls what Satan interposes and thus God authenticates His revelations — God all-knowing and all-wise. God's aim is to make Satan's insinuations an occasion to test those who are diseased in heart or whose hearts are hardened — those who perpetrate the wrong are in open schism — and also that those to whom knowledge is given may realise that it is the truth from your (s.) Lord and thus put their faith in it with hearts humbly submissive to Him. Truly God guides believers into a straight path, while those who deny will continue to be in doubt of it until the Hour overtakes them suddenly or the punishment of a forlorn Day. The dominion on that Day will be God's, judging between them.

Those who have believed and done good deeds will be in gardens of delight: those who have denied and taken our signs as false — theirs will be a doom of shame.

Those who have emigrated in the way of God and been killed or suffered death God will then certainly provide for them well. For God is the supreme provider. He will assuredly give them entrance, to their utmost satisfaction. For God is all-knowing and forebearing.

So it will be. Anyone who has acted in retaliation proportionate to what was inflicted on him and is then again victimised, God will certainly come to his aid. God is the One who pardons and forgives.

Surah 22.52-60

BEFORE your (pl.) time established ways have gone into limbo. Go out through the land and see what happened in the end to those who denied the truth. This is clear evidence to mankind and guidance: it is admonition for those who are devout God-fearers. Do not weaken and give way to grief: you are the ones to prevail — if believers you be!

Surah 3.137-139

IT is an evident triumph We have achieved for you (s.), God's purpose being to forgive what has been wrong in you in the past and what may yet be, thus making good His grace upon you and guiding you into a straight path. God aids you strongly towards victory.

It is He who caused the *Sakīnah* to come down into the hearts of the believers so that, out of faith's experience, they might grow in faith. God's are the armies of the heavens and of the earth — God who is all-knowing and all-wise. He wills to bring believers, men and women alike, into gardens with flowing streams, there to dwell eternally, and to absolve them of their evil deeds. That — in the sight of God — is a great goal to attain.

The dissemblers, men and women alike, those — of both sexes — who offer false worship, and all who think thoughts of falsehood about God, He wills to punish. They are the very hub of evil. God's wrath rests on them. He has laid them under a curse and made *Jahannam* ready for them. An evil destiny is theirs. God's are the armies of the heavens and of the earth — God who is all-strong and all-wise.

We have sent you (s.) as a witness, a preacher and a warner, so that you

251

(pl.) might believe in God and His apostle, that you might honour and revere Him and celebrate His praise morning and evening.

Those who pledge their allegiance to you (s.) pledge their allegiance to God. The hand of God is over their hands. Anyone who breaks his oath does so to his own hurt, but whoever fulfills what he has pledged to God for him God will have an ample reward.

Those of the desert Arabs who absented themselves from the venture will tell you: 'We were occupied with our material and domestic affairs. So pardon us.' They say with their lips what is not in their hearts. Say: 'Who will avail you anything should God's will entail either hurt or help in respect of you? God is well aware of what you are doing. Indeed, you guessed that the apostle and the believers would never come back again to their families — which was to you an attractive notion. You had such foul surmises in your hearts because you are a worthless lot!' For those who do not believe in God and His apostle, deniers of the truth, We have made ready a burning Fire (*al-Saʿīr*).

To God belongs the kingdom of the heavens and of the earth. Whom He will He forgives and whom He will He punishes. God is ever forgiving and merciful.

When you set forth in quest of booty those who hold themselves back from the venture will say: 'Let us go along with you,' intending to change the ordinance of God. Tell them: 'You will certainly not go along with us, as God has already decreed.' To which they will reply: 'Obviously you are grudging us out of jealousy.' They are people of very limited intelligence. Say to those of the desert Arabs who loitered behind: 'You will be summoned to face a people of far greater prowess anon. These you will have to engage in battle unless they become Muslims. God will repay you handsomely if you obey but if you turn tail then as you did earlier He will afflict you with heavy punishment.'

The blind, the lame and the sick are exempt from action and from any reproach. Anyone who obeys God and His apostle, God will bring into gardens with flowing streams and any who turn away He will painfully requite. When, under the tree, the believers pledged their fealty to you (s.) God took pleasure in them, knowing their hearts. He sent the *Sakīnah* down upon them and made an impending victory their reward, with ample booty which they were able to take. God is all-strong and all-wise.

God has given you promise of great gains in war coming into your hands, the early materialisation of which He has ensured, holding off from you the hands that were hostile, in order to constitute a sign for believers and to guide you into a straight path. There are also gains which you have not been able to secure that God has already brought within reach. God has all things in the disposal of His power. Though the unbelievers fought against you they have turned back, finding as they did so neither friend nor helper. This has been the way of God in times past and you (s.) will never find the way of God to change. It was He who held them back from you and you from them in the valley of Mecca, after He had brought about your victory over them. God was vigilant over all you did.

It was they who denied the faith and debarred you from the sacred mosque and impeded the offering from reaching the intended place of sacrifice.

Had believers and unbelievers (in Mecca) been clearly identifiable as such, We would have inflicted a painful punishment upon the latter. However, there were believing men and believing women there whom you did not know — these, in that context, you might otherwise have struck down, thus incriminating yourselves unknowingly in a guilty crime against them. Thus God brings whom He wills into His mercy.

The unbelievers set their hearts fanatically against you — the very fierce fanaticism of *Al-Jāhiliyyah.* God caused His *Sakīnah* to come down upon His messenger and upon the faithful and He made the word of true godliness to constrain them, as befitted their worth and their aptitude. God has knowledge of all.

Truly God has made good the vision to His apostle, namely that you will indeed enter the sacred mosque, God being willing, and that, in full security and unafraid, with head shaven and hair cut short. God had knowledge that was denied to you (pl.). He has, moreover, granted you a victory soon to be yours.

He it is who has sent His apostle with guidance and the religion of truth, which He wills to make victorious over all religion. God is the all-sufficient witness.

Muhammad is the apostle of God. Those who are with him are sternly against deniers of the faith and compassionate among themselves. You (s.) see them kneeling and prostrating in prayer, desiring to experience God's goodness and grace. The marks of their devotion in prostration are traced on their faces. Their character has its likeness in the Torah and again in the Gospel where they are compared to corn-seed which sprouts into a shoot and, growing strong and tall, stands firmly upright to the delight of the sowers. At such believers the deniers of the faith only kindle to anger. God pledges, to those of them who come to faith and perform deeds of righteousness, forgiveness and a great reward.

Surah 48

THEIR desire is to extinguish the light of God with the words they mouth. But however averse it may be to the faith-deniers, God perfects His light — He who has sent His apostle with guidance and with the religion of truth, to make it prevail over all religion, however hateful they find it who practice plural worships.

Believers! Shall I indicate to you a transaction that will save you from painful chastisement? You believe in God and in His messenger, you strive in the way of God with your property and with very selves — a course of action which is best for you, if only you realised. He will forgive your transgressions and bring you into gardens with flowing streams, into fine abodes in the gardens of Eden. That is the ultimate triumph — and there is another too, on which you set your hearts — aid from God and a victory soon to come. So give (s.) good news to the faithful. *Surah 61.8-13*

IF the hypocrites and those who are sick-hearted, together with the dissidents in Medina, do not desist, We will surely kindle your (s.) zeal against them and in no time you will have them for neighbours no longer. A curse on them! where-ever they are found they shall be seized and put to death. That is God's way with those who before now have passed away, and in the way of God you (s.) will find no variance. *Surah 33.60-62*

BELIEVE in God and in His apostle: what He has brought into your possession expend for His sake. Those among you who have believed and have put their goods to His service receive ample reward. How does it come about that you fail to believe in God when the messenger is calling you, in your Lord's Name, to such belief and He has made covenant with you — if believers you are? He it is who sends down upon His servant clear revelations to bring you out from dark shadows into the light. For God is gentle and merciful towards you. Why, then, should you not spend of yourselves in the way of God, to whom belongs the heritage of the heavens and of the earth? Those who gave to the cause and did battle prior to the conquest (of Mecca) are not to be thought on a level with others: they are superior in honour and standing to those who gave and who battled later. To each and all God has pledged what is good and fair, God is watchful over all you undertake. *Surah 57.7-10*

FROM God and His apostle — a *Barā'ah*, a proclamation respecting the termination of the pledge into which you had entered with those who worship pseudo-gods. 'Have free passage in the land for four months. Take note: there is no frustrating God within your power and God brings low those who deny the faith.'

From God and His apostle — an announcement to all mankind on the day of the Great Pilgrimage. 'God hereby renounces all ties with the polytheists, as does His apostle. If you turn penitently, well and good it will be for you and if you turn away, be aware there is no frustrating God.' Give (s.) word to those who deny the faith that there is a terrible punishment. Exempted, however, are those polytheists with whom you have entered into pledges and who have not subsequently failed in any way in their undertakings with you, and have not allied with anyone against you. With these, fulfill the covenant they have with you until it expires. God loves those who live in His fear. When the sacred months (of truce) have elapsed, take the sword to the polytheists where-ever you find them. Capture them, besiege them, and take them in ambushes where-ever you can. If they repent, perform the prayer-rite and bring the *Zakāt*, let them go their way. God is ever forgiving and merciful. If any of the false worshippers seeks your protection, give him sanctuary in order to hear the word of God. Then see that he reaches a place of security. This is because they are a people long ignorant.

How could there possibly be a covenant on God's part or on that of the apostle with those who are idolatrous people, other than those of them around the sacred mosque, with whom you covenanted? Keep faith with them as long as they keep faith with you. God loves those who fear Him.

How, again, beyond this exception, could there be a covenant since, were they to get the better of you, they would have scant respect for their bond with you or for any protected status. They give you verbal satisfactions while at heart they are hostile, and — by and large — they are evil-minded. They have sold the revelations of God for a cheap sum and impeded the way of God in the sheer evil of their activities. They do not hold to any pledge or agreement made with a believer. They are the sort who flout everything. Even so, if they repent, perform the prayer-rite and bring the *Zakāt*, they will be your brethren in religion. We make the revelations explicit for those who will comprehend. But if, after entering into covenant, they flout their pledge and revile your religion, then fight to the death these captains of unbelief for whom no bond is sacred, in hope they may call a halt.

Are you not bound to fight against those who have broken their solemn pledges and were determined to drive the apostle out, initiating the conflict with you? Are you somehow cowed by them? It is God whom you have more right to fear — if believers you are! Then take the fight to them. God will afflict them at your hands. He will confound them and give you victory over them. Thus He will heal the inward feelings of believing people and assuage the anger in their hearts. God relents towards whom He wills, God ever aware and ever wise. Did you (pl.) suppose that you would somehow be left immune, before God knew your mettle as participators in the *Jihād*, taking none but God and His apostle and fellow-believers as your resource? God is ever watchful over your doings.

Polytheists have no right to enter or administer the mosques of God while they bear witness against themselves in their denial of faith. Their deeds avail them nothing. The Fire is their eternal destiny. The man who believes in God and in the last Day is the one to frequent and occupy the mosques of God — the man who perfoms the prayer-rite, brings the *Zakāt* and fears God alone. It is such who may hope to be among the rightly guided.

Have you assumed that the watering of the pilgrims and the management of the sacred mosque have the same worth as a believer's faith in God and the last Day and his *Jihād* in the cause of God? With God these are not commensurate. God does not guide people who commit evil. Those who believed and emigrated and have struggled in God's cause with their possessions and in their persons have greater standing with God. It is these who are the blessed achievers. Their Lord gives them the glad word of His mercy and grace, of gardens awaiting them where they will find abiding bliss, dwelling there eternally. For with God there is great reward.

Believers! Do not accept your fathers and your brethren into your friendship if unbelief rather than faith is what they hold dear. Any of you who take them as allies are inculpated as wrong-doers. Say: 'If anything is dearer to you than God and His apostle and the struggle for His cause — whether your fathers, your children, your brethren, your wives, your clan, the properties you have acquired, the commerce you suspect may diminish, and the haunts of which you are so fond — attend the fulfilment of God's decree. God does not guide degenerate people.'

Surah 9.1-24

THOSE with whom you (pl.) have entered into covenant and then every time break their bond, having no fear of God, if you encounter them in the course of fighting handle them so as to strike panic into those at the rear of them — a worsting they may remember. If, at the hands of any group, you (s.) suspect an act of treachery, make formal renunciation of your treaty. God has no love for traitors. Let no unbelievers think they will elude Us. That is far beyond their capacity. Make ready against them armed force and mounted cavalry to your utmost ability, whereby to engender fear in the enemy — God's enemy and yours, and among others also of whom you do not know, though God knows who they are. Whatever you have to lay out in the cause of God He will repay to you and you will suffer no injustice. If they incline to peace, you be minded for it too. Put your trust in God: He hears and knows all. If they are simply wanting to trick you that way, God is sufficient for you. It is He who aids you with His victory and with the believing people, those whose hearts He has bonded together. Such heart-unison you (s.) could not have brought about had you spent everything in the whole world. But God, who is all-strong and all-wise, He made them single-hearted.

Prophet! God is sufficient for you and who-ever follows you among the believers. *Surah 8.56-64*

GOD came to your aid in many places, as on the day of Hunain when your great numbers, which occasioned you such satisfaction, availed you nothing. Despite the breadth of the terrain you were caught in tight ambush and retreated in a rout. Then God brought His *Sakīnah* down upon His apostle and upon the faithful: He sent down armies invisible to you and inflicted loss on the unbelieving forces — the condign retribution of those who deny the faith. God will yet relent towards those whom He so wills — God, forgiving and merciful.

Believers! The polytheists are altogether unclean. They are not to come near the sacred mosque after this year. If you are apprehensive that poverty will result, God of His goodness will enrich you as He wills. God is all-knowing and all-wise.

Fight against those who do not believe in God nor in the last Day and who do not hold forbidden what God has prohibited and who do not adhere to the religion of truth, being among those to whom the Book was given. Do so until they pay the *Jizyah* (tax on tolerated minorities) personally, once they have been reduced to submission. *Surah 9.25-29*

THERE are those of them who defame the prophet: 'He hears too much!' Say: 'Such ears as his are good for you.' He believes in God and trusts the believers and he is a mercy to those of you who believe. For those who

257

disparage God's apostle there awaits a painful punishment. To ingratiate themselves with you they swear in God's name when it is more to the point that they should please God and His apostle — if believers they truly are. Do they not realise that whoever resists God and His apostle the Fire of *Jahannam* awaits him, as a dwelling evermore, and the ultimate ignominy?

The hypocrites are fearful that a surah may be sent down against them, telling them out loud what is in their hearts. Say: 'Keep up your derision! The very thing you are dreading God will bring about.' If you interrogate them they will certainly say: 'We were merely engaging in a light banter.' Say: 'Was it God and His revelations and His apostle you were holding up to mockery? Make no excuses: you have denied the faith after professing it. If We forgive one party among you We will requite another. For they are indeed guilty.' Hypocrites, both men and women, are all of a kind: they incite to dishonourable things and forbid what is honourable. They are tight-fisted and oblivious of God — and He has no mind for them! The hypocrites are downright villains.   *Surah 9.61-67*

PROPHET! Carry the *jihād* to those who deny the faith and the hypocrites. Be rigorous with them. For *Jahannam* they are bound, a wretched destiny. They swear to God that they said nothing, but in truth it was a word of unbelief they did say. They denied even after their *islām* but the real objective they intended they did not achieve. There was nothing they had to avenge themselves about except that God and His messenger — out of His bounty — had brought them enrichment. If they repent it will be better for them, but if they turn away God will afflict them with fearful punishment in this present world and in the hereafter. They will find none on earth to be either protector or succourer to them.

Among them there are those who thus pledge to God: 'If He gives us His bounty we will assuredly give freewill alms and conduct ourselves as righteous people.' But when He did bestow His bounty on them they proved to be miserly hoarders and in their obdurate way they retracted. Consequently He caused hypocrisy to root in their hearts against the Day of their encounter with Him, having withheld from Him what they pledged and for their habitual lying. Have they not realised that God knows their secret thoughts and their whispered words? and that He is omniscient of the unseen realms?

Those who denigrate and deride the believers who volunteer their freewill offerings and the believers who can find only their exertions to offer, God holds in contempt and painful retribution awaits them.

Seek forgiveness for them or forebear to do so, but whether you (s.) do so seventy times over, God will never forgive them. For they have denied both God and His messenger. God does not guide ungodly people.

Those who were left behind were happy enough to be squatting in the rear when the apostle went forth. They were thoroughly averse to laying out their wealth and exerting themselves in God's cause. They said: 'Do not go to fight in the heat.' Say: 'The Fire of *Jahannam* is much hotter, did they but realise!' Let them laugh awhile: they will for sure weep much in the requiting of their deserts.

If God brings you safely back to any of them — a group that requests leave of you to go on expedition, tell them: 'Never will you go out with me: never will you fight an enemy with me. On the first occasion you were satisfied to sit passively. Go on sitting with the non-combatants in the rear.' Never pray for any single one of them at his death nor stand beside his grave. They have belied God and His messenger and died in their sins. Do not allow their wealth or their children to arouse your admiration. God's purpose with them is to afflict them in this world and their souls forfeit in the state of unbelief.

When a surah was sent down: 'Believe in God and share in *jihād* with the messenger,' the men of wealth among them asked your (s.) leave, saying: 'Let us stay out with the non-combatants.' They were satisfied enough to remain with those behind. A seal has been set on their hearts and they do not comprehend. But the messenger and the believers with him took up the *jihād* with their property and their persons. Theirs are the good things: they are the ones to attain success. God has made ready for them gardens with flowing streams in which they for ever abide in the great triumph of bliss. *Surah 9.73-89*

IT is not in the interests of the people of Medina nor of the bedouin Arabs who are around them to hold back from participation with God's apostle or to esteem their own souls more precious than his. For a good deed is recorded in their favour whenever they undergo thirst or fatigue or hunger in the way of God and at every step they take which vexes the unbelievers and for every advantage they gain over the enemy. God does not let the reward of well-doers run to waste: For there is no occasion when they expend anything, whether small or large, and no time when they cross a valley, but that it is recorded of them, so that God may afford the best reward for these deeds of theirs. *Surah 9.120-121*

THE retribution to requite those who war against God and His messenger and who persist in their corrupt ways in the land is that they be put to the sword or be crucified, or be mutilated by severing hands and feet on alternate sides, or be expelled from the land — utter humiliation for them in this present world and a dreadful doom in the hereafter — except those who repent before you have them in your power. Know that God is merciful and forgiving.

Believers! Hold God in reverent awe and make it your desire to draw near to Him: give yourselves to the *Jihād* in the way of God. It may be you will have good success.

The unbelievers — had they in possession all that is in the earth and the same again to ransom them from the retribution of the Day of resurrection, it would not be accepted from them. Theirs will be dire punishment. They will long to come out of the Fire, but they will not emerge from it. Theirs will be a lasting doom.   *Surah 5.33-37*

THE sole obligation of the messenger is the delivery of the message. God knows what you (pl.) disclose and what you conceal. Say: 'What is foul and what is good are in no way comparable, even though you (s.) may find fascination in much that is foul. So hold God in reverent awe, you (pl.) who are blessed with perception, and maybe you will truly prosper.

Believers! Do not enquire about things which, were they to be disclosed to you, would be harmful for you. If you are asking about them while the Qur'ān is being sent down they will be shown to you. God absolves you over this: for He is forgiving and forbearing. People before you asked such questions and later became unbelievers because of them.

It is no ordinance from God by which cattle have been named for idols — *bahīrah, sā'ibah, wasīlah* and *hām* — it is the false invention of pagan unbelievers foisted upon God, most of whom are devoid of understanding.

When they are bidden to come to the revelation which God has sent down to the apostle, they reply: 'What our forebears followed is good enough for us!' What — though their forebears knew nothing and had no guidance?

Believers! You are responsible for your own souls. If you are rightly guided those in error can do you no harm. To God is your returning, one and all, and He will have you know of your doings.   *Surah 5.99-105*

THESE are the ones who buy error at the price of guidance. But this merchandising of theirs has brought them no profit, and guidance has eluded them. They can be likened to men who kindled a fire, and when it was shedding light around them God deprived them of its illumination and left them in a darkness where they could see nothing. Deaf, dumb and blind, there is no way back for them.

Or they are like a cloudburst in the sky, accompanied by darkness, thunder and lightning. In fear of death they put their fingers in their ears at the thunderclaps. God besets the unbelievers on every side. The lightning almost blinds them in its sudden brilliance: they pick their way in its flashes, halting when the dark is black around them. Had God so willed He could have taken from them both hearing and sight. For God has all things in the disposal of His power.   *Surah 2.16-20*

MARCH out, whether light or heavy of heart (*or* of weapons) and struggle with your possessions and in your persons in God's cause. That will be well for you — if only you understood. They would readily have followed you (s.) had the objective been handy and the expedition specific, but the distance was too arduous for them. They will swear by God saying: 'Had we been able, we would have sallied forth with you (pl.).' God knows they are outright liars, destroying their own souls.

May God pardon you (s.). Why did you give them permission until it became clear to you who were the ones speaking truthfully and you knew who were the false? Believers in God and the last Day do not ask from you exemption from the *Jihād* with their possessions and themselves. God knows those who are truly God-fearers. Those who want you to exempt them are those who withhold belief in God and the last Day, they of doubting heart and given to vacillation. Had they really willed to join the campaign they would have made some preparation for it. God detested having their participation in the venture and so made them sluggish. The word was: 'Sit down with the stay-at-homes!'

Were they to take the field with you they would add nothing to you but confusion, stirring up sedition among you by their comings and goings. Indeed there are some of you who have an ear for them. God knows who are the evil-doers. They have before now been instigators of sedition, overturning what you (s.) had in hand, until the truth arrived and the decree of God came into clear light — much to their chagrin. There were many of their number whose cry was: 'Let me off, and do not put me on the spot!' Have not such already fallen into sedition? All around the unbelievers *Jahannam* stands encircling.

If things go well with you, they take it ill and if some calamity happens to you they say: 'We took precautions earlier,' and turn away delighted. Tell them: 'Nothing befalls except what God has prescribed for us. He is our protector. Let believers place all their trust in Him.' Say: 'Are you anticipating with respect to us anything other than the two good outcomes (victory or martyrdom)? For our part we are anticipating God's visitation on you, namely a painful retribution at His hand and by our hands. Wait then! we will be waiting too!'

Say: 'Whether you are contributing willingly or involuntarily, it will never be accepted from you. You are a corrupt set of people.' What stands squarely in the way of anything being acceptable from them is the very fact that they deny faith in God and in His apostle, only perfunctorily do they perform the prayer-rite and only with feelings of aversion do they contribute to God's cause.

Do not be (s.) enamoured of their property or their children. By these God wills to bring them punishment in this present life and their souls to depart this life in a state of unbelief. They take oaths in God's Name that they are one with you. In fact they are not one with you at all. The truth is they are a craven people who, if they could, would find a refuge in caverns or bolt-holes, and make a hasty run there.   *Surah 9.41-57*

CERTAIN desert Arabs made excuses, seeking exemption for themselves from combat. Others gave the lie to God and His apostle and stayed where they were. Such unbelievers will undergo painful retribution. There is no reproach to the weak, or the sick or those with no resources to spend in the cause, provided they are sincere with God and His apostle. Nor is there any onus on those whose actions are right. God is forgiving and merciful. Nor again is there onus of those who, when they came to you (s.) asking for mounts on which to ride, were told by you that you could find none for them. These turned away, their eyes brimming with tears of sorrow because they had no resources to give. But there is onus on those who pleaded exemption though they had ample resources. They were happy enough to be left behind with the rest. Ignorant in themselves, God sealed their hearts. They will still be offering excuses to you when you return. Say: 'Never mind more excuses: we will never believe what you say. God has informed us all about you. God will be seeing all you do, and so will His apostle, and anon you will be brought before the One who knows things unseen and things manifest, and He will rehearse to you all your doings.'

On your return to them from the campaign they will swear to you in

God's Name just to get you to leave them alone. Well, leave them alone. They are a squalid lot whose abode is *Jahannam*, the penalty they have fully earned. Or they will swear to you ingratiating themselves with you. Even were you to favour them God would in no way grant His favour to a people of such corruption.

The desert Arabs are very obstinate in unbelief and hypocrisy, and very liable to defy the limits God has prescribed by revelation to His messenger — God who is all-knowing and all-wise. Some desert Arabs regard what they expend in God's cause as levied on them and they are anticipating some adverse turn in your fortunes. The adverse turn will be theirs — God heeds and knows. Others, however, among the desert Arabs who believe in God and the last Day regard all that they lay out as a means of approach to God and of the prayers of the apostle. Indeed, it will be such a means of access for them. God will usher them into His mercy. For God is forgiving and merciful.

Precedence belongs to those who were the pioneer emigrants (*Al-Muhājirūn*) and their Medinan allies (*Al-Ansār*) and those who have emulated them in well-doing. With these God is well-pleased, as they with Him. He has made ready for them gardens with flowing streams in which they will dwell eternally — which is the supreme destiny. Among the neighbouring tribes around you there are dissemblers, and people, too, in Medina who are brazen hypocrites. You do not know who they are: We know them and will bring them into twofold punishment, before consigning them to final retribution.

There are others who have acknowledged their evil doings, though they have a mixed record of good and bad actions. God may relent towards them: for God is forgiving and merciful. Take (s.) from what they own as an offering for God's cause, whereby to purify and cleanse them. Pray over them. Your prayer will be a solace for them. God hears and knows. Do they not realise that God indeed accepts repentance from His servants and receives freewill offerings? For God the merciful responds to penitence.

Say: 'Act. For God and His apostle will see your action, as will the believers. You will finally be brought before Him who knows things unseen and things manifest and He will give you to know of your doings.' There are others held in abeyance pending the decree of God, whether it be their punishment or their receiving God's clemency. God is all-knowing and all-wise.

Concerning those who have taken a mosque of their own with hostile intent, to induce unbelief and disunity among believers and to act as a base of operation for those who have from the first resisted God and His apostle — though they swear emphatically that they intend nothing but good — God witnesses what liars they are — you must not set foot in it. Only a mosque founded on God's true fear from its very first day is worthy for you to set foot in, a house of worship where there are men whose love is set on purity. God loves those who purify themselves.

Who is better — one who has founded his building on the true fear of God and His good pleasure, or one who has founded what he builds on the edge of a river-bank crumbling into the under-cutting stream, thus toppling him with it into *Jahannam's* fire? People of the evil way God does not guide. What those disaffected ones have erected will remain to plague them with misgiving, if it does not lacerate their very hearts! God is all-knowing and all-wise. From the believers God purchases their very selves and their possessions, the price of the garden. They do battle in God's cause, they kill and are killed themselves. It is a pledge God undertakes in truth, in the Torah, in the *Injīl*, and in the Qur'ān. Who is more true to covenant than God? So find joy in the bargain you have made with God: to do so is the supreme achievement. Such are they who repent, who worship, give praise, live as pilgrims, who kneel and prostrate in prayer, who enjoin what is right and repudiate what is proscribed, and who observe the limits God has set. So tell (s.) the believers the glad news.   *Surah 9.90-112*

IT is not appropriate that all believers, to a man, take the field. Let there be an element, from within each company that takes the field, who give themselves to fuller competence in the principles of religion and who can apprise their people returning to them from the field so that these may be alerted.

Believers! Fight the unbelievers in your vicinity: let them find you dealing with them sternly. Know that God is with those who truly fear Him.

Whenever a surah has been sent down there were those saying: 'Which of you has this conduced to greater faith?' As far as believers are concerned, it has conduced to greater faith and they rejoice for it. But as for those of sickly heart it has only accentuated their evil, adding yet more. They have died in their unbelief.

Do they not see that they are being put to the test time and again? Yet they are still without repentance, nor do they call God to mind. Whenever a surah is sent down, they look at one another as if to ask: 'Is there really anyone who has us in view?' Then they go off. Witless lot that they are, God turns their hearts off too.

Truly there has come to you an apostle from among your own selves, one who takes with heavy heart the distress you undergo, one who watches over you, with gentleness and compassion towards believers.

If they turn away, say: 'God is sufficient for me. There is no god but He. In Him have I put my trust. He is the Lord of the great Throne.'

Surah 9.122-129

THE desert Arabs say: 'We have believed.' Say(s.): 'You have not believed: you should rather say: "We have become Muslims" (or: "We have surrendered.") Faith has not entered your hearts. If you obey God and His messenger, He will not let you forfeit any of your deeds. For God is forgiving and merciful. Believers are those who, having believed in God and His messenger, do not doubt further but strive in the way of God (*Jihād*) with their possessions and their persons. These are the ones who are truly sincere.'

Say: 'Do you want to teach God about your religious practices when God knows all things in the heavens and on earth and God fully comprehends all that is?'

They imagine they are doing you (s.) a favour in becoming Muslims. Tell them: 'Do not consider your *islām* a favour done to me. It is God who does good to you in having guided you to faith, that is, if what you say is sincere. God holds the secret of the heavens and of the earth, and everything you do is open to His sight.'

Surah 49.14-18

BELIEVERS! Take due precautions and advance either in separate companies or all together. There are those among you who drag their feet terribly. When adversity strikes, such a one will say: 'God has been good to me, in that I was not present among them,' whereas if there comes to you from God some good success, he will surely say — as if there had never been any question about the love between you and him: 'Would I had been there with them: I would have achieved a splendid victory.'

Let those go to war for God's cause who sell the life of this present world for that of the world to come. For whoever fights in the way of God, whether he himself is slain or is victorious, We will in due time greatly repay.

What is amiss with you that you do not go to war in the cause of God and of the feeble folk, men, women and children, who are pleading: 'Our Lord, bring us out from this city of oppressors and raise up for us, of Your mercy, a champion. Send us a friend in our need from Your presence.' Those who have come to faith do battle in the cause of God, while those who deny the faith do battle for the cause of *Tāghūt*. Fight then against the intimates of Satan. For puny are the wiles of Satan.

Have you (s.) not noticed how a group among those who had the summons: 'Restrain yourselves, fulfill the prayer-rite and bring the *Zakāt*' became fearful when told to do battle in God's cause — as much in fear of men as they are of God! or even more so. They say: 'Our Lord, why have You laid on us the order to fight? If only You would grant us respite a little while.' Tell them: 'The enjoyment of this present world is brief. The world to come is better for those who truly fear God and you will not be wronged even as much as the line on a date-stone. Where-ever you may be death will overtake you even were you in fortress towers.'

When some happy thing occurs for them, men will say: 'This is from God.' If some evil chance strikes them they say: 'This is your (s.) doing.' Tell them: 'All is from God.' What ails these people? They hardly understand a thing said to them.

Whatever good happens to you (s.) is from God and whatever evil happens to you it is from yourself. We have commissioned you an apostle to mankind, and God is sufficient witness. Whoever obeys the apostle has obeyed God and whoever turns away — We have not sent you to them as one in charge of them.

They say: 'We are all attention!' But when they have gone out from your presence some of them spend all night busy with thoughts other than what you said. God records in writing their dark cogitations. So give them a wide berth and put your (s.) trust in God — God the sufficient trust.

Will they not give their minds to reflect on the Qur'ān? Had it come from elsewhere and not from God they would surely have found in it much contradiction.

When word of anything, whether to do with security or fear, comes their way, they broadcast it. If they would just refer it to the apostle and to those of their responsible leaders, these whose business it is to gather and apply intelligence would know what course to take.

But for the goodness of God over you and His mercy all but a few of you would have gone after Satan.

So fight in the cause of God — you (s.) are responsible for yourself alone — and urge the believers on. It may be that God will restrain the power of the unbelievers. For God has greater might and He is more stern to repel. Whoever commits himself on behalf of what is good finds himself sharing in it and whoever commits himself on behalf of what is evil will share liability from it. God presides over all things.

Surah 4.71-85

How does it come that you are in two minds about the hypocrites, when God has repudiated them for their deserts? Do you want to guide those whom God has led astray? Whoever God misguides for him you (s.) will never find a path. They would love to have you (pl.) reject the faith as they have done, so that you would be at one with them. Do not take them as friends unless they emigrate in the way of God. If they then revert, seize them and kill them where-ever you find them. Do not take any of them as an ally or a friend, except those who have ties with a people with whom you have a mutual covenant or those who come over to you because they are loathe of heart to make war on you or to fight against their own people. Had God so willed He would certainly have given them superiority over you and they would have gone to war against you. Thus, if they keep clear of you and do not make war against you, and if they offer you peace, God leaves you no occasion to confront them in hostility. You will find others who desire to enjoy security from you and from their own people, who nevertheless succumb to the temptation of beligerence every time it presents itself. So if they do not keep clear of you, nor offer you peace, nor restrain their hands, then seize them and kill them where-ever you encounter them. Against such as these We have given you a clear authority so to act.   *Surah 4.88-91*

Do you (s.) not know that the sovereignty of the heavens and of the earth belongs to God? Whom He will He punishes and whom He will He forgives. God has everything in the disposal of His power.

Apostle! Do not let those grieve you who are bent on surpassing one another in their unbelief, those who say with their lips: 'We have believed,' when there is no faith from their hearts, and the Jews who give their ears to what is false and listen to other people who do not listen to you. They distort what is said to wrest it from its meaning: what they say is: 'If such and such is the message brought to you, accept it. But if it is not, then be on your guard.'

Anyone whom it is God's will to bring to the test concerning some evil, you (s.) can in no way avail that man anything before God. These are the people whose hearts God has not willed to cleanse. Theirs is degradation in this present world and great retribution in the world to come, listening as they do to what is false and avidly devouring what is illicit. If they come to you (s.) judge between them or turn from them. If you turn away from them, they cannot harm you in any way. If you do give judgement between them, do so with justice. God loves those who deal justly. Yet, how is it that they come to you to give judgement when the Torah is theirs in which are God's judgements, and even so they turn away? Such people are no believers!

Truly We have sent down the Torah, wherein are guidance and light, according to which the prophets who had surrendered themselves gave judgement to those who are Jews, and so also did the rabbis and the learned scribes, by that part of the Book of God entrusted to their keeping and to which they were witnesses. So have no fear of men: fear Me and do not barter My revelations for a paltry sum. Whoever does not judge by what God has sent down they are denying the truth . . .

To you (s.) We have sent down the Book with truth, confirming the Scripture already in possession and determining its meaning. Accordingly judge between them by what God has sent down and do not follow what they lust after, diverting you from the truth that has come to you.

For each of you We have assigned a divine law and a rule of life. Had God so willed He could have made you a single nation. However He has willed to put you to the test respecting the revelation brought to you. Strive to excel in good things. To God is your return all of you, when He will give you to know about the things over which you were at variance.

Judge (s.) between them by what God has sent down and do not follow their desires: be on your guard lest they beguile you away from some part of God's revelation to you. If they turn away, realise that God wills to afflict them for some transgression of theirs. Mankind, for the most part, are sin-corrupted. Could it be that they want the sort of judgement obtaining in the *Jāhiliyyah*? Who can be better than God in the role of judging, as people of sure conviction must know?

Believers! Do not take Jews and Christians for friends — they are friends of themselves and any one of you who allies himself with them becomes one of them. God does not guide people who are committing evil.

You (s.) notice those who are diseased in heart all eagerness to associate with them, saying: 'We are afraid some change of fortune may happen to us.' What may happen is that God will give us the victory, or something He will ordain, and then they will regret having had such thoughts within them. Believers will ask: 'Are these the ones who swore in God's Name most solemn oaths that they would indeed be on your side?' Their doings have come to nothing and they are themselves brought to nought.

Believers! Any one of you who apostacises from his religion — well, God will in due course bring on a people whom He loves and who love Him, who will relate to the believers in all humility and be sternly against those who deny the faith, and who will strive in the way of God, not fearing reproach from any quarter. Such things are God's gift of grace which He grants to whom He wills. God is infinite and ever wise.

Your real ally is God and His messenger, and the believers — those who perform the prayer-rite and bring the *Zakāt* and who bow in worship. Whoever allies with God and His messenger, these — with the believers — are God's party, and the victors.

Believers! Do not take into alliance those who hold your religion in derision as a thing of jest, be they those who had the Scripture before you or outright unbelievers. Fear God, if believers you are! These people take it as a joke when you make the call to prayer, and they jest at it. That is because they are senseless folk.

Say: 'People of the Book, do you have any case against us except our believing in God and in what has been sent down to us and what had been revealed earlier?' Most of you are evil-minded.

Surah 5.40-44 and 48-59

OF old We took a covenant with the people of Israel and We sent messengers to them. Every time a messenger came to them with a message not congenial to them they would say that some of the messengers were liars and they would murder others. They assumed that nothing to disquiet them would come of it and thus they grew blind and deaf. Afterwards God turned towards them, and again many of them became blind and deaf and God was cognisant of their every deed.

Surah 5.70-71

BECAUSE of the wrong-doing of those of Jewish allegiance and for their having turned many back from the path of God We prohibited good things to them which had been made lawful. This was also for their taking usury though forbidden to them and their consuming the property of people deceptively.

For those of them who are unbelievers We have made ready painful punishment, but for those of them who are steadfast in their knowledge and believers in what has been revealed to you (s.) and revealed before your time, and who perform the prayers and bring the *Zakāt*, being believers in God and the last Day We have a great reward to bestow.

Surah 4.160-162

SURELY they are unbelievers who allege that God is the third of three! There is no god but One. If they do not cease saying such a thing these unbelievers will most surely be seized with a painful retribution. Will they not repent before God and seek His forgiveness? God is forgiving and merciful.

You (s.) will indeed find the Jews and those who hold with associate gods the people most strongly hostile to the believers, while you will find the closest to the believers in affection to be those who say: 'We are *Nasārā*,' — the reason being that among them are priests and monks, and they are not a people given to arrogance. When they listen to the revelations sent upon the apostle you (s.) see their eyes filling with tears at their realisation of the truth, when they say: 'Our Lord, we have believed: write us among the witnesses. How shall we not believe in God and in the truth which has come to us and not yearn that our Lord might bring us in with the righteous?'   *Surah 5.73-74 and 82-84*

HAVE you (s.) not seen those to whom a part of the Scripture has been granted bartering it for error and wanting you (pl.) to stray from the true path? God knows well who are your enemies and God suffices as the One to have on your side and as the complete source of help.

Some of the Jews' allegiance distort words from their meaning, saying: 'We have heard but we refuse to heed. You had better listen to us — what is beyond your comprehension! Attend to us!' — thus twisting words with their tongues and making false imputations about the faith. It had been better for them, and more appropriate, if they had said: 'We hear and obey. Hear what we say,' — making a play on words with a good sense against the bad earlier. But God has cursed them for their unbelief. There is scant faith in them.

You to whom the Book was brought, believe in what has been revealed, confirming the truth of what is with you from earlier times, lest We eliminate you altogether and make a total end, having them accursed as We did the men of the Sabbath, when the decree of God was brought to pass.

God does not forgive the ascription of a partner to Himself: a lesser sin than that He forgives to whom He wills. He who ascribes associates to God contrives a great sin. Have you (s.) not seen those who preen themselves on their purity? Rather it is God who makes pure whom He wills. Men will not be wronged by Him as much as a hair's breadth.

Look (s.) how they invent lies against God — which is self-evidently a gross sin. Have you not seen those to whom a part of the Scripture has been granted believing in *Jibt* and *Tāghūt*, pagan objects of worship, and saying to the unbelievers: 'These are better guided as to the right way than the believers are!'? Such are they whom God has cursed. He whom God curses, for him you (s.) can find no helper.

Have these some share in sovereignty? Had they, indeed, they would not give people even the line on a date-stone! Is it that they are envious of what God has granted to people from His bounty? For We bestowed on the family of Abraham the Book and the wisdom and We granted him a great kingship. *Surah 4.44-54*

WHOEVER argues with you (s.), about the truth from your Lord, after the knowledge which has come to you, say to them: 'Come, we will call together our sons and yours, our women-folk and yours, and we ourselves with all of you; we will pray and invoke the curse of God on those who are lying. The truth of the whole matter is this, and there is no god save God, and God is the all-mighty, the ever-wise.' If they turn away God knows well enough who are the people in the wrong.

Say: 'You people of the Book: come now to a formula acceptable to each of us, namely that we worship God alone and do not ascribe divinity to any but He and that we take no others as lords beside God.' If they turn away then say (pl.): 'Bear witness that, for our part, we are surrendered to God, (we are *muslimūn*)'. *Surah 3.61-64*

THERE is an element among the people of the Book who would love to have you led astray. It is only themselves, however, whom they misguide, though they do not realise it.

People of the Book, why do you deny the revelations of God to which you yourselves are witness?

People of the Book, why do you clothe the truth in falsehood and knowingly conceal the truth?

There are certain among the people of the Book whose line is to say: 'Believe in what has been sent down to these believers when day begins and deny it at the close of day. It may be they will return. Trust only him who follows your religion.' Say to them: 'The guidance is God's guidance: it is open to anyone to have been given the like of what you have received.' They may well argue with you in the very presence of your Lord. Say then: 'It is in the hand of God that His bounty lies: He bestows it on whom He wills. God is infinite and wise. He singles out for His mercy whom He will: God is the Lord of great goodness.'

271

There are those among the people of the Book who, if you entrust them with much treasure, will pay it back to you and there are others who, if you trust them with a mere dinar, will not repay it unless you stand over them all the while. This springs from their saying: 'We are under no obligation to the *ummiyyūn* (the "gentiles"),' thus deliberately attributing a false thing to God. By contrast, it is those who keep His covenant and truly fear Him who are the devout whom God loves. For those who barter the covenant of God and their own treaties for paltry gain are the ones to have no part or lot in the world to come. On the Day of resurrection God will not address them, nor even look upon them, nor will He purify them. Theirs is a painful doom.

There is a party of them who twist the Scripture when they quote it, so that you (pl.) think what they are saying is authentically from the Book when it is not. They say that it is from God when it is not from God, thus attributing falsehood to God — and that knowingly.

It is not for any human person to whom God gives the Book and wisdom to rule and prophethood, then to tell people: 'Be servants to me, rather than to God,' but: 'Be devoted to God as Lord by the fact of your steady teaching in the Book and your being occupied in its study.'

He gives you no command to adopt angels and prophets as lords. Does He order you into unbelief after you have become *muslimūn*?

When God undertook His covenant with the prophets He said: 'Seeing I have brought you a Book and wisdom, when there comes to you a messenger confirming the truth of the revelation you have already, you are certainly to believe in him and aid him to victory. Are you so agreed and do you undertake My charge?' They said: 'We accept so to do.' 'Then bear witness to it,' He said, 'and I will witness with you. Whoever, henceforward, dishonours this pledge, they are workers of evil.'

Do you desire some other religion than God's when it is to Him that all surrender in the heavens and in the earth, whether willingly or unwillingly, and to Him all must return? *Surah 3.69-83*

SAY: 'People of the Book, why do you deny the revelations of God when God Himself is witness to your deeds?'

Say: 'People of the Book, why do you debar from the path of God those who have believed therein, wanting to make it crooked, when you are yourselves witnesses of it and God is in no way unalert to what you are doing?'

Believers! If you obey a party among those who have received the

Book they will bring you back from your faith into unbelief again. And how can you deny the faith when God's revelations are rehearsed to you and His apostle is in your midst? He who holds fast to God is the one who has been guided into a straight path. *Surah 3.98-101*

Is it always the case that when they enter into a covenant a section of them casts it aside? Indeed, most of them are without faith. When a messenger came to them from God, confirming the truth of what they already had, a section of those who had been given the Scripture put that Book of God behind their backs as if they had no knowledge at all.

They followed the same course as that which the satans adopted in what they said against the kingship of Solomon. For it was not Solomon himself who denied the truth, but the satans who did so, inculcating sorcery in the people and the arts bestowed in Babylon on the two angels, *Hārūt* and *Mārūt*. Those two angels did not teach these practices to any one without first warning him: 'We are in fact testing you, so do not deny the truth.' From these two angels people learn how to occasion strife between a man and his wife, though they do not work harm thereby on anyone except by leave of God. People learn, too, what works harm to themselves and is profitless to them, having realised that whoever purchased this skill would have no part or lot in the hereafter. For what they sold themselves for was a wretched evil business, did they but know. If only they had believed and truly feared God the recompense from God would have been far better — had they but known. *Surah 2.100-103*

MANY of the people of the Book desire to make you revert from the faith you hold into unbelief. They do so out of envy within themselves, after the truth has been made clear to them. Even so, forgive and hold off, until God brings about what He ordains. God has everything in the disposal of His power. Perform the rite of prayer and bring the *Zakāt*. Whatever good deed you send ahead to your souls' account you will find it with God. For God is watchful over your every deed.

They have said: 'No one will ever enter the garden unless he be a Jew or a Christian.' These are their wishful notions. Say: 'Produce your evidence, if what you are saying is the truth. No! whoever surrenders his being to God, and is a doer of good, his is the reward with his Lord. For such there is nothing to fear nor will they be in sorrow.'

The Jews say: 'The Christians — there is nothing in their faith!' while the Christians say: 'The Jews — there is nothing in their faith!' Both cite the Book. Ignoramuses talk the same sort of language. God will judge between them on the Day of resurrection respecting their disputations.

Who perpetrates a greater evil than he who bars access to the places of God's worship where His name is in the minds and on the lips of men, and whoever works to bring them to destruction? It is not for such people to enter them, unless it be in fear. In this present world there is humiliation for them and in the world to come a great punishment.

Surah 2.109-114

SAY: 'If the mansion of the hereafter with God is reserved for you alone to the exclusion of other peoples, then be ardent for death — if you mean what you say.' But they will never be eager to die because of what they have sent on ahead by their deeds. God is well aware of those who perpetrate evil.

You (s.) will find them of all people the most covetous of life, even more than the pagan idolators. Any one of them would like it were he to have a life span of a thousand years — though being spared for such a long reprieve would not save him from the retribution. God is watchful over all they do.

Say: 'Whoever is an enemy of Gabriel — who by leave of God has brought this Qur'ān down upon your heart, confirming what was earlier, as guidance and good tidings for those who believe — whoever is an enemy of God, His angels and His messengers, of Gabriel and Michael, God certainly is an enemy of these unbelievers. Truly We have sent down to you (s.) clear revelations. It is only evil-doing reprobates who deny their truth.

Surah 2.94-99

THERE is no place for compulsion in religion. The right has been clearly distinguished from the false. Whoever gives the lie to the *Tāghūt* and who affirms his belief in God has laid hold of the most sure hand-hold which will never break. God hears and knows all.

God is the befriending guardian of believers. He brings them out from the shadows of dark into the light, while those who disbelieve have the *Tāghūt* for their guardians, who take them out from the light into the shades of darkness. These are the habitués of the Fire where they abide for ever.

Surah 2.256-257

BELIEVERS! Hold God in awe and believe in His apostle and He will grant you a double share in His mercy — God is ever forgiving and merciful — so that the people of the Book may know that they have no perquisite on God's grace. For grace is in God's hand and He bestows it on whom He wills, the God of great goodness.   *Surah 57.28-29*

TODAY those who repudiated your religion as false have despaired, so have no fear of them. Fear only Me. Today I have brought your religion to completeness and fulfilled My grace to you. It is My will and My good pleasure that Islam be your religion.   *Surah 5.3 (part)*

WHEN God's help comes about, and conquest, and you have seen people come crowding into the religion of God, then sing the praise of your Lord and seek His forgiveness. To be merciful was ever His wont.
          Surah 110

بسم الله الرحمن الرحيم

F. Faith and Religion

IN THE Name of the merciful Lord of mercy. Truly, by the transience of time, loss is ever the lot of mankind, save for those who believe and do righteously, who counsel one another in the truth, who counsel one another to patience. *Surah 103*

IN THE Name of the merciful Lord of mercy. Say: 'I take refuge with the Lord of the daybreak, from the evil of what He has created, and from the evil of the enveloping darkness, and from the evil of those who bind their spells, from the evil of the envier and his envy.' *Surah 113*

IN THE Name of the merciful Lord of mercy. Say: 'I take refuge with the Lord of men, the King of men, the God of men, from the evil of the whispering insinuator who whispers in the hearts of men, from jinn and men.' *Surah 114*

THOSE who follow the apostle, the unlettered Prophet, (the *Ummī*) whom they will find noted among them in writing in the Torah and the *Injīl*, who enjoins well-doing on them and forbids them what is evil. He makes lawful for them the things that are good and prohibits for them the things that are foul. He rids them of their burdens and of the fetters they wore. Those who believe in him, honour him and make his cause their own, following the light sent down with him — surely these are the ones who triumph. *Surah 7.157*

ALIF, Lām, Mīm. God — there is no god but He, the ever-living, the ever-real who reigns. He has bestowed the Book upon you (s.) from on high in very truth. It is in confirmation of what has anticipated it earlier.

276

He sent down the Torah and the *Injūl* as guidance to mankind. He has now sent down the final decisive Scripture.

For those who deny the revelations of God there awaits heavy retribution. God is great in strength and avenging power is His. There is nothing that is hidden from Him in earth or in heaven. It is He who gave you form in your mothers' wombs according to His will. There is no god but He, all-powerful and all-wise.

It is He who sent down upon you (s.) this Book. There are revelations within it which are quite categorical and explicit. These are the Book in its essential meaning and nature. Other verses employ metaphor and analogy. Those who in heart incline to deviant ideas have a habit of following these metaphorical parts with a will for discord and tendentious exegesis. God alone it is who knows the interpretation of it. Those who are well-grounded in the knowledge of it say: 'We have put our whole faith in it: it is all from our Lord.' It is only those endowed with real perception who take it to heart.

Our Lord, do not let our hearts err after You have guided us: grant us mercy in Your presence. For truly You are the giver of grace. Our Lord, it is You who gathers mankind to a judgement day which none can doubt. What He has pledged God does not fail to fulfill.   *Surah 3.1-9*

No! I swear by the where and whither of the stars — a tremendous oath did you but comprehend — this is truly a gracious Qur'ān, in a hidden Book which only those who are purified shall touch, a revelation from the Lord of all being.   *Surah 56.75-80*

Hā, Mīm. Hereby the Book that brings light to bear. We have sent it down on a night that is blessed — for it has been Our wont to give warning — a blessed night in which everything is, by command of Ours, duly ordered in wisdom — for it has been Our wont to communicate to man — in act of mercy from your (s.) Lord who sees and knows all, Lord of the heavens and of the earth and all they encompass, if only you knew it for certain.

There is no god but He, who gives life and makes to die, your (pl.) Lord and the Lord of your fathers of old time.

But no! they are doubters, merely playing around.   *Surah 44.1-9*

ALIF, Lām, Mīm. This is the Book where doubt has no place: it is guidance to the God-fearing, those who believe in the world unseen, who perform the prayer-rite and lay out of the substance We have provided for them, who believe in what has been sent down in revelation to you (s.) and in what has been sent down in revelation before you, and who are convinced of the reality of the last Day.

It is these who are possessed of their Lord's guidance, these who truly prosper. *Surah 2.1-5*

ALIF, Lām, Mīm. These are the revelations of the Book whose wisdom is guidance and mercy to those who will the good, those who perform the rite of prayer and bring the *Zakāt*, and who are firmly convinced of the reality of the last Day. It is these who are within their Lord's guidance: it is they who truly prosper. *Surah 31.1-5*

THIS is a glorious Qur'ān, engraved where it is well-guarded. *Surah 85.21-22*

GOD has sent down the best of all texts, a Book which is self-consistent and uses re-iteration. Those who fear their Lord are seized with physical trembling at it until flesh and heart alike yield to the remembrance of God. Such is the guidance of God who guides by it whom He wills. He whom God leads astray — there is no guide for him!

In this Qur'ān We have drawn every sort of parable for mankind: it may be they will take thought. It is an Arabic Qur'ān, free from all distortion, so that they may perhaps become indeed God-fearers.

One parable God gives you concerns a man with several masters quarrelling over him and another man who belongs exclusively to one. Are these two to be regarded as in the same case? Praise be to God. But the majority do not understand. *Surah 39.23, and 27-29*

THESE are the revelations of the Qur'ān and of an illuminating Scripture, guidance and good tidings to those who believe, who perform the prayer-rite and pay the *Zakāt* and who are convinced of the last Day. As for those who do not believe in the last Day, We have made all their doings attractive in their own eyes and they flounder blindly. It is they for whom a grim retribution waits and in the hereafter theirs will be the sorest loss.

And you (s.) — yours is the Qur'ān received from the presence of One who is all-wise and who knows all.   *Surah 27.1-6*

ALIF, Lām, Rā. These are the signs of the Book, the arbiter of wisdom. Do men find it surprising that We should have inspired a man of themselves: 'Warn humanity and bring good news to those who believe as to the standing they have with their Lord for their sincerity,' while the unbelieving say: 'This fellow is plainly a spell-binder!'?

Your Lord is God, who created the heavens and the earth in six days, then seated Himself on the Throne, disposing all things. There are none to intercede unless He has given leave.

This is the truth to you — God your Lord. Then worship Him. Will you not give thoughtful heed? It is to Him you return, one and all. The promise of God is true. He originates the creation and renews it again, in order with equity to reward those who have believed and done righteously. For those who have denied the truth there awaits a boiling drink and a grim retribution for their unfaith.   *Surah 10.1-4*

MEN find allurement in lustful desires for women and children, for accumulated hoards of gold and silver, for horses of fine fettle, cattle and land. These are pleasures of this present life. It is with God that the finest haven is found.

Say: 'Shall I tell you what is better than all these? — gardens where streams flow below, immortal abiding and pure companions and the good pleasure of God — the boon in the presence of their Lord of those who fear God. God has His servants ever in His sight — servants whose words are: "Our Lord, we have believed, forgive us, then, our transgressions and make us secure from the pain of the Fire," — servants who are steadfast, truthful and devout, liberal in alms, and who seek forgiveness at the dawn of day.'

Religion as God wills it to be is surrender (*al-islām*). It was only after knowledge had come to them that those who had received the Book fell to disputing out of mutual jealousy. Whoever denies the revelations of God will find that God is swift to the reckoning. If, then, they are in altercation with you (s.) say: 'I have surrendered my whole being to God and those, likewise, who follow me,' and say also to those to whom the Book came and to the *ummiyyūn* (the unscriptured): 'Have you surrendered? (have you become muslims?)' If they surrender they are rightly guided and if they turn away your (s.) only task is to deliver the word. God has His servants ever in His sight.

Say: 'If you (pl.) love God then follow me: God will love you and forgive you your sins. God is ever forgiving and merciful.' Say: 'Obey God and His apostle. If you turn away — God has no love for unbelievers.' *Surah 3.14-17, 19-20 and 31-32*

BELIEVERS! Hold God in awe — the godly fear that is properly His. Do not let death take you save when you are in surrender as *muslimūn*. Take firm hold, all of you, on the rope of God: do not break up into divisions. Be mindful of the grace of God to you, how you were formerly enemies and He united your hearts in mutual bonds so that, by His grace, you became brothers. When you were on the brink of a fiery abyss He saved you from it. Thus God makes evident to you His signs so that you may find guidance.

Let there be a single nation of you, sounding the call to good, enjoining what is of honour and forbidding what is reprobate. It is such who truly prosper. Do not be like those who have fallen away from each other and differed after the clear evidences had come to them. For such there is a dire retribution. *Surah 3.102-105*

HUMANITY was one single nation, to whom God sent prophets as heralds of good news and warners too. And with them He sent down the Book with the truth by which the things over which mankind had come to be at odds might be decided. Yet the very people to whom it was given fell, out of mutual jealousy, into disagreement over it after clear proofs had come to them. God guided those who believed to the truth concerning which, by His leave, they were allowed to be at variance. God guides those whom He wills into a straight path. *Surah 2.213*

ANY revelation of Ours which We abrogate or cause to be forgotten We bring a better in its place or one similar. Have you (s.) not understood that God has the power to do everything? Do you not know that the kingdom of heavens and of the earth is God's and that, apart from God, you (pl.) have neither friend nor helper? Or do you (pl.) want to question your apostle as Moses earlier was questioned? Whoever accepts a denial of the faith in exchange for belief has indeed fallen into error away from the right path. *Surah 2.106-108*

IF THEY would but hold upright on the true way, We would assuredly give them a fount of waters, thus putting them to the test. Whoever turns away from the remembrance of his Lord We will make to pass through sharp punishment. The mosques are God's: do not make invocation to any but God. When the servant of God stood calling upon God people almost pressed in throngs around him. Tell them: 'I call upon my Lord and ascribe divinity to none but Him.' Say: 'The issue of harmful evil or sound direction in respect of you is not one that lies within my power.' Say: 'No one can ever render me immune from God, nor — aside from Him — have I any place of refuge. My sole task is to bring His messages to you from God. For whoever repudiates God and His messenger there is waiting the fire of *Jahannam*, the eternal abiding place.'

Surah 72.16-23

FULFILL the rite of prayer from the going down of the sun till the night becomes dark and observe the dawn-recital. Witnesses gather around the dawn-recital. As for the night, keep vigil then as a work of piety which exceeds your duty, for which your Lord may raise you to a station of high honour, and pray: 'O my Lord, make my coming in true and honest and my going out true and honest and from Your presence grant me Your enabling power.' Say: 'The truth has come; falsehood has come to nought. Falsehood is bound to vanish away.'

We send down the Qur'ān as healing and mercy to those who believe though, for the wrongdoers, it only spells greater ruin. When We are gracious to man he turns away and shows indifference, while, if evil befalls him, he lapses into despair. Say: 'Everyone reacts according to his own fashion. Your Lord well knows who is guided aright in his way.'

They question you (s.) about the Spirit. Say: 'The Spirit is within the explicit authority of my Lord. Very little knowledge is available to you concerning this.'

Had We so willed We could indeed have withdrawn what We have inspired in you by revelation, in which case you would have found no one to fill the role for you against Us, save by some act of mercy on your Lord's part. His goodness is great toward you.

Say: 'Were humans and jinn to join their forces to bring about the like of this Qur'ān they would never produce anything comparable — no, not for all their mutual aid. In this Qur'ān We have set forth for mankind every sort of expression of meaning. Yet most men only persist in their obduracy.'

Surah 17.78-89

YOUR Lord knows how you, and those who take your part, hold station for two thirds of the night, or maybe a half or a third. It is God who measures night and day and He knows you would in no way stint your vigil. He has turned towards you (pl.), so together recite the Qur'ān, so far as you may readily do. He knows that some among you may be sick, others on their journeys in the land in quest of God's bounty, while others are fighting in the way of God. So recite as far as you are readily able, perform the prayer-rite and bring the *Zakāt*, lending to God a worthy loan. For whatever well-doing you remit to your soul's account you will find with God a greater reward and an ampler good. Seek God's forgiveness. For God is a merciful forgiver.   *Surah 73.20*

GIVE your whole being devotedly to the things of faith as a man of pure religion, the faith God made proper to mankind by His creation of them — that creation of God in which no change occurs. Such is the authentic religion. But most of mankind is ignorant of the fact.

Turning ever to God, hold Him in reverent fear, fulfill the rite of prayer, and have no truck with plural worship. Do not be party with those who have divided religion and made separate sects, each of whom takes partisan pleasure in their own.   *Surah 30.30-32*

BELIEVERS! Remember God in frequent recollection. Celebrate His praise at dawn and in the evening. It is He who sends down blessing upon you, as do His angels, to bring you forth from the shadows into the light. He is merciful to those who believe. On the day when they meet Him a greeting of 'Peace' will be their welcome. He has made ready for them a gracious reward.

O Prophet, We have sent you as a witness and a bearer of tidings, as a warner and as one who calls men to God — all by His divine commission, and as a shining lantern. So give glad word to those who believe that there awaits them from God a great bounty. Do not yield anything to those who deny the faith and the hypocrites. Disregard their truculence and put your trust in God. God is all the reliance you need.

Surah 33.41-48

DO NOT be (s.) in any doubt about what these people are worshipping. They simply persist in the worship their fathers followed aforetime. We shall indeed requite them for their deserts — and no mitigation. We brought Moses the Scripture and there was contention over it then and, but for a decree already made on your Lord's part, judgement would have decided the issue among them. For they were certainly in doubt and scepticism concerning Moses. Your Lord requites each and all for their actions — actions of which He is thoroughly aware. So keep your (s.) integrity as you have been commanded, and likewise those with you who have turned to God. Do not behave perversely. For He is vigilant over all you do. Do not lean toward those who deal unjustly lest the Fire take you, and then no succour would avail you. For you have no source of security except in God.

Perform the rite of prayer at each end of the day, as well as during the early hours of the night. Good deeds overcome evil ones — a right reminder for the rightly minding!

Endure patiently. God does not let the reward of those who act rightly fail. *Surah 11.109-115*

BELIEVERS! When you enter upon the rite of prayer, wash your face and the hands up to the elbows: wipe your head and also your feet up to the ankles. If you are in a state of ritual impurity, make a complete purification. Should you be sick or en route in travel or any of you have come from having a bowel discharge or from sexual intercourse, and in these circumstances you can find no water, have recourse to fine clean soil and wipe face and hands with it. God does not have it in His will to require of you what is vexatious. He wills only to purify you and to fulfill His grace toward you, so that you may find it in you to be grateful.

Remember God's grace towards you and the covenant bond with which He bound you, when you said: 'We have heard and we obey.' So hold God in reverent fear. God knows well the thoughts in the heart.

Believers! Be resolute in your allegiance to God, staunch witnesses for justice. On no account let hatred against any people cause you to be perverted from what is just. Deal justly. To do so is the nearest thing to the fear of God. Hold God in reverent fear. God is aware of all your doings.

God has promised to those who have believed and who practise righteous dealing that forgiveness is theirs and a great reward. Those who disbelieve and count Our revelations false, they are denizens of *Jahannam*. Believers! Remember the grace of God toward you when there were people making physical threats against you and He restrained their hands from harming you. Fear God, then: let believers put their trust wholly in God. *Surah 5.6-11*

BELIEVERS! Do not come to the rite of prayer in a drunken state before you know what you are saying, nor in a state of ritual impurity before you have undergone full purification, unless, that is, you are en route in a journey. If you are unwell or travelling, or you have come from having a bowel discharge or you have had sexual intercourse, and then find no water available, have recourse to fine clean soil: wipe your faces and your hands. God absolves and forgives. *Surah 4.43*

RIGHTEOUSNESS does not consist in the mere act of facing on the *qiblah* of the east or of the west. They have the true righteousness who believe in God and the last Day, in the angels and in the Scripture and the prophets, who spend their substance — prize it lovingly as they may — on their own kinsfolk, and orphans, the impoverished, the wayfarer and those who beg, and on the ransoming of slaves. Theirs is true righteousness who perform the prayer-rite and pay the *Zakāt*, who fulfill their word when they have given a promise, who endure patiently under distress and hardship and, in time of danger. These are the ones whose faith is genuine: these are the truly God-fearing people. *Surah 2.177*

BELIEVERS! Seek help in patient steadfastness and the act of prayer. God is with those who patiently endure. Do not say of those who are killed in God's cause: 'They are dead and gone.' On the contrary, they are alive — though unseen by you. We will assuredly put you to the test of anxious fears, of hunger and poverty of goods, loss of life and yield of crops. Nevertheless bring (s.) joyful word to those who patiently endure, those who say when calamity overtakes them: 'We are God's and to God do we return.' On these rests the benediction of their Lord and His mercy. These are the truly guided. *Surah 2.153-157*

MAKE the prayers your watchful care, including the middle one. Stand before God in utmost reverence. Should you suspect danger, pray as you go, walking or riding. When you are out of danger, remember God who has made you to know what was unknown to you. *Surah 2.238-239*

TO Him alone is prayer in its reality. Those who are invoked apart from Him make no answer at all — no more than if one were stretching out hands towards water to bring it to his mouth, but it never comes to mouth. The prayer of the unbelievers is nothing but delusion.
Surah 13.14

IT is not for the prophet and the believers to seek forgiveness from God for those who hold with gods they associate with God Himself, even though they are their near-of-kin, after it has been shown to them that they are denizens of *Al-Jahīm*.

Abraham's prayer for forgiveness on behalf of his father was by warrant of a promise he made to him. He disowned liability for him when it was made clear to Abraham that his father was an enemy of God. Abraham was tender-hearted and kind. *Surah 9.113-114*

MAN was created with a restless anxiety. When evil befalls him he commiserates with himself but when good comes his way he arrogates it jealously to himself. It is not so with those who pray, who are constant in their prayers, who acknowledge in their possessions the right of the poor and the deprived, who hold the Day of judgement to be real, standing in awe of the retribution of their Lord. For there is no certain immunity from the retribution of their Lord. They keep themselves chaste, finding their sexual fulfilment only with their wives and the slave-women in their charge. Thus they are free of reproach, for it is transgressors who desire to go beyond that. They keep their trusts and covenants loyally, hold firmly to their testimony and are watchful over their prayers. These will be honoured in the gardens of Paradise. *Surah 70.19-35*

THE apostle believes in what is sent down to him from his Lord, and the believers, each and every one, believe in God and His angels, in His books and His messengers. We make no distinction between any of His messengers. They said: 'We hear and we have obeyed. Our Lord forgive us: to You is our final destiny.'

God does not hold any soul accountable except what is within its own capacity. To each what the soul has earned, and the tally against it what it has itself acquired.

Our Lord, do not hold it against us if we forget and do wrong. Our Lord, do not tax us with the burden like that You laid upon those who lived before us. Lord, do not burden us with what is beyond our ability to bear. Pardon us and forgive us: have mercy upon us. You are our Master: come to our aid against the people who deny the faith.

Surah 2.285-286

WHEN you are making an expedition anywhere you will not be at fault in curtailing the act of prayer, if you have reason to suspect the unbelievers of some evil design against you. For that these deniers of the truth are at enmity with you is plain enough. When you (s.) are in the midst engaging in the prayer rite, let a number of them stand with you retaining their weapons by them. When these have performed the prayer let them make cover for you, while the other part who have yet to pray come forward to pray with you, taking due precaution and retaining their arms. The unbelievers would dearly like you to be negligent about your weapons and your equipment in order to fall upon you in a sudden attack. However, there is no reproach on you in putting your weapons aside in the event of rain or in case of sickness. Yet be ever alert to danger. God has made ready a bitter humiliation for those who deny the faith.

When you have completed the prayer-rite, keep God in constant recollection, whether you are sitting or standing or lying down. When your minds are at rest from apprehensions fulfill the prayer-rite. For the regular act of prayer is a sacred obligation upon believers in its prescribed times.

Do not grow faint in your ardour against the foe. You may be undergoing distress, but they are also in like case with you. In God you have a hope such as they in no wise possess. God is all-knowing and all-wise.

We have brought down to you (s.) the Book with the truth so that you may judge between the people by what God has made you to see. Do not enter any plea on behalf of those who break faith. Seek forgiveness from God. For God is ever forgiving and merciful. Do not take up the cause of those who play false with themselves. God has no love for those evil folk who practice treachery, who may well conceal their mischief from man, but never from God. For He is present among them as they talk darkly by night of things He would never approve. God has the measure within His knowledge of all their actions. You (pl.) may indeed take up their cause in this present life. But who will argue for them before God on the Day of resurrection? Who will be their reliance then?

Nevertheless any one who commits evil or wrongs his own soul and then seeks forgiveness from God, will find God forgiving and merciful. Any person with a tally of wickedness against his name alone bears whatever it brings upon him. God is all-knowing and all-wise. Any one who commits a sin or transgression and foists it off on some innocent party carries a guilty onus of calumny and flagrant evil.

But for the goodness and mercy of God toward you a faction of them would have been at pains to implicate you (s.) in wrongdoing. But they merely led themselves astray without injuring you (s.) at all. God has sent down upon you the Book and the wisdom and has made you to know what was beyond your knowledge. Great is the goodness of God upon you.   *Surah 4.101-113*

THOSE only are true believers in Our revelations who, on recital of Our signs, bow down in prostration and celebrate the praise of their Lord. It is not such as these who assume arrogant attitudes. In mingled fear and aspirations they rise from their beds in invocation of their Lord and they lay out in charitable works what We have given them for provision. No soul knows what things, yet hidden from them, await them to their entire delight in reward for their deeds. Is there, then, any comparison between a believer and a man of evil ways? They are in no sense on the same level. For those who have believed and done good deeds there are waiting gardens of repose in which to be guests, in recognition of their deeds, whereas the Fire is the destined abode of those who have dealt corruptly.   *Surah 32.15-20a*

SAY: 'We believe in God and in what He has revealed to us and His revelations to Abraham and Ishmael, to Isaac and Jacob and the tribes, and in what was brought to Moses, Jesus and the prophets, from their Lord. We do not discriminate between any of them and to God do we surrender. Any one who desires other than surrender (*islām*) as religion, it will never be accepted of him and in the world to come among the losers he will be.'   *Surah 3.84-85*

BY the Mount Sinai, by a Book surely penned, on parchment unrolled. By the well-peopled house and the roof rearing high over all. By the sea brimming wide. The doom of your (s.) Lord is near to befall, the doom which none can avert.   *Surah 52.1-8*

AND then We caused you (s.) to enter upon a path of Our divine authority. So pursue it and do not follow the vain wishes of those who are devoid of knowledge. They could never be of the least avail to you in defiance of God. Those who play false may be friends of each other but God is the Friend of those who are truly God-fearing.

Insights for mankind is this Qur'ān, guidance and mercy to people of resolute conviction.

Do those who have committed evil deeds assume that We will have for them the same reckoning as for those who have believed and done good deeds, as if they were of equal standing in their living and their dying? They judge falsely who think so.

God created the heavens and the earth for truth's sake so that every soul might be repaid their own deserts, none being the victim of injustice. Have you (s.) not taken stock of those who made a god of their desires, whom God leads astray in their perceptions, sealing ears and heart alike, and casting a veil upon the eyes? Who then will guide such as these, taking up after God? Will you not give due heed?

What they say is: 'There is nothing but our life here in this present world. We die and we live. It is merely time which brings us to nothing.' How bereft they are of all comprehension; following mere guesswork! When Our revelations are rehearsed to them their one contention is to say: 'If you are telling the truth, bring back our forefathers.' Say: 'God it is who gives you life and then causes you to die. Then He will gather you together to the Day of resurrection.' That is beyond doubt, despite the ignorance of most people.

To God belongs the kingdom of the heavens and of the earth. On the very day when the Hour dawns those who called it all false will be the losers.   *Surah 45.18-27*

GOD and His angels call blessing upon the prophet. O you who have believed, you also call blessing upon him and greet him with a greeting of peace. Those who malign God and His messenger the malediction of God is upon them here in this present world and in the hereafter, God has made ready for them a fearful retribution. Those who insult believers, men and women, with undeserved charges bear the heavy guilt of slander and self-evident wickedness.   *Surah 33.56-58*

YOU who have believed, fasting is decreed for you as it was for those who came before you, with a view to a deep sense among you of devotion to God. The fast proceeds through a set period of days. Any of your number who is sick or on a journey must observe a like sequence of other days and, in the event of their being able to undertake the feeding of some needy person, that may be for them a way of making it good. When anyone, of his own free will, outdoes what is enjoined that is certainly to his own good. For, when you fast, you do good to yourselves, did you but realise it.

The month of Ramadān was the time in which the Qur'ān was sent down as guidance for mankind, with clear evidences of the guidance it constituted, and as the criterion. So then, any of you, observing the incidence of the month, let him take up the fast throughout it. Any one who is ill or on a journey should fast that number of other days. God's will is that you should be at ease. He does not desire hardship for you, but to have you make good the ordained number of days and magnify God in His having thus guided you, and all with due gratitude.

If My servants question you (s.) concerning Me, in truth I am near. I answer the call of the suppliant who cries to Me. So let them hearken to Me: let them believe in Me that they may be rightly led.

It is made lawful for you to have intercourse with your wives during the nights of the fast. Your sexuality is like a seemly garment, theirs to you and yours to them. God knows how you were mistakenly depriving yourselves and He has turned towards you and released you. So then consort with them and desire what God has ordained for you. Eat and drink until there appears to you, as you watch, the white streak of dawn against the blackness of the night. At that point resume the fast until nightfall. However, do not consort with your wives at any time you are withdrawn for devotion in the mosques.

These are the bounds God has set. Keep well within them. Thus does God make clear His revelations to mankind that they may hold Him in due and reverent fear. *Surah 2.183-187*

SAY: 'Sure is the truth God has spoken.' Follow, then, the faith-community of Abraham, a man of pure faith, who was no polytheist. The very first house of prayer established for humanity was that at Bakkah (Mecca) — a blessed house for the guidance of all the worlds. The place where Abraham stood, it is replete with clear signs and evidences. Who-ever enters there finds security. To make pilgrimage to the house is a duty men owe to God, on condition they have the capacity to take the journey thither. As for those who deny the faith, God is rich enough beyond all the worlds. *Surah 3.95-97*

AL-SAFĀ and Al-Marwah are certainly places God has made to be signs, so that anyone going on the pilgrimage to the house, or who is performing the lesser pilgrimage, is in no way at fault if he does a circuit around them both. For anyone obeying his own prompting for a good end can be assured that God, who is all-wise, is ready with recognition.

Surah 2.158

PERFORM the pilgrimage, and the *'Umrah* (lesser pilgrimage). If you find yourselves prevented, then make what offering you can readily afford. Do not shave your heads until the offering has reached the place where it should properly be. Should any among you be sick or have a head injury, let him keep a fast in lieu of the shaving of the head, or else make a voluntary act of almsgiving or perform a ritual sacrifice. Where all is secure and well with you, and any of you are participating in the *'Umrah* and the pilgrimage in sequence, let them offer what-ever they readily can or — in the event of inability — make a fast of three days during the pilgrimage and a further seven days after returning, that is ten full days in all. This applies to those whose people are not domiciled around the sacred mosque. Hold God in reverent awe and realise that God is stern in His retribution.

The pilgrimage takes place in the given months with which you are familiar. Whoever undertakes the pilgrimage in them should refrain throughout from sexual intercourse, from all that is obscene and contentious. God knows full well the good you do. Make due provision, remembering that the best provision of all is a true devotion to God. You who are gifted with perception, keep Me ever in godly fear. It is, however, no fault in you to have a mind for profitable things at God's good hand.

When you are in the throng running from 'Arafāt, remember God as you come near the sacred monument (at Muzdalīfah). Remember Him too as the One who guided you when, aforetime, you were indeed in error. Then press onward within the surging throng as it moves swiftly forward. Seek the forgiveness of God — God who is forgiving and merciful. When you have fulfilled your pilgrim rites have God's Name in remembrance, even as you remember your own fathers, or yet more fervently.

There are those folk whose plea to the Lord is for the things of this present world. Such have no part in the world to come. Others make their prayer: 'Our Lord, give us good things both in this world and in the world to come, and protect us from the doom of the Fire.' It is such who have as their portion the deserts they have themselves earned. God is swift in His accounting.

Remember God during the appointed days. He who in haste fulfills them in two days will not be incurring guilt, nor is there any wrong in taking longer, given that all such truly fear God. So hold God in reverent awe in the knowledge that you will all be gathered unto Him.

Surah 2.196-203

As for those who, having denied the faith, close off the very way to God and to the sacred house of prayer which We have established for mankind as the equal possession of those who frequent it locally and of those who repair to it from afar, We will make them to taste painful punishment and, with them, those also who make it their aim to violate and flout its sanctity. When We assigned the site of the ancient house to Abraham his solemn charge was: 'On no account bring false gods into the worship that is only Mine. Cleanse My house for those who perform the circuit round it, and for those who fulfill their prayer, standing, kneeling and in prostration. Proclaim pilgrimage to it among the people who will come to you on foot or on mounts of every kind, making their way through deep defiles. Coming, they will be aware of all they stand to gain as, during the prescribed days, they make devout recollection of the Name of God, reciting it over the beasts of the flock with which God has supplied them. His command is: 'Eat of their flesh and feed the poor in their distress.' Subsequently, let them terminate their ritual state, fulfill the vows they have undertaken and make the circuit of the ancient house. Such is their duty. Whoever holds sacred the solemn directives God has laid down will find good therein to his soul from his Lord.

Cattle have been made lawful for you, except those parts indicated to you. Be at pains to avoid all the filthiness that stems from idolatry and shun all false talking, as those who are of pure faith before God and do not alienate God's worship from Him to pseudo-gods. For anyone who lets false worship usurp God's is as if, falling headlong from heaven, he is snatched away by the birds or borne along by the wind to some far-away place.

Furthermore, any one who holds in high reverence the symbolic rites ordained by God does so from a heart-felt sense of devotion to God. Though, for a due period you derived benefit from the animals you sacrifice, their final destination is the ancient house. For every community We have ordained a sacred rite in which to name the Name of God over the animals of the flock He has bestowed upon them. Your Lord is

One God: to Him be surrendered and bring good news to the humble whose hearts are filled with awe at the mention of the Name of God and who bear patiently whatever befalls them, who fulfill the prayer-rite and expend of their substance given at Our hand. As for the beasts of sacrifice, We appointed them for you as God's symbols for your good. Recite, then, the Name of God over them when they are lined up in sacrificial order and, after ritual slaughter, eat of their flesh and feed the needy — the quiet, contented ones as well as those who are clamorous. It is thus that We have placed the beasts within your power, laying on you the onus of gratitude. It is not their sacrificed flesh which avails with God, nor their shed blood. Only reverent awe on your part avails with Him. To that end He has made them subject to you, so that you might magnify God for all the guidance He has granted to you. To those who do well bring (s.) the glad word. *Surah 22.25-37*

BELIEVERS! Fulfill your covenants. The beasts of the flock are made lawful for you, except as indicated to you. Hunting is not allowable while you are in the pilgrim's sacral state. God makes His decree in line with His will.

Believers! Do not profane the symbolic rites of God, nor the sacred month, nor the animals of offering, nor the garlands they bear, nor those repairing to the sacred house seeking their Lord's goodness and His acceptance of them. You may hunt game only after your pilgrim hallowing is terminated.

Do not allow your detestation of those who impeded your access to the sacred house of prayer to lead you into acts of aggression. Help one another to righteousness and godly piety: do not co-operate for evil-doing and hostility. Fear God — God who is strong to requite. . . .

God has made the Ka'bah to be the sacred house, a holy edifice for mankind — the sacred month, too, the offerings and the garlands they carry are sacred symbols, whereby you may know how God's knowledge embraces everything in the heavens and the earth. For God knows all. Be aware that God is strong in retribution and that God is also forgiving and merciful. *Surah 5.1-2, 97-98*

THERE is a clue which He presents to you from your own relationships. Would you yourselves regard the slaves in your hands as participants with you in what We have given to you as provision of yours, as if you and they were equals respecting it? Do you hold them in the same sort of respect that you have for one another? On these lines We clarify things significant — given people who will use their intelligence.

Yet, for all that, the evil-doers follow their own appetites in their ignorance. Who is going to guide those whom God leads astray? For them there are no saviours. *Surah 30.28-29*

WHEN affliction befalls people they call upon their Lord and turn to Him but then, when He visits them with His mercy, some of them take to other gods in their thoughts alongside their Lord, in their ingratitude for what We have bestowed on them. Well, then, enjoy it now: the time will come when you will know! Have We ever sent down to them any authority which had anything to say about the associate deities they avow? When We let people experience mercy they delight in it, but when evil overtakes them for what they have themselves contrived, they fall into despair. Have they not realised that it is God who extends His provision to whom He wills or gives it sparingly? Truly there are signs in that fact for believing people. *Surah 30.33-37*

As for man, when his Lord tests him by having brought him into honour and gracious living, his comment is: 'My Lord does well by me.' However, when He tries him by stinting His provision, then he says: 'My Lord humiliates me.'

No, the fact is you (pl.) have no regard for the orphan, you are not urgent about feeding the destitute, you consume what comes in inheritance like gluttons and you have an inordinate love of wealth. *Surah 89.15-20*

WHO says a better thing than the man who sounds the call to God, who does what is right, and says: 'I am among those who surrender to God.' (*muslimūn*)?

What is good and what is evil are in no way commensurate. Return evil with some better thing and, so doing, you (s.) will make the one with whom you are at enmity to become like a close friend. Only those who have patience can attain this, and any such, reaching it, come to possess great good fortune.

If some prompting from Satan comes to you (s.) seek refuge with God who listens and who knows all. *Surah 41.33-36*

IT is God who created and sustained you, who then causes you to die and brings you alive again. Have any of those whom you partner with Him in your cult ever done so in any way at all? Glory and majesty be to Him, immune from all your false ascriptions. Corruption is evident on land and sea by the deeds of men's hands and He has them taste, in part, the entail of their deeds so that perhaps they may turn again.

Say: 'Go abroad in the land: see the doom of those who were before you — most of whom were idolators. Set your (s.) face to the one true religion before there come a Day from God which there is no averting. On that Day there will be a great divide of mankind. His unbelief will be upon the unbeliever, and he who has done good — all such will have ensured themselves a resting-place. So God out of His bounty rewards those who have believed and done righteously. He has no love for those who deny the faith.' *Surah 30.40-45*

YOU who have believed, obey God and His messenger and do not turn away when you are listening to him, nor be like those who said: 'Yes! we have heard what you say,' when they do not listen at all. Those who are deaf and dumb and devoid of all reason are the vilest of beasts in God's sight. Had God known any good in them He would have endowed them with hearing. Had He given them hearing, they would have turned away in refusal.

You who have believed, answer the call of God and His messenger when He calls you to what is very life for you, and know that God stands between man and his heart and that it is to Him you will finally be gathered.

Be on your guard for a temptation which does not come uniquely upon those of you who commit wrong, and know, too, that God punishes with great severity.

Remember when you were few and despised in the land and in fear that people would seize you violently, how God found a refuge for you and fortified you with His aid and provided you with good things, so that you might be thankful.

Believers! Do not betray God and His messenger nor knowingly betray the trusts placed in you. Be aware that your goods and your children are a temptation for you and that there is a great reward with God.

Believers! If you truly fear God He will grant you a *furqān* and will divest you of your evil ways and forgive you. God is infinite in His goodness. *Surah 8.20-29*

BELIEVERS! Be resolute in the doing of justice, as witnesses to God, even though it be against yourselves, your parents or your kinsfolk, and whether it concerns rich or poor. For what has to do with God is more relevant than wealth or poverty. Do not follow your own desires into perversion of what is right. If you act in bias or prejudice God is well aware of what you are doing.

Believers! Believe in God and in His apostle, and in the Book which He has sent down upon His apostle and in the Book He sent down aforetime. Whoever repudiates faith in God, and His angels, His Books and His messengers, and in the last Day, has indeed gone far into error.

Those who have believed, then denied the faith, then believed anew and denied again and go still further in their unbelief God will not pardon, nor guide them in the way.

What occasion would God have to punish you if you are thankful and have come into faith? God is ever responsive to gratitude and knows all.

God has no love for public talk about what is wrongly done, unless it be by the one who has been wronged. God is One who listens and knows. If you do good in an open way or if you keep it hidden or if you forgive some evil deed, God pardons and has all things within His power. *Surah 4.135-137 and 147-149*

بسم الله الرحمن الرحيم

G. Society and Law

SET up no other deity alongside God lest you find yourself in shame and desolation. Your Lord has commanded that you serve none but Him.

Show kindness to parents, whether one or both of them reaches old age with you. Do not be round or impatient with either of them but speak kindly words to them. Lower to them tenderly the wing of humility and say: 'My Lord, have mercy on them as they nurtured me when I was little.' Your Lord knows well what is in your hearts, if you be true of soul. He is forgiving to those who seek Him.

Give to the kinsman his due and to the needy and the wayfarer and do not squander your substance, for squanderers are brothers of the satan. Satan is ever thankless to his Lord. If you have to turn away from them, as you yourself are anticipating your Lord's mercy for the wherewithal, then at least speak to them kindly.

Do not have your hand chained to your neck: yet do not be open-handed to utter excess or you will end up with reproach and destitution. Your Lord gives with bountiful hand and with sparing hand to whom He wills. Truly He knows and observes His servants.

Do not kill your children for fear of poverty. We will provide for you and for them. To kill them is a most grievous sin.

Come not near to adultery which is foul and an evil way. Do not kill any man — a deed God forbids — except for rightful cause. If a man is slain unjustly, We have appointed to the next of kin the right to satisfaction. But let him not carry his retaliation beyond the due, for there is counter-retaliation.

Handle the property of the orphan with all integrity, until he comes of age, seeking only its improvement.

Keep your bond. For you are accountable.

Give full measure when you measure and weigh with just scales. That is better and fairer in the end.

Do not pursue things of which you have no knowledge. Hearing, sight and heart — all these faculties of a man will be held responsible.

Do no strut proudly on the earth. You cannot cleave the earth nor match the mountains in stature. All such ways are evil with your Lord. All this is given you by revelation of the wisdom of your Lord. Set up no other deity alongside God, lest you be cast into *Jahannam*, reproached and desolate. *Surah 17.22-39*

THE believers — theirs is the true well-being — they who are humble in their acts of prayer, turning away from idle vanities, who are active in the fulfilment of *Zakāt* and are careful to keep their sexual activity solely to their wives or to those whom they rightfully possess, thus remaining free from reproach, whereas those whose desires go beyond these restraints are in transgression. Believers are diligent in their trusts and covenant, faithfully observing their prayers. It is they who are the inheritors — the heirs of Paradise, where they will forever dwell. *Surah 23.1-11*

GOD commands justice and well-doing and generosity towards one's kinsfolk. He forbids what is shameful and all that flouts right-dealing, and cupidity too. It may be you will mind His constant admonition.

Fulfill the covenant of God into which you have entered. Do not break your oaths after you have pledged yourselves by them and have made God your surety. God knows your every deed. Do not be like the woman who breaks her strong yarn and frets all the strands that make it so, by swearing oaths in order to deceive each other, in a situation where one party has superior numbers to another. God is simply putting you to the test in that context. He will surely make clear to you on the Day of resurrection all that was at issue between you.

Had God so willed He could have made you one single community. But whom He wills He lets go astray and whom He wills He guides aright. You will surely be interrogated about your doings.

Do not undertake your pledges as a means to mutual deception, lest the foot that was firmly set should start to slide and you taste the evil of having subjected to frustration the way of God, thus incurring great retribution.

Do not sell the covenant of God for a paltry price. Did you but know, the reward you have with God is better by far. What is yours is transient but the things of God abide. In very truth We will recompense those who patiently endure, measuring their reward by the finest of their deeds. To anyone — man or woman — who has done righteously, being a believer, We will in truth grant a good life and give the recompense fitting to their finest deeds. *Surah 16.90-97*

GIVE to those near of kin what is rightly due to them, and also to the needy and the wayfarer. For those whose desire is to the face of God this is the most fitting way, and it is they who truly prosper. Any increment you get from dealing in usury in material transactions represents no profit in the sight of God. What you give in *Zakāt*, however, desiring the face of God, means your participation in doubled reward.

Surah 30.38-39

FAR removed from the Fire he shall be who lives in awe of God, who gives what he owns as an act of purification and in no case in expectation of a favour being repaid but solely out of his desire for his Lord's countenance, the Lord most high. His blessedness to come is sure.

Surah 92.17-21

ONE who knows full well that what has been revealed to you (s.) from on high is the truth, is he to be held like one who is blind? It is only those gifted with perception who realise and remember. It is they who fulfill their covenant with God and do not go back on what is pledged. What God has commanded to be held together they do so hold, revering their Lord and fearing the evil of the reckoning. These exercise patience, desiring the face of their Lord. They fulfill the prayer-rite and they lay out from Our bounty to them, both in secret and in public, repaying evil with good. Theirs will be the consummation of the glad hereafter.

Surah 13.19-22

THOSE who read the Book of God, who perform the prayer-rite and from Our provision for them lay out on behalf of others, both anonymously and openly — they are the ones who can look for a commerce that cannot fail, seeing that He will pay them their full due and more also, from His beneficence. He is forgiving and gracious to the grateful.

What We have inspired in you (s.) from the Book is the very truth, confirming previous Scriptures. God is ever aware of His servants: He sees all. *Surah 35.29-31*

THEY question you as to what they should be ready to expend. Say: 'In your expenditures for charity the first claim must be that of parents and near relatives, of orphans and the deprived and the wayfarer. God is well aware of what you do in the matter of such benefaction.' *Surah 2.215*

THOSE who expend their possessions in the way of God may be likened to a grain of corn bearing seven ears, each with a hundred grains. God gives multiple increase to whom He wills — God who is infinite and all-knowing. Those who expend what they own for the sake of God and do not then proceed to make such expenditure on their part a matter either of their munificence or of reproach to others — their reward is with their Lord. No fear need be theirs, neither shall sorrow come their way. A kindly word and a forgiving attitude are better than a charitable action which brings hurt in its train. God is altogether rich and full of forbearance.

Believers! Do not nullify your charitable deeds by posing as munificent or by painfully embarrassing others, as do those who expend their wealth just to be seen of men, with no faith in God and the last Day. These are to be likened to a nearly bare rock whose scanty soil is left quite denuded after a storm of driving rain. Such people derive no profit at all from their amassings. God does not guide people who deny the faith.

The apt parable, however, for those who expend their wealth out of a desire for simply pleasing God and for their own confirmation of faith, is of a garden set on a hill, receiving copious rain and yielding double fruitage — or, if not a storm of copious rain, dew itself suffices. God takes note of all your deeds.

Would any of you like to own an orchard of date-palms and vines with streams flowing through it and containing all kinds of fruits, and find, when overtaken by old age, that those born to him were useless weaklings, and then live to see it blasted by a fiery wind and quite consumed?

It is in this way that God makes clear His signs to you: it may be you will ponder them well.

Believers! Expend for others of the good things you have gained and of the yield We have brought forth for you from the earth. Do not select for your charitable expenditure worthless produce such as you would not accept for yourselves, unless it were with averted eyes. Know that God is of infinite wealth and worthy of all praise.

Satan threatens you with poverty and constrains you to foul ways. God's promise to you is of His forgiveness and generosity. God is infinite and wise. He grants wisdom to whom He wills, and anyone to whom wisdom is granted has become possessed of great good. Yet only men of insight mark this well in their thoughts.

Whatever expenditures you undertake, whatever vows you pledge, God knows full well. For those who are perverse there is no source of succour.

If you do your charitable actions in the open, it is well. But if you do them in hidden ways and give to the poor, that will be better still for you. It will atone for some of your bad deeds. God is well aware of all your doings.

It is not your (s.) responsibility to give them guidance: rather God guides whom He wills. Whatever you (pl.) expend for others' good is good for you, so long as your expending is done in the sole desire for the face of God. What you thus lay out will be fully repaid to you and you will not be wronged.

Let your giving in alms be for the poor and for those who labour under limitations in pursuing the way of God, in that they are not able to travel abroad in the land — people whom the ignorant might suppose to be wealthy because they practice self-restraint. That, indeed, is the distinguishing feature by which you recognise them. For they are not given to persistent soliciting of alms. Whatever you lay out in well-doing God is well apprised of.

Those who spend what they possess in charity, by night and by day, whether secretly or publicly, have their reward with their Lord. They have no need to fear, nor shall they grieve.   *Surah 2.261-274*

THERE are some among them who find fault with you (s.) over the free-will offerings. If they are recipients they are well content, but if they are not given anything from these alms their anger kindles. Would they had been well content with what God and His messenger have brought them and had said: 'For us God Himself is all-sufficing. God out of His goodness will supply us, and His messenger will also. It is to God that our desire turns.'

Alms freely given are for the poor and the destitute, as well as for those whose work it is to operate them, and for those whose hearts may thereby be constrained to faith. They are also for the ransoming of slaves, for debtors, for any endeavour in God's cause, and for the wayfarer. Such is the ordinance of God — God all-knowing and all-wise.   *Surah 9.58-60*

WORSHIP God and do not elevate anything at all to share His worship. Deal kindly with your parents and your kinsfolk, with orphans and the poor, as well with the neighbour near of kin as the neighbour not your kin, with the companion beside you, with the wayfarer and the slaves in your charge. God has no love for the conceited and the boastful, those who — being themselves niggardly — lay miserliness on others, concealing what God has generously put in their possession. We have made ready for deniers of the faith a punishment to bring down their arrogance.

Nor has God love for those who lay out of their substance in alms in order to be seen of men, believing neither in God nor in the last Day. Anyone who makes Satan his bosom-friend has, to be sure, acquired a wretched one! And what would they have incurred had they believed in God and in the last Day and expended in alms out of God's provision for them? God knows them through and through. God does not do any atom's weight of injustice to anyone: a good deed He will double, granting great reward from His own grace. *Surah 4.36-40*

Do they assume that by the material wealth and children We accord them We are inciting them to compete with each other for the good things of life? No! they are uncomprehending. Those who stand in fear of their Lord, who believe in the revelations of their Lord and who associate no pseudo-deities with God and give what they give with hearts alive to the dread of their impending encounter with their Lord — it is they who compete for good things and overtake them.

We do not hold any soul to account except within its own capacity and before Us there is a Book which speaks the truth. They will not be wronged. *Surah 23.55-62*

We have laid upon man the duty of kindly devotion towards his parents. In pain his mother bore him and in pain gave him birth. Thirty months long was the burden of him through pregnancy and weaning. At length, in the full maturity of his forty years, he says: 'My Lord, constrain me to gratitude for all the blessedness You have granted me, and my parents: dispose my heart to well-doing acceptable in Your sight and let me have integrity in my offspring. To You have I turned in penitence, with those who are surrendered in their *islām*.' These are the ones whose best deeds We will take with acceptance, passing over their evil-doings and numbering them among dwellers in the garden of Paradise — fulfilling the promise pledged in truth to them.

As for him who addresses his parents with abuse, saying: 'Are you really telling me that I will be back to life again, when whole generations before me have perished?' even while his parents are imploring God's help and saying: 'For pity's sake, believe: the promise of God is true,' to which he answers: 'That is just a lot of balderdash, legends from old time,' — it is such people against whom will be realised the same condemnation spoken against nations that have already perished, jinn and human alike, who are indeed lost. For all have their status determined according to their deeds, none being subjected to injustice.

This word to those who have denied the faith on the day when they confront the Fire: 'You have had your fill of the good things of this present life and have taken your pleasure in them. You are requited this day with retribution and with humiliation for all your arrogant behaviour on earth, counter to the truth, and for all your base doings.'

Surah 46.15-20

TRULY We granted wisdom to Luqmān: 'Be thankful to God,' he said. 'For who-ever gives thanks his gratitude is to his own soul's good. Whoever denies all thankfulness — well! God is infinitely rich and worthy of all praise.'

Luqmān on occasion said to his son in admonition: 'Dear son of mine, never ascribe divinity except to God. For thus to commit *shirk* is a grievous wrong.' And We have laid upon man the care of his parents, the mother who bore him in much weakness and pain. Two years long were his infant needs. Be thankful, then, to Me and to those parents of yours. It is to Me that all things move as their goal.

But should your parents exert pressure on you to commit *shirk* by ascribing to Me things of which you have no knowledge, do not obey them. Nevertheless hold with them in well-doing in this present life, following the path of one who turns to Me. To Me is your ultimate returning, when I will give you to know all your deeds.'

'My dear son, God will disclose it, though it weigh no more than a mustard seed and be somewhere within rock or anywhere in the heavens or the earth. For God sees through all subtleties and discerns all.'

'Dear son of mine, perform the prayer-rite, enjoin what is worthy and proscribe what is unworthy. Endure with patience whatever befalls you. Such is the staying-power that masters things. Do not turn your cheek away from people in disdain and do not strut about the earth with lofty airs. God is no lover of the haughty and the boastful who-ever they be. So behave yourself modestly and lower your voice. The harshest of all sounds is the braying of the ass.'

Surah 31.12-19

BLESSED be He who has ordained constellations in the heaven, setting among them a lamp and a moon to give light. It is He who has made night and day in their sequence, as any perceive who have a will to take thought or who desire to be grateful.

It is the servants of the all-merciful Lord who go about the earth in modesty and who answer: 'Peace' when accosted by those who talk to them rudely. It is they who spend the night in their Lord's presence, prostrate and standing in prayer and saying: 'Our Lord, release us from the anguish of *Jahannam*. For grievous indeed is the suffering there: it is a place of dire evil and a wretched haunt.' True servants, when they expend their wealth, are neither extravagant nor niggardly, but keep the mean there is between the two. They do not invoke another god alongside God. They do not take human life — something God has made unlawful — except for just cause. They do not commit fornication. He who commits these sins will meet his due penalty and retribution will be doubled to him on the Day of resurrection, in a perpetual reproach — the penitent alone being excepted who believes and does what is right. It is such as these whose wrong-doings God will replace with good deeds, seeing that God is forgiving and merciful. Whoever repents and does righteously, his is a true repentance towards God.

God's servants are those who do not bear false witness and when they encounter idle talk maintain an honourable demeanour. When they are reminded by the signs of their Lord they do not collapse as if they had neither hearing nor sight. Their prayer is: 'Our Lord, grant us in our wives and children the joy of our eyes and let us be exemplary for the God-fearing.'

These will have as the reward for their steadfastness the high station in heaven, where they will receive the greeting and welcome of peace, dwelling there eternally. Goodly is that dwelling place and worthy that abode!

Say: 'You who have denied the faith, though there be no prayer of yours to Him, it matters not to my Lord. In time to come what must be will be.'   *Surah 25.61-77*

ALL that has come your way is merely the passing satisfaction of life in this present world. What is with God is better and more lasting, in respect of those who believe and whose trust is in their Lord, who steer clear of heinous sins and deeds of shame and, when moved to anger, are ready with forgiveness. These respond to the call of their Lord: they fulfill the rite of prayer and regulate their affairs by mutual counsel. They lay out for others from the provision We have made for them. When anything comes their way which violates their rights they take concerted action against it. The principle of equivalence is to be followed in the requital of evil. Anyone, however, who relents and reconciles has his reward with God. God is no lover of those who transgress.

But those who take up retaliatory action when wronged are in no way culpable. It is only those who deal wrongfully with people who are to be reprehended — those who flout the right and commit outrage in the land. There is for them a grievous retribution. And who-ever exercises patience and practices forgiveness — that is the staying power which masters things.   *Surah 42.36-43*

BELIEVERS! In what has to do with God and His apostle usurp no priority for yourselves. Hold God in reverent awe — God who hears and knows. Believers! Do not raise your voices above that of the prophet and do not address him in loud tones as you would one another, lest all your works — unbeknown to you — should come to nothing. Those who lower their voices in the presence of God's messenger are the ones whose hearts, through God's testing discipline, have attained to piety. Forgiveness is theirs and great reward.

Those who call out to you (s.) outside your private apartments are people who, for the most part, are unintelligent. Had they the patience to wait until you come out to them, it would be much better for them. God is all-forgiving and merciful.

Believers! If any wanton person comes to you with some rumour look well into it, lest you bring people into distress by your ignorant neglect, and then undergo regret for what you have done.

Know that in your midst is the apostle of God. Were he to comply with what you bid him in most things, it would certainly spell trouble for you. But God has made faith precious to you and given your hearts an appreciation of its beauty, rendering unbelief, wickedness and rebellion hateful to you. It is such who are rightly guided, through the goodness and grace of God — God who is all-knowing and all-wise.

Should two parties among believers be at war with each other, you (pl.) are to reconcile them to each other. Then if one persists in violence against the other, fight against that party until they adhere to the ordinance of God. If they come into line, make reconciliation between the parties justly. Deal with them all in fairness. God loves those who act equitably. Believers are brothers one of another. So make (pl.) peace between that pair of brothers of yours, with due fear of God, and mercy may be yours.

Believers! Do not let one group set another group to ridicule, who may well be the better folk than they. Likewise let no women scorn other women who may well be better than themselves. Do not decry one another or revile one another with name-calling. It is a foul thing, once

faith has come, to use offensive names. Those who do not repent of this
are surely perpetrating wrong.

Believers! Keep away from overmuch suspicion. For, in some cases,
suspicion is wicked. Do not spy on one another nor engage in calumny
against one another. Would any one of you like to eat the flesh of his
dead brother? Surely not: you would loathe it. So fear God. God is
indeed responsive to repentance and all-merciful.

Humanity! Truly We have created you male and female and made you
to be nations and tribes in order that you might know each other. Truly
the noblest among you in God's sight are those who fear Him most. God
knows and observes all.   *Surah 49.1-13*

WOE to those who act fraudulently, who exact their full measure when in
receipt from others, yet give short measure when they reckon out or
weigh out for others. Do such people not realise that they will be raised
to life again for the great Day — the Day when mankind will stand before
the Lord of all being?   *Surah 83.1-6*

THOSE who feed themselves on usury will have no standing. They will
be in no better state than that of a victim deranged by the touch of Satan.
It is their saying: 'Trade itself is just a sort of usury' which makes them
so, whereas God has made commerce entirely lawful and has proscribed
usury. So anyone to whom admonition from his Lord has come and who
desists from usury may retain his past profits. The matter in his case will
rest with God. But whoever reverts to usury — the Fire will be their
destiny eternally. God nullifies usury and blesses free-will offerings with
yield of interest. God has no love for anyone denying the faith and going
on in an evil way.

Those who believe and do righteous deeds, who fulfill the prayer-rite
and bring the *Zakāt*, have their reward with their Lord. They have no
need to fear nor will they find sorrow.

Believers! Hold God in reverent fear and forsake all remaining forms
of usury — if you are indeed true believers. For, if you do not do so, then
understand that God and His apostle are at war with you. If you repent,
your original capital shall be yours and you will not be either committing
or suffering injustice. If, however, the debtor is in difficult circumstances, let there be a delay, pending an easier situation. Should you
remit the debt as a free act of charity be sure that this will be best for you
— if you only knew it so. Be alive to fear of the Day when you will be

brought back to God, when every soul will be paid in full for what he has earned and none shall be wronged.

Believers! When you enter into mutual contracts of loan and debt for a stated term, set it down in writing, with a scribe to write out exactly the terms between you. No scribe shall refuse to write in accordance with what God has taught him. Let him set things down in writing, with the one undertaking the debt dictating to him. Let him do so in the fear of God his Lord and not make the sum less than it is. Should the man contracting the debt be feeble-minded or weak, or cannot dictate for himself, let his representative do so with all honesty. Let two witnesses be called, being men, or, if not two men, then one man and two women, being witnesses satisfactory to you. Thus, if one of the women makes a mistake the other can bring it to her notice. The witnesses are not to refuse whenever called upon. Do not disparage this practice of writing things down, be they small or great, and the term involved. For, in the sight of God, this is the procedure most conducive to justice, most reliable for evidence and for avoidance of dubiety on your part. However, in the case of merchandise actually transacted between you on the spot, there is no onus on you of wrongdoing if you do not have it down in writing. Have witnesses when you are trading with one another. Scribe and witness must not be made to incur liability, and if you do bring harm on them the iniquity will be yours. Hold God in reverent fear. God will teach you. God has all knowledge.

Should you be travelling and cannot find a scribe, let pledges be made and taken. When one places his trust in another let him who is trusted fulfill that trust and let him be devoted to God, his Lord. Do not conceal evidence. Any one who does so has an evil heart. God knows full well what you are about.

To God belongs all that is in the heavens and in the earth. You may disclose what is in your own souls or you may conceal it — either way God reckons with you concerning it. Whom He will He forgives and whom He will He punishes. For God has supreme power over all things. *Surah 2.275-284*

BELIEVERS! Do not be gluttonous, feeding on usury, doubling by compound interest. Hold God in awe and then you may prosper. Fear, too, the Fire made ready for those who deny the faith. Obey God and the apostle that you may find mercy. Press on mutually towards the forgiveness of your Lord and to attain a garden as wide as the heavens and the earth, made ready for those who fear God, who give of their wealth whether in prosperity or adversity, who control their anger and pardon their fellow men. In truth God loves those who are doers of good, those who, should they commit some shameful act or work some evil against their own souls, remember God and seek His forgiveness for their transgressions (for who but God is the forgiver of sins?) and who do not knowingly persist in their wrongdoing. These have their reward — forgiveness from their Lord and to abide for ever in gardens with flowing waters. How surpassing is the reward of those who do so!

Surah 3.130-136

As for the person who steals, man and woman, cut off their hands — the penalty their deed incurs — as a punishment to deter, of God's ordaining. God is almighty and wise. The one who repents after his evil deed and makes amends, God accepts his repentance. For God is forgiving and merciful.   *Surah 5.38-39*

BELIEVERS! Do not proscribe as unlawful those wholesome things which God has made lawful for you and do not transgress the rightful bounds. God has no love for those who overstep the limits. Partake of God's provision for you of lawful, wholesome things and hold God in reverence. He it is in whom you believe.

God will not take you to task for oaths you have foolishly made but He will take you to task for things you have quite deliberately sworn to. Such oaths in earnest are atoned for by feeding ten needy folk with food comparable to how you normally feed your own families, or by clothing those ten, or else liberating one captive slave. Anyone who has not the wherewithal — then a fast of three days. This is the way of expiation for the oaths you have sworn. Keep, then, the oaths you swear. Thus God makes His revelations clear to you, that you may be grateful.

Believers! Intoxicants and games of chance, idolatrous practices and divining by arrows are an abomination, the handiwork of Satan. Avoid them altogether and it may be you will find you prosper. By intoxicants and games of chance Satan desires to occasion enmity among you and hatred and to deter you from the remembrance of God and from the act of prayer. So will you not refrain? Obey God and obey the apostle and be on your guard. If you turn aside then realise that the sole duty of Our messenger is simply the message in all its clarity.

On those who believe and do righteously there is no fault in respect of what they eat, so long as they believe, fear God and do good works —

again, so long as they hold God in awe, believe and do righteously and live worthily. For God loves well those who lead good lives.

Surah 5.87-93

THEY enquire from you (s.) about intoxicants and games of chance. Say: 'In both there is great evil, as also some advantage for mankind. The evil is greater than the benefit.'

They ask you what they should lay out in charity. Say: 'All you generously can.' So God makes His signs clear to you so that you may ponder how they bear on this world and the next.   *Surah 2.219-220a*

BELIEVERS! Eat of the good things with which We have provided you and give thanks to God — if indeed it is His worshippers you are! However, carrion, blood and the meat of swine are prohibited to you as well as that over which any other name than God's has been invoked. But if anyone is driven by necessity, without deliberate intent and not going beyond his need, there will be no sin incurred by him. God is forgiving and merciful.   *Surah 2.172-173*

BELIEVERS! . . . For bidden to you are carrion, blood and the flesh of swine, and any meat slaughtered in any other name than God's, also animals that have been strangled, killed by a heavy blow or by a fatal fall, or by being gored to death or savaged by a beast of pray — unless you have yourselves actually killed it under due form. Also prohibited are all animals slain on idolatrous altars.

You are forbidden also the use of divining arrows, which is a sinful act. However, he who in extreme hunger is driven to transgress, not deliberately intending to commit evil, God is forgiving and merciful.

They enquire of you as to what is permissible for them. Say: 'The good things of life are made lawful for you. Eat also of what is taken for you by those hunting animals whom you have trained for that purpose out of the knowledge in which God has educated you, invoking the Name of God over it in due fear of Him. God is swift to the reckoning. This day all wholesome things are made lawful for you, as is the food of those who had the Scriptures already, just as your food is made lawful for them.

Surah 5.1, 3a, 4-5a

EAT, then, of the good things made lawful to you from God's provision and give thanks for the grace of God — if it is indeed He whom you worship. He has forbidden to you carrion flesh, blood and the flesh of swine, whatever, too, has been sacrificed in any other name than God's. However, anyone who is under urgent necessity, not acting out of mere desire or flagrantly, God is forgiving and merciful. Do not say with glib and lying tongue of yours: 'This is lawful and this is prohibited,' forging a falsehood against God. Those who attribute their lies to God will find no prosperity — only a brief pleasure and then a painful torment.

As for the Jews, We prohibited to them what We have already related to you (s.). We did them no wrong: it was their own selves they wronged. Your Lord, then, is truly forgiving and merciful to those who did evil in their ignorance, subsequently repented of it and put things right.   *Surah 16.114-119*

SAY: 'I (s.) do not find in all that has been revealed to me anything forbidden one to eat, save carrion, blood which is shed, or the flesh of swine — which is an abomination — or that which is profaned by the name of a pseudo-god. Whoever is in urgent need, however, and not acting out of desire or flagrant wilfulness — to such your Lord is forgiving and merciful.'

To those of the Jewish religion We have prohibited any beast that has claws and also the fat of oxen and sheep save for the fat on their backs, in their entrails or adhering to their bones. This We made so in requital for their obduracy. What We are saying is the truth of the matter. If they accuse you (s.) of untruth say: 'Your Lord is all-embracing in His mercy but His might will not be turned aside from people who are set on evil.'

Those who commit *shirk* will say: 'Had God so willed we would not have been worshippers of pseudo-gods, nor would our fathers. Nor would we have laid anything under ban as unlawful.' It was likewise that their predecessors also were gainsayers until they experienced Our severity. Say: 'Have you any actual knowledge you could adduce for us? It is only conjecture you are following: you are doing nothing but guess.' Say: 'It is God who has the conclusive case. Had He so willed He would have guided you, one and all, aright.' Say: 'Bring forth your witnesses, those who are saying that "God has prohibited such and such." Though they say so, do (s.) not join them in affirming so, nor follow the vain ideas of those who deny Our revelations and who have no faith in the last Day, bringing their Lord on to an equal level with gods many.'

Say: 'Come, I will give you word as to what your Lord has indeed made unlawful for you, namely that you should not hold anything as divine but your Lord alone, that you deal kindly with your parents, that you do not kill your children out of fear of poverty — for We will provide both for you and them — that you avoid all shameful conduct, whether open or secret, that you do not take life, except for just cause — for God has made life sacred. Such is what He commands you: it may be you will realise all intelligently. Lay no hand on what belongs to the orphan until he comes of age, unless it be to enhance it. Operate in all justice with your measures and scales. We only lay upon anyone what he is able to fulfill. Be equitable in all you say, even though it relates to a near kinsman, and keep your covenant with God. All this is His charge to you: it may be you will have a retentive mind for it. This is My path of rectitude. Follow it then: do not take other paths lest they divert you from His path. All this is His charge to you: it may be you will hold all in reverent and godly fear.'   *Surah 6.145-153*

EAT from that over which the Name of God has been invoked, if you are those who believe in His revelations. And why is it that you do not eat that over which God's Name has been pronounced, when He has made it clear in detail what He has forbidden to you, unless you are acting under duress? Many are led into error by their ignorant desires. Your (s.) Lord well knows those who are transgressors.

Forsake both the outward manifest sin and the hidden secret one. Truly those who accumulate evil-doing will be requited for their deserts.

Do not eat what has not had the Name of God pronounced over it. To do so is an abomination. The satans incite those who have truck with them to dispute with you (pl.). You would be idolators if you were to follow what they say.   *Surah 6.118-121*

THEY assign to God a portion of the crops and cattle of His creation, saying: 'This is God's' — at least so they claim — 'and this is for our deities.' What they offer to those associate-deities of theirs does not reach God while what they render to God goes the way to those pseudo-deities. It is an evil ordinance to which they hold.

Likewise, those pseudo-deities have made many of those who ascribe divine reality to them, as if partners with God, regard infanticide as something to be commended — to their own ruin and making an utter travesty of what goes with them for religion.

Had God so willed they would not have done so. Keep away (s.) from them and their machinations.

They say: 'These cattle and crops are forbidden: No one should eat of them unless we will it so.' So their demand runs, and they claim, too, that such and such cattle are not to be used for burdens nor have God's Name pronounced over them. All this is so much fabrication of theirs for which God will requite them.

They also say: 'What is in the wombs of these cattle is reserved for our men-folk and forbidden to our women. But if it is stillborn then both may share in it.' He will requite them for what they allege: He is wise and all-knowing.

They are lost who kill their children in their blind stupidity and folly and who forbid things God has provided them, foisting falsehoods on God. Far have they gone in error, astray from all guidance.

Surah 6.136-140

MANKIND! Revere and obey your Lord who created you from one single soul and thence created his partnering mate and from those two dispersed abroad a large progeny of men and women. Be then truly devoted to God in and through whom you seek your mutual relationships: let your reverence hallow the womb. God is watching over you.

Give to orphans their possessions and do not substitute worthless things to replace what is good. Do not appropriate their property, treating it as your own — a heinous crime to commit. If you fear that you cannot deal fairly with the orphans, then take to wife such women as may seem good to you, that is two, three or four, and if you fear that you cannot treat them equitably, then one only, or from the female slaves under your charge. This will be likely to obviate unfair dealing on your part.

Give women their marriage portion as a free-will gift. But if they freely give back part of it to you take it with happy satisfaction.

Do not give property, for which God has made you responsible, over into the hands of the feeble-minded, but provide for them out of it and clothe them, using kindly words. Keep orphans under discipline until they attain marriageable age. If you find them to be of sound judgement, hand their possessions over to them. Do not eat what is theirs yourself, wastefully or in haste to beat their coming of age. Let a guardian who is rich refrain from any interest of his own, and a guardian who is poor take only what is deemed right. In handing over their possessions let there be

311

witnesses on their behalf, God being the all-inclusive witness keeping reckoning.

Men shall have a share in what parents and close relatives leave behind and women have a share in what parents and close relatives leave behind, whether it be little or large, a share is laid down. If those who also have kinship, and orphans and the needy are present when the inheritance is divided make provision for them from it and speak to them in a kindly way. Let those who could well be apprehensive for their own offspring left in weakness have a true sense of their duty to God and give voice to it pointedly. For those who criminally devour the property of orphans gobble up fire into their own bellies and will burn in a blazing hell.

Surah 4.1-10

THEY enquire from you about orphans. Say: 'The improvement of their situation is the ideal thing. If you have their affairs involved with your own do as brothers should. God knows how to tell a corrupt handler from an honest one. Had God so willed He could have brought you into affliction. God has all strength and wisdom.' *Surah 2.220b*

GOD directs you to deliver all that has been put into your trust to those to whom it belongs. When you (pl.) judge between people exercise your judgement justly. Excellent is what God exhorts you to do. God hears and perceives all.

Believers! Obey God and obey the messenger and those of your number invested with authority. If in anything you are at variance with one another refer it to God and the apostle, if you do indeed believe in God and in the last Day. To do so is the best way and the finest resolution of what is at issue. *Surah 4.58-59*

ONE of His signs is the fact that He has created partners in marriage to be yours from your own selves, so that, dwelling with them, you might find rest and He has ordained a mutual tenderness and compassion, wherein truly there are signs for thoughtful people. *Surah 30.21*

BELIEVERS! Do not enter houses other than your own unless you have asked leave and have greeted the people there. This is for your good: perhaps you will have an alert mind for it. If you find no one present in a house, do not go in until there is permission. Should you be told: 'Go away,' then do so. This is more seemly for you. God has knowledge of all you do. However, there is no harm in your entering houses that are not dwellings but serve some public function. God knows the things done on your part — both open things and hidden things. Tell the believers who are men to be chaste in their looking and to keep their sexual impulses under control — a restraint that will make to their greater purity. For God is aware of all they have in hand. And tell the believing women-folk to be chaste in their looking and to keep their sexual instincts under control, not parading their charms beyond what is chastely seen but drawing their veils over their bosoms. Let them not display their charms except to their own husbands, or fathers, or sons, or husbands' sons, their brothers, brothers' sons or sisters' sons, or their own women-folk, the slaves in their charge, or their male servants who are without sexual capacity, or children ignorant of the embarrassment of women's nakedness. Let them not draw attention to their hidden charms by the way they tap with their legs. All of you, men and women, turn penitently to God, O believers, and true well-being may be yours.

Take in marriage those among you who are single, and those of your slaves, both male and female, who are worthy. If they are poor, God of His goodness will enrich them. God is infinite, knowing all. Let those who find no means to marry live in continence until God of His goodness affords them what they need. As for those in your charge who desire a deed of emancipation write one out for them accordingly, assuming you know well of them and let them have means out of the wealth God has brought to you. Do not, out of lust for the fleeting gains of this present world, force the slave girls in your charge into prostitution when their desire is to keep themselves pure. In the event any do so force them God, after such coercion, will be forgiving and merciful.

Surah 24.27-33

Do not take in marriage women who are pagans, worshipping pseudo-gods unless they first come to faith. Truly a slave-girl who is a believer is better than a woman avowing false gods, even though you find her more alluring. Do not give your women-folk in marriage to men who worship what usurps the place of God, until they come to faith. A believing slave makes a better husband than an idolatrous pagan, even though the latter impresses you. The call of such is to the Fire, whereas God invites you to the garden, and to forgiveness by His dispensation. He discloses His revelations to mankind: it may be they will give them due thought.

313

They enquire from you concerning menstruation. Say: 'It is a trying condition. So leave the women to themselves during their monthly periods and do not resume intercourse until they are cleansed. When they are cleansed resort to them again as God has directed you to do. God loves those who keep themselves pure.'

Women are to you as a field of tillage. So, as you will, come to your fertile field, effectuating what you purpose for yourselves in all the reverence due to God, knowing that it is your destiny to meet Him. Give good tidings to the believers.

Do not let your pledges by oath in God's Name serve as a bar to what is virtuous and godly and what makes for right relationships among people. God hears and knows all. God will not take you to task for thoughtlessness in what you swear but He will hold you to account for what you have actually resolved in your hearts. God is forgiving and He forebears.

Four months of waiting is the period prescribed for those who have said on oath that they are not consorting with their wives and if, in that time, they decide to consort again God is forgiving and merciful. But if they are determined on divorce God hears and knows all.

Women, on being divorced, must let three menstrual periods pass without co-habiting. It is not lawful for them to conceal what God may have brought about in their wombs — if they believe in God and in the last Day. During this interlude their husbands have every right to take them back again if they desire to be reconciled. The wives also have rights of their own comparable to those their husbands have over them, in all fairness, while men's rights take precedence over theirs. God is all-strong and all-wise.

Divorce between the parties may be pronounced and revoked twice and after that either the marriage holds good honourably or is dissolved in mutual fairness. It is not lawful for you to reclaim possession of anything you have given to your wives, unless either party has a fear they may not be observing the prescribed limits set by God. In the event you fear that you are not within the bounds of God no blame shall attach to either over what the women may yield back for the sake of her release. These are the rules God has prescribed. Do not violate them. Those who do transgress God's bounds — they are acting wickedly.

If a man divorces his wife decisively it is not lawful for him to re-marry her unless she has first taken some other husband in marriage who has in turn divorced her. In that event there is nothing to preclude their return to each other, given that they are both of the opinion that they can conform to the rules God has decreed. These — the bounds God has set

— He has clearly indicated to people who comprehend. Thus, when you have pronounced divorce of the women and they have attained their term, either decide to keep them in all fairness or else release them altogether in a proper manner. Do not retain them against their will, maliciously. For anyone doing so sins against himself. Do not take God's revelations frivolously: call to mind God's grace upon you, the Book and the wisdom He has sent down to you from on high, admonishing you thereby. Hold God in awe and realise that God has knowledge of everything.

When you have divorced your wives and they have attained their term do not hinder them from taking husbands for themselves if satisfactory agreement has been reached between them. To this every one of you is exhorted who believes in God and in the last Day. It is the course of action most conducive to purity and integrity among you. God knows and you do not know.

Mothers, following divorce, shall suckle their children for two full years, if it is their wish to complete the suckling period. Their maintenance and clothing is incumbent on him whose issue they are in all fairness. For no soul is put to charges other than he can duly bear. A mother shall not be distrained on account of her child nor the man whose issue the child is. The like responsibility devolves upon his heir. However, if the parents, after consultation, want mutually not to have the mother wean the child, no blame attaches to them. But if you do opt to seek other suckling for your children you will incur no reprobation, provided you take proper steps in entrusing to another what has been given to you. Fear God, knowing that God takes cognisance of your every deed.

As for those of you who die leaving wives behind, these widows shall be in waiting for a period of four months and ten days. When they come to the completion of that time, you are under no liability for what they may do in due seemliness concerning themselves. God is aware of all you do. Nor is there any wrong on your part in respect of any proposal of marriage to these women or in secretly entertaining the idea during that period. God knows that you will disclose it to them. Do not, however, make secret troth to them, conversing only with them in gentle courtesy. Do not decide on the bond of marriage until the period lawfully prescribed has ended, in the knowledge that God knows all that is in your souls. Fear Him, therefore, and realise that God is forgiving and that He forebears.

There is no reproach on you if you divorce women with whom you have not yet consummated marriage or settled a dowry on them.

315

Nevertheless, make provision for them — the man of affluence according to his means, the impoverished according to his, in all fairness. Such is the obligation on those disposed to act well. If you do so divorce them before consummation of marriage and you have settled a dowry on them, give them half of what you have settled on them, unless they forego their right or the husband who holds the marriage bond foregoes his. To forego what is due in this way is closer to true piety. Do not forget mutual kindness. God is watchful over all your actions.

Let those of you who die leaving widows make bequest to their wives of one year's maintenance without requiring them to quit their dwellings. But if they depart of their own accord you are under no liability for their personal decisions honourably taken. God is all-strong and all-wise. Divorced women have right to maintenance in a fair way. This is an obligation upon those who truly fear God. In this way God makes clear to you His revelations: it may be you will respond intelligently.

Surah 2.221-237 and 240-242

BELIEVERS! It is not lawful for you to gain some inheritance through your wives by forcibly retaining them, nor to put them under duress to recover anything you may have given them, except when they have committed some grave and open act of immorality.

Dwell together with your wives in all honour. If you take to disliking them, it may well be that the very point of your dislike is something God has meant for your great good. If you desire to exchange one wife in place of another do not take away from the first anything at all from the treasure you may have given her. Would you take it away by slander and sheer, plain wickedness? How could you take it back when you have consorted in sexual intimacy and the wife has had from you a solemn pledge? Do not marry any women whom your fathers have had in marriage, excepting past occasions of this practice, for it is an indecent, reprehensible thing, conducive to evil.

Forbidden to you for marriage are your mothers and daughters, your sisters, your paternal and maternal aunts, your brother's daughters, your sister's daughters, your mothers who have suckled you, your sisters who have suckled you, your wives' mothers, your step-daughters, being in your care and born of the wives with whom you have consummated marriage (but if you have not consummated such marriage there is no blame in marriage to them), the spouses of your sons whom you have yourselves begotten. You are forbidden to have two sisters together in marriage, excepting those from the past already so. God is forgiving and merciful. Forbidden also to you are married women, save for those whom your right hands possess. Such is the ordinance of God binding on you. All other women outside these prohibited are lawful for you to seek out with your possessions, in due wedlock and not in fornication. Give them the dowries due to them in law, considering what you have of them in satisfaction. But if, after doing so, you agree together to vary the settlement there is no reproach on you. God is all-knowing and all-wise. If any of your number are unable to afford to take in marriage believing free-women, let him marry believing slave-girls within your charge. God knows best about your faith: you all belong together. Marry them with the permission of their people and give them their wages fairly as in honourable wedlock, not as paramours nor secret concubines. But if, when in wedlock, they commit adultery, the penalty is half that applicable to married free-women. This liberty to marry captive women is there for those of you who are afraid that otherwise they will fall into sin. It is, however, better for you to be patient. God is forgiving and merciful. God wills to make these things plain to you, to guide you into the patterns of those who were before you, and to turn to you in mercy. God is all-knowing, all-wise. God wills to turn to you in mercy while those who follows their lusts want to get you far away into deviance and excess. God wills to make things lighter for you. For man was created a weak creature.

Men take responsibility for women in view of the differing capacities, one over the other, with which God in His goodness has blessed them, and of what men outlay from their possessions. Virtuous women, therefore, are quietly dutiful, keeping in their care those hidden things which God guards. As for those women whose refractoriness you suspect, first admonish them, then have them go to separate beds, and beat them. If they come round to obey you, seek no more occasion against them. God most high is most great.

If you fear that a breach is coming between a couple, appoint an aribiter from his people and another from hers, if they are both willing for a reconciliation. God will bring them into agreement. God is all-knowing, ever wise.   *Surah 4.19-28 and 34-35*

O PROPHET! When you (pl.) divorce your women-folk, do so in accordance with the waiting period. Calculate the *'iddah* precisely, in due fear of God your Lord. Do not expel them from their homes, nor shall they leave of themselves, except in cases where they have committed some grave and open act of immorality. Such are the prescribed bounds set by God. Whoever transgresses God's bounds does evil to himself. You do not know — it may be that God will bring something to pass in the sequel. So when they have completed the waiting period retain them in all fairness or else separate from them in all fairness. Have two just men of your own number be witnesses and you yourselves witness before God. Such is the admonition for those who believe in God and in the last Day. Whoever truly fears God, He will make for him a way through and provide for him from sources he never envisaged. For whoever puts his trust in God, God will prove all sufficient. For God achieves what He purposes and for all things God has determined the measure.

As for those women who are ceasing menstruation — and you are in doubt here — their waiting period shall be three months, and those who have not yet begun menstruation likewise. As for those who are pregnant, their waiting period ends when they give birth. For whoever fears Him God will ordain restful relief in his situation. All this is God's command sent down to you (pl.) from above. God will acquit of his wrong-doing whoever truly fears Him and make great his reward.

Lodge women in the divorcing period in your own abodes and in the same style as yourselves. Do not put them under any pressure with a view to distressing them. If they are pregnant, lay out for them until they are delivered. If they suckle the child for you, pay them their wages. Take mutual counsel in an honourable way and if some difficulty between you arises, seek out some nursing mother instead. Let the man of means lay out of his wealth and let the man with scant resources at least expend what God has given him. God does not make any one chargeable beyond what He has granted him and God will bring ease and rest for pain and stress. *Surah 65.1-7*

THEY ask you (s.) for a ruling (*fatwā*) about women. Say: 'God gives you ruling concerning them and brings you what is rehearsed to you in the Book concerning female orphans whom you desire to marry, while not giving them what is decreed for them: ruling also relating to children who are weak and helpless and as to your duty to treat orphans with all justice. Whatever doing of good there is on your part God is fully apprised of it.'

If a woman fears antipathy from her husband or desertion of him, there is no harm in their seeking an amicable solution between them: reconciliation is a better thing, seeing that the human soul is prone to self-seeking. If you act generously and hold God in reverent awe, truly God has all your actions under His steady cognisance.

You will never be able to treat wives with equal fairness, however eager you may be. Do not let yourselves by inclined wholly to one so that you leave another forlorn in a state of suspense. If you set matters right in due fear of God, God is truly forgiving and merciful. But if husband and wife separate God, out of His abundance, will enrich each of them. For God is infinite and all-wise. To God belongs all that is in the heavens and in the earth — God who is ever rich and ever praised.

Surah 4.127-131

GOD has heard the words of her who pressed her case to you (s.) concerning her husband, when she complained to God. God hears all that you (dual) have had to say between you. God hears and sees all.

Those of you (pl.) who separate from their wives by the (pagan) formula of *Zihar*, dubbing their wives their 'mothers', are saying something scandalous and false. 'Mothers' they are not. Only they are mothers who actually gave them birth. God is willing to pardon and forgive. Those men who repudiate their wives with this formula and then retract what they said, let them set free a slave before they take and touch each other again. This you are enjoined to do. He who finds no way to free a slave, let him fast for two successive months before they take and touch each other again. He who cannot do so let him feed sixty poor folk. Thus you will show that you believe in God and His apostle. Those are the ordinances of God. Painful retribution awaits those who deny the faith.

Surah 58.1-4

BELIEVERS! If you take believing women in marriage and then divorce them before consummation of the marriage, you have no need to reckon any interlude in respect of them. Make appropriate provision for them and let them go happily.

Prophet! We have made your wives lawful for you, to whom you have paid dowries, and also those female slaves whom God has given you as spoils of battle. He has also made lawful for you the daughters of your paternal and maternal uncles, and the daughters of your paternal and maternal aunts, who have emigrated with you, and any believing women who gives herself freely to the prophet, should the prophet desire her in marriage — this being exclusively your right and not that of other believers. We have indicated what We have enjoined on them as to their wives and female slaves. The purpose of this is that no blame should attach to you. God is forgiving and merciful.

You are free to refrain as you wish from any of your wives or to have them resort to you. Should you seek out any of them anew after you have kept from them awhile, there is no reproach to you in so doing. Indeed, they will be the more consoled, and not grieve, in the satisfaction you afford them all. God knows what is in your (pl.) hearts — God who is ever wise and forbearing.

It is not allowable for you to take further wives, nor for you to change those you have for others — though their beauty delights you — excepting your female slaves. God is vigilant over all things.

Believers! Do not enter the house of the prophet unless leave is given you. Invited to a meal, do not come before time to wait for it to be made ready. Enter when invited and when you have eaten, disperse promptly, not hanging around for talk's sake. That would be tiresome for the prophet — he being diffident about asking you to leave. God, however, is in no way diffident about what is true and right.

If you are making any request to his wives, do so from behind a curtain — a more salutary way both for you and them. It is no business of yours to cause distress to God's messenger, nor is it for you to take his wives in marriage after him — never! In the sight of God to do so would be an enormity.

Remember, when you do anything in the open or in concealment, God has knowledge of all things.

There is nothing wrong with his wives being in the company of their fathers, or their sons, or their brothers, or their brothers' sons or sisters' sons, or their own women folk, or their slaves. Be truly devoted to God. God is witness to everything. *Surah 33.49-55*

PROPHET! Tell your wives, your daughters and the women folk of believers to draw their veils closely around them. This will facilitate their being identified for who they are and will save them from molestation. God is forgiving and merciful. *Surah 33.59*

GOD has promised those of you who have believed and done good deeds that He will surely make them come to power in the world just as He vested power in their predecessors, and that He will certainly establish their religion on their behalf — the religion He has approved for them, and that in place of the fear they knew He will give them security. Me alone they worship, repudiating all deities made associate with Me. Henceforth those who do not believe are evil reprobates.

Perform the rite of prayer and bring the *Zakāt* and obey the apostle, that mercy may be yours. Do not imagine that the unbelievers can avail anything against God in the world. Their abode is the Fire — a wretched destination!

Believers! There are three times of day when your slaves and those of yours who have not yet attained to puberty should ask due leave to do so before entering on your privacy, namely before the dawn prayer, when you lay aside your garments at high-noon, and following the prayer of evening — these being the three daily occasions when you are in undress. Otherwise, at other times there is nothing wrong either for you or for them in going in and out in attendance on each other without explicit leave. In this way God makes His revelations clear to you — God all-knowing and all-wise.

When your children reach the age of puberty let them ask leave of you at all times, just as those did who came of age before them. So God makes His revelations clear to you — God all-knowing and all-wise.

Women who are past child-bearing and those who have ceased to anticipate marriage incur no blame if they leave off their garments, provided they are not flaunting charms. Yet to refrain from doing so is better. God hears and knows all.

There is nothing reprehensible on the part of blind people, or lame people, or sick folk, eating in your houses, nor on your own part. The same applies to the houses of your fathers and mothers, your brothers and sisters, your uncles and aunts of either side, and to the houses where you hold the keys, or to the house of your friend. You may eat all together or in separate groups without any fault incurred. When you enter houses salute each other with a greeting from God, blessed and good. Thus God elucidates His revelations to you — maybe you will comprehend.

Only they are believers who believe in God and His apostle and who, accompanying him on some matter concerning the whole, do not go until they have asked his permission. Only those who do so ask leave of you (s.) prove themselves believers in God and His apostle. Should their request for permission from you concern some private thing, give it to whom-ever you will and seek God's pardon for them. God is forgiving and merciful. Do not treat the call the apostle makes among you as being like the calls you have one upon another. God knows well those of you who slink away under cover. Let them be warned who go counter to His command lest some trial befall them or some painful punishment.

Do not all things in the heavens and in the earth belong to God? He knows where you stand and the Day when they will be brought back to Him, when He will acquaint them with all their deeds. God knows all things. *Surah 24.55-64*

GOD has not given to any man to house two hearts within himself. Nor has He made your wives whom you repudiate with the formula of *Zihar* to be in fact your mothers. Nor has He made the sons you have adopted the sons of your own bodies. Your calling them so is merely talk you are mouthing. God says what is truth and He guides you to the right way.

Call your adopted sons by their actual fathers, this being more just in God's sight. If you do not know who their fathers were, take them as your brothers in religion and as your wards. Unintended mistakes on your part incur no reproach but only what is deliberate from your hearts. For God is truly forgiving and merciful. The prophet has a closer relationship to the believers than they have to each other. His wives are their mothers. In the Book of God those who have blood relationship are closer to each other than believers and those who participated in the *Hijrah* — though you should act in kindness toward all your associates. This too is set down in the Book. *Surah 33.4-6*

BELIEVERS! When women believers come over to you as emigrants, examine them. God knows well about their faith. If you have ascertained that they are indeed believers, do not send them back to the unbelieving people to whom they are no longer lawful. Nor are those who deny the faith lawful to them. Return to the unbelieving men whatever they have expended. There is nothing reprehensible in your marrying such women, provided you have given them their payments.

Do not persist with the ties to women who deny the faith. Ask only what you have laid out for them, just as the other men demand what they have expended. This is the decree of God who judges between you — God who is all-knowing and all-wise. If any of your wives have gone over to the unbelievers with anything that you have expended on them, reversing the situation when you had accessions, give to those whose wives have deserted the equivalent of such expenditure. Fear God in whom you believe.

O Prophet! when women who are believers come to you to swear allegiance and pledge that they will not acknowledge any deity save God, nor commit adultery, nor kill their children, nor engage in any slander falsely schemed up by their own devices, nor go against you in any worthy thing, then accept their allegiance and seek for them the forgiveness of God. For God is forgiving and merciful.

Believers! Do not take as friends those people who are under God's wrath, who have given up all hope of the world to come, just as those deniers of the faith who have disowned all faith concerning the dead in their tombs. *Surah 60.10-13*

A SURAH which We have sent down and Our explicit instructions therein laid down, with very clear revelations We have sent down from on high for your steady recollection.

The adulteress and the adulterer — beat each of them with a hundred lashes: do not allow any feeling of pity for them to deter you carrying out what is a matter of God's religion, if you really believe in God and the last Day. A group of believers are to witness their punishment.

He who engages in sexual union adulterously does so only with a woman who, likewise, is committing fornication. She is thereby in *shirk*, disowning God's sovereignty. In turn she is one whom only an adulterer takes, he being also one who flouts God's law in *shirk* — a thing altogether forbidden to believers.

Anyone who alleges adultery on the part of a moral woman and fails to present four witnesses should be flogged with eighty lashes. Never again accept witness from them. Such people are totally depraved, unless it be those who subsequently repent and make amends. God is forgiving and merciful.

Those who accuse their own wives of adultery and have only themselves as witnesses, let each one of them swear by God four times that he has spoken the truth and the fifth time invoke the curse of God on himself if he is lying. Punishment of the wife shall be averted if she swears four times that he is lying and the fifth time invokes the wrath of God upon herself if he is telling the truth. *Surah 24.1-9*

BELIEVERS! Do not walk in the footsteps of Satan. For whoever follows in Satan's footsteps, Satan inveigles him into what is foul and evil. But for the goodness of God towards you and His mercy not one of you would ever have come to be pure. God cleanses whom He wills. God sees and knows all.

Do not let those of you who are favoured with good life and ample means set themselves against helping their kinsmen, the poor, and emigrants in the way of God. Let them relent and forgive. Do you not yearn that God will be forgiving to you — God who is forgiving and merciful?

Those making allegations against chaste women, believers, who have been careless, are accursed in this world and in the next. A great retribution is theirs on the Day when their own tongues, hands and feet will witness against them concerning their deeds. On that Day God will pay them their due in all justice, and they will know that God is the enlightening truth.

Corrupt women go with corrupt men and corrupt men with corrupt women. Wholesome women go with wholesome men and good men with good women. For these are known as innocent of all that is alleged of them. Forgiveness and gracious provision are theirs.   *Surah 24.21-26*

THOSE of your women-folk who are guilty of immorality, call to witness against them four of your people and if these testify to that effect confine them in their houses until death takes them or until God provides a way for them. When any couple among you commits an immoral act, punish them both. If they repent and behave well, let them be. God is merciful and receives repentance. However, repentance towards God avails only in respect of those who commit evil in ignorance and promptly repent. To such God turns in mercy — God all-knowing and all wise. Repentance does not avail in the case of those who do evil deeds right up to the approach of death, and then one says: 'Now I repent,' nor yet for those who die in unbelief. For these We have made ready a painful punishment.   *Surah 4.15-18*

IT is laid down for you that when death approaches any of you and he is leaving any wealth behind him, he should bequeath it fairly to his parents and kinsfolk. This is a duty on those who fear God. If anyone changes such bequest after having heard it, the sin thereof will be only upon those responsible for such changes. God hears and knows all.

However, if any one suspects some partiality or evil-doing on the part of the testator and secures a settlement between those involved, no wrong will attach to him. God is forgiving and merciful.

Surah 2.180-182

GOD commands you as follows concerning your children. The males shall inherit the equal of two females. But if there are more than two females they shall have two thirds of what the testator leaves. If there is only one she shall inherit half. The parents shall each inherit one sixth of what he leaves if the deceased has left a child. But if he has left no child and the parents are his only heirs, his mother shall have a third. If he has brothers, his mother shall have a sixth, after the settlement of any debts he may have left and bequests he may have made. You do not know whether it is your parents or your children who represent the great benefit to you. So this is the ordinance from God. God is all-knowing and all-wise.

You are to have half of what your wives leave, if they die childless. If they leave any issue, you have a quarter of their estate, after payment of their debts and any legacies they may have made. Your wives have a fourth of what you bequeath, if you have no issue. But if you do have issue, then they shall inherit one eighth of your estate after payment of legacies made and of your debts.

If a man or a woman leave neither parents nor children and have a brother or a sister, then each of these two shall have a sixth, but if there are more brothers and sisters they are to share equally in one third of the inheritance, after payment of any bequests made and debts incurred, given that these are not calculated to defraud the heirs. This is what God commands. God knows all and He forebears.

These are the rules, not to be infringed, as set by God. Those who obey God and His apostle, He will bring into the gardens where running streams flow to dwell eternally — the triumphant climax. Those who disobey God and His apostle and transgress the bounds He has set He will usher into a Fire — an eternal abode. His will be a dire punishment. *Surah 4.11-14*

Do not covet the good things which God has bestowed on some of you more fully than others. To men a share of what they have earned and to women a share of what they have earned. Ask of God, then, from His store of goodness. For God has knowledge of all things.

For everyone We have appointed inheritors of what a man leaves — parents and kinsfolk and those with whom bonds have been contracted. So make over to them their shares. God is witness over everything. *Surah 4.32-33*

THEY will ask you (s.) for directive. Say: 'God gives you this ruling concerning those who leave no heir in the direct line. Should a man die childless but has a sister, she inherits one half of his estate, and a brother shall inherit one half from a sister without issue. If there are two sisters they shall inherit two thirds of what he leaves. If there are brothers as well as sisters, the male has the share of two females. God makes this clear to you, lest you err. And God has knowledge of everything.'

Surah 4.176

BELIEVERS! When death draws near to any of you, when you are to make bequest let there be witnesses present with you — two persons, men of probity, from among you and, if you are en route in the land and the onset of death comes upon you, then two others not of your people.

Have them on hand after the prayer-rite and let them both take an oath before God, if you are in any way dubious about them, pledging: 'We will not take any bribe, though it were for some relative's sake, nor will we conceal what is witnessed before God. For then we would be indeed transgressing.'

But if, subsequently, it transpires that the two witnesses have become justly suspect of such false dealing, then two others shall take their place from among those whose interests the suspicion against the former ones concerns. Let these two swear before God: 'Truly our testimony is more true than that of these two. We have not transgressed what is right. For then we would indeed be evil-doers.'

In this way it is more likely that they will bear true and proper witness or they will fear that the oaths they have sworn will be refuted by the oaths of others. Fear God and heed. God has no guidance for people of evil mind.

Surah 5.106-108

BELIEVERS! Retaliation is prescribed for you in cases of murder — the freeman for the freeman, the slave for the slave, the woman for the woman. But in the case of a homicide being pardoned by the brother, reparation must be made appropriately and the due compensation transacted kindly. This is an alleviation from your Lord and a merciful thing. But whoever acts aggressively afterwards will incur a painful retribution.

In the law of retaliation there is life for you — you who are endowed with intelligence. Perhaps you will let the fear of God prevail.

Surah 2.178-179

BELIEVER should not kill believer, unless it be by mistake. Whoever kills a believer accidentally let him set free a slave who is a believer and pay blood money to the victim's family — unless they forego it as an act of charity. If the man killed belonged to a people in hostility to you, himself a believer, the reparation is just the freeing of a believing slave. If the victim belonged to a people with whom you have a treaty, blood money is paid to his family and a believing slave is to be freed. Any one lacking the means to do those things shall fast two successive months. This is the penance God wills — God all-knowing and all-wise.

Anyone killing a believer deliberately — *Jahannam* is his requital, where he will be eternally, the wrath of God upon him, and His curse. God prepares for him a great retribution. *Surah 4.92-93*

WE laid down for them (in the Torah) the principle of an eye for an eye, a nose for a nose, an ear for an ear, a tooth for a tooth, and retaliation for wounds. But if any foregoes retaliation as an act of charity it will be an expiation for sins done. Whoever does not judge by what God has sent down they perpetrate evil. *Surah 5.45*

WHEN you are greeted with a salutation respond with one of even greater courtesy, or else return it equally. God has all things in His careful reckoning. God, there is no god but He. He will indeed assemble you on the Day of resurrection. Of that there is no doubt. Whose word could be truer than God's? *Surah 4.86-87*

MAN (*or* 'the messenger') has a succession of attendants accompanying him both before and behind and guarding him, through God's command. God does not change a people's state of affairs unless they change what is in themselves. If God has willed evil for a people there is no averting it. Apart from Him there is no protector. *Surah 13.11*

WITH God the number of the months is twelve by the Book of God on the day when He created the heavens and the earth. Four of the months are sacred. That is the true abiding law of God. Do not then commit wrong against yourselves in respect of them. Make total war on the pagans, with their plural worship, as they make total war on you, in the knowledge that God is on the side of the God-fearing. To tamper by postponement with the sacred months aggravates the act of unbelief and, that way, the unbelievers are led astray. They count such inter-calation permissible one year and they forbid it another year, conforming to the number of months which God has made sacred while, in effect, permitting what God has forbidden. The evil of these doings of theirs they present to themselves as a fine thing. God does not guide such an unbelieving people.

You who have believed, what ails you when you are bidden: 'Go forth in the path of God,' you are weighed down to the very ground? Is it that you find your satisfaction in the life of this present world rather than in the hereafter? Enjoying the life of this world is a scant thing in relation to the life hereafter. If you do not go forth to fight He will requite you with grievous chastisement and exchange you for another people. Him you cannot frustrate. For God has disposing power over all things.

Surah 9.36-39

بسم الله الرحمن الرحيم

H. Unfaith, Judgement and the Last Things

THE deeds of those who give the lie to the faith are like a mirage in the desert. A thirst, a man thinks it to be water until he approaches it, only to find nothing. God he does find — ready there to pay his account in full — God who is swift to the reckoning.

Or their deeds are like the darkness in the deep of the ocean, under cavernous waves, billow upon billow, and dark serried clouds rearing above — a darkness so dense that a man could scarcely see his own hand in front of him. To whom God assigns no light, no light has he.

Surah 24.39-40

ANGUISHED shall the Day be when the trumpet is sounded — a Day bringing no ease to those who deny the faith.

Leave him to Me whom I alone have created, endowing him with ample resources, with sons for living proof, and generously paving his way. And he covets the more from Me! He shall not have it! To Our revelations he has been stubbornly hostile. I will make his path steep and toilsome. Busied with his thoughts, he laid his plans. Death take him, how he schemed! Death take him, how he schemed! He surveyed the scene, with a frowning look and an angry scowl. He turned away in aversion and arrogance. He said: 'This is nothing but a mere man saying things, nothing but trumped-up magic.' I will consign him to *Saqar's* fire. *Surah 74.8-26*

ON that Day you will see every people kneeling, every people being called to its Book. Today you will be requited for your every deed. Here is your Book, that tells the truth against you. All that you have ever done We have been recording in a register.

Those who have believed and done righteously their Lord will usher

329

into His mercy — the supreme and open climax. But for those who have denied the faith the word is: 'Were not Our revelations read to you? You proved arrogant and a race of sinners.' When it was said: 'The promise of God is true and of the Hour there is no doubt,' you said: 'We have no notion what the Hour may be: we have nothing but surmise. We are in no way convinced.' The evils they have done will be made apparent to them and what they scoffed about will encompass them. It will be said: 'Today We put you out of mind as you put from your mind the encounter of this very Day. The Fire shall be your abode, with none to come to your help; and all this is so because you took God's revelations for a joke. The life of this present world proved your deceiver.' On that Day they will not come forth from it, nor will they be reinstated in grace. *Surah 45.28-35*

INCREASING, multiplied wealth is your besetting pre-occupation all the way to the tombs. But anon you will realise, anon you will realise. If only you did realise and that with utter certainty! For sure, you would see *Jahannam*'s fire. You will indeed see it with your very eyes. Then — on that Day — you will certainly be interrogated about the real satisfaction! *Surah 102*

HAVE you pondered the man who defies as lies the duty of religion — namely the man who rejects the orphan and feels no constraint to feed the destitute?

Woe to those who do their prayers but in their very prayers are heedless, who want only outward seeming and withhold the wherewithal from those in need. *Surah 107*

WOE to every sleuth with his slander, his defamation! amassing material things and counting his hoard — a wealth which he thinks has made him immortal! Never! He will for sure be flung to *Al-Hutamah*. Have you any conception of what *Al-Hutamah* is like? It is the Fire of God, kindled and mounting over the hearts of men. It will close in upon them as if it were a vault on rearing columns. *Surah 104*

DOOM on the hands of Abū Lahāb: doom on the man (the Father of Flame). His wealth has availed him nothing, nor all his gains. He will burn in a fire — flame be its name — his wife, too, that carrier of calumnies, with a twisted halter round her neck. *Surah 111*

THOSE who deny the faith say: 'The Hour will not overtake us.' Tell them: 'Yes! it will indeed come upon you, by my Lord who knows the things unseen. Nothing in heaven or on earth escapes Him, be it no more than the weight of an atom.' There is nothing — be it smaller, or greater, than that — but it is noted in a Book where all is manifest, to the end that He may reward those who have believed and done righteously. For such there is forgiveness and a generous benefaction. Those who set themselves against Our revelations to refute them will suffer painful and punishing retribution.

Those to whom knowledge has been given recognise that what has been sent down to you (s.) from your Lord is indeed the truth, guiding into the way of the Lord of all might and praise. Those who deny the faith say: 'How about it? Shall we point you to a man who will tell you that you will find yourselves in a new creation after you have been rent and crumbled into dust? Has he foisted a falsehood upon God or has some jinn possessed him?' On the contrary — and those who do not believe in the last Day are grievously far gone in error. Have they no mind for what confronts them and what follows them in heaven and on earth? Were it Our desire We would sink them into the earth or bring down on them a darkness from heaven. Every penitent servant will recognise all that this signifies.

Surah 34.3-9

MAN never tires of asking what is good. If, however, evil afflicts him he is disheartened and falls into despair. Yet if, after experiencing hardship, We let him taste some mercy on Our part, he is sure to say: 'This was my due, anyway: I don't imagine that last Hour will ever happen. But if I am made to live again and brought before my Lord what I have with Him will surely be good alright!'

Those who denied the faith We will certainly inform of all their deeds and make them to taste of hard punishment.

When We deal graciously with man he turns away and holds aloof. It is when evil touches him that he prays profusely.

Say to them: 'Have you considered? If this was from God and you then denied it could any be in deeper error than those in open breach with God?'

We will show them Our signs in the horizons and in themselves, that it may be evident to them that this is the truth. Does it not suffice you that your Lord is witness over all things? Does He not encompass everything, that they should thus be in doubt that it is with Him they have to do?

Surah 41.49-54

BY the heaven and by the night star — that star of piercing brilliance which baffles all comprehension — there is a watcher likewise over every soul.

Man does well to realise out of what he was fashioned. For he was brought into being from a fluid in orgasm from the loins and from within the breast. So then God is well able to bring a man back from death again, on a Day when all secrets are sifted and man stands without power or succour.

Here is no jesting message but a word that is absolutely critical, as sure as the return of heaven's rain and the answer of the fertile earth.

The gainsayers are hatching their conspiracies. But let them be for a while: I have My plot too! *Surah 86*

HE sends down waters from the heaven and wadis flow to capacity, the flood bearing a swirling scum just like the scum that comes when men kindle a fire to smelt some piece of ornament or utensil. Such is God's likening of the true and the false. For the scum goes away like the waste it is, while the pure water, the true metal, which are of benefit to man, abide in the earth. Thus God makes use of parables.

Those who respond to their Lord shall have what is good and those who do not respond to Him, though they possessed all that is in the earth, and the like of it again, and would offer it as a ransom — would find it an evil reckoning, with *Jahannam* their abode, a very bed of wretchedness. *Surah 13.17-18*

WE have sent down upon you (s.) the Book, with truth to mankind. Anyone who follows the right path serves well his own soul, while he who errs from it serves himself ill. You (s.) are not accountable for them.

At the point of death God takes human souls: in the sleep of death He takes the living. He takes hold of those upon whom He has passed the decree of death: others He leaves mandated until their prescribed term comes — wherein are signs for people with thoughtful minds.

Have they taken intercessors for themselves other than God Himself? Say: 'Despite the fact that these have no avail whatever and do not even understand?' Say: 'Intercession belongs with God wholly and altogether. His is the sovereignty of the heavens and of the earth. To Him at length you are brought back.'

There is an onset of disgust in the hearts of those who do not believe in the last Day when God as One is named, yet they register joy at the mention of the usurping pseudo-deities. Say: 'O God, Giver of being to the heavens and the earth, knowing the realm that is hidden and the visible world, You will judge between Your servants about all that was in contention among them.'

Were those who do wrong possessed of all the world and a like world as well, they would be sure to offer it as a ransom from the dire evil of the punishment on the Day of resurrection. For they will be shown, on God's part, things of which they never reckoned. The evil deeds they have accumulated will be made evident to them and the reality they made a mock of will overwhelm them.

When distress afflicts man he invokes Us. Yet when We accord him grace, then he says: 'This has come to me because of my *savoir faire*.' The fact, rather, is that it was a test — a fact few understand. Many of those who lived in earlier times said the same thing but all that they gained was of no avail to them at all. The evil deeds they had accumulated brought calamity on them and on these present perpetrators of evil. Their tally of wrongdoing will bring affliction on them too and they are powerless to escape. Do they not know that on whom He wills God freely bestows His provision or is scant with it. Those who believe will surely find the signs there.

Say: 'Servants of Mine, you who have indulged in excesses, to your own guilt, do not despair of God's mercy. For God forgives transgressions — inclusively, being ever forgiving and merciful. Turn, then, to your Lord, surrender yourselves to Him, before retribution overtakes you, when there will be no help for you. Follow the goodly revelation sent down to you (pl.) from your Lord before punishment suddenly overtakes you unawares and some soul should say: "Alas for me — things done and left undone, before God, and scoffer that I was!" Or someone should say: "If only God had guided me I would truly have been God-fearing:" or should say at the sight of the retribution: "Would I could go back a second time to be among those who live rightly." But No! God would say: "My revelations came to you and you treated them as lies: you became arrogant and joined the ranks of unbelief."'

On the Day of resurrection you (s.) will see those who said about God that it was all lies, their faces blackened. Is there no abode in *Jahannam* for the proud? God will deliver those who fear Him by virtue of their deserts. No evil shall touch them nor shall they grieve. God is the Creator of all things and over all things He holds authority. His are the keys of the heavens and of the earth. It is those who count the revelations of God to be falsehood who are the losers.

Say: 'You *Jāhiliyyah* people! Is it something other than God that you bid me to worship? It has already been revealed to you (s.), as to those before you. All that you do will most certainly spell futility and loss if you give to others the worship that is solely God's. No! serve God alone, in the ranks of the grateful.'

Their comprehension of the reality of God was all awry. On the Day of resurrection He will hold the whole earth in the hollow of His hand and with His right hand roll up the heavens. Glory be to Him: supreme in His transcendence above all their associate gods. The trumpet will be sounded and all in the heavens and in the earth will fall down awestruck, save those whom God wills otherwise. And the trumpet will sound again and they will stand and gaze. The earth will be aglow with the light of her Lord, the Book will be set in place, prophets and witnesses will be brought forward: with justice shall all be judged and none shall have injustice. Every soul will be requited for its deeds. For God knows everything they did. To *Jahannam* will those be driven in throngs who denied the truth. At their approach the gates will be opened and the keepers will say to them: 'Did not messengers come to you from your midst, reciting to you the revelations of your Lord and warning you that you would have to face this Day, your Day?' They will reply: 'Yes, indeed.' The retribution told against deniers of the faith will then be realised in fact. A voice will be heard: 'Enter the gates of *Jahannam*, an eternal sojourn.' How dire the abode of the proud and arrogant.

Those who have feared their Lord in true piety will be conducted in their throngs to the garden. On their approach, the gates will be opened and the keepers will say to them: 'Peace be upon you: you have well done. Enter here eternally.' And they will say: 'Praise be to God who has made good His promise to us and has given us the earth for our inheritance to dwell where-ever we desire in the garden. Blessed is the reward of those who wrought.' You (s.) will see the angels encircling the Throne, celebrating the praise of their Lord. With justice shall judgement be done among them and 'praise be to the Lord of all being' will be the theme.   *Surah 39.41-75*

BY throes that overwhelm, by energies ever at work, by buoyancies borne in space, by precursors passing already, by forces disposing what must be — on the Day when the blast convulses the world and there follows a blast yet again, on that Day all hearts will be filled with agitation and all eyes with dread.

They ask: 'Are we in truth to be returned to our former state even though we have become wasted bones?' 'That,' they say, 'would be a pointless recurrence.' One single, arresting cry — and there they are, stark awake!   *Surah 79.1-14*

WHY, when life's breath comes into the very throat of the dying and there and then you are watching (We are nearer to him than you are, though you see Us not), why do you not cause that breath to return, if you are indeed not in fee to Us, if you mean what you say?

If he is one of those who are drawn near to God, then blessing and bliss will be his and a garden of grace. If he is among whose who are the community of God's right hand, he will be greeted with 'Peace be to you', by those at His right hand. But if he is among those who gave the lie to the faith and wandered in error, then his reception will be in waters of boiling fire and in *Jaḥīm* he will burn. This is verily the certain truth. Then praise the name of your (s.) Lord, the mighty One.

Surah 56.83-96

GOD invites into the house of peace and whom He will He guides to a straight path. To those who have done what is good — goodly reward and more besides. Nothing to stint or humiliate them shall come into their experience. They are the denizens of the garden, dwelling there eternally. Those whose deeds are a tally of evil-doing will find evil for reward in comparable measure. They will be covered in disgrace and, having none to defend them from God, a pall as of the night's own black darkness will descend upon them. They are the denizens of the Fire, abiding eternally.

On the Day We muster all mankind We will say to those who ascribed divinity to pseudo-gods: 'To your place — the place of your associated gods!' Then We will set them at a remove from those pseudo-gods of theirs who will say to them: 'Your worship had no register in us. God is sufficient witness between us and you to that fact. We were entirely oblivious of your worship.' Every soul will there comprehend what deeds were past and done. To God their Master, God the Truth, will all be brought back again and all their minds' inventions shall leave them stranded.   *Surah 10.25-30*

WERE you within sight, you would see how, when God brings to their dying those who have rejected faith, the angels buffet them on their faces and their backs, saying: 'Taste the Fire's anguish in requital for all your hands have sent on here ahead of you.' God is in no way unjust to His servitors.   *Surah 8.50-51*

SAY: 'My Lord, if You will to have me witness the retribution promised them then, my Lord, do not assign me with the evil-doing people.' Truly We are indeed able to let you witness what We promised them. Repay evil with a better deed. We are fully cognisant of all they are imagining.

My Lord! I seek refuge with You from all satanic promptings to evil and I seek refuge with You, Lord, from their very presence.

Only when death comes to any one of them will he say: 'My Lord, send me back again to life: let me return. It may be that I will act righteously where formerly I defaulted.' On no account! That is mere talk on his part. For behind them there is a barrier, in place until the Day of their resurrection.

When the trumpet is sounded there will be no ties of kinship among them on that Day and no asking help from one another. Those whose scales are heavy are the ones who will be in blessed state and those whose scales are light — their very souls are forfeit and in *Jahannam* will they abide eternally. The Fire will scorch their faces and livid will their appearance be. 'Were My revelations not recited to you,' the Lord will ask, 'and you treated them as lies?' They will say: 'Our Lord, things went hard with us and that is why we lost our way in sin. Lord, bring us out from here: if we ever go back to sin again, we will, indeed, be wicked men.' He will say: 'Away where you belong! talk no more to Me. Among My servants there was a group who said: "Our Lord, we have believed, forgive us, then, and have mercy on us. For You are the supremely merciful One." But those people you made a laughing-stock, so that your ridicule of them made you lose all mindfulness of Me, so bent were you on deriding them, this day I have rewarded them for their patient attitude. They have come through victoriously.'

He will say: 'How many years have you lived on earth?' They will answer: 'A day or perhaps part of a day. Ask those who have kept count.' He will say: 'Indeed you spent but a brief time there — if only you had realised how brief! Did you really think that We had created you pointlessly and that you would not be returned to Us again?' Exalted be God, the King, the Truth: there is no god but He, the Lord of the gracious Throne. He who calls upon another god beside God — a god of whose being he has no evidence — his reckoning is with his Lord. Those who deny the faith will never prosper.' Say: 'My Lord, forgive and have mercy: You are the supremely merciful One.'   *Surah 23.97-118*

HAD they no perception that it was We who made the night for their repose and the day for vision, with signs in that fact for any people minded to believe? On the Day when the trumpet is sounded all the denizens of heaven and earth will be seized with terror except those whom God exempts. Each and all will come in abject humility. You (s.) will see the very mountains you deem so solid and immoveable — God's handiwork who made all things to perfection — drifting off like clouds. He is entirely aware of all your deeds. Whoever comes before Him with good done from it he will have greater good and on that Day will be secure from fear. Whoever comes with deeds of evils will be cast crestfallen into the Fire. 'Is your requiting anything other than your deeds' deserts?'   *Surah 27.86-90*

ON the Day when the earth is convulsed in an earthquake and earth casts forth her burdens and men say: 'What has befallen her?' — on that Day will the earth publish her storied past, the tale of all that was, as her Lord inspires her to tell. On that Day shall mankind come forth in manifold diversity, to be shown their deeds. He who has wrought even an atom's weight of good shall see it and he who has done an atom's weight of evil shall see it.   *Surah 99*

BY the chartered winds in their familiar courses and tempests in their stormy pride; by the dispersing, fructifying rain-clouds; by all that deciphers and discerns, that brings home a reminder as plea or as warning — all that you are promised will assuredly happen — when the stars are blotted out, when the heaven is torn apart, when the mountains are crumbled into dust and when the apostles are brought to rendezvous. For what day is their time set? — for the Day of decision.

Would that you realised what the Day of decision means! Woe be on that Day to those who think and call it false! Have We not caused ancient peoples to perish and subsequently have others follow them? For thus it is We deal with guilty sinners. Woe be on that Day to those who think and call it false! Have We not fashioned you from a fluid you hold cheap, lodged by Us in a safe receptacle for a set term? So Our power has willed and excellent is Our competence.

Woe be on that Day to those who deny its truth! Have We not made the earth a habitation alike for the living and the dead, rearing thereon the lofty mountains and appointing fresh waters for you to drink?

Woe be on that Day to those whose deny its truth. 'Get you to the very place you have been calling a lie! Get you to the three-pillared shades that are no shade or respite from the flame which throws out sparks like burning timber-sparks falling in cascades of yellow.'

Woe be on that Day to those who call it lies. It is a Day on which they will come to an end of words, when no leave will be given them to make excuse. Woe be on that Day to the deniers: it is the Day of decision. 'With those of old time We have assembled you. If you have any devices now, try them on Me!' Woe be on that Day to those who think it all lies!

Those who truly fear God will dwell among shades and fountains, with fruits at their hearts' desire. 'Eat and drink, and joy attend you, by virtue of your deeds. It is thus We reward those who do rightly.'

Woe be on that Day to those who give the lie to the truth. 'Eat and enjoy yourselves awhile, you guilty ones!' Woe be on that Day to those who deny the truth, who, on being summoned to prostrate in prayer, make no prostration. Woe be on that Day to the deniers of the faith. After this, in what word will they have faith? *Surah 77*

THE Day of decision has its appointed time decreed — the Day when the trumpet is sounded. In throngs you will come: the heaven will be opened, its gates turning: the mountains will be carried away and dissolve like a mirage; *Jahannam* will lie in wait like an ambush, a place for the rebellious and their haunt for long years, where they shall taste no cool water nor refreshing drink but only boiling waters and bitter tears — their due requital.

They were not looking for their reckoning but totally rejected Our revelations. Everything We had ledgered in a book. 'Taste, then, your retribution — a retribution which, on Our part, can only intensify!'

For those who truly fear God there is sure triumph, sheltered gardens and vineyards, buxom companions and a cup of overflowing delight. No idle talk will be heard there and no deceiving. Such is your (s.) Lord's recompense, a bounty and a reckoning from the Lord of the heavens and of the earth and all within them, the all-merciful — He to whom they have no prerogative to speak on that Day when the Spirit and the angels stand rank on rank. Nor shall they address the all-merciful save him to whom He gives leave, saying only what is truth.

Such is the Day of truth. Who-ever so wills let him then repair to his

Lord. We have given you warning of a retribution near at hand, a Day when man shall witness what his own hands have earlier wrought, when the unbeliever will say: 'Would that I were dust!'   *Surah 78.17-40*

BY the dust-laden winds and the rain bearing clouds, by the coursers gliding swiftly and bearers of benison by God's command, all that you (pl.) are promised is faithful and true: the judgement is imminent. By the heaven with its highways of the stars, you talk in conflicting minds. Perverse in his reason is the pervert from the truth. Death to those who invent falsehoods, darkening and dazed with bewilderment and asking: 'When is this Day of judgement?' It is a Day when they will be in the tribulation of the Fire. 'Taste your tribulation — the thing you had tauntingly wanted to hurry on!'

Those who truly fear God will dwell in gardens and by fountains, receiving all their Lord bestows on them, being aforetime well-doers. They would sleep only a little at night and at dawn seek the pardon of God. In their possessions the suppliant and the deprived had due share. For those who are firm in faith there are signs in the world and within your own selves. Can you not see? And in the heavens is your provision and all that you are pledged. By the Lord of the heaven and of the earth, this is very truth — as true as your ability to speak.   *Surah 51.1-23*

NO! I swear by the Day of resurrection. No! I swear by the self-incriminating soul. Does man consider that We will not re-assemble his bones? For sure, We are well able to make good again his very fingers. Yet man wills to deny what lies ahead of him, querying: 'When will this Day of resurrection happen?' But when his sight is dazzled, the moon is eclipsed, and when sun and moon collide — on that Day man's question will be: 'Whither to flee?' Futile! There is no refuge. Your (s.) Lord alone that Day is the haven to seek. On that Day man hears the tally of all he has done from first to last. Man will be clear evidence against himself, excuse himself as he may.   *Surah 75.1-15*

THE Hour draws near: the moon is split in two. Seeing a portent they turn away, saying: 'Still the same old sorcery!' They have denied the truth and followed their own whims. But everthing will come to a decisive issue. Warnings have come their way calculated to give them pause, and wisdom too, in all its range. But warnings proved unavailing.

Turn (s.), then, away from them. On the Day when the one with the summons calls them to an inconceivable fate, they will emerge from their tombs with downcast eyes, as if they were a flurry of locusts, and go crowding towards the one who summons them — unbelievers, crying: 'Grim is this Day.'   *Surah 54.1-8*

THE imminent Hour, striking! Ah! the dread striking! What can make you realise the imminent Hour, striking? — the Day when mankind will behave like flies swarming wildly and the mountains will swell like wool that is teased by the carder's hand.

Then he whose deeds are heavy in the scales shall be in a state of blissful life and he whose deeds weigh light in the scales — the abyss of *Hāwiyah* will take him to herself. What can make you realise what *Hāwiyah* is like? — a raging fire.   *Surah 101*

WHEN the sun is wrapped in darkness; when the stars come plunging down; when the mountains are moved and the camels, big with young, are left abandoned; when the wild beasts are gathered in droves; when the very seas overflow; when human souls are paired with what is theirs; when the infant girl, buried alive, will be asked for what sin she was murdered; when the scrolls are unrolled and the heaven above is rolled away, *Jahannam* is kindled to a blaze, and the garden is brought near — then, on that Day, a soul will know what life's yield it has to show.
                                          Surah 81.1-14

WHEN the heaven is rent asunder, heeding her Lord and bound to His bidding; when the earth is levelled and, casting out everything within her, is resolved into an empty void, in heed to her Lord and bound to His bidding; it is then, O man, that you will in truth encounter your Lord to whom you have long been toiling and straining. For him who then is given his book in his right hand there will be a gentle reckoning. With delight he will turn around to his own people. As for him who is given his book from behind his back, he will call down destruction on himself and in *al-Saʿīr* will he burn — he who lived among his people well-satisfied, supposing he would never return before God. His Lord, however, was watching him all the while.

I swear by the glow of sunset, by the night and all that night enfolds, by the moon at the full, you pass on from one state into another. What is it, then, about them that makes them unbelieving, that they fail to prostrate themselves in worship when the Qur'ān is read to them? Instead, those who deny the faith treat it all as lies. God knows well their hidden thoughts. So give (s.) them word of a painful retribution, except for those who believe and do righteous deeds. Theirs will be a reward that never fails. *Surah 84*

WHEN the blast is heard on a Day when a man will flee from his brother, from his mother and his father, from his wife and sons — on that Day every man will be solely absorbed in what is at stake about him. The faces of some that Day will be radiant with laughter and happiness. But other faces that Day will be laden with dust and dark with gloom. Those are the unbelievers, the ones who play false. *Surah 80.33-42*

IMMINENT is the retribution of your (s.) Lord and none can turn it aside — a Day when a great rocking shall seize the heaven and a thrusting motion the mountains, and woe will it be on that Day to those who belied the truth while immersed in their follies. They will be harried that Day into the fire of *Jahannam*. 'This is the very fire you thought and said was all lies. Is this fire mere magic or is it that you have no eyes? Burn in its flames. Whether you endure with patience or otherwise, it is all the same. You brought it all upon yourselves because of your deeds.'

Those truly devoted to God are in gardens and bliss, delighting in all their Lord has bestowed upon them. Their Lord will make them secure from the pains of *Jahannam*. 'Eat and drink delightsomely of the very reward of your deeds.' They are seated at ease on couches, row on row. We will wed them with companions whose eyes are lustrous wide. Those who have believed and whose progeny have followed them in the faith We will unite with their offspring. We will in no way deprive them of what they have wrought. Every man has the liability for what he personally has acquired. We will amply furnish them with fruits and food, after their hearts' desire, as they pass from hand to hand the cup that makes for neither idle talk nor bent of sin. Youths in attendance, as fair as secret pearls, will circulate among them. In mutual exchange they will ask one another about their lives and say: 'We were always apprehensive when we were aforetime among our people. But God has been gracious to us and has preserved us from the fiery wind of chastisement. We were calling upon Him then and He is indeed the all-benign, the all-merciful.' *Surah 52.7-28*

WHEN the trumpet is blown, a single blast, on that Day the earth and the hills will be borne upwards and shattered at a single blow, and on that Day the dread act will be enacted. The rending heaven on that Day will totter in frailty and on its borders shall the angels stand, eight of them on that Day bearing up the Throne of your (s.) Lord, before whom on that Day you (pl.) will be arraigned, with not one secret of yours hidden away.

Then he who is given his record in his right hand will say: 'Here, read my book: it was in my thoughts that I would have to face my reckoning.' His will be a blissful state in a celestial garden with clustered fruits ready to his hand. 'Eat and drink (pl.) to hearts' content, reward for all you did before now in days that have passed.'

Then he who is given his record in his left hand will say: 'Would my record had not been brought to me, that I had no knowledge of my reckoning. Would that death had closed all. Everything I had is of no avail to me now. All that I could command is perished from me.' Take him and bind him and then in *Jahīm* let him burn. Fasten him in a chain seventy cubits long. He did not believe in God most great and felt no urge to feed the destitute. Today he is here without a single friend, nor anything to eat but putrid things — fit food only of sinners!

Surah 69.13-37

WE have given you from Our presence a *dhikr*. On the Day of resurrection he who turns away from it will incur the burden of so doing — a burden to be borne eternally — a grievous burden to all such on the Day of resurrection, the Day of the trumpet sounding, the Day when We assemble guilty sinners, their looks aghast, and saying to each other with bated breath: 'It is a mere ten days we have had elapse.' We know well what they talk of and how the more judicious among them say: 'It is only a single day you have passed.'

They put questions to you (s.) about the mountains. Tell them: 'My Lord will scatter them as dust and leave only a bare and level plain, where you will see neither devious defiles nor any rugged places. On that Day men will heed and follow the summoner's call — no devious note in him! — and all voices will be hushed in the presence of the all-merciful. Nothing but a faint murmuring will you (pl.) hear. No intercession will avail on that Day, save his to whom the all-merciful gives leave and whose word He approves. He knows what is ahead of them and what is behind them, while they have no such comprehension. All faces will be bowed in humiliation before the all-living One, the Eternal. He who is laden with evil-doing will be confounded and he who has accomplished deeds of righteousness, being a believer, shall have no fear of being wronged or ill-used.'   *Surah 20.99-112*

THE trumpet is sounded: it is the Day of which dread warning was given. Each and every soul comes attended by an escort urging it on and by a witness. 'You were negligent of this. But We have taken the wraps off you and now today your sight is keen.' And one self within him will say: 'This was always with me as a reality.'

'Throw, throw into *Jahannam* every obdurate unbeliever, every one who impedes the good, transgresses and persists in doubt and who sets up another god alongside God: cast him to condign punishment.'

His other self says: 'Our Lord, it was not I who provoked him to sin: in his own waywardness he was far gone.'

The Lord said: 'Do not remonstrate together in My very presence. I had already given you My sharp warning. There is no changing what I have spoken. I do My servants no wrongful thing.'

On that Day We will say to *Jahannam*: 'Are you filled?' and it will respond: 'Are there yet more to come?'

Into close proximity with the devout God-fearers the garden will be brought, with the words: 'Here is the reality of the promise made to each and every penitent, careful in law-abiding, fearing the all-merciful in the great unseen, and coming with a contrite heart. Enter here, in peace: this is the Day of immortal life.' There they have what they desire and with Us there is ever more yet.   *Surah 50.20-35*

INDEED they deny the Hour and for those who deny the Hour We have made ready *al-Saʿīr*. When *al-Saʿīr* sees them afar off, they hear its crackling and its roar. When fettered together, they are thrown into a confined area within it, they pray to perish there and then. 'Cry not today to be made to perish once! Cry for many perishings!'

Say: 'Is that better? or the garden of endless life promised to the truly pious for their reward and a final destiny?' Dwelling eternally, they enjoy all their desire — a pledge your (s.) Lord is responsible to fulfill.

On that Day when He will gather them, and the entities too which they worshipped to the exclusion of God, He will say to the latter: 'Was it you who misled these servants of Mine or was it they who strayed from the path?' They will say: 'Glory to You: it was in no way right for us to have adopted any object of loyalty other than You. You granted them and their fathers a life of ease to the point that they forgot the divine *Dhikr* and they became a worthless people.'

The entities you worshipped have given the lie to you concerning what you (pl.) say: you cannot avert your doom nor find any succour. We will bring any of you in wrong-doing to a heavy retribution.

We sent no messengers before your (s.) time who did not eat their food and frequent the markets. We have made it so that some of you are a source of testing to others, whether you are steadfast to endure. Your (s.) Lord observes all.

Those who do not expect to encounter Us are saying: 'How is it that angels have not been sent down to us, or that we do not see our Lord?' They pride themselves in the arrogance of their souls and are altogether presumptuous. On the Day when they do see the angels there will be no good news for them then, those guilty sinners! They will cry: 'Debarred! debarred!' We will proceed to deal with every deed of theirs and scatter their doings like dust.

But those who belong in the garden will find themselves that Day in a happier abode and delightsome — a place of noon-day rest. On that Day the heaven with the clouds will be sundered and the angels will be sent down in splendid array and to the all-merciful the sovereignty, the true sovereignty, will belong that Day. It will be a grim Day for the unbelievers — the Day when the wrong-doer will gnaw his hands and say: 'Would I had taken the way with the apostle. Woe is me! would I had not taken such-and-such for friend! He led me astray away from the remembrance of God after it had come to me. Satan — the inveterate traitor to man.'   *Surah 25.11-29*

THIS is your (pl.) nation-community, one single community, and I am your Lord: so worship Me. But what was ordained for them they have broken by schisms among themselves. To return to Us is the destiny of each and all. Whoever has done good deeds, being a believer, will not find his endeavours denied: We Ourselves are his recorder. Anathema is laid upon a community We have caused to perish: there will be no coming again for them, until Gog and Magog are loosed, swarming down from every hillside and the promised truth draws near. Then — there are the unbelievers, their eyes wild with terror, saying: 'Woe betide us! We were heedless of all this! We were evil people.'

Both you and what you worshipped in the stead of God are fuel for *Jahannam*, whither you shall go. If these objects of worship had been gods they would not have found their way here, where all abide for ever. Wailing is their lot and naught shall they hear.

But those to whom already the good reward is given from Us — they are far removed from thence. Not the least sound will they hear, dwelling evermore in that which their souls desire. The awesome terror shall not grieve them. Angels will welcome them: 'This is your Day — the Day you were promised, the Day when We will roll up the heaven as the rolling up of the scroll for the records.' As We inaugurated a first creation We will renew it again — a pledge upon Ourselves. Thus will We do. Truly have We written in the Book of Psalms, after the earlier *Dhikr*: 'Verily the earth is the heritage of My righteous servants.' (Psalm 37.29.) This is a pronouncement for a people who worship. We have sent you(s.) entirely as a mercy to the worlds.   *Surah 21.92-107*

HAVE you (s.) not realised that God created the heavens and the earth in truth? If He so wills He will remove you (pl.) and bring into being a new creation — a proceeding presenting no difficulty for God!

Before God all will present themselves together to judgement. The weak will say to the masterful: 'We were your followers, can you succeed in mitigating for us the doom of God?' They will reply: 'Had God guided us we would have guided you. It is all one for us now, whether we are restive or patient. We have nowhere to turn for refuge.'

When the issue had been decided, Satan will say: 'God promised you in a promise that was true: I made a pledge to you and defaulted on you. I simply put my call to you, when I had in fact no authority in respect of you, and you responded to me. Do not reproach me: blame yourselves. I cannot help you, nor can you help me. I can do nothing about your cries for help, nor you about mine. What, before, you ascribed to me of divine rank I denied.'

For those who commit wrong there is painful retribution. But those who believe and do righteously will be ushered into gardens where streams flow and where they will abide eternally, by leave of their Lord. The greeting they have there is: 'Peace.'

Have you (s.) not noted the likeness God has drawn in a parable — a good word being like a good tree, its root firm and its branches reaching toward heaven, yielding its fruit each season by leave of its Lord? So God sets forth parables for mankind so that they may reflect on them — and the parable of a corrupt word like a corrupt tree, uprooted from the ground for lack of solid hold? With the surely grounded word God establishes believers in the life of this present world and in the hereafter. God leads astray those who work evil. God does what He will.

Have you (s.) not noticed those who offered only ingratitude and unfaith in exchange for the grace of God and conveyed their people into the house of doom —*Jahannam* consuming them, an abode of wretched despair? They set up rivals against God, misguiding people from His way. Say: 'Take your fill!: the Fire will be your final destiny.' Say: 'Tell My servants who believe to fulfill the rite of prayer and expend both secretly and openly from the bounty We have bestowed on them 'ere a Day come when there will be no transactions of business or friendship.' *Surah 14.19-31*

THOSE who conceal what We have sent down as clear revelations and guidance, after We had made them clear to mankind in the Book, God sets His malediction on them and cursed they are by the lips of all who reject them, except those of them who repent and make amends and give clear evidence thereof. I relent towards those, for I am open to penitence and merciful.

But those who deny the truth and die in their unbelief the curse of God and the angels and of mankind at large remains on them — so abiding eternally. Retribution shall not be lightened for them and they will have no reprieve.

There are people who adopt objects of worship rivalling and excluding God Himself. These they love with the love due to God Himself, but the believers in God love Him more ardently. Would that the evil-doers might see — before they face the retribution — how all power is entirely God's and that God is stern in punishment on the Day when 'gods' to whom they adhered will exonerate themselves from their followers, the Day when, seeing the retribution, all their hopes will be shattered. These false worshippers will say: 'Would we had a chance to return: we would disown them as they have disowned us.' Thus will God show them their deeds, weighing upon them in bitter remorse, and from the Fire they will not emerge. *Surah 2.159-162 and 165-167*

WHAT can make you realise *Saqar* as it is! It neither exempts nor spares: it is a scathing signal to mankind. Nineteen guards are stationed above it. Only angels have We appointed to be custodians of the Fire. Their number serves only for puzzlement to try those who deny the faith and to give certitude to those to whom the Book has been given and for the increase in faith of those who have believed — thus effectively to free the heirs of Scriptures given, and the believers, from all doubt, while those whose hearts are sick with unbelief go on asking: 'What does God intend by this figuration?'

Thus God causes whom He wills to go astray and whom He wills He guides aright. Only He knows the hosts your (s.) Lord commands. Its whole significance is to be an admonition to mankind.

Or else! By the moon, by retreating night, by the brightening morn, *Saqar* is supremely a dire warning to mankind, to every one of you, whether he chooses to press ahead in the van or to be a laggard in the rear. Every soul is surety for its own entail of deeds, save those who belong on the right hand. In gardens of Paradise they will ask the guilty sinners: 'What has conveyed you into *Saqar*?' and they will say: 'We never prayed, nor did we feed the destitute. We took our fill with the rest and it was our habit to deny the Day of judgement, until the one certainty — death — overtook us.' No intercessor's interceding will profit them.

What can ail them that they turn away from this urgent word, as frightened asses fleeing from a lion? Indeed, every man of them wants to have scriptural scrolls of his own unrolled for him. But no! never. They have no awe of the hereafter. No! this — here — is an urgent word for whoever will take it to heart. Only as God wills so will they give it heed. He is worthy of all reverent devotion and forgiveness befits Him.

Surah 74.27-56

HAVE you (s.) heard tell of the event set to bear down overwhelmingly on all? It will be a Day of downcast faces, people toiling and straining in the toils of a scorching fire and made to drink from a steaming spring. No food is theirs save the cactus-thorn from which no sustenance is found and no hunger appeased.

And there are faces that Day radiant with delight in the satisfaction of endeavour, people in a noble garden where no idle talk is heard, where a flowing fountain plays, where couches are set with goblets ready to hand, where silken cushions are laid and carpets spread.   *Surah 88.1-16*

WHEN the great disaster supervenes, on that Day man will bring back to mind all his effort in life. *Jahannam* will be disclosed for all to see. *Jahannam* will then be the abode of those who have violated the right and hankered after this present life. But the garden will be the abode of those who have held in godly fear the majesty of their Lord and restrained their souls from base desire.

They question you (s.) about the Hour: 'When will it drop anchor and arrive?' What word do you have of that? Your Lord only knows when it will finally come. You are simply a warner to any who stand in fear of it. On the Day they see it, it will be as if they had been only a single evening, or forenoon, away from it.   *Surah 79.34-46*

NO! Truly the recording book of the workers of iniquity is there in *Sijjīn*. What can make you realise *Sijjīn* for what it is? — a book with its written text. Woe be on that Day to those who think and call it lies, who deny the reality of the Day of judgement — and only they who are wicked and hostile do so deny it! When Our revelations are rehearsed to them they say: 'Just tales from folk of long ago!' Far from it! All their acquisitions in life have worked a corrosion in their hearts. No, indeed! On that Day they shall be barred from the presence of their Lord and then in *Jahīm* will they burn. They will be told: 'This is the very thing you used to say was false.'

But the recording book of the righteous is in *'Illiyyūn* and what will give you to understand *'Illiyyūn*? a Book with its written text, seen by those who are brought near to God. The righteous truly are in bliss. Reclining on couches, they take in the scene. In their very faces you (s.) recognise the glow of happiness as they are given wine to drink — a wine of pure vintage and well sealed, redolent of musk, and mixed from the fountain of *Tasnīm* — let all who aspire to reach it bring their aspirations into play. For it is a fountain which those drink of who are brought near to God.

Wicked doers used to make a mock of believers, winking at one another as they passed them by. When they returned among their own kin they were full of jests and whenever they saw them they would say: 'These fellows are all misled.' They were not commissioned, however, to be in charge over them. On this Day, though, it is the believers who have the laugh on those who denied the faith as, at ease on their couches, they behold the scene. Shall not unbelievers be rewarded for their doings?
                                                           Surah 83.7-36

FOR those who repudiate faith We have made ready chains and fetters and *al-Saʿīr*. The righteous will drink from a chalice blended from *Kāfūr* — a fountain of waters for the refreshment of the servants of God who draw forth its copious flow. They fulfill their vows and hold in awe a Day so comprehensive in the evil it portends. For love of Him they give food to the destitute, the orphan and the captive. 'We feed you,' they say, 'mindful only of the face of God. We want neither reward nor thanks on your part. We stand in fear of the Day of our Lord — a Day full of grim foreboding and anguish.' Thus God has made them secure from the evil of that Day and made them to experience delight and gladness, rewarding their patient endurance with Paradise where, in silken attire, they take their ease on couches and sense no heat of sun or grip of biting cold. The shades of the garden overhang them with clusters of fruits drooping gently to their reach. Silver vessels and crystal goblets are passed round to them — silver-like glasses with a capacity it is theirs to decide. A cup drawn from the fountain called *Salsabīl*, with its flavour of ginger, is afforded them to drink. Immortal youths attend upon them, the very sight of whom would remind you of strewn pearls and every sight of that scene is a vision of bliss and sovereign authority. The raiment of the blessed is fine green silk and rich brocade and their adornment bracelets of silver. Their Lord gives them a pure drink, saying: 'This is your reward: your lives' endeavour finds welcome and recognition.'

Surah 76.4-22

WHO is there to lend a generous loan to God that He may return it to him twofold, making his a rich reward? A Day is coming when you (pl.) will see believers, men and women, their light gleaming before them, greeted on the right hand with the words: 'Glad news to you this Day — gardens with flowing streams, and you eternally within them — the supreme triumph.' It is a Day when the hypocrites, men and women, say to those who believed: 'Wait for us, and let us take from your light!' For answer they will hear: 'Go back yourselves and seek out your own light.'

A wall will be erected between them, with a gate, on the inner side of which there is mercy and on the outer side retribution. The excluded will cry out: 'Were we not with you?' to which those within reply: 'Yes, truly, but you were the source of your own undoing. You prevaricated and doubted, you were deluded by vain desires, until the command of God came about and the arch-deceiver deluded you about God. This Day no ransom will be taken for you nor from any who denied the faith. The Fire is your dwelling place, your master now — a wretched destiny!'

Surah 57.11-15

WHEN the heaven breaks apart and the stars are strewn around, when the seas break through their shores, when the tombs are heaped in ruins, every soul of man will know its accumulated deeds from first to last.

Yet you (pl.) deny the reality of the judgement. There are guardians keeping vigil over you, noble beings keeping record, who know your every deed. The righteous will dwell in bliss. The evil-doers will be in *Jahīm*, in the burning on judgement Day and there will be no absconding for them.

What can make you (s.) realise the Day of judgement as it is? Again, what can make you realise the Day of judgement — the Day when there is no soul that can avail another soul. For the authority on that Day is God's alone.　　　　　　　　　　　　　　　　　　　*Surah 82.1-5, 9-19*

SOME questioner queries the impending doom on the deniers of the faith — the doom none can avert — from God whose are the *Ma'ārij* by which the angels and the Spirit ascend to Him on a day that measures fifty thousand years.

Keep yourself (s.) in noble patience. They consider that Day far distant: We see it near at hand — the Day when the heaven will be like molten brass and the mountains like shreds of wool, when bosom friends shall not enquire of one another though they be in plain sight, each to each. The guilty soul will yearn on that Day if only he could redeem himself from doom by his sons, his wife, his brother or his kinsfolk who shelter him, even all the people of the earth together, could it but avail to save him. But no! *Lazā* awaits, to enflame him. It summons those who rejected and gave no heed, who amassed wealth and hoarded it.

　　　　　　　　　　　　　　　　　　　　　　　　　Surah 70.1-18

BUT what, when the earth is crushed and crumbled into dust and your (s.) Lord comes, and the angels, rank on rank, and *Jahannam* is brought into view on that Day? On that Day man will recall what he has been. But what will the realisation avail him? He will say: 'Would that for my very life I had reckoned earlier for this Day!' None requites as God does on that Day: none can bind as He binds.

'O soul at rest, return to your Lord, welcomed in His welcoming. Enter among My servants, enter My Paradise.'　　　　　*Surah 89.21-30*

Appendix:
The Chapters of the Qur'ān

1	Al-Fātihah	'The Opener'
2	Al-Baqarah	'The Cow'
3	Āl-'Imrān	'The House of 'Imrān'
4	Al-Nisā'	'Women'
5	Al-Mā'idah	'The Table (of Food)'
6	Al-An'ām	'Cattle'
7	Al-A'rāf	'The High Vantage Points'
8	Al-Anfāl	'Spoils of War'
9	Al-Taubah	'Repentance'
10	Yūnis	'Jonah'
11	Hūd	'Hūd' (an early prophet)
12	Yūsuf	'Joseph'
13	Al-Ra'd	'Thunder'
14	Ibrāhīm	'Abraham'
15	Al-Hijr	'Al-Hijr' (a locality in Arabia)
16	Al-Nahl	'The Bee'
17	Al-Isrā'	'The Night Journey'
18	Al-Kahf	'The Cave'
19	Maryam	'Mary'
20	Tā Hā	'Tā Hā' (two Arabic Letters)
21	Al-Anbiyā'	'The Prophets'
22	Al-Hajj	'The Pilgrimage'
23	Al-Mu'minūn	'The Believers'
24	Al-Nūr	'The Light'
25	Al-Furqān	'The Criterion'
26	Al-Shu'arā'	'The Poets'
27	Al-Naml	'The Ants'
28	Al-Qisas	'The Story'
29	Al-'Ankabūt	'The Spider'
30	Al-Rūm	'The Byzantines'

31	Luqmān	'Luqmān' (The Wise man of the Fables)
32	Al-Sajdah	'Prostration'
33	Al-Ahzāb	'The Confederates'
34	Sabā'	'Sheba'
35	Al-Fātir	'The Originator'
	or: Al-Malā'ikah	or: 'The Angels'
36	Yā Sīn	'Yā Sīn' (two Arabic Letters)
37	Al-Saffāt	'The Serried Ranks'
38	Sād	'Sād' (an Arabic Letter)
39	Al-Zumar	'The Throngs'
40	Ghāfir	'A Forgiver'
	or: Al-Mu'min	or: 'The Believer'
41	Fussilat	'Verses clearly set forth'
42	Al-Shūrā	'Counsel'
43	Zukhruf	'Ornaments of Gold'
44	Al-Dukhān	'Smoke'
45	Al-Jāthiyah	'The Kneeling'
46	Al-Ahqāf	'The Sand Dunes'
47	Muhammad	'Muhammad'
48	Al-Fath	'Victory'
49	Al-Hujurāt	'The Private Apartments'
50	Qāf	'Qāf' (an Arabic Letter)
51	Al-Dhāriyāt	'Dust-laden Winds'
52	Al-Tūr	'The Mount' (Sinai?)
53	Al-Najm	'The Star'
54	Al-Qamar	'The Moon'
55	Al-Rahmān	'The All-Merciful'
56	Al-Wāqi'ah	'The Imminent and Ineluctable'
57	Al-Hadīd	'Iron'
58	Al-Mujādalah	'The Pleading'
59	Al-Hashr	'Gathering for Exile'
60	Al-Mumtahanah	'Being Tested for Faith'
61	Al-Saff	'The Ranks'
62	Al-Jumu'ah	'The Congregation'
63	Al-Munāfiqūn	'The Hypocrites'
64	Al-Taghābun	'Respective Deserts on the Day of Resurrection'
65	Al-Talāq	'Divorce'
66	Al-Tahrīm	'The Prohibition'

67	Al-Mulk	'The Sovereignty'
68	Al-Qalam	'The Pen'
69	Al-Haqqah	'The Reality'
70	Al-Ma'ārij	'The Ways of Ascent'
71	Nūh	'Noah'
72	Al-Jinn	'The Jinn'
73	Al-Muzzammil	'Wrapped in a Mantle'
74	Al-Muddaththir	'He who is enmantled'
75	Al-Qiyāmah	'The Resurrection'
76	Al-Insān	'Man'
	or: Al-Dahr	or: 'Time'
77	Al-Mursalāt	'Messengers in the Sending'
78	Al-Nabā'	'The Tiding'
79	Al-Nāzi'āt	'Throes that overwhelm'
80	'Abasa	'He Frowned'
81	Al-Takwīr	'The Darkened Sun'
82	Al-Infitār	'The Shattering'
83	Al-Mutaffifin	'The Defrauders'
84	Al-Inshiqāq	'The Sundering'
85	Al-Burūj	'The Constellations'
86	Al-Tāriq	'The Night Star'
87	Al-A'lā	'The Most High'
88	Al-Ghāshiyah	'The Overwhelming Event'
89	Al-Fajr	'The Daybreak'
90	Al-Balad	'The Land'
91	Al-Shams	'The Sun'
92	Al-Lail	'The Night'
93	Al-Duhā	'The High Noon'
94	Al-Sharh	'The Opening of the Heart'
95	Al-Tīn	'The Fig'
96	Al-'Alaq	'The Sperm Cell'
97	Al-Qadr	'Power'
98	Al-Bayyinah	'The Clear Evidence'
99	Al-Zalzalah	'The Earthquake'
100	Al-'Ādiyāt	'The War Steeds Charging'
101	Al-Qāri'ah	'The Imminent Hour Striking'
102	Al-Takāthur	'Multiplied Wealth'
103	Al-'Asr	'The Transience of Time'
104	Al-Humazah	'The Slanderer'
105	Al-Fīl	'The Elephant'
106	Quraish	'The Quraish'

107 Al Mā'ūn		'Wherewithal for the Needy'
108 Al-Kauthar		'Abundance'
109 Al-Kāfirūn		'Deniers of the Truth'
110 Al-Nasr		'Succour'
111 Al-Masad		'Rope for a Halter'
112 Al-Ikhlās		'Sincere Religion'
113 Al-Falaq	The Two Refuge	'Break of Day'
114 Al-Nās	Seekers	'Men'

For the most part the chapter (Surah) names in the Qur'ān are drawn from words in the initial verse or verses, or from central terms, objects, or incidents, occurring in the body of the Surah. Two are from the Names of God, five refer to places and eleven to persons or people noted in the text. Four use letters of the Arabic alphabet. Twelve invoke the splendour of nature and at least fifteen denote aspects of the final Judgement. While reference to the Qur'ān by Surah Titles is preferred by Muslims, numerical reference is more convenient for other readers.

The Arabic letters in Surah titles and in initial verses have caused some puzzlement to newcomers. Apart from the six letters occurring in four Surah titles (20, 36, 38 and 50), there are two sets of five letters, six sets of three, two of two, and a solitary 'n' heading Surah 68, though not its title. The most frequent are 'h' and 'm', 'a' 'l' 'm', and 'a' 'l' 'r'. The five which head Surah 42 are written in groups of two and three, not as five — as is the case with Surah 19. In oral reading the letters are pronounced individually and not as they would be when read within a word. In all they number just half of the Arabic alphabet, i.e. fourteen letters. Called *al-Muqatta'āt*, the 'separate letters', they have intrigued commentators and theologians and there is no conclusive solution to their significance. Some stay with that fact and see the letters as signifying the ultimate mystery of revelation by which language characters 'carry' divine truth. Quranic eloquence in the 'matchless Qur'ān' being the vehicle of divine revelation, perhaps the letters are meant as a kind of challenge: 'Here is the raw material of language, bring a surah like it.'

A more mundane theory suggests that the letters belong to salient words in the chapters and are used to denote them. One needs to keep in mind that in Arabic it is not the initial letter that signifies (thanks to the prevalence of prefixes) but 'root' consonants from the triliteral form. Whether they have any practical connections with the collecting of the fragments of the Qur'ān it is impossible to say.

Some ingenuity has been expended on them, notably on the 'kāf', 'hā', 'yā', ''ain', 'sād', of Surah 19, the Surah of Miriam, narrating the nativity of Jesus. The sequence could yield 'king of the Jews 'Īsā of Nazareth', i.e. the inscription over the Cross.

Glossary

'Ād   An ancient tribe to whom Hūd (q.v) was sent and on whom condign retribution came. pp.125, 126, 129, 172, 228

Ahmad   Surah 61.6 has this word, 'more praised,' either as a synonym for Muhammad from the common root: *hamada*, or as an adjective. In either case in the passage it refers to one coming after Jesus with this fuller renown. Many Muslims read this as a foretelling of Muhammad while holding that Christians misread it as the promise of the Holy Spirit. p.169

Amr   'Command,' the divine 'let there be' which gave existence to the universe: also the initiating by divine authority of the word, and words, of the Qur'ān coming down through the several heavens into Muhammad's utterance. Also the moral directive by which mankind is guided. pp.90, 100, 109, 119, 188, 204, 277, 339

ansār   'The aiders' i.e. the Muslims within Medina who facilitated the reception of the *muhājirūn* or emigrants from Mecca during and after the Hijrah. pp.234, 242, 263

Al-Aqsā   lit. 'the farthest,' referring in Surah 17.1 to the sacred sanctuary to which Muhammad was 'carried' on 'the night journey,' usually understood to be Jerusalem, where on Temple Mount it is one of the twin mosques, Al-Masjid al-Aqsā. p.204

Al-Asmā' al-Husnā   'The most excellent Names of God' — traditionally ninety-nine in number, recited on the *sibhah* or 'rosary.' They are central to Islamic theology. pp.87, 200, 206, 226

'Arafāt   The plain and mountain, with the one name, east of Mecca and the furthest point in the pilgrim ceremonies of the annual *Hajj*, where the pilgrims perform 'the standing' and sermons are given. p.290

Āyāt (pl)   The term for a verse of the Qur'ān: it also denotes the 'signs' in the natural order and prophetic story by which mankind is alerted to the truths of God. Recurring throughout the Qur'ān: see especially e.g. pp.95, 97, 100f, 146f, 169, 173, 174, 250, 280, 312, 331

balāgh	The communication of the revealed message, enjoined on Muhammad in the pre-Hijrah time as his sole duty, the *hisāb*, or 'reckoning,' belonging to God. Post-Hijrah Islam moves into active propagation. pp.108, 123, 170, 185, 238, 260, 280, 307
Barā'ah	The first word of Surah 9 promulgating an edict of disavowal on the part of God and the Prophet of any existing contracts made with pagan tribes and giving notice of their termination. It followed the capitulation of Mecca and preceded the expedition to Tābuk. p.255
Al-Bayān	One of the titles of the Qur'ān, as that which manifests, elucidates, reveals and illuminates the truth. *Al-mubīn*, 'making clear,' derived from the same root is a frequen. descriptive of the Scripture and its contents. Both lucidity and discernment are meant. pp.93, 251
Bismillāh	The invocation of the Name of *Allāh*, in the form: 'In the Name of God, the merciful Lord of mercy.' It prefaces every Surah except Surah 9 which is sometimes read as following on Surah 8 and not as separate. The *Bismillāh* precedes every act of Muslim piety and e.g. pp.85, 87, 93, 159, 276
Al-Dhikr	Another title of the Qur'ān, as that which 'reminds,' or stirs recollection: also the act, and the mystic discipline, of such recollection. e.g. pp.130, 149, 165, 178, 183, 187, 192, 203, 209, 218, 247, 323, 344
Dhū al-kifl	lit. 'the owner of the pledge,' an anonymous prophet noted in Surahs 21.85 and 38.48 where he is linked with Ismā'īl, Idrīs and Elisha. pp.160, 161
Dhū-al-Qarnain	lit. 'the owner of the two horns,' figuring in Surah 18.83f and usually identified with Alexander the Great, pp.175, 176
Dīn	'Religion' and religious duties; also 'judgement' at the Last Day. There are five 'pillars' of *Dīn*, i.e. witness, prayer, almsgiving, fasting and the pilgrimage. e.g. pp.180, 190, 214, 229, 233, 253, 257, 275, 279, 282, 294
Falāh	'Wellbeing,' 'prosperity,' 'realised good.' Figures in the call to prayer: 'Come ye . . . to the good.' e.g. pp.101, 248, 280, 297
fatwā	A formal legal opinion or decision, given by one so qualified, a *muftī*. p.318
fitnah	A significant term meaning hostility, overt or covert, to Islam and Muslims. It means 'persecution' when these are emerging in Mecca, and 'sedition' when the Muslim cause succeeds from Medina. The root sense is of anything that constitutes a 'test' or a 'trial.' It may even cover what wife and children are to reluctant warriors. e.g. pp.229, 233, 234, 238, 261

357

fitrah	In Surah 30.30, the natural disposition of mankind for which Islam is properly the apt and right religion. p.282
Al-Furqān	Another of the titles of the Qur'ān as the criterion by which truth and right guidance are 'discerned' by that which 'discriminates' or 'separates' the true from the false. The Battle of Badr was *Yaum al-furqān*, as the day of signal 'accreditation' of the Muslim cause. pp.189, 233, 249, 277, 289, 294
Al-Ghaib	The hidden and unseen, what is beyond human ken yet is the theme of revelation: all that has to do with God and the Last Day. pp.86, 88, 96, 107, 114, 115, 175, 178, 195, 209, 211, 213, 237, 247, 249, 262, 263, 278, 317, 331, 333, 343
Hadīth	Tradition told and treasured about the Prophet and affording a second source of law after the Qur'ān, leading to the *Sunnah* or path of right guidance.
hanīf, pl: hunafā'	A word of uncertain origin, used of 'pure faith' antecedent to Islam, as exemplified by Abraham, as dissenting from traditional idolatry. pp.118, 121, 122, 214, 215, 222, 231, 282
Hajj	The statutory great pilgrimage to Mecca in the month of pilgrimage, and the ceremonies through the appointed days. pp.255, 289, 290, 291
Al- Haqq	The true, the real: one of the divine Names. e.g. pp.182, 203, 205, 271, 336
haram	The sacred enclave at the heart of Mecca enclosing the Ka'bah. pp.193, 194
Hārūt	With Mārūt: a pair of angels in Surah 2.101 (or possibly kings) who practised sorcery in Babylon of whom there are stories also in Jewish Midrash. p.273
hāwiya	Surah 101.9, the intense fire in the abyss of hell. p.340
Hifz	The art of memorising the Qur'ān for faithful recital.
Hijrah	The emigration of Muhammad's followers and himself from Mecca to Medina, the event which begins the Islamic calendar and constitutes the fulcrum of Islam. pp.226, 228, 230, 242, 322
hittatun	In Surahs 2.58 and 7.161, a plea or word the Israelites were directed to use on entering the land, a term denoting release from the burden of sins. p.154
Hūd	One of the lesser prophets sent to the tribe of 'Ād. Inexplicably, the same word is used of Jews in the Qur'ān, suggesting a possible link between the two. pp.125, 126, 138
hukm	Judgement and decision, one of the terms denoting the Qur'ān, a decree or decretal giving the ultimate verdict. p.223

Al-hutamah	In Surah 104, another of the names of hell, the fire which shatters as it consumes. p.330
Iblīs	Arabicising 'diabolos' the name of the Devil, al-Shaitān. pp.94f, 118, 202
'iddah	The calculating (lit.) of days and months in menstruation to tell the period within which divorced women may not remarry, for fear of confusion of paternity. p.317
I'jāz	The term used to denote the matchless, inimitable quality of the Qur'ān as truth and as Arabic, constituting the 'miracle' of the Scripture given to Muhammad understood to have been 'illiterate.'
ikhlās	'Sincerity,' worship of God free from all *shirk* (q.v.), the purity proper to an undivided worship, the quality within a true *Dīn*. e.g. pp.105, 190, 191, 212, 231
īlāf	The organising and marshalling of the Meccan caravans in Surah 106, root meaning 'to compose' applied also to writing, p.180
'Illiyūn	Surah 83.18-19, contrasted with *sijjīn* (q.v.) the place in the heights of celestial writ, the book, or books, of virtuous record. p.348
Il-yāsīn	A form of the name of Elijah in Surah 37.130, Yā Sīn is the title of Surah 36, formed from two Arabic letters. Ilyās (Elias) is a current form of this prophet's name. p.160
Imām	Normally in Sunnī Islam, the leader of ritual prayer and, in Shi'ah Islam the successor and heir to 'the light of Muhammad.' Used, however, in Surah 28.41 of the 'lords' in Egypt at the time of the Exodus. p.150
Īmān	The act of faith partnering the fulfilment of *Dīn*, in Islam. Distinguished in Surah 49.14 from a purely formal, political submission or *islām*. p.265
Injīl	Arabicised form of the Greek *euaggelios*, or evangel: the Scripture understood to have been given to 'Isā (Jesus) as messenger. pp.121, 163, 253, 264, 276, 277
Iram	Surah 89.7, the name of a lost city, famed capital of the tribe of 'Ad, or that — or another — tribe (Aram ?). p.129
islām	As a common noun, the act of faith and surrender making the *muslim*: as a proper noun the historic faith via Muhammad. e.g. pp.169, 275, 279, 287
Istighfār	Seeking the forgiveness of God in repentance, with a sense of the protection that wards of evil. e.g. pp.115, 116, 125, 127, 157, 190, 199, 337
Istighnā'	The pretension by which mankind suppose themselves autonomous and in no need of divine trust or mercy. p.177

Glossary

itmi'nān	Tranquillity or rest in the peace and will of God. pp.125, 167, 212, 232, 238, 286, 350
Jahannam	The most frequent of the names of hell (cf Gehenna, and the Valley of Hinnom where fire consumed Jerusalem's garbage.) e.g. pp.95f, 118, 147, 162, 190f, 202, 204, 212, 217, 229, 232, 247, 251, 258, 261, 263, 281, 283, 297, 303, 327, 330f
Jāhiliyyah	The state of 'ignorance' prior to the revelation of the Qur'ān and the 'wildness' which characterised it. The term is also used currently by Muslims to denote unworthy, nominal Islam. pp.236, 244, 245, 253, 268, 333
Al-Jahīm	The blazing fire of hell. pp.249, 285, 335, 342, 350
Jibt	An idol of the Meccans, named in Surah 4.51, linked with Taghut, a worthless delusion. p.271
Jih⁻d	Endeavour in the way of God, on behalf of Islam. Signifies military struggle but also inward discipline in pursuit of Falāh (q.v.). pp.156, 226, 227f, 240, 244, 254, 256, 258f, 265f, 328
Jinn	Invisible demons and spirits, mainly demonic but also helpful to mankind. They are recipients of the revelation and are judged. e.g. pp.93, 158, 160, 180, 215, 276, 281, 331
Ka'bah	The cube shaped shrine at the heart of the great Mosque in Mecca around which pilgrims in the Hajj circulate in the ritual ceremonies. The focal point of Muslim prayer, linked with Adam and Abraham in Islamic faith and cleansed of its idols by Muhammad after his victory over the Quraish. p.292
Kāfirūn	Unbelievers, those who repudiate the revelation, a word occurring some 130 times.
Kāfūr	Surah 76.5 a sweet and fragrant drink of the blissful, the term referring either to the source or the flavour. p.348
Khilāfah	The 'dominion' over the natural order given to mankind, despite angelic demur about the divine wisdom in such entrustment to fickle creatures. Man's deputy-ship on behalf of God, his vice-regency. e.g. pp.96, 97, 107, 157
Al-Kitāb	The Book, the Qur'ān, but also previous Scriptures and also the ledger of personal deeds at the Last Day, the record of human destiny. pp.102, 117, 143, 145, 155, 160f, 182, 187f, 196, 209, 210, 215, 217, 231, 246, 248, 257, 268, 271, 276, 286, 295, 322, 329f
Kufr	The sin, unbelief and unfaith of the kāfirīn. e.g. pp.110, 160, 164, 229, 237, 256, 267, 272, 280, 304
Lazā	In Surah 70.15 another of the names of the Fire. p.350

Glossary

Luqmān	An ancient sage, identified by some with Aesop of the fables, or Solomon, he gives his name to Surah 31 where he is noted imparting righteous wisdom to his son. p.302
Al-Ma'ārij	The ways of ascent to God, in Surah 70.3, to which the word provides the title. Some translators have, oddly, 'the stairs.' There may be a reminiscence of Jacob's ladder. p.350
marad	'Sickness,' a frequent term in reference to the hearts of unbelievers. pp.227, 228, 235, 240, 250, 254, 264, 347
Mārūt	One of a pair with Hārūt (q.v.). p.273
Al-Marwah	With Safa the points between which the 'running' takes place in the *Hajj* at Mecca, linked with Hagar's desperate search for water rewarded at the well of Zamzam. p.290
Millah	The community e.g. of Abraham, as identified by its worship. Also used, e.g. in Surah 7.88, of a pagan cult-community. pp.92, 122, 132, 139, 172, 174, 215, 240, 289
Al-mīzān	The scales in which deeds are weighed (Surah 42.17) as to their worth, and in 55.7f the balance in the divine ordering both of the physical and the moral worlds. pp.93, 208, cf138, 249
Muhājirūn	The emigrants who took part in the Hijrah from Mecca to Medina to be received and succoured there by the *ansār* (q.v.). pp.230, 234, 235, 242, 251, 256, 263, 324
Munāfiqūn	'Hypocrites,' those guilty of *nifāq* or double-dealing whether as an organised party, or otherwise, in the encounters between Islam and the Quraish after the Hijrah. e.g. pp.227, 228, 230, 235, 239, 242, 254, 258, 261, 267, 349
Muslimūn	'Muslims,' holding *Īmān* and duly fulfilling *Dīn*, differentiated totally from the *mushrikūn* (idolaters), the *khāsirūn* (losers) and the *kāfirūn* (deniers of the faith). pp.107, 123, 149, 159, 190, 191, 193, 207, 210, 216, 270, 272, 280, 293, 301
Nasārā	The Quranic term for 'Christians' echoing the name of Nazareth. pp.121, 245, 246, 270, 273, 274
Qadr	Lit. 'measure,' or 'determinant,' the divine decree of destiny: applied to Surah 97 to 'the night' of the Qur'ān's bestowal into time. p.177
Qāri'ah	The cataclysm, or thundering summons announcing the final, or other, Judgement. pp.129, 223, 340
Qarīn	The self's 'mate' or 'other self' always attendant on the living and 'matching' their good and evil. No alibi at the last. Surah 43.36 and 38. pp.199, 343, cf301
qatl	'Killing' or 'slaughter' seen, in the cause of Islam, as a lesser evil than *fitnah* (q.v.). pp.229, 232, 233, 257, 264, 267

361

Qiblah	The Muslim direction of prayer: originally toward Jerusalem, after the Hijrah toward Mecca. pp.149, 230, 231, 284
qist	Fair dealing, the scale of truth and justice: equity and that which it awards. pp.93, 98, 138, 220, 249, 267, 279, 283, 295, 310, 318
Qistās	The instrument to determine *qist*, a balance. pp.138, 296
Al-Rabb	'The Lord God' usually with '. . . of the worlds,' in power, control, sovereignty, and nourisher. Among the most frequent of divine Names. On almost every page.
Al-Rahmān al-Rahīm	Two divine Names from the common root of 'mercy,' the first God's mercy essentially His, the second that mercy actively His. Forms the *Bismillāh* (q.v.). Throughout the Qur'ān.
Al-Rasūl	The title and dignity of Muhammad as final 'messenger,' 'envoy' and 'apostle' of God. (Pl. *rusul* used also of other prophet spokesmen). Throughout the Qur'ān.
Al-Raqīm	A term in Surah 18.9 concerning the Seven Sleepers of Ephesus secreted in their cave: probably meaning an inscribed tablet on which details of them were recorded, or the name of the dog who figures in the story, or of the locale of the cave itself. p.173
Rauh-ullāh	A term used by Jacob in Surah 12.87, as a variant of *Rūh-ullāh*, 'the spirit' of God, or of the divine mercy of which the faithful do not despair. p.136
Al-Rūh	'Spirit' the divine agency within the revelation of the Qur'ān, in annunciation to Mary, Jesus being described as His (i.e. 'God's spirit,' and 'a spirit from Him.') The power at work in all divine emissaries. pp.165, 167, 168, 169, 177, 188, 206, 244, 281, 338, 350
Sabr	The quality of patient endurance awaiting divine help and vindication, tenacity under adversity. e.g. pp.103, 110, 150, 156, 157, 161, 178, 200, 214, 223, 235, 283
Al-Safā	See Al-Marwah, locales in the pilgrimage rites. p.290
Al-Sa'īr	Another of the titles of the fire of hell. pp.158, 193, 197, 252, 340, 343, 348
Al-Sakīnah	The re-assuring peace brought by a sense of divine presence and succour as experienced by prophets and by Muhammad: tranquillity. Cf. Heb. *Shekhinah*). pp.156, 226, 251, 253, 257
Salāt	The ritual prayer of Islam with prostrations, five times daily. 'Perform (*uqīmū*) the prayer' recurs repeatedly.
Sālih	A 'minor' prophet sent to the tribe, Thamūd. pp.127, 128, 129, 138

Sallā 'alā	The formula used in Surah 33.56 directing the faithful to 'call down blessing' on Muhammad as God also does. pp.282, 288
Salsabīl	A paradisial spring of sweet water (Surah 76.17). Some suggest it is a compound word — *sal sabīl*, or 'ask the way': or a name to rime with *zanjabil* (ginger) in the previous verse. p.349
Al-Samad	One of the Names of God, found only once, i.e. in Surah 112 where it must be read in apposition to the following phrase: 'unbegetting, unbegotten,' having all resources in Himself, and so 'eternal,' 'self-subsistent.' p.87
Al-Sāmirī	In Surah 20.85f blame for the sin of the golden calf is laid on one so named, either 'the Samaritan,' or some 'foreigner' liable to such deviance and pagan impulses. p.148
Saqar	The fire of hell. pp.329, 346, 347
Saum and Siyām	Fasting, the fourth 'pillar' of *Dīn*. pp.244, 245, 288, 289
Shahādah	The act of confessing faith in God alone and Muhammad His *Rasūl*. A *shahīd* is one so confessing: also a martyr.
Al-Shaitān	The angel who demurs at the *khilāfah*, or 'dominion' given to the creature man and defies God by refusing to prostrate before Adam. The word is also made plural, signifying demons corrupting and misleading mankind. pp.95, 96, 101, 130, 133, 134, 140, 144, 159, 172, 173, 178, 185, 205, 207, 221, 232, 235, 237, 243, 248, 266, 323
Al-Sharī'ah	The sacred law of Islam, lit. 'the path' of right and obligation, as derived from the Qur'ān and the Sunnah. p.287
Shirk	The supreme sin of plural worship and of alienating from God to pseudo deities the trust, appeal, obedience or devotion due to God alone inalienably. e.g. pp.195, 302, 309, 310, 323
Shu'aib	A prophet-messenger from Madyan, sometimes identified, though not convincingly, with the Biblical Jethro. Details are closely akin to those of Muhammad's situation before the Hijrah. pp.137, 138, 139
Shukr	Gratitude, a frequent theme of the Qur'ān as due from mankind in the light of the innumerable 'signs' (*āyāt*) (q.v.) of divine goodness in nature and revelation. Antonym of *kufr* (see: *kāfirūn*). Ingratitude is a form of atheism.
Sibghah	Lit. 'dipping' or 'dyeing,' and applied in Surah 2.138 to 'baptism' understood there as 'truth-initiation.' p.122
Sidrah	A tree of Paradise, the shady lote-tree noted in Surah 53.16 in the context of Muhammad's experience receiving the Qur'ān. Also figures in 34.15 where the context is the terrain at Ma'rib famed for the bursting of its great dam. pp.178, 201

Glossary

Sijjīl	Surah 105.4, which records the discomfiture of Abraha's army attacking Mecca at the time of Muhammad's birth. *Sijjīl* taken to mean 'clay tablets' on which (root meaning) decrees were written. Were they stone missiles, or is the sense metaphorical, destruction by divine decree? p.202
Sijjīn	In Surah 83.7 where the next clause identifies it with a written record: perhaps the place where the record is housed, or its contents 'prisoned' i.e. indelibly set down. p.348
Sunnah	The path or way followed by the faithful, divine ordinance, so, in turn, the corpus of Islamic 'guidance.' pp.185, 224, 245, 253
Tanzīl	The 'sending down' of the contents of the Qur'ān 'piecemeal' whereby the heavenly Book comes to the Prophet's lips.
Tāghūt	Like Jibt, a pagan object of worship. pp.266, 271, 274
Taqwā	The fundamental Muslim quality of 'awe' before God, piety, duty, devoted avoidance of evil. e.g. pp.105, 112, 120, 137, 164, 167, 171, 221, 230, 232, 237, 238, 243, 248, 275, 280, 283, 304
Tasbīh	Glorifying God, with Takbīr (the saying of *Allāhu akbar*) the basic theme of Islamic praise.
Tasnīm	Surah 83.27 notes this fountain in Paradise, with its 'uplifting' waters of benediction. p.348
Tauhīd	The affirming of the unity of God. pp.87, 111 and throughout
Tawakkul	The act of reliance upon God. e.g. pp.149, 171, 172, 178, 196, 223, 230, 233, 237, 248, 257, 262, 265, 266, 283
Ta'wīdh	The seeking of refuge in God from evil and wrong. e.g. pp.216, 221, 276, 326
Taurāt	The Torah given to Moses for the Jews who are enjoined to keep faith with it and accused of disloyalty and distortion. pp.121, 164, 167, 169, 247, 253, 264, 268, 276, 277, 327
Thamūd	An Arabian people from before Muhammad's time, to whom Sālih was sent and whose ruin in unbelief provides salutary warning for Muhammad's hearers. pp.127, 128, 129, 130, 139, 172, 228
Ukhdud	The pit, or trench, of burning fire traditionally associated with the Jewish ruler Dhū Nuwās' persecution of Christians in Najran prior to the rise of Islam. p.202
Ummah	The 'nation' or people of Islam in their unity as Muslims beyond ethnic, tribal, local or other 'units' thereof. pp.122, 222, 230, 268, 280, 297, 344
Umm al-Kitāb	'The mother (lit.) of the Book,' the eternal counterpart of the Qur'ān on earth. pp.197, 223

Ummī	Adjective applied to Muhammad in Surah 7.157-158, as a messenger to those without Scripture who is one among them. By others taken to mean his total 'illiteracy.' pp.187, 226, 272, 276, 279
'Umrah	The lesser pilgrimage to Mecca, performed outside the time of *Hajj* and with fewer ceremonies. p.290
Wahy	The state of 'inspiration' in which 'revelation' happened to the Prophet, the enabling both of awareness and language conveying it. pp.113, 130, 178, 197, 223, 279, 297, 298
Al-Yaqīn	'The utterly certain,' death and the Last Day. pp.219, 315, 330, 347
Al-Zabūr	The psalms, scriptures given to David. pp.114, 157, 188, 345
Zabāniyah	'The guards of hell' or 'officials of retribution.' p.177
Zakāt	The obligatory alms-payment, the third 'pillar' of Islam. e.g. pp.88, 153, 228, 231, 246, 255, 266, 269, 273, 278, 282, 284, 297, 305, 321
Zann	'Supposition' in an evil sense, surmise that misleads. pp.120, 170, 215, 221, 236, 252, 305, 309
Zihār	A pagan form of dismissal of wives in divorce reproached in Surah 58. pp.319, 322
Zulm	A frequent Quranic term in various derivatives, meaning the denial of what is due, injustice, violation of rights, wrong-doing to self, to others and to God. e.g. pp.120, 169, 179, 228, 229, 269, 302

General Index to the Qur'ān Readings

Some terms and themes — God, mercy, power, apostle and others — are present on almost every page. An exhaustive Index would be over-taxing. It is hoped that this General Index, with the indexed Glossary, will enable readers to locate the place and frequency of their concerns.

Index to Omitted Passages

The letter column notes the section(s) to which, broadly, the omitted passages pertain.

The page(s) column indicates the location in included passages of identical and kindred themes or subject matter and illustrates where the import of the excluded ones is present in allusions or turns of phrase (in the Arabic) that correspond. Highly selective as these page references are, they exemplify how the topics and nuances of omitted verses are readily accessible within the abridgement. The page listing is in no way intended as adequate cross-reference.

An English Concordance to the Qur'ān is available for users of Arberry's translation in: *A Concordance of the Qur'ān*, Hanna E. Kassis, University of California Press, 1983.

A total of some 1,800 verses (around thirty per cent) are in this listing. It will be clear that no accent or concern of the whole has been elided. Urgency and strong reiteration were in the very fabric of Muhammad's task, no dimension of which is missing here. The hope is to give unfamiliar readers a readier occasion of discovering the impact of its salient themes and of the tenacity which sustained them. Forty-nine Surahs are unabridged.

Verse reference for omitted passages	Related section(s)	Close parallels
Surah 2		
6- 15	E and H	pp.227, 228, 267
23- 29	E and H	pp.90, 219, 341
39- 66	C and H	pp.139-156
72- 86	C	pp.173, 246, 248
87[a]	C	p.145
88- 93	E	pp.152, 269, 271
104-105	E	pp.272, 273
116-123	E	pp.104, 195, 211, 221, 245, 268, 342
168-171	E and H	pp.188, 282, 308
174-176	E	pp.261, 272
188-189	G	pp.289, 305
204-212	E	pp.87, 332

Verse reference for omitted passages	Related section(s)	Close parallels
80- 84	C	pp.123f
90-126	C	pp.139-143, 145-150
179-188	D and F	pp.87, 106, 218
Surah 8		
36- 37	H	pp.197, 220
52- 55	C	p.150
Surah 9		
35	H	pp.225, 338
68- 72	C	pp.113-126, 137, 138
115-119	E	pp.87, 199, 250, 346
Surah 10		
7- 9	H	pp.345, 350
11- 14	D	pp.153, 200, 205, 209, 212
31- 36	B and D	pp.89, 91, 98, 104
71- 82	C	pp.114, 117, 139f
Surah 11		
1- 11	D	pp.100, 104, 199, 210, 225
15- 24	D	pp.171, 213
69- 83	C	pp.122, 123, 125
96-108	C and H	pp.139, 140, 149, 345, 347
116-119	C	p.215
Surah 13		
1	F	See pp.354, 355
23- 29	D and H	pp.108, 238, 345, 350
34- 35	H	pp.344, 350
41- 43	D	pp.210, 212, 266
Surah 14		
5- 8	C	pp.139f, 246, 247, 254, 274, 282
42- 52	H	pp.340f
Surah 15		
24- 25	H	pp.197, 217, 220, 291, 294, 335, 343
44- 84	C and D	pp.122, 123, 124, 128, 350
Surah 16		
19- 47	D and H	p.334
61- 76	B and D	pp.108, 172, 200
84- 89	D and H	pp.182, 206
106-113	D and H	pp.240, 268, 295
Surah 17		
40- 42	D	pp.206, 281
58- 72	C	pp.96, 103, 110, 128, 130, 270, 340, 342

Index to Omitted Passages

Verse reference for omitted passages	*Related section(s)*	*Close parallels*
38	C	pp.125, 126, 127, 128
53- 63	D and H	pp.193, 198, 293, 296, 345, 350
Surah 30		
11- 16	H	pp.335, 338
20	B	pp.165, 190
54- 60	D and H	pp.192, 278, 332
Surah 31		
6- 11	B and D	pp.100, 108, 194
Surah 32		
1- 14	B and D	pp.98, 106, 177, 190, 278
20^b- 30	D and H	pp.114, 239, 274, 337, 338
Surah 33		
63- 71	C and D	pp.148, 152, 334, 335
Surah 34		
22- 42	B, D and H	pp.108, 332, 342, 344
51- 54	H	pp.342, 343
Surah 35		
4- 11	D and H	pp.98, 110, 177, 190, 192, 332, 343
18- 28	B and F	pp.100, 106, 184, 204, 216
32- 37	H	pp.345, 350
Surah 36		
48- 67	H	pp.329, 343, 347, 350
Surah 37		
19- 82	C and H	pp.114, 329, 350
139	C	pp.161, 162
149-179	D	pp.195, 206, 211, 225
Surah 38		
12- 16	C	pp.114, 125, 126, 127, 129, 137
27- 29	B and D	pp.104, 226, 227, 266
49- 70	A, B and H	pp.86, 96, 97, 343, 350
Surah 39		
13- 22	D	pp.125, 180, 213, 216, 223
24- 26	D and H	pp.225, 338
30- 40	H	pp.193, 201, 220, 235
Surah 40		
5- 6	C	pp.108, 116, 117
10- 33	B, C, D and H	pp.104, 143, 145, 150, 154, 335
35- 54	C	pp.150, 204, 334
69- 85	D and H	pp.99, 108, 137, 173, 209, 224

Verse reference for omitted passages	Related section(s)	Close parallels
Surah 58		
5- 6	G	pp.157, 302, 328
Surah 60		
1- 9	C and E	pp.118, 248, 285, 293
Surah 61		
2- 5	C and E	pp.145, 149, 265
Surah 63		
9- 11	D and E	pp.116, 238, 254, 294, 299
Surah 64		
5- 10	C, D and H	pp.137, 197, 294, 333, 343
Surah 65		
8- 10ª	H	pp.229, 344
Surah 67		
6- 24	B and H	pp.101, 197, 217, 350
Surah 68		
33- 47	D and H	pp.203, 333
Surah 69		
11- 12	C	pp.113-117
Surah 72		
1- 15	D	pp.104, 211, 277, 281
Surah 73		
11- 19	C and H	pp.139, 335, 337, 338, 341, 342
Surah 75		
20- 40	B and H	pp.98, 99, 110, 117, 181, 190, 305, 341, 347
Surah 78		
1- 16	B and H	pp.99, 100, 103, 145, 146, 342
Surah 85		
17- 20	C	pp.127, 129, 143, 149, 150, 261, 286
Surah 91		
11- 15	C	pp.127, 128, 129
Surah 92		
14- 16	H	p.350

(Surahs unabridged are:
1, 12, 20, 27, 48, 49, 52, 57, 59, 62, 66, 70, 71, 74, 76, 77, 79, 80, 81, 82, 83, 84, 86, 87, 88, 89, 90 and 93 to 114.)

Index to the Surahs and Verses

127-131	G	pp.318-319		**Surah 7**		
135-137	F	p.295		1- 9	D	p.209
147-149	F	p.295		10- 30	B	pp.97-98
157-159	C	p.170		54- 58	B	p.109
160-162	E	p.269		65- 72	C	p.126
163-166	C	pp.113-114		73- 79	C	p.128
171-172	C	p.169		85- 89	C	p.139
176	G	p.326		127-156	C	pp.150-153
				157	F	p.276
Surah 5				158	D	p.187
1- 2	F	p.292		159-171	C	pp.154-155
3ª	G	p.308		172-174	B	p.98
3ᵇ	E	p.275		175-178	C	pp.172-173
4- 5ª	G	p.308		189-191	B	p.98
6- 11	F	p.283		191-206	D	pp.221-222
12- 16	E	p.246				
17	C	p.169		**Surah 8**		
18- 19	E	pp.246-247		1- 19	E	pp.232-233
20- 26	C	p.154		20- 29	F	p.294
27- 32	C	p.113		30- 35	D	pp.224-225
33- 37	E	p.260		38- 49	E	pp.233-234
38- 39	G	p.307		50- 51	H	p.336
40- 44	E	pp.267-268		56- 64	E	pp.256-257
45	G	p.327		65- 75	E	pp.234-235
46- 47	C	p.166				
48- 59	F	pp.268-269		**Surah 9**		
70- 71	E	p.269		1- 24	E	pp.255-256
72	C	p.168		25- 29	E	p.257
73- 74	E	p.270		30- 34	E	pp.245-246
75	C	p.166		36- 39	G	pp.327-328
82- 84	E	p.270		40	E	p.226
87- 93	G	pp.307-308		41- 57	E	pp.261-262
97- 98	F	p.292		58- 60	G	p.300
99-105	E	p.260		61- 67	E	pp.257-258
106-108	G	p.326		73- 89	E	pp.258-259
109-120	C	pp.167-168		90-112	E	pp.262-264
				113-114	F	p.285
				120-121	E	p.259
Surah 6				122-129	E	pp.264-265
4- 20	D	pp.209-210				
33- 36	D	pp.210-211				
42- 45	C	p.173		**Surah 10**		
56- 62	D	p.211		1- 4	F	p.279
74- 82	C	pp.118-119		5- 6	B	p.100
95-101	B	p.104		10	A	p.92
102-103	A	p.89		15- 23	D	pp.212-213
104-117	D	pp.214-215		24	B	pp.100-101
118-121	G	p.310		25- 30	H	p.335
136-140	G	pp.310-311		37- 70	D	pp.219-221
145-153	G	pp.309-310		83- 93	C	pp.149-150
154	C	p.145		94- 99	C	p.161
155-165	D	pp.215-216		100-109	D	pp.213-214

Index to the Surahs and Verses